P9-CMY-689

CHINA MODERNIZES

CHINA MODERNIZES

Threat to the West or Model for the Rest?

Randall Peerenboom

OXFORD
UNIVERSITY PRESS
Great Clarendon Street, Oxford OX2 6DP
Oxford University Press is a department of the University of Oxford.
It furthers the University's objective of excellence in research, scholarship,
and education by publishing worldwide in
Oxford New York
Auckland Cape Town Dar es Salaam Hong Kong Karachi
Kuala Lumpur Madrid Melbourne Mexico City Nairobi
New Delhi Shanghai Taipei Toronto
With offices in
Argentina Austria Brazil Chile Czech Republic France Greece
Guatemala Hungary Italy Japan Poland Portugal Singapore
South Korea Switzerland Thailand Turkey Ukraine Vietnam
Oxford is a registered trade mark of Oxford University Press
in the UK and in certain other countries
Published in the United States
by Oxford University Press Inc., New York

First published 2007

British Library Cataloguing in Publication Data
Data available
Library of Congress Cataloging in Publication Data
Data available
Typeset by Newgen Imaging Systems (P) Ltd., Chennai, India
Printed in Great Britain
on acid-free paper by
Clays Ltd., St Ives plc., Suffolk
ISBN 0–19–920834–4 978–0–19–920834–0
1

To Rayne and Nico—BD&SF

Preface

This book builds on and complements my previous work on legal reforms in China and law and development in Asia. In *China's Long March toward Rule of Law*, I examined competing conceptions of rule of law, several of them at odds with the liberal democratic version of rule of law found in Euro-America. I provided a detailed analysis of China's legal reforms, adopting an institutional approach to assess the progress China had made in improving its legal system and the obstacles to further progress. Despite the occasional comparison to the institutions or laws of other legal systems, the focus was squarely on China.

While working on that book, I became interested in the extent to which the nonliberal variants of rule of law could also be found in other countries, particularly other Asian countries. I also became increasingly interested in the extent to which China was confronting similar issues as other developing countries, and whether anything could be learned from their experiences. This led to an ongoing collaborative effort with some of the leading scholars on Asian legal systems to produce a series of volumes examining the role of law in Asia countries, the first two volumes being *Asian Discourses of Rule of Law* and *Human Rights in Asia*. An overview of the series and its goals and methodology is available at **http://papers.ssrn.com/sol3/papers.cfm?abstract_id=445820**.

These projects in turn highlighted several issues that became central to this work, including the importance of wealth to virtually all indicators of human rights and well-being, including rule of law and good governance; the wide variation within Asia; and, despite the variation in Asia as a whole, the notable success of several East Asian states that followed a largely similar developmental path.

This book then places China's efforts to modernize within a broader comparative context, emphasizing in particular how well China does relative to other countries at its income level across a wide range of areas, with the exception of civil and political rights.

There are heated debates in the popular press and policy-making circles about whether China's rise will be peaceful, as Beijing would have us believe, or whether a rising China will pose a military and economic threat to the West, and undermine support for democracy and human rights around the globe, as many US politicians and defense industry players would have us believe. While acknowledging that a geopolitical shift in power of this magnitude will inevitably cause friction and that at times a hardheaded pragmatic approach will be required when interests conflict, this book seeks to bridge the gap in understanding that now exists on a range of issues, and thus to mitigate tensions and create a firmer foundation for mutual trust.

To that end, I describe the views of the Chinese government and citizens on a number of controversial issues, as evidenced in official government statements and in public opinion polls. There have been many debates about the advantages or disadvantages of liberal democracy or Asian values. These debates could have been sharpened by moving beyond grand statements, posturing polemics, and inflamed rhetoric to concrete issues bolstered by broad comparative, empirical, and historical studies. I rely on empirical studies to demonstrate differences in values across a range of issues, and, more importantly, to test many of the grandiose claims about the alleged benefits of globalization and democratization.

This book is not an exercise in ideal theory. I do not begin with the hypothetical assumption that we are all hiding behind a veil of ignorance and do not know whether we are likely to be rich or poor, citizens of the world's sole reigning superpower or citizens of the up and coming challenger. Nor do I ask what would be the best political system if people were always rational and reasonable, or more altruistic, or less nationalistic. Such philosophical works have their place. But this work takes the world as it is.

While the book relies heavily on empirical studies, normative claims or judgments are inevitable given the subject matter. Some factual or descriptive claims will imply or lead to a normative judgment, such as that China is being held to double standards on human rights issues (and this should stop), or that globalization has led to increased inequality (and this should be redressed), or that democratization at low levels of wealth has failed to produce the positive benefits claimed by democracy advocates (and thus democratization should be postponed until higher levels of development).

In other cases, some claims may be more purely normative, and not amenable to resolution based on empirical evidence. A few words about my own normative preferences may be in order, as readers may wonder where I stand on some of the normative issues raised in the text. To the extent that broad labels are useful, I am a communitarian-leaning pragmatist who emphasizes economic development and the elimination of poverty as essential for human dignity. More technically, for what it's worth, I am a nonfoundational pragmatic arealist, a nonnaturalist, a moderate metaethical relativist, a noncognitivist, and a pluralist (see Peerenboom 2003*b*).

I support, in broad stroke, democracy, rule of law, human rights, freedom of speech and religious practice, and equality for women, and oppose torture and arbitrary detention, as I think most people do in China. However, I question the way in which some of these laudable goals are promoted, including the feasibility and normative appropriateness of some of the methods; the timing and priority assigned to their realization relative to the realization of other social goods; and the details of how these broad goals are to be interpreted and implemented in practice—as again do most people in China. On the whole, I find the arguments in favor of the kind of communitarian or collectivist approach to rights issues found in some Asian countries (especially those where the collectivist orientation leads to greater economic equality) more persuasive, and the results on the whole more attractive, than the liberal approach as practiced particularly in the United States.

To put it simply, and to gloss over what liberalism might be like if normative philosophers engaging in ideal theory had their way, liberalism tends to benefit the more talented, smarter, or already well-off individuals in a society at the expense of the vast majority. In contrast, communitarianism benefits the vast majority, albeit at times to the detriment of exceptional individuals. In some cases, individuals work hard and deserve what they get. But often they enjoy unfair advantages, including being born male, or white, or rich, or 7 feet tall with long arms. As a white male with the resources and good fortune to attend decent schools—not to mention the good fortune to have been born in the world's sole superpower at the height of its powers—I stand more to gain personally from liberalism and the belief that we deserve all we can get. But we do not have to hide behind a veil of ignorance to know that doesn't make it right.

Randy Peerenboom
July 2005

Acknowledgements

I have incurred many debts of gratitude in completing this book, none of which I will be able to adequately discharge here. Research for this book and for related conferences has been supported by grants from the Asian Foundation, Ford Foundation, University of California Pacific Rim Research Foundation, UCLA Council on Research, UCLA Academic Senate, and the US–China Business Council. A Fulbright research grant gave me the opportunity to complete this manuscript while I delved more deeply into reforms of administrative detention and criminal law. The library team at UCLA Law School once again provided the kind of support that one dreams about but never expects to actually enjoy.

Various draft chapters and articles from which parts of this book have been drawn were presented at Oxford, Cambridge, Georgetown, Columbia, University of Washington, Syracuse University, Indiana University, Hong Kong University, University of Melbourne, Griffith University, Australian National University, University of New South Wales, National University of Singapore, the Hoover Center at Stanford, Yale Law School, the University of Law and Politics in Beijing, and Sciences Po in Paris. I thank the participants in the seminars, conferences, and workshops for their comments. Daniel Bell, Michael Dowdle, James Feinerman, Paul Gewirtz, Tom Ginsburg, Martin Krygier, Maximo Langer, and several anonymous reviewers, were kind enough to read and comment on all or parts of this manuscript or earlier versions of chapters.

I must thank Benjamin Liu, Gao Wei, Yang Liu, Joshua Hodus, Jenny Lentz, and Joseph Doherty for their help in tracking down obscure materials, data collection, statistical analysis, and the preparing of tables. My recent empirical turn would not have been possible without Joe.

Diane LeCover has throughout the years been extraordinarily helpful in preparing manuscripts, shipping books and documents, and countless other ways. My thanks also to Sarah Caro of Oxford University Press for her enthusiastic support of this project.

None of this implicates any of these kind souls in any of the shortcomings and errors herein.

I also thank family and friends for bearing with me as I bored them with lengthy discussions of half-thought ideas or ignored them as I sat in front of my computer typing away—although my clever daughter Rayne did figure out the best way to reach me was to send repeated MSN messages, while my younger son Nico took the more direct approach of plopping down in my chair and not moving.

This book draws in places on articles published in the *Georgetown International Law Review, Cornell International Law Journal, China Journal, Duke International Law Journal, Northwestern Law Review, Columbia Journal of Asian Law* and chapters that have appeared in books published by Cambridge University Press and RoutledgeCurzon. My thanks to the publishers for permission to reprint passages from those works.

Contents

Abbreviations

ASEAN	Association of Southeast Asian Nations
BERI	Business Environment Risk Intelligence
BC	Beijing Consensus
BJP	Bharatiya Janata Party
CAT	Convention Against Torture
CCP	Chinese Communist Party
CECC	Congressional-Executive Commission on China
CEDAW	Convention on the Elimination of All forms of Discrimination Against Women
CPL	Criminal Procedure Law
DR	detention for repatriation
EAM	East Asian Model
ECHR	European Court of Human Rights
ETIM	East Turkestan Islamic Movement
ETL	education through labor
ETLO	East Turkestan Liberation Organization
FDI	foreign direct investment
GATT	General Agreement on Tariffs and Trade
GDI	Gender-related Development Index
GDP	gross domestic product
GNI	gross national income
HDI	Human Development Index
HPI	Human Poverty Index
ICC	International Criminal Court
ICCPR	International Covenant on Civil and Political Rights
ICESCR	International Covenant on Economic, Social, and Cultural Rights
ICS	individual case supervision
ICRG	International Country Risk Guide

IFI	international financial institution
IMF	International Monetary Fund
IP	intellectual property
KMT	Kuomintang
LDP	Liberal Democratic Party
MFN	Most Favored Nation
MNC	multinational corporation
NCCC	National Counter Corruption Commission
NGO	nongovernmental organization
NPC	National People's Congress
PAP	People's Action Party
PBOC	People's Bank of China
PPP	purchasing power parity
PRC	People's Republic of China
PTS	Political Terror Scale
RMB	renminbi
SOE	state-owned enterprise
SPC	Supreme People's Court
SR	Special Rapporteur
TAR	Tibetan Autonomous Region
TRIPs	Trade-Related Aspects of Intellectual Property Rights
UNDP	United Nations Development Programme
WC	Washington Consensus
WTO	World Trade Organization

CHAPTER ONE

Introduction: two opposing views of China

Two sharply opposing popular images of China prevail today. Skyscrapers, urban professionals in Italian suits dashing in to Starbucks for their morning latte, streets filled with shiny new BMWs—this is the positive face of the self-confident China seen in glossy advertisements beamed around the world on CNN. This is the rising superpower predicted to have the world's largest economy by mid-century, if not by 2020.[1]

The envy of developing countries, this China has in the last twenty-five years lifted several hundred million people out of poverty, built a functional legal system virtually from scratch and emerged as a powerful actor on the international stage. Modern yet proud of its past, this China is eager to host the Olympics and show off the best of both contemporary and traditional China. With a foreign policy based on peaceful coexistence and the 'Four No's'—no hegemony, no power politics, no military alliances, no arms race—this China is much more popular around the world than the United States and roughly as popular as France, Germany, and Japan.[2]

On the other hand, there is the much darker image of China as a brutal authoritarian state that violently oppresses its citizens, an anachronistic throwback to the Cold War era. This China arrests political dissidents, censors the Internet, and imprisons courageous lawyers who try to help families thrown out of their homes by profiteering developers eager to build the next skyscraper. Far from self-confident and tolerant, this China is defensive and nationalistic, quick to find insults to 'the dignity of the Chinese people' in every difference of diplomatic opinion, prone to xenophobic anti-Westernism and violent protests against Japan stemming from wartime violations more than half a century ago. With rapidly rising military budgets and army generals eager to attack Taiwan should it declare independence, this China is a threat to geopolitical stability. With a financial system teetering under the weight of bad loans, inefficient state-owned enterprises bloated with excessive employees, and weak government institutions riddled by corruption, this China is hardly an economic miracle. It is rather a relatively poor developing country in which more than 40 per cent of the population live on less than $2 per day, peasants are crushed under the heavy burden of illegal taxes, retirees are unable to collect their pensions from insolvent employers, and millions lack access to medical care and minimal social welfare. With over 3,300 mining accidents claiming 5,986 lives in 2005 alone, and sixteen of the world's twenty most-polluted cities, its economic growth has come at the expense of worker safety and the environment. This China is politically unstable, with the regime lacking legitimacy and besieged by protesters demanding economic redress, social justice, and political change. This China, pundits tell us, is on the verge of collapse.[3]

These two conflicting popular views parallel two equally conflicting views in the academic literature on law and development, globalization, and modernization. The positive view sees China as a paradigm for developing states in this era of globalization and the envy of industrialized states with its high growth rates. The critical view sees China as challenging the central assumptions of the dominant legitimating narrative of Western states today that combines free markets based on neoliberal economic policies with constitutional democracy, rule of law, good governance, and a liberal interpretation of human rights.

China as problem?

At a conference in New York in early spring 2005 on 'Legal Evolution Toward a World Rule of Law: Development of Legality and Constitutional Democracy Worldwide,' China was included in a panel on problematic cases, as often happens at such conferences, along with Africa, the Mid East, and Latin America—which is to say, along with most of the world. Let us set aside for the moment the irony of holding such a conference in the US, with the US taken as the model for global rule of law, when US hegemony and exceptionalism have done so much to undermine the possibility of a genuine international rule of law.[4] Let us also set aside for the moment the fundamental divide between the largely successful West and the mostly unfortunate Rest. The question remains whether China is indeed a problem case, and if so, what kind of problem.

For some, the problem is that China has enjoyed remarkable economic growth in the last several decades, apparently without the benefit of 'the rule of law' and clear and enforceable property rights.[5] China's success calls into question the wisdom of spending billions of dollars on promoting rule of law and good governance modeled on the legal systems and political institutions found in Euro-America. Accusing the apostles of the revamped law and development movement of myth-making, New York University Law Professor Frank Upham claims that 'this new rule of law orthodoxy linking formalist legal regimes and economic development ignores the empirical evidence and is ultimately counterproductive. Not only does the formalist rule of law as advocated by the World Bank and other donors not exist in the developed world, but attempting to transplant a common template of institutions and legal rules into developing countries without attention to indigenous contexts harms preexisting mechanisms for dealing with issues such as property ownership and conflict resolution.'[6]

For others, the problem is political in nature. China has resisted the third wave of democratization, and remains officially a socialist state, albeit a unique twenty-first century version of a socialist state that has endorsed a market economy and rule of law. Some fear that 'since China is an increasingly important and influential country in world affairs, China's continuous antidemocracy diplomacy would have a significant impact on the diffusion of . . . democracy throughout the world.'[7] Indeed, some believe that Russia's recent tilt toward authoritarianism reflects the influence of China's model of 'markets without democracy.'[8]

For still others, the main problem is human rights. Not only does China have a poor record on civil and political rights. Critics fear that unlike Japan, which during its economically powerful years did not attempt to challenge the Western powers, China is likely to take advantage of its growing economic and geopolitical influence to defend and advocate, even in the face of Western opposition, rights policies and a normative vision of the world at odds with current rights policies based on secular liberalism. This is already beginning to happen, they contend, most notably in the heavily politicized debates over 'Asian values' and China's attempts to influence the policies and restructuring of the UN's Human Rights Commission. As a result, critics accuse China of adopting a strategy of divide and conquer where the concept of universality is sliced up 'little by little, region by region, to the point where there are few teeth left in the UN human rights monitoring and implementation mechanisms.'[9] We are, in short, heading for a 'clash of civilizations.'[10]

For others the problem is that China is an outlaw regime that undermines geopolitical stability through the sales of ballistic missiles to rogue states, contributes to the proliferation of weapons of mass destruction, and threatens US hegemony and military superiority. This view assumes that authoritarian regimes are a greater threat to world peace than democracies.[11] It is also based on the historical observation that the rise of a new power has generally resulted in conflict and geopolitical instability. Accordingly, the US and its allies must prepare now for the coming conflict with China, with debates as to whether the best way to do that is by trying to contain China or by engaging China in the hopes that a more interdependent and prosperous China will eventually join the fold of peace-loving liberal democracies.[12]

China as paradigm?

In contrast to this critical view of China, the opposing view sees China as a paradigm for developing states, a twenty-first-century, technologically leapfrogging variant of the East Asian developmental state that has resulted in such remarkable success for Japan, South Korea, Hong Kong, Singapore, and Taiwan.[13] This view rests on six pillars. Not all who believe China may be a model for developing states endorse all six pillars or assign the same weight to them. They are listed in roughly ascending order from least to most controversial. The final three points are more forward-looking, and hence speculative.

First, the government has adopted a pragmatic approach to reforms. While embracing market reforms, China resisted the attempts of international financial institutions and foreign experts to engage in shock therapy, pursuing instead a more gradual pace of reform. Rather than blindly following the advice of the IMF or the World Bank, the government has taken care to adapt basic economic principles to China's current circumstances. This has led Nobel prize winner Joseph Stiglitz and Harvard economist Dani Rodrik among others to praise China for its wise policy choices and measured approach.[14] Similarly, China has sought to develop its own variant of socialist rule of law compatible with its current form of government and contingent circumstances, including existing cultural norms and level of institutional development, rather than attempting to import wholesale the liberal democratic form of rule of law found in Euro-America—or at least found in self-congratulatory civic textbooks in Euro-America.

Second, contrary to neoliberal prescriptions, the state has actively intervened in the Chinese economy and played a key role in setting economic policy, establishing functional government institutions, regulating foreign investment, and mitigating the adverse effects of globalization on domestic constituencies. This is consistent with a longstanding view that developing states need a strong state, which fell out of favor in the era of Reagonomics and Thatcherism, and the emerging revisionist view in this era of globalization that it is time to bring the state back in.[15]

Together, these first two points form the economic core of what some have provocatively if somewhat misleadingly called the 'Beijing Consensus,' in contrast to the equally provocative and somewhat misleading 'Washington Consensus.'[16] The Beijing Consensus (BC)—like the Washington Consensus (WC) and related terms such as neoliberalism and market fundamentalism—mean different things to different people, reflecting a lack of consensus even as to content, much less as to the superiority of any particular approach.

The original 'Washington Consensus' proposed by John Williamson in 1989 included: (1) fiscal discipline: reduction of budget deficits to a non-inflationary level; (2) redirection of public expenditure priorities toward fields offering both high economic returns and the potential to improve income distribution, such as primary health care, primary education, and infrastructure; (3) tax reforms to lower marginal rates and broaden the tax base; (4) interest rate liberalization and transition to market-determined interest rates (Williamson later broadened this principle to include financial liberalization); (5) a competitive exchange rate; (6) trade liberalization; (7) abolition of barriers to foreign direct investment; (8) privatization of state-owned enterprises; (9) deregulation to abolish barriers to entry and exit; and (10) secure property rights.

Rodrik added ten elements to what he took to be an augmented WC in the 1990s: (1) improvement of 'corporate governance'; (2) curbing corruption; (3) flexible labor markets; (4) adherence to WTO rules; (5) adherence to international standards in the financial sector; (6) 'prudent' liberalization of cross-border capital transactions; (7) fixed or floating exchange rates; (8) independent central banks/ inflation targeting; (9) social safety nets; and (10) poverty reduction.[17]

Neoliberalism, sometimes referred to as market fundamentalism, is widely used but seldom strictly defined. For present purposes, it refers to: (1) promotion of a global economy based on free trade policies; (2) belief in the view that the state is to play a minimal role in the economy limited to ensuring basic security and providing the necessary infrastructure to facilitate transactions and administer justice, with a corresponding emphasis on deregulation and privatization; and (3) belief in the trickle down effects of economic growth both between and within states.[18]

The Beijing Consensus, in addition to a pragmatic approach to reforms and support for a larger role for the state in guiding the economy and ensuring equitable growth, has been used to refer to market reforms without democracy, an emphasis on self-determination to prevent powerful international actors from unduly influencing

China's development choices, and—more problematically, as we shall see—a wholesale rejection of the WC.[19]

Joshua Cooper Ramo, who popularized the term 'Beijing Consensus,' describes China as 'marking a path for other nations around the world who are trying to figure out not simply how to develop their countries, but also how to fit into the international order in a way that allows them to be truly independent, to protect their way of life and political choices in a world with a single massively powerful centre of gravity.'[20] In his view:

> [The BC] replaces the discredited Washington Consensus, an economic theory made famous in the 1990s for its prescriptive, Washington-knows-best approach to telling other nations how to run themselves. The Washington Consensus was a hallmark of end-of-history arrogance; it left a trail of destroyed economies and bad feelings around the globe. China's new development approach is driven by a desire to have equitable, peaceful high-quality growth, critically speaking, it turns traditional ideas like privatisation and free trade on their heads. It is flexible enough that it is barely classifiable as a doctrine. It does not believe in uniform solutions for every situation. It is defined by a ruthless willingness to innovate and experiment, by a lively defense of national borders and interests, and by the increasingly thoughtful accumulation of tools of asymmetric power projection. It is pragmatic and ideological at the same time, a reflection of an ancient Chinese philosophical outlook that makes little distinction between theory and practice.[21]

The third pillar in the China as paradigm construction is that China has pursued economic reforms before democratization, as did other East Asian states (and for that matter America and Western European countries). Advocates of this approach support their position in part by pointing to the problems in Russia, the Philippines, Indonesia, and a host of other failed states that put political reforms ahead of economic reforms and democratized at low levels of wealth before rule of law and functional government institutions were established.[22] Broader empirical studies discussed in Chapter 2 provide considerable support for the view that democratization at lower levels of wealth is in general not likely to lead to development, and may hinder growth. Granted, poor authoritarian regimes on the whole are not likely to be all that much better at sustaining growth.

However, not all authoritarian regimes are the same. Authoritarian regimes that follow the East Asian model by investing in human capital and institutional development—as China is doing—have been remarkably successful.

Fourth, while China has acknowledged the importance and legitimacy of human rights, it has also challenged the alleged universal consensus on human rights issues, or at least the consensus among much of the cosmopolitan elite in economically advanced Western liberal democracies. Given the deeply entrenched view in China that even universal rights are contingent on local circumstances, Beijing is unlikely to attempt to impose its own particular solutions to complex issues on other countries. Nevertheless, it may seek a shift in normative orientation toward a more flexible, contextual approach, with greater toleration for nonliberal, communitarian, or collectivist approaches to rights issues. But whereas liberal critics see such policies as a dangerous threat to the legitimacy of human rights, supporters see China's position as a necessary corrective to the hegemony of liberalism and the neo-imperialistic tendencies of the Western-centric human rights movement.

Fifth, and in a more speculative vein, neo-authoritarians, New Confucians, communitarians, and other critics of liberalism hope that China may one day provide a viable normative alternative to the formal democracy and liberalism that have failed to resolve the very pressing issues of social inequality and human well-being for so many people in rich and poor countries alike.

A sixth aspect to China's rise to power that is attractive to developing countries is its emerging foreign relations policy. At the core of this policy is an importance attached to sovereignty, self-determination, and mutual respect that allows countries to develop on their own terms and in their own ways, freed from the priorities established by the G7 and the conditionalities imposed by international financial organizations. Demanding that reforms be 'country-owned and country-led,' developing countries from Asia to Africa have enthusiastically endorsed these concerns, which are central to Beijing's pragmatic approach.[23] A related, more speculative aspect of China's foreign policy is the professed intent to coexist peacefully with other countries and avoid power politics and the pursuit of narrowly defined national interests. While developed and developing countries alike may hope that China's rising will be peaceful (*heping jueqi*), how to be an honorable superpower is clearly not an issue that smaller, less powerful countries will themselves ever confront.

There is now ample evidence that other countries are looking to China for inspiration. Vietnam has closely followed the economic, legal, and political reforms in China, and modeled its foreign investment regime on China's. Laos, still a single party socialist state, followed China's lead in implementing market reforms beginning in the mid-1980s, resulting in higher growth rates despite a dip during the Asian financial crisis. Iran and other Middle Eastern countries have invited experts on Chinese law, economics, and politics to give talks to government officials and academics. These countries, hardly liberal democracies, favor China's approach of state-led economic reforms with limited political reforms. They, along with democratic developing countries in Latin America and Africa, have also taken heed of China's pragmatic approach to reforms.

China itself has attempted to persuade other countries to follow its lead. Government officials regularly lecture their trading partners in other developing states on the need to open their markets, establish rule of law, battle corruption, and promote good governance. Beijing welcomes delegations from other countries throughout the world to come discuss, study, and see for themselves the benefits of the Chinese approach to reforms. In 2004, China and World Bank jointly hosted the Shanghai Global Learning Process. More than 1,200 participants from 117 countries attended the conference to discuss what other countries could learn from China's experience and to share their own experiences. The government has also sought to influence others through aid programs and foreign investment. It has set up 27 Confucius Institutes around the world, with plans for over 100 more, at an annual cost of $200 million to teach Chinese language and culture. The government also provides scholarships to students from developing countries for study in China. In addition, Beijing has entered into numerous bilateral and multilateral agreements to promote exchanges and provide technical development assistance.

What then are we to make of China? Is China a failure, an authoritarian relic from another era? Or is it a success story? Is it perhaps a bit of both? Is it simply too early to tell? Is China a dangerous aberration likely to lead struggling developing countries back into the darkness of despotism or a shining pagoda on a hill showing them the way to prosperity and the good life? As China modernizes, will it adopt the institutions and values found in Euro-American liberal democracies? Or will China develop its own variants of modern institutions and its own distinctive normatively attractive ideology? Would a nonliberal but economically and militarily powerful China be a threat to Euro-America and its regional neighbors or be able to coexist peacefully?

China in comparative context

This book seeks to address these issues, and to do so by placing China within a broader comparative context. China's size, rich traditions, and rising superpower status make it possible for scholars, commentators, and politicians to focus on China alone. While in-depth studies of China or particular aspects of China are obviously necessary, such studies may ignore global trends, miss opportunities to take advantage of comparative scholarship, and ultimately lead to one-sided, misleading or incomplete appraisals. A broader perspective is essential if we are to understand the complex reality of China today, avoid the demonization of China, and accurately assess China's performance to date in its quest for modernization.[24]

The choice of standards will often determine the outcome of the assessment. Sometimes the actual performance of China's government institutions or its human rights record are compared against idealized accounts of good governance and rule of law that no country lives up to, or the normatively inspiring yet frequently violated idealistic standards championed by human rights activists. But to compare the actual to the ideal is to compare apples and oranges. Accordingly, this study will rely heavily on empirical studies to demonstrate how China does relative to the actual performance of other countries.

Another approach is to compare China's human rights record and the performance of its legal system and government institutions with the record and performance of much wealthier countries. As we shall see, however, rule of law, good governance, and virtually all rights including civil and political rights are highly correlated with wealth. Comparing China to much wealthier countries leads to the unsurprising conclusion that China has more problems: there are more deviations from the rule of law; government institutions are weaker, less efficient, and more corrupt; and citizens enjoy fewer freedoms while living shorter and more impoverished lives. More revealing is how well a country does compared to the average country in its income class. While not ignoring the performance of richer and poorer countries, this study will pay particular attention to how well China has done relative to other lower-middle income countries.

How one assesses China will also depend on one's views about modernity and globalization. Thus a second goal of this book is to situate China's quest for modernization within the general debate about these topics. Modernization and globalization have their champions, and their critics. The affirmative school emphasizes the normative attractiveness of a democratic society governed in accordance with rule of law in which individuals have the necessary freedom and security to flourish and pursue their own conceptions of the good life. Neatly summarizing this view, Howard-Hassman suggests that globalization's 'medium and long term effects may well be positive, as it impels social change that will result in greater moves to democracy, economic redistribution, the rule of law, and the promotion of civil and political rights. Capitalism is a necessary, though hardly sufficient condition for democracy; democracy is the best political system to protect human rights.'[25]

In contrast, rather than taking the stirring inspirational rhetoric of modernity at face value, the more critical perspective emphasizes the empirical and normative limits of the current legitimating narrative. The more extreme critics portray globalization, neoliberal market capitalism, rule of law, liberal democracy, and human rights as new forms of imperialism and colonialism—the latest in a long series of attempts by developed states to impose their values on developing states in order to ensure the structural reforms needed to facilitate resource extraction and trade, and thus serve their own interests.

Many human rights issues implicate deep moral commitments, including religious views, traditional gender roles, different notions of freedom and autonomy, and fundamental beliefs about the relationship of the individual to the state and other members of society. Given differences in fundamental commitments, critics argue the liberal-leaning human rights movement is in danger of becoming the new religion, the latest crusade, a modern day inquisition, while others portray the movement as a well-intentioned if benighted hegemony at best, or malicious strong-arm politics and cultural genocide at worst.[26] Noting that international human rights organizations share a fundamental commitment to the proselytization of Western liberal values, the well-known human rights scholar Makau wa Mutua points out that people in economically undeveloped, non-Western societies are portrayed as ignorant savages victimized by malicious government leaders who must by saved by enlightened Western rights activists.[27]

More moderate critics accept that parts or all of the modernist program may be desirable. However, they see development as a constant negotiation between universal values and principles—often abstractly stated—and concrete local conditions. They therefore accept, and often celebrate, that the hallmarks of modernity—free markets, rule of law, democracy, and human rights—come in different varieties. They also point out that in the real world, all good things need not and unfortunately often do not go together. Much of the world has failed to benefit from globalization, to consolidate democracy, to implement rule of law, and to protect human rights.

The main beneficiaries of 'free trade' have been already wealthy developed countries. Between 1950 and 1990, 57 out of 83 countries with a per capita income of less than $2,000 remained equally poor or became even poorer, while all but seven of the fifty-two countries with higher incomes at least doubled their income, and none became poorer.[28] By 2000, after another decade of free trade, fifty-four developing countries were poorer than in 1990.[29]

Using various methodologies to measure inequality, seven out of eight studies by leading economists found that global income inequality has increased.[30] The gap is significantly larger if one excludes China and India, which account for much of the growth in developing states.

Although measures of global income equality raise a number of contentious issues, the difference between rich and poor countries is so grotesque as to shock the conscience. Global income inequality is greater than the gap between rich and poor even in the most inegalitarian countries.[31] The average income in the twenty richest countries is thirty-seven times that of the poorest twenty countries, with the spread doubling in the last forty years.[32] The income of the richest 1% of the people is greater than the income of 57% of the rest of the people in the world.[33] Despite such gross inequality, aid from developed countries actually fell in the 1990s.

Adding insult to injury, developed countries continue to impose unfair trade conditions on developing countries, more than offsetting the minimal amounts of aid and debt relief granted poor countries. Agricultural subsidies in rich countries alone amount to more than $350 billion, six times the total amount of official developmental assistance and sixteen times the amount of aid to Africa.[34] At the same time as developed countries are pushing developing countries to reduce tariffs on manufacturing products, they themselves continue to impose tariffs on products for which developing countries enjoy a competitive advantage. The average tariff on agricultural products is 14% in the US and 22% in the EU, although tariffs on particular products may be as high as 400%.[35] These subsidies and tariffs mainly aid large agribusiness interests at the expense of poor people in developing and developed countries. Small farmers receive only 4% of the amount the US and EU spend on agricultural subsidies, while 70–80% goes to the richest 25% of landowners and farming conglomerates. The subsidies and tariffs add $1,500 to the annual food bill of a family of four.[36]

Rich countries also protect domestic manufacturers by imposing discriminatory quotas or invoking anti-surge clauses that trigger higher tariffs or a ban on further imports when imports of textiles or other such products meet a certain threshold. They also limit labor flows from developing countries, which according to UNDP estimates could generate more than $150 billion annually.[37] Meanwhile, the Agreement on Trade-Related Aspects of Intellectual Property Rights (TRIPs), imposed on developing countries as one of the prices for admission to the WTO, results in large transfers from the rest of the world to a handful of developed countries.[38]

The cost of all these discriminatory anti-free-trade policies is high. Leveling the playing field would increase income in developing countries by as much as $350 billion, the equivalent of the income of all Sub-Saharan Africans together, and lift as many as 140 million people out of poverty.[39]

The wide gap in wealth between—and within—countries has devastating consequences for the rights and well-being of billions of people in poor countries. Every year, more than 10 million children die of preventable diseases, some 30,000 a day.[40] In some countries, one-third of the children will not live to the age of 5. Human development levels decreased between 1990 and 2000 in twenty-one countries, while life expectancy declined in thirty-four, and primary school enrollment dropped in twelve. Excluding China, the number of poor people actually increased by 28 million in the 1990s.[41]

Developed countries are beginning to take poverty more seriously, although perhaps not seriously enough. The Millennium Declaration signed by 189 countries in 2000 and the Monterrey Consensus in 2002 laid out an ambitious agenda for rich and poor countries to work together to eliminate poverty and achieve sustainable development. At long last, millions of people would no longer die because they lacked patented HIV medication; children would no longer go hungry while farmers in rich countries were paid not to grow crops; and universal education would ensure that all boys and girls had a fighting chance to succeed. Unfortunately, developed countries have often failed to match their rhetoric of a war on poverty with actions. Surveying the landscape at the end of 2004, John Boughton, the Assistant Director of the IMF's Policy Development and Review Department, and Zia Qureshi, Senior Advisor to the World Bank's Global Monitoring Secretariat, concluded: 'Overall, developed country actions to date have fallen well short of the Monterrey Vision. Progress seriously lags commitments in most areas. This must change quickly if the world is not to fall further behind in its efforts to achieve policy goals.'[42]

While fully acknowledging the failure of African governments to uphold their end of the bargain, the Commission on Africa was even more blunt in taking the developed world to task for their failure to deliver on their promises:[43]

> Pledges of 'education for all' have gone unfunded. So have commitments on HIV and AIDS. Initiatives to curb corruption are unratified and unimplemented. The world says 'never again' after every major atrocity, but turns a blind eye to the trade in small arms. Codes of conduct by multinational companies remain mere exercises in public relations. Trade rules are applied vexatiously. Promises on aid are seen as impossible targets. Debt forgiveness schemes are hedged about with intractable restrictions. Wealthy nations make well-intentioned pledges at international conferences only to later decide that the promises, or their timetable, were unrealistic. Goals are set, reset, and recalibrated yet again so that all the rich world ends up doing is mitigating the extent to which it has failed. The gap between promises and reality never closes. Today the world community has before it another great pledge . . .

Against the backdrop of global demonstrations to Make Poverty History, G8 leaders promised once again in the summer of 2005 to increase aid and to do more to reduce poverty. However, aid in most countries will still fall short of the Millennium Declaration goal of 0.7% of GNI, with OECD countries continuing to spend ten times as much on the military as development assistance.[44]

There are of course many reasons why countries have failed to develop. Blaming globalization, free markets, and the failure of rich countries to provide adequate assistance is too simple. Corrupt and incompetent governments in developing countries have also played a role in the failures. Nevertheless, the international financial institutions' economic prescriptions have clearly not produced the anticipated results. The financial liberalization promoted by the IMF and the World Bank has led to volatile securities markets and banking crises, including in Asia. Even the World Bank has acknowledged that not all has gone according to plan: 'All past episodes of surges in capital flows to emerging markets have ended in severe international financial crises. Hard landings rather than soft landings have been the rule.'[45] Looking back over the decade of the 1990s, the World Bank concluded that 'whereas in recent years many of the developed countries were able to take advantage of globalisation, the effects on many developing and transition countries have been perverse.'[46]

The failure of so many countries to achieve sustained economic growth has caused reformers in developing countries to reconsider the wisdom of dogmatic adherence to neoliberal economic principles and the WC, to reject the assumption that one-size-fits-all in terms of democracy, human rights, rule of law and institutional reforms in favor of a more contextual approach, and to question the motives of the rich in pushing the poor to remake themselves in the image of contemporary Euro-America. As the Commission on Africa pointedly observed:

> There is also scepticism in some quarters about the developed world's insistence that the continent should follow an economic and political prescription which some Africans perceive as differing from the ones followed by the industrialised world in its own development. Developed countries, they argue, did not get where they are now through the policies and the institutions that they recommend to Africa today. Most of them actively used policies such as infant industry protection and export subsidies—practices that are now frowned upon, if not actively banned, by the World Trade Organisation (WTO). In addition, development did not grow from the adoption of democracy; history shows that matters often proceeded the opposite way round. Why, say some Africans, should we be denied the very policy instruments used by Europe and America for their own development? 'Is there a hidden agenda or conspiracy?', they ask.[47]

Taking up where dependency theory left off, some critics in developing states have portrayed the attempts of the US and other developed states to promote democracy as motivated by economic self-interest rather than concern for people in developing countries. Formal democracy along with rule of law, enhanced transparency, and a market operated on neoliberal economic principles serves the interests of MNCs.

> After supporting authoritarian regimes throughout the world (from Somoza to Marcos to Mobutu) for decades, why has international capitalism now

begun to support democracy? . . . It is not an accident that the intensification of Western demands for democratization go hand-in-hand with demands for trade liberalization, privatization and other forms of deregulation. The Western push for democratization can be read as part of the process of opening up the South for Northern investment and trade.[48]

There *is* something suspicious about the US and other Western powers preaching democracy and freedom for all. After all, in the past these same countries actively subverted democratic regimes in Guatemala, Nicaragua, and Chile that rejected business as usual in favor of more radical popular agendas that called for nationalization of foreign-invested companies, protection of domestic industries, better salaries and working conditions for labors in companies owned by foreign multinationals, and reallocation of resources from the wealthy to the poor. Nowadays, the US opposes populists such as Hugo Chavez in Venezuela, Evo Morales in Bolivia, and Luiz Inacio Lula da Silva in Brazil who reject neoliberal policies and oppose a 'free trade' zone for the Americas. The US and its allies also continue to support authoritarian regimes such as Saudi Arabia and the decidedly nonliberal Pakistan when it is in their economic and geopolitical interest to do so. And the US has tolerated without much protest election fraud and other gross abuses of the democratic process in countries from Haiti to Zanzibar, while condemning the flawed process in Iran when it produced a leader not to the administration's liking and then cutting off aid to Hamas after its landslide victory in Palestinian elections.

On the other hand, one problem with this view is that it assumes MNCs prefer democracies to authoritarian states. But China's success in attracting foreign investment suggests most investors are more concerned about political stability than regime type—and thus unlikely to welcome democratization at lower levels of wealth. Rather than being complicit in a grand conspiracy to exploit developing countries for their own economic gain, the broad public in the West is more likely to support the promotion of democracy abroad out of the genuine if misguided belief that democracy will lead to economic development and resolve many of the problems of human suffering and poor governance in developing countries.[49]

Globalization enthusiasts had hoped that imitation, the diffusion of best practices, and the mobility of trade and capital would lead to a convergence on the institutions and practices of advanced Western liberal democracies. Clearly this has not happened, at least not to the extent predicted by advocates of globalization.

It is true there has been a global trend toward market-based economies. However, rather than all states converging on a similar form of market economy with common institutions, policies, and modes of production, distinct varieties of capitalism have arisen as a result of the embeddedness of institutions, cultural differences, and dissimilarities in the political economy.[50] Convergence or divergence is largely in the eye of the beholder, and depends on which countries and indices one examines, and the time frames one assumes.[51] Nevertheless, there has undeniably been more convergence among developed states than developing states thus far.[52] The UNDP observes that for 'the majority of countries the globalization story is one of divergence and marginalization.'[53]

The picture is roughly the same for rule of law and good governance. The authors of the World Bank's ongoing study of good governance conclude that there is no evidence of 'any significant improvement in governance worldwide, and if anything the evidence is suggestive of a deterioration, at the very least in key dimensions such as rule of law, control of corruption, political stability and government effectiveness.'[54]

Even supporters of globalization acknowledge the problems and the risks. In his spirited defense of the overall benefits of economic globalization, Columbia University's Jagdish Bhagwati recognizes problems with financial liberalization and intellectual property rules, and wisely recommends that governments take steps to protect those who lose out in the transition.[55] While calling for more rather than less globalization, *Financial Times* editor Martin Wolf laments the gross hypocrisy of rich countries in their treatment of developing countries, complains that international financial institutions have been captured by special interests, and criticizes the WTO's single undertaking, which requires developing countries to submit to the full range of policies favored by rich countries to become a member. He also concedes that successful Asian countries adopted policies that nurtured infant industries.[56] Meanwhile, a US National Intelligence Council report warned that globalization will be rocky, leading to chronic financial volatility, widening income gaps, deepening economic stagnation, political instability, and cultural alienation. This will in turn foster ethnic, ideological, and religious extremism, with an accompanying increase in violence and terrorism.[57]

Given the many problems confronting developing countries, China may seem to offer a new model for development, albeit one that challenges aspects of the dominant legitimating narrative being exported by Western countries and the international financial institutions they control.

Thus, a third goal of this book is to critically analyze both views of China as paradigm for developing countries and China as enfant terrible, a threat to the West, and a problem case for law and development and modernization theories. I shall argue that China is now following the same general path—modified slightly in light of the realities of the twenty-first century—of other East Asian countries that have achieved sustained economic growth, established rule of law, and usually developed constitutional democracies, albeit not necessarily liberal democracies.[58] This appears to be the most successful 'model' for relatively large countries in the contemporary era to achieve high levels of economic growth, implement rule of law, and eventually democratize and protect the full range of human rights through some form of constitutionalism.[59] East Asia stands out as the one eye-catching regional exception to the general pattern of successful West versus unfortunate Rest.

At this stage of development, China is meeting or exceeding expectations on most measures. Most notably, economic growth has been phenomenal. Official growth rates may be inflated, and there are many weaknesses in the economy. Nevertheless, no one denies that China's economic performance has been anything short of impressive thus far, particularly in light of the disappointing performance of so many other developing countries.

Moreover, consistent with the experiences of other countries in Asia and elsewhere, the legal system has played a greater role in economic growth in China than often suggested by those who belittle the importance of rule of law for development, and it is likely to play an even greater role in the future.[60] China has made significant progress in a short time in improving the legal system, having essentially begun from scratch in 1978.[61] China's legal system now outperforms the average in its income class on the World Bank's rule of law index.[62] Considerable progress has been achieved in strengthening other institutions as well, including people's congresses and government agencies. Despite an inevitable increase in social tension as a result of economic reforms, China has remained relatively stable, notwithstanding—or perhaps because of—the brutal crackdown on demonstrators in 1989.

Chinese citizens are also generally better off. Most live longer; more are able to read and write; most enjoy higher living standards. Notwithstanding the repeated attempts by the US and its allies to censure China for human rights violations and the steady stream of reports from human rights groups claiming deterioration in rights performance, China outperforms the average country in its income class on most major indicators of human rights and well-being, with the notable exception of civil and political rights.

In sum, China's performance across a range of variables from economic performance to elimination of poverty to the establishment of a functional legal system and government institutions is on the whole demonstrably superior to the performance of most African, Middle Eastern, and Latin American countries with which it is often lumped as a problem case. At least at this stage, China is, despite its problems, an example of a relatively successful developing country.

Whether China will ultimately prove as successful as some of its East Asian neighbors, and whether its rise will be peaceful or not, remains to be seen. Many lower income countries make some initial progress and show improvement in terms of economic growth, institutional development, and good governance given low starting points. However, once they reach the middle income level, they get bogged down. Powerful interest groups capture the reform agenda, opposing further reforms or pushing for reforms that do not benefit the broad public. Economic growth slows or reverses. The reform momentum is dissipated. Some states settle into a stable but dysfunctional holding pattern, while others sink into chaos and become failed states. As discussed in Chapter 6, there are signs that China is beginning to experience the middle income blues.

Even assuming China does follow other East Asian countries into the upper ranks of wealthy, well-governed countries, the process of development will take decades if not longer to reach a relatively stable equilibrium, after which change will continue, albeit in less dramatic fashion, just as it does in Euro-America. Moreover, capitalism, rule of law, democracy, and human rights are sufficiently contested in theory and varied in practice that the final outcome in China cannot be specified at this point—much to the chagrin of those who would press their own version of liberal democracy on China. As China negotiates modernity, and indeed postmodernity, it may very well give rise to one or more novel varieties of capitalism, rule of law, democracy, and human rights. On the other hand, there is enough minimal determinate content to each of these four aspects of modernity to provide a teleological orientation to the process that is likely to survive into the next decades, barring extraordinary catastrophes that change radically the nature of contemporary society.

Is China then a paradigm? I shall argue there are aspects of China's experience that may be useful for other countries. However, China's developmental path does not provide a detailed blueprint to be followed slavishly by other developing states today for a variety of practical and normative reasons.

The East Asian Model (EAM) has come back into vogue since countries in the region rebounded from the Asian financial crisis. Notwithstanding debates about whether the model contributed to or impeded economic growth and the wisdom of particular policies, the general economic approach appears sound. The experience of China and other Asian countries also suggests that good institutions and rule of law are important once a country reaches a certain level of wealth. More controversially, the East Asian experience suggests that democracy may need to be postponed and limitations imposed on civil and political rights in the name of social stability and growth.

Even assuming the soundness of the EAM, other countries may not be able to, or may not want to, follow it. Having democratized, most developing states will not be able to restrict civil and political rights in the name of social stability and economic growth in the way China and other East Asian states have. Citizens of other developing countries may also object that the tradeoff is unnecessary in their case or not worth it. In addition, other countries may not have the political or economic power to resist external pressures to open the domestic economy to foreign competition in the way China has.

More fundamentally, each country faces unique challenges and opportunities. Along the way, many particular choices are made. Some institutions gain power, some lose power; some segments of society are made better off as a result of reforms, others are made worse off. Accordingly, the story of modernization or law and development in any given country is inevitably a story of *politics*—and largely local politics at that. Thus, it is not likely that any single model will apply everywhere. At minimum, the model would need to be adapted in light of local conditions. Indeed, the key to the East Asian success has been the willingness to be pragmatic.

China is certainly different than many developing countries in terms of size, political power, the nature of the political system, and the degree to which it can control its own economic destiny. Nevertheless, despite the differences among successful Asian countries and between Asian countries and other countries, mutual learning is still possible. Thus a fourth goal is to explore what China can learn from other countries engaged in the process of development, democratization, and modernization, and conversely what lessons China offers other developing—and perhaps even developed—states.

Organization of this book and chapter synopses

The general structure of the book tracks the four main pillars of modernity, taking up in turn China's path of economic development and variety of market-capitalism, human rights, rule of law, and democracy. More specifically, Chapter 2 begins to situate China's quest for modernity within a broader comparative context by comparing China's path of development to the East Asian Model.

The Model is drawn from the experiences of the five most successful East Asian countries: Singapore, Japan, Hong Kong, Taiwan, and South Korea. It is stated at a relatively high level of abstraction to underscore areas of commonality among all or most of these countries. The ensuing discussion highlights important dissimilarities among them. I also draw comparisons to countries in Asia and elsewhere that have been less successful.

Chapters 3 to 6 examine China's performance on a number of rights measures and other indicators of human well-being relative to that of other countries. Chapter 3 presents a brief overview of the PRC government's official human rights policy and then turns to China's record on *personal integrity rights* and *civil and political rights*. Chapter 4 examines *social and economic rights* and other indicia of quality of life including poverty, infant mortality, life expectancy, primary school enrollment, and government expenditures on education, health, and the military; *law and order and social stability* as reflected in crime rates and the number of drug users, suicides, divorces, and young mothers; *women's rights*; and *cultural and minority rights*. The *quality of governance*, measured in terms of regulatory effectiveness, regulatory quality, rule of law, and control of corruption, is postponed until Chapter 6.

The multi-country statistical studies used to place China within an overall comparative framework are complemented by a more detailed discussion of particular issues in each area to provide a more complete picture of the rights situation in China.[63] To avoid any confusion—and the bogeyman of being accused of being an apologist for a repressive regime—let me be clear. Despite China's relatively strong performance on a number of indicators given its level of wealth, there are still many people living in relative and absolute poverty; justified concerns about the rights of laborers, migrant workers, women, and minorities; serious shortcomings in criminal justice; major weaknesses in certain aspects of the legal system; widespread corruption; frequent abuse of state power, and a host of other good governance issues.

The government has generally acknowledged these shortcomings, and continues to take steps to address them, although it has been less forthright about defending the severe restrictions on the exercise of civil and political rights when the exercise of such rights is perceived as threatening to social and political stability.[64] However, as the more detailed discussion demonstrates, most of these issues are factually, legally, politically, economically, and normatively contentious, and defy easy solution, especially for such a large developing country as China. Not surprisingly, and with some considerable justification, government officials and even reform-minded academics have expressed impatience with the international human rights community for failing to appreciate the complexity of the issues. They also claim that the critics discount the progress China has made in improving people's living standards and expanding citizens' freedoms while exaggerating the severity of its problems by focusing on the relatively few cases involving political dissidents. Many also take exception to what they see as heavy-handed attempts to impose simplistic solutions that are normatively biased toward liberalism and likely to be counterproductive given China's history and traditions, level of economic development, and current legal and political institutions.

China is routinely subject to censure as one of the worst violators of human rights by the United States and the international human rights community, despite its superior performance to other countries at its income level on most indicators. Chapter 5 argues that China is subject to a double standard, and considers several explanations why.

Chapter 6 examines institutional development in China. The primary objective is to examine the legal reform process in China and what China's efforts to implement rule of law reveal about our understanding of the relationship between law and development. Accordingly, I apply our current conceptual tools for describing, predicting, and assessing legal reforms to the experiences in China. In general, our descriptive metaphors tend to oversimplify the reform process and fail to address the issue of prediction. Our ability to predict success and failure and derive useful policy recommendations is limited by the abstractness of existing indicators for measuring rule of law. And our ability to assess legal reforms meaningfully is complicated by competing and contested standards and the long time frame for reforms to take hold. Nevertheless, there has been some progress in understanding and explaining the relationship between law and development, and further studies will continue to shed more light on the process. It would be a mistake to prematurely give up on the revival of law and development, just as it was a mistake for American academics to abandon ship in the earlier round of law and development in the 1960s and 1970s. This chapter also underscores the inherently political nature of reforms, and the importance of adopting a pragmatic approach.

A second objective is to discuss why China is experiencing the middle income blues, and what can be done about it.

Chapter 7 examines the ongoing debates about democracy. Many of the countries in Asia and elsewhere that democratized at lower levels of wealth have encountered difficulties sustaining economic growth, achieving political stability, and consolidating democracy. In contrast, East Asian countries that democratized at higher levels of wealth have been more stable and prosperous. Not surprisingly, Chinese leaders and most citizens have concluded that the main issue at this stage is not democracy but stability and economic growth (albeit with greater concern for social justice), and that democratization would be counterproductive. However, since China will most likely eventually democratize, I consider what type of democracy is likely to take hold.[65] I suggest some form of nonliberal elitist democracy found in other Asian countries is most likely in China as well.

Chapter 8 considers the implications of China remaining a socialist state or democratizing for economic growth, rule of law, human rights, and geopolitical stability. While no one can predict the future, democracy is clearly no panacea, and will not resolve many of the pressing issues China now faces or necessarily make the world a safer place.

Chapter 9 concludes with some thoughts on the challenges China faces in replicating the success of other East Asian countries, and on the utility of the East Asian Model for other countries.

CHAPTER TWO

Déjà vu all over again: China and the East Asian Model

The strong economic performance of Japan and the other Asian Tigers, combined with the dismal results of developing countries elsewhere, led to intense debates in the 1980s and early 1990s about an East Asian Miracle, and the possibility of other countries following an East Asian Model.[1] The Asian financial crisis in 1997 cast doubt on the Miracle and the viability of the Model. Champions of the affirmative view of modernity and the superiority of Euro-American institutions, practices, and values rushed to attribute the financial crisis to cronyism, bad governance, and the very same 'Asian values' that were considered earlier to be one of the reasons for success. Alan Greenspan jumped into the fray, opining that the crisis had accelerated the trend toward American-style neoliberal capitalism and away from the competing EAM: 'What we have here is a very dramatic event towards a consensus of the type of market system which we have in this country.'[2] Meanwhile, the fall of Suharto and subsequent democratization in Indonesia, the strengthening of democracy in Thailand, and the higher pre-crisis growth rates in the Philippines put advocates of the view that a strong (soft-authoritarian) ruling regime was necessary to ensure economic growth and stability on the defensive.

As Asian economies fought their way back to prosperity, supporters of the EAM mounted a counterattack. Most of the countries that had followed the model were not the ones hardest hit by the crisis.

Among the countries to first follow the EAM and thus the most wealthy and developed, Taiwan, Hong Kong, and Singapore escaped relatively unscathed; only South Korea was devastated. Among the more recent generation of countries to follow the EAM, China and Vietnam were not directly impacted to a significant degree. Neither country had democratized or engaged in rapid financial or capital market liberalization. In addition to South Korea, the hardest-hit countries were Indonesia, Malaysia, Thailand, and the Philippines. Indonesia, Malaysia, and Thailand are borderline cases for the EAM. Malaysia and Indonesia had for decades imposed few restrictions on capital account transactions and had largely deregulated the financial sector. Thailand, which democratized at a relatively low level of wealth by the standards of the EAM, also gave in to liberalization pressures. The Philippines, one of the more dysfunctional states in Asia, never followed the EAM. It too however had leapt on the financial liberalization bandwagon.

Stiglitz, Williamson, and many others in Asia have argued that it was not the model but rather the premature dismantling of the model, and in particular a precipitous turn to financial and capital market liberalization, that led to the crisis, just as rapid liberalization has led to crises in other regions.[3] Even critics of the Asian developmental state acknowledge that attributing the crisis to Asian cronyism was much too simple.[4] Why, after all, had cronyism not produced a financial crisis earlier? Nor could problems across the region be explained solely by reference to weak financial systems, poor corporate governance or industrial policy.[5]

In any event, Asian countries bounced back relatively quickly. Meanwhile, China and Vietnam continued to grow at a blistering pace. Moreover, some of the Asian countries that recovered did so by ignoring the advice of the IFIs to one degree or another. Malaysia and Vietnam imposed currency controls. Hong Kong spent billions to prop up the currency. Thailand, South Korea, and Indonesia set up special agencies staffed by technocrats to solve financial and corporate governance problems, liquidate insolvent financial institutions, and manage their assets.[6] Thailand actively promoted the development of small businesses.[7] South Korea pumped money into a public–private project to support high-tech start-ups.[8] It is true

Thailand and especially South Korea also accepted much of the advice of the IMF. In fact, they had little choice, as the IMF demanded concessions as the quid pro quo for bailing them out. South Korea, for example, opened its capital markets to foreign investors, improved its stock markets, and privatized many state-run or state-owned companies. Nevertheless, they continued to show signs of divergence typical of the East Asian variety of capitalism.[9] Malaysia's response was more effective, faster, and less painful in terms of decreases in employment and real wages than the IMF approach.[10] The IMF was also criticized for various policy blunders, most notably prescribing tight fiscal policies based on crisis intervention models developed for the very different conditions of Latin American countries where high budget deficits were the norm rather than the balanced budgets or surpluses of Asian countries.

In further support of the continued utility of the EAM, Asian business practices and values played an important role in the recovery. The high incidence of family businesses and the relational nature of much business in Asian countries, for instance, helped cushion the shock by providing a social welfare network in countries where the social security system is typically weak and by making it possible to raise capital to start over. Quite apart from the debates about the crisis and its causes, supporters have argued that there are still many aspects of East Asian capitalism worth maintaining, including 'the combination of rapid economic growth with decreasing poverty and income inequality; companies that emphasize the interests of workers, local communities and the national good and take a more long-term view regarding the need to make profit; and rapid modernization that preserves social stability and civil harmony.'[11]

In short, the economic recovery in Asia along with China's march to superpower status have again sparked interest in the EAM. To be sure, there are still doubters. Some skeptics questioned the miracle even before the Asian financial crisis.[12] Similarly, some economists have noted that China's official growth rates are overstated and that China's growth has resulted in large part from productivity improvements mainly from reallocation of labor from low to high productivity sectors, in particular from agriculture to manufacturing and services.[13] Long-term growth however requires an increase in productivity within individual sectors. According to World Bank studies, only one-fourth of China's growth resulted from improvements in each sector.[14]

Other commentators have also questioned whether there was anything special about Asia's success. Some argued that in fact Asian states followed basic neoclassical principles and intervened very little. Other skeptics allowed that there was considerable deviation from such principles, as the works of specialists demonstrated,[15] but questioned whether an interventionist developmental state was the reason for success.[16] On this view, the success was due to other factors: US support in Japan, Taiwan, and South Korea; favorable international economic conditions; or 'Asian values' and the impact of Confucianism, which led to an emphasis on education, hard work, personal savings, a nationalistic desire for a strong state, and a willingness to sacrifice personal interest in the name of the overall good. The World Bank cited a number of factors: sound macroeconomic management, including fiscal discipline and control of inflation; high levels of private domestic investment, domestic savings, and investment in education; agricultural policies that increased productivity; promotion of exports; flexible labor markets; limited price distortions; openness to foreign technology; a demographic transition from high to low birth rates; politically insulated and reasonably compensated technocratic leaders; a business-friendly environment; and selective state interventions subject to strict performance criteria—although the Bank was ambivalent at best about the positive value of state interventions that deviated from 'the neoclassical' model.[17] No doubt many factors were involved. Nevertheless, the success of Asia as a region is still remarkable. That this success is due to a variety of factors, some of them context specific, in no way diminishes the achievement, though it may make it more difficult for other regions to follow their lead.

John Williamson, the economist who first articulated the principles of the 'Washington Consensus,' has acknowledged that successful East Asian states deviated from some of his ten principles to one degree or another.[18] They generally followed the WC with respect to fiscal discipline; the redirection of public spending to education, health, and infrastructure; tax reforms to lower rates and increase the base (and to encourage foreign investment or promote exports); competitive exchange rates;[19] and secure property rights. However, they were more circumspect about trade liberalization, privatization, deregulation, interest rate liberalization, and financial liberalization.

Williamson acknowledges that his emphasis on trade liberalization was at odds with the policies that led to growth in East Asia. In general, Japan, South Korea, and Taiwan imposed numerous limits on foreign direct investment and imports, whereas Singapore and Hong Kong, and now China, have been more open. Williamson points out however that he did not take a position on how fast countries should reduce protective measures, and he now allows that there may be occasions when protection of infant industries makes sense. He also acknowledges that the results of privatization have been mixed, and that privatization has had no consistent effect on wages, prices, output quality, or employment. Whatever the economic merits, he concedes privatization is widely unpopular with the public because of problems with corruption and the sale of domestic assets to foreign companies (the latter also a major concern in the US, first with Japan in the 1980s and now with China). Williamson now also concedes that interest rate liberalization should come at the end of the process of financial liberalization, and must be accompanied by financial supervision.

One of the key remaining areas of contention is over industrial policy. Williamson disagrees with Stiglitz and others who attribute the East Asian success to allocation of resources to particular industries. Rather, he believes that the Asian financial crisis demonstrated the problems with this approach, including high debt to equity ratios and the large number of bad loans. However, he now also believes that there may be a role for government in promoting a national innovation system and in igniting an investment boom by subsidizing particular investments.

The renewed interest in the EAM has given rise to several new issues. Even assuming there is an EAM, is China following it? Have economic globalization and democratization undermined China's ability to follow the developmental state path of earlier countries? Why have other Asian states failed to achieve the same impressive results? Is the model applicable to other Asian states or elsewhere? Are there ways of mitigating the negative aspects of the EAM?

The East Asian path to constitutional democracy

The economic aspects of the EAM have drawn the most attention. However, the EAM—a notion which admittedly serves a useful purpose only at a high level of generalization and conceals considerable diversity when subject to closer scrutiny—involves the sequencing of economic growth, legal reforms, democratization, and constitutionalism, with different rights being taken seriously at different times in the process. I will focus more on the relationship between economic growth and these other factors than on the purely economic aspects of the EAM, in part because others have discussed the economic aspects at length, and in part because the assessment of China's performance to date requires the broader perspective.

The EAM involves:

(i) an emphasis on economic growth rather than civil and especially political rights during the initial stages of development, with a period of rapid economic growth occurring under authoritarian regimes;

(ii) a pragmatic approach to reforms, with governments following some aspects of the WC and rejecting or modifying others; in particular, with governments adopting most of the basic macroeconomic principles of the Washington Consensus for the domestic economy; rejecting or modifying the neoliberal aspects that would greatly reduce the role of the state through rapid privatization and deregulation, with the state also more active in reducing poverty and in ensuring minimal material standards to compete in a more competitive global economy;[20] and modifying the prescribed WC relationship between the domestic and global economy by gradually exposing the domestic economy to international competition while offering some protection to key sectors and some support to infant industries;

(iii) as the economy grows and wealth is generated, the government invests in human capital and in institutions, including reforms to establish a legal system that meets the basic Fullerian requirements of a procedural or thin rule of law;[21] over time, as the legal system becomes more efficient, professional, and autonomous, it comes to play a greater role in the economy and society more generally;

(iv) democratization in the sense of freely contested multiple party elections for the highest level of office is postponed until a relatively high level of wealth is attained;

(v) constitutionalism begins to emerge during the authoritarian period, including the development of constitutional norms and the strengthening of institutions; social organizations start to proliferate and 'civil society' begins to develop, albeit often a civil society with a different nature and political orientation than in Western liberal democracies, and with organizations with a political agenda subject to limitations; citizens enjoy economic liberties, rising living standards for the vast majority, and some civil and political rights although with limitations especially on rights that involve political issues and affect the control of the regime; judicial independence remains limited, with the protection of the full range of human rights and in particular civil and political rights suffering accordingly;

(vi) there is greater protection of civil and political rights after democratization, including rights that involve sensitive political issues, although with ongoing abuses of rights in some cases and with rights frequently given a communitarian or collectivist interpretation rather than a liberal interpretation.

This very roughly describes the arc of several Asian states, albeit with countries at various levels of economic wealth and legal system development, and with political regimes ranging from democracies to semi-democracies to socialist states.[22] South Korea and Taiwan have high levels of wealth, rule of law compliant legal systems, democratic government, and constitutionalism. Japan does as well, although it is a special case given its early rise economically and the post-war colonial influence of the US on legal and political institutions. Hong Kong, Singapore, and Malaysia are also wealthy, with legal systems that fair well in terms of rule of law, but are either not democratic (Hong Kong) or are nonliberal democracies dominated by a single party (Singapore and Malaysia). Thailand, less wealthy than the others, has democratized, but has a weaker legal system and, under Prime Minister Thaksin, adopted policies that emphasize growth and social order rather than civil and political liberties.[23] China and Vietnam are at an earlier stage. They are lower-middle and low income countries respectively, and have legal systems that outperform the average in their income class but are weaker than the rest. They remain effectively single-party socialist states, with varying degrees and areas of political openness.

There are also examples of less successful paths in Asia (and elsewhere). Some involve countries that democratized at lower levels of wealth: Indonesia, India, the Philippines, and Cambodia. Others involve authoritarian systems that failed to invest in human capital and institutions: North Korea, Laos, and Myanmar. The latter tend to have thc weakest legal systems and to be mired in poverty, with all of the human suffering that entails.[24] When authoritarianism fails, it fails badly.

The mutual reinforcement of rule of law and economic growth

Five East Asian countries or jurisdictions rank in the top quartile on the World Bank's rule of law index: Singapore, Japan, Hong Kong, Taiwan, and South Korea. This is an astonishing achievement given the well-documented failures of the earlier law and development movement and its more recent reincarnation under the banner of rule of law and good governance.[25] Apart from North American and Western European countries, Australia, and Israel, the only other countries in the top quartile are Chile and French Guiana from Latin America, Slovenia as the lone (non)representative from Eastern

Europe, and a handful of small island states and oil-rich Arab countries.[26]

The seemingly random countries in this odd grouping have one thing in common: wealth. All of the countries in the top quartile of the World Bank rule of law index, including the East Asian countries, are high or upper-middle income countries. This is consistent with the general empirical evidence that rule of law and economic development are closely related ($r = .82$, $p < .01$—see Table 2 below), and tend to be mutually reinforcing.[27] Notwithstanding theoretical arguments for and against the claim that rule of law contributes to economic development, the empirical evidence is surprisingly consistent and supportive of the claim that implementation of rule of law is necessary though by no means sufficient for sustained economic development.[28]

Asia is often considered to be an exception to the general rule requiring rule of law for sustained economic growth.[29] However, the role of law in economic development in Asia is frequently underestimated because of the tendency to elide rule of law with democracy and a liberal version of rights that emphasizes civil and political rights.[30] Although the political regimes may not have been democratic and the legal systems may not have provided much protection for civil and political rights in some cases, the Asian countries that experienced economic growth generally have scored high with respect to the protection of economic interests and the facilitation of economic transactions. A survey of economic freedoms in 102 countries between 1993 and 1995 found that seven of the top twenty countries were in Asia.[31] Economic freedoms include protection of the value of money, free exchange of property, a fair judiciary, few trade restrictions, labor market freedoms, and freedom from economic coercion by political opponents. Six states—Japan, South Korea, Taiwan, Hong Kong, Singapore, and China—experienced sustained growth over 5% for the period from 1965 until 1995.[32] The legal systems of these countries measure up favorably in terms of economic freedoms and rule of law, with the possible exception of China.

However, even in China, the legal system has improved significantly in the last twenty-five years, particularly in the commercial area. In contrast, the legal systems of most of the low growth countries are among the weakest in the region. Table 1 presents a percentile ranking of Asian legal systems based on the World Bank's rule of law index for the years 1996 and 2002.[33] Countries with better legal systems tend to have higher growth and more wealth, and vice versa. The relationship between GDP and rule of law is actually stronger in the Asian region ($r = .91$) than for countries overall ($r = .82$), as indicated in Table 3 below.

Despite such consistent and seemingly overwhelming evidence, there are still good reasons to be cautious in reaching broad conclusions about the relationship between rule of law and economic growth. Defining and measuring rule of law remains an issue.[34] Several of the main empirical studies relied on subjective measures from three sources, the ICRG and BERI surveys and the World Bank rule of law index.

The relationship between rule of law and economic growth also appears to be nonlinear.[35] Rule of law may not be necessary or as significant where a country is very poor and the economy is largely rural based. A formal legal system that meets the standards of rule of

Table 1. World Bank Rule of Law Rankings (percentiles)

Country	2002	1996
Singapore	93.9	99.4
Japan	88.7	88.0
Hong Kong	86.6	90.4
Taiwan	80.9	84.3
South Korea	77.8	81.9
Malaysia	69.6	82.5
Mongolia	64.9	70.5
Thailand	62.9	71.1
China	51.5	37.3
Vietnam	44.8	34.9
Philippines	38.1	54.8
Indonesia	23.1	39.8
Cambodia	20.1	16.9
North Korea	14.7	13.9
Laos	12.9	4.8
Myanmar	2.1	5.4

Source: The World Bank Group, Governance Matters In: Governance Indicators for 1996–2002. All tables and figures using this dataset were based on data as reported in 2003. **www.worldbank.org/wbi/governance/govdata2002**.

law is costly to establish and operate. In some cases, norms of generalized morality, social trust, self-enforcing market mechanisms, and informal substitutes for formal law may provide the necessary predictability and certainty required by economic actors for a fraction of the cost.

Formal and informal law, public ordering and private ordering are complementary in many ways. Family businesses, networks of personal relationships, and private orderings exist in all legal systems, although the cultural, economic, political, and economic context may vary from one country to the next, leading to differences in the degree of importance or variations in particular practices.[36] Since they are not perfect substitutes, each can support and help overcome the weaknesses of the other. In general however, relationships and social networks, clientelism, corporatism, and informal mechanisms for resolving disputes, raising capital, and securing contracts are at best imperfect substitutes. Once a country reaches higher levels of economic development, the costs of a formal legal system are easier to bear. It is no accident that richer countries have better legal systems.

Critics who challenge the relationship between rule of law and economic development often note that in some cases courts have played a minor role in enforcing contracts or resolving disputes, and emphasize that these other informal institutions may provide substitutes for formal court proceedings. While true, such substitutes operate against a background of law, and often could not function without the possibility of ultimately turning to the courts should other means for resolving the dispute fail. Furthermore, dispute resolution is only one of the economic functions of a legal system. The legal system also performs an enabling function by creating the basic infrastructure for transactions, including markets, security exchanges, mortgage systems, accounting practices, and so on. Of course, a legal system that is compliant with rule of law serves many laudable functions other than promoting economic growth, including limiting arbitrary acts of government and promoting fairness and justice.

Rule of law is an ideal, which admits of degrees. Obviously the legal systems in the prosperous Asian countries were not always so well developed. As critics note, legal systems in Asia deviated to one degree or another from the rule of law ideal. The legal systems—relative to their current state if not to the weakest legal systems in the region—were slow and inefficient, in some cases corrupt, and frequently set up a variety of barriers to civil litigation.[37] Administrative officials were often allowed considerable discretion, particularly in Japan where administrative guidance played a crucial role in the development state.

On the other hand, the amount of discretion compatible with rule of law is a hotly contested issue. Legal systems everywhere allow for administrative discretion, and employ a variety of legal, social, institutional, and political means for restraining and checking the discretion of bureaucrats. Chan highlights the role of 'inclusionary institutionalism' in Asian developmental states. Industry groups, consultative committees, and social networks provided a channel for the flow of interaction back and forth between the state, industry, and society. They thus helped nondemocratic governments overcome information problems, allowing them to respond effectively to changing economic conditions. In addition, the system performed a commitment function, creating a structure of rights and expectations that reduced uncertainty and bolstered investor confidence. 'By making information available to all, by ensuring policies are transparent, and by creating a forum for mutual interaction and feedback, the [system] eliminated uncertainty and mistrust on the one hand, and on the other erected a de facto constitutional framework in which co-operative economic decision-making is guaranteed.'[38]

The nature of the system varied from country to country. In Japan, a 'pervasive consensual, consultative style' of administrative guidance developed where government agencies worked closely with key industrial actors; in Korea, the government at times more aggressively orchestrated events in command-like fashion; and in Taiwan, where small and medium-sized businesses played a greater role, the government relied more on arms-length incentives to steer private firms while promoting development of new fields or industries through the sponsorship of research and development. In all cases, networks of formal and informal relationships played a key role.[39]

Thick conceptions of rule of law—which incorporate into the conception of rule of law different elements of political morality, including different varieties of capitalism with their corresponding conceptions of the proper role of the state (such as the development state as opposed to the minimalist neoliberal state, the limited liberal state, or the most expansive social welfare or progressive state)—will differ with respect to issues such as administrative discretion and administrative law more generally.[40]

The legal systems in Japan, Taiwan, South Korea, Hong Kong, Singapore, and now China during their period of growth were still stronger and more functional than other legal systems in the region. Critics often speak of the 'lack' or 'absence' of rule of law during the period of high growth, as if rule of law were a discrete variable and either present in perfect form or completely absent. This way of speaking suggests that the legal system was wholly dysfunctional, imposed no limits whatsoever on administrative discretion or state actors, or provided no relief for private parties seeking to settle disputes. But surely the legal system did not just suddenly jump into the top quartile of countries on the World Bank rule of law index. Even most critics allow that the legal system played some role in the economy, and acknowledge that practices such as administrative guidance existed in a regulatory environment that included legal limits as well as political, institutional, and economic constraints. Of course, growth rates might have been even higher had the legal systems been stronger.

The role of the legal system has naturally changed over time, and is still continuing to change. As the legal systems became stronger and more professional, they have played a greater role in both economic and noneconomic matters. In Japan, poor economic performance and the Asian financial crisis have led to the restructuring of the bureaucracy and attempts to curtail administrative guidance, which is now subject to tighter legal restrictions and judicial review. Globalization and domestic pressures have also led to proposals to overhaul the legal profession and legal education, a hot issue in South Korea as well.

Perhaps most worrisome for policy-makers, implementing rule of law and achieving economic growth are complicated tasks. Even those at the center of the new law and development movement acknowledge the persistent difficulty in operationalizing the relation between law and development, and the inability to specify with any reasonable degree of certainty precisely what is required at what stage for economic development. The problem in a nutshell is that rule of law is consistent with considerable institutional variation. The general principles of a thin rule of law are too abstract to provide determinate advice on issues such as what the proper standing requirements should be for civil litigation, how many lawyers there should be and whether they should be allowed to charge contingency fees, or whether courts should adopt a purposive or positivist form of interpretation.

To complicate matters further, the rule of law agenda has continually expanded. During the 1990s, in addition to the procedural and institutional features of a thin rule of law, the new law and development movement, spearheaded by international financial organizations and development agencies, incorporated under the banner of rule of law the substantive principles of the WC. [41] Faced with dismal results in many countries, including the financial crisis in Asia and a notable negative impact on social services and the most vulnerable in Latin American countries and elsewhere, development agencies and human rights activists then joined forces to expand the program even further to take in a broader range of concerns, and thus built into the rule of law and good governance agenda democracy, human rights, and the particular norms and institutions of liberal democracies.[42]

The result has been greater conceptual confusion, with rule of law becoming a slogan to advance whatever substantive agenda or wish-list of rights the speaker chooses. Not surprisingly, in Asia and elsewhere, countries at low levels of wealth that have taken on the broader agenda and attempted to democratize and implement a full range of social and economic as well as civil and political rights have often experienced disappointing results.

Investment in human capital and institutions

Performance on human rights standards, including measures of civil and political rights, and other indicia of human well-being, is highly correlated with wealth.[43] As Figure 1 graphically depicts and Table 2 demonstrates, wealth is highly correlated with social and economic rights ($r = .92$),[44] women's rights as measured by the Gender Developmental Index ($r = .93$),[45] good governance indicators such as government effectiveness ($r = .77$), rule of law ($r = .82$), and control of corruption ($r = .76$), civil and political rights ($r = .62$),[46] and even physical integrity rights though to a lower degree ($r = -.40$).

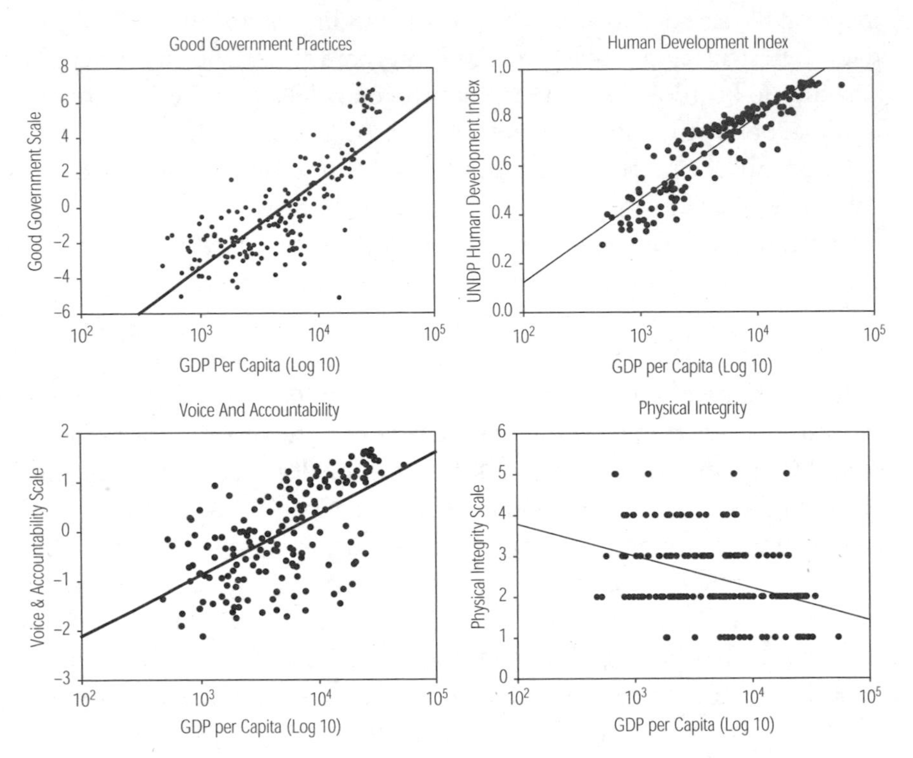

Fig. 1. Wealth Effect (GDP) on Rights Performance

Sources: Good Government Practice combines the World Bank Governance Indicators for Rule of Law, Government Effectiveness, and Control of Corruption. Human Development Index: UNDP, Human Development Report 2003, *Human Development Indicators*. **http://hdr.undp.org/reports/global/2003/indicator/index.html**. Voice and Accountability: World Bank Governance Indicators for 1996–2002. Physical Integrity: Mark Gibney, *Political Science Terror Scale*. **http://www.unca.edu/politicalscience/faculty-staff/gibney_docs/pts.xls**. GDP figures are from the World Bank Group, World Development Indicators, World Development Indicators (CD-ROM, current through 2003).

As countries become wealthier, they generally protect all rights better. Asian countries are no exception.

CIVIL AND POLITICAL RIGHTS

The World Bank's Voice and Accountability scale incorporates a number of indicators measuring various aspects of the political process, civil liberties, and political rights, including the right to participate in the selection of government representatives and the

Table 2. Correlation of Wealth and Measures of Development

Measure	Region								
	All	Africa	Asia	Australia and Pacific	Caribbean	Former Soviet Influence	Latin America	Middle East	Western Europe
Human development index (HDI) 2001	0.92**	0.88**	0.93**	0.97**	0.86**	0.97**	0.88**	0.93**	0.94**
Gender-related development index (GDI) 2001	0.93**	0.87**	0.92**	0.98*	0.89*	0.97**	0.90**	0.92**	0.83**
Rule of Law	0.82**	0.58**	0.91**	0.95**	0.90**	0.81**	0.64**	0.89**	0.92**
Government Effectiveness	0.77**	0.49**	0.90**	0.98**	0.92**	0.85**	0.69**	0.78**	0.91**
Control of Corruption	0.76**	0.55**	0.88**	0.96**	0.81**	0.83**	0.67**	0.77**	0.86**
Voice and Accountability	0.62**	0.29	0.50*	0.94**	0.75*	0.73**	0.34	0.18	0.85**
PTS 2002 (AI & State)	−0.40**	−0.22	−0.42	−0.74	−0.71*	−0.21	0.10	−0.25	−0.48*
N	174	41	19	6	10	20	20	15	23

Cell entries are Pearson's *R* coefficients. Dependent variable is natural log of GDP per capita $*p < .05$, $**p < .01$.
GDI source: UNDP **http://222.undp.org/hdr2003/pdf/hdr03_HDI.pdf**. Data are as of March 2003. The data are now available at **http://hdr.undp.org/statistics/data/indic/ indic21811.htinl**.
For calculation of the GDI, see **http://hdrc.undp.org.in/APRI/metho/GDI.htm**.

independence of the media.[47] The East Asia region falls squarely in the middle among all regions as shown in Table 2. However, there is a considerable range within the Asian region as indicated in Figure 2. Japan and Taiwan score reasonably well, though not as high as the US and France, whereas Vietnam and China are in the lowest 10%. The differences in performance are largely consistent with variations in levels of wealth, although clearly ideology, the nature of the political system, and others factors also play a role. Low income democratic India and Indonesia, for example, score higher than lower-middle and low income socialist China and Vietnam.

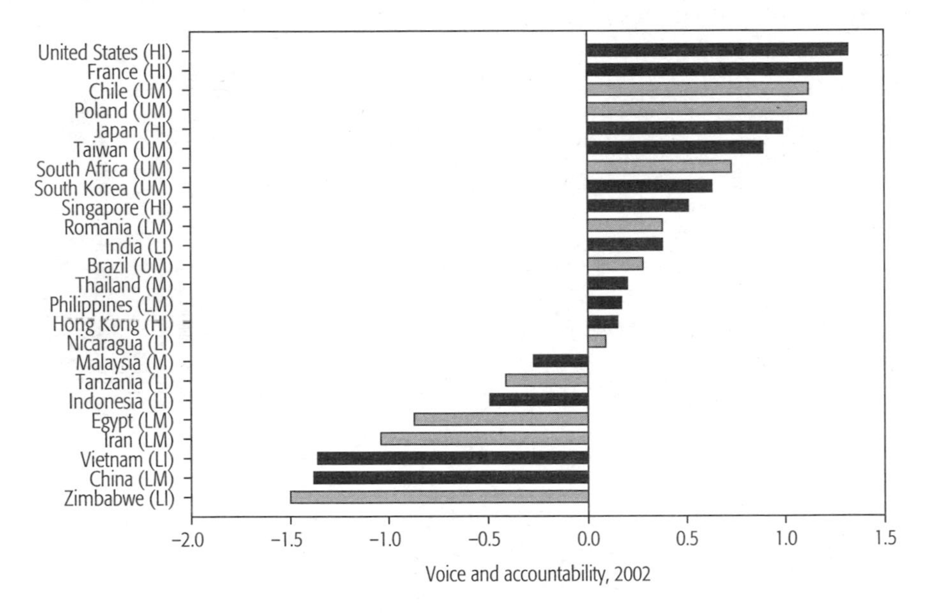

Fig. 2. Civil and Political Rights: Voice and Accountability 2002

Notes: LI refers to lower income countries; LM to lower-middle income; M to middle income; UM to upper-middle income; HI to high income. I have used World Bank income categories; however, the following countries have been ranked differently according to the World Bank and the UNDP:

Country	World Bank	UNDP
Taiwan	HI	UM
South Korea	UM	HI
Malaysia	M	UM
Brazil	UM	LM
South Africa	UM	LM

Sources: World Bank Governance Indicators for 1996–2002 (2003).

On the whole, however, East Asian countries with a Confucian influence, even if democratic, tend to do poorly relative to income level on civil and political rights.[48] Japan, Taiwan, Singapore, Malaysia, Hong Kong, China, and Vietnam all underperform relative to income.[49] In contrast, South Korea, India, the Philippines, Thailand, and recently Indonesia outperform the average in their income class.[50] Moreover, even the most democratic regimes in the region score somewhat lower than the more liberal US and France.

In contrast, Asian countries tend to do much better, both relative to civil and political rights and also to other countries in their income group, on economic rights and other quality of life indicators such as education, infant mortality, life expectancy, law and order, and social stability (see Figure 3 and Table 4). East Asian governments also tend to outperform other countries in their income group on good governance measures (see Tables 2 and 7).

POVERTY REDUCTION

China and other Asian governments have attacked the bias of the international rights community in emphasizing civil and political rights over the right to subsistence, economic rights, and the right to development. Their superior performance on these other measures suggests that at least they are not simply being hypocritical. There is still considerable room for improvement of course, and critics would take issue with the assumption that there must be any tradeoff between protecting civil and political rights and ensuring growth and development.

Figure 3 presents the rankings for UNDP's Human Development Index based on data for 2002. The HDI measures the average achievement in a country in three basic dimensions: a long and healthy life based on life expectancy at birth; education and knowledge measured by adult literacy and combined primary, secondary, and tertiary enrollments; and a decent standard of living as measured by GDP per capita ($PPP). As one would expect, wealthier countries everywhere, including in Asia, generally have higher HDI rankings, with wealth constituting a more important factor than the nature of political regime.

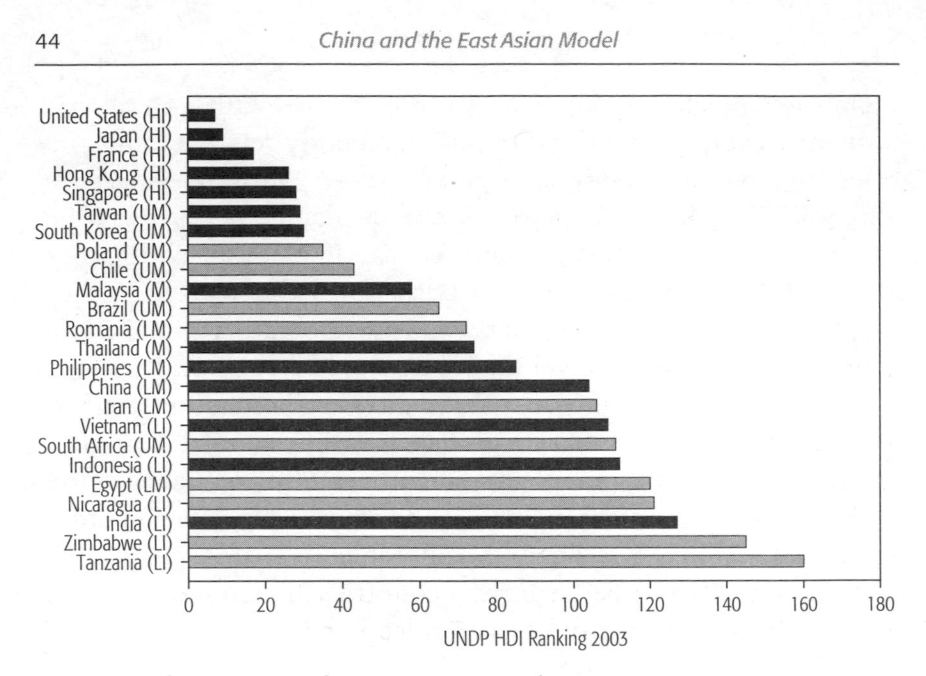

Fig. 3. Social Economic Rights: UNDP HDI Ranking 2003
Source: UNDP *Human Development Indicators* (2003).

However, the general composite measure fails to tell the whole story. Higher levels of economic development and riches for some are consistent with an impoverished life for many others. Asia as a region has been relatively successful over the last decade in reducing poverty, defined as the admittedly minimalist standard of living on less than $1/day. In contrast, poverty in other regions has increased or remained more or less the same.[51]

The performance of the East Asian region is somewhat deceptive in that the results are skewed by the remarkable performance of China, which lifted 12% of its population out of poverty in just nine years. To be sure, even within China, poverty remains an issue, as discussed in Chapter 4.[52]

Table 3 shows three ways of measuring human poverty. One approach measures the percentage of the population below the national poverty line defined as what that society considers necessary to satisfy basic needs. Because countries will set the poverty line at different levels, a wealthier, welfare-conscious country may have a high percentage living in poverty and appear poorer. The second approach measures the percentage of the population below uniform poverty lines of $1 and $2 per day. Even when adjusted for purchasing

Table 3. Poverty Index

Country and Human Development Indicator Rank		Human poverty index (HPI-1)		Population below income poverty line (%)			HPI-1 rank minus income poverty rank
		Rank	Value (%)	$1 a day 1990–2001	$2 a day 1990–2001	National poverty line 1987–2000	
26	Hong Kong (HI)	–	–	–	–	–	–
30	South Korea (HI)	–	–	<2	<2	–	–
58	Malaysia (UM)	–	–	<2	9.3	–	–
43	Chile (UM)	3	4.1	<2	8.7	17.0	1
28	Singapore (HI)	6	6.3	–	–	–	–
65	Brazil (LM)	18	11.4	9.9	23.7	–	−8
74	Thailand (LM)	24	12.9	<2	32.5	13.1	12
104	China (LM)	26	14.2	16.1	47.3	4.6	−13
85	Philippines (LM)	28	14.8	14.6	46.4	36.8	−6
106	Iran (LM)	31	16.4	<2	7.3	–	18
112	Indonesia (LI)	33	17.9	7.2	55.4	27.1	5
109	Vietnam (LI)	39	19.9	17.7	63.7	–	−4
121	Nicaragua (LI)	44	24.3	82.3	94.5	47.9	−34
120	Egypt (LM)	47	30.5	3.1	43.9	16.7	18
111	South Africa (LM)	49	31.7	<2	14.5	–	31
127	India (LI)	53	33.1	34.7	79.9	28.6	−9
160	Tanzania (LI)	59	36.2	19.9	59.7	41.6	5
145	Zimbabwe (LI)	90	52.0	36.0	64.2	34.9	14

Sources: Columns 1–2 (Human poverty index): UNDP, *Human and Income Poverty: Developing Countries*. **www.undp.org/hdr2003/indicator/pdf/hdr03_table_3.pdf**.

HPI rank is determined on the basis of the HPI-1 values. The HPI value is a composite score based on standard of living measurements including life expectancy (probability of death before age 40), education level (adult illiteracy rate), access to water (population without sustainable access to water), and access to food (children underweight for age). The aggregation rule is specified in Technical Rule 1 of the UNDP 2003 report, at **http://hdr.undp.org/reports/global/2003/pdf/hdr03backmatter2.pdf**.

Columns 3–5 (Population below income poverty line): World Bank, 2003, World Development Indicators (CD-ROM, current through 2003), **http://hdr.undp.org/reports/global/2003/pdf/hdr03backmatter2.pdf**.

The final column is calculated on the basis of ranking data in columns 1 and PPP$I data in column 3. A positive final column figure indicates that the country performs better in income poverty than in human poverty, a negative the opposite.

power parity (PPP), this income-based approach cannot fully capture actual differences in the standard of living of poor people. While the first two approaches measure consumption and income, a third approach measures the impact of poverty directly. The Human Poverty Index quantifies poverty in terms of life expectancy, access to food and water, and education as measured by literacy rates.

Ultimately, it pays to look at the three measures concurrently. For example, in comparison to other countries at its income level, China has a relatively large number of people living on less than $1 day.[53] But the actual standard of living in China, as measured by the HPI, exceeds countries with higher income such as Iran and South Africa.

Asian countries vary dramatically in levels of poverty. India is by far the worst, though poverty remains a problem in Vietnam, Indonesia, the Philippines, China, and Thailand. However, some countries are doing fairly well in reducing poverty relative to the number of people with very low incomes, including China, the Philippines, and Vietnam. Others have been doing poorly, especially Thailand but also Indonesia, although Thailand has improved recently under Thaksin.

Of course, relative and even absolute poverty remains an issue in developed countries as well. About 9% of the population lives on less than $2/day in middle income Malaysia. Surprisingly given the communitarian rhetoric of Lee Kuan Yew, Singapore's poverty ranking is out of line with its income level and HDI ranking. By way of comparison, the US has the highest rate of poverty at 15.3% when measured by the UNDP's higher HPI-2 standard for developed countries. More than 17% of the population in the US is income poor, with the poverty line set at 50% of the median adjusted household disposable income.[54] While GNP reached a historic high in the United States in 1990, having grown over 25% in a decade, child poverty increased by 21% to where one in five American children lived in poverty.[55] Almost 30% of the poor had no medical insurance in 1991. The lack of medical insurance results in 18,000 premature deaths every year.[56]

ECONOMIC 'RIGHTS' AND OTHER INDICATORS OF HUMAN WELL-BEING: INFANT MORTALITY, LIFE EXPECTANCY, AND LITERACY RATES

Table 4 on infant mortality, life expectancy, and education demonstrates that wealth and war matter, with richer and less war-prone Asian countries outperforming many African countries. Interestingly, Japan, Hong Kong, and Singapore outperform the significantly wealthier US in terms of infant mortality and life expectancy.

Table 4. Infant Mortality, Life Expectancy, and Primary School Enrollment

Infant mortality rate (per 1,000 live births) 2001		Life expectancy at birth (years) 2001		Net Primary School Enrollment Rate (% eligible age children) 2000–1	
Hong Kong (HI)	3	Japan (HI)	81.3	Japan (HI)	100
Japan (HI)	3	Hong Kong (HI)	79.7	France (HI)	100
Singapore (HI)	3	France (HI)	78.7	Hong Kong (HI)	98
France (HI)	4	Singapore (HI)	77.8	Taiwan (UM)	99
South Korea (HI)	5	United States (HI)	76.9	South Korea (HI)	99
Taiwan (UM)	6	Chile (UM)	75.8	Poland (UM)	98
United States (HI)	7	Taiwan (UM)	75.6	Malaysia (UM)	98
Poland (UM)	8	South Korea (HI)	75.2	Brazil (LM)	97
Malaysia (UM)	8	Poland (UM)	73.6	United States (HI)	95
Chile (UM)	10	Malaysia (UM)	72.8	Vietnam (LI)	95
Romania (LM)	19	China (LM)	70.6	Singapore (HI)	91
Thailand (LM)	24	Romania (LM)	70.5	Romania (LM)	93
Philippines (LM)	29	Iran (LM)	69.8	Philippines (LM)	93
Vietnam (LI)	30	Philippines (LM)	69.5	China (LM)	93
Brazil (LM)	31	Nicaragua (LI)	69.1	Egypt (LM)	93
China (LM)	31	Thailand (LM)	68.9	Indonesia (LI)	92
Indonesia (LI)	33	Vietnam (LI)	68.6	Chile (UM)	89
Iran (LM)	35	Egypt (LM)	68.3	South Africa (LM)	90
Egypt (LM)	35	Brazil (LM)	67.8	India (LI)	83
Nicaragua (LI)	36	Indonesia (LI)	66.2	Thailand (LM)	85
South Africa (LM)	56	India (LI)	63.3	Nicaragua (LI)	81
India (LI)	67	South Africa (LM)	50.9	Zimbabwe (LI)	80
Zimbabwe (LI)	76	Tanzania (LI)	44	Iran (LM)	74
Tanzania (LI)	104	Zimbabwe (LI)	35.4	Tanzania (LI)	47

Sources: Column 1 (Infant Mortality Rate): UNICEF (United Nations Children's Fund), *The State of the World's Children* (2003), **www.unicef.org/sowc03/tables/table1.html**. For Hong Kong's infant mortality rate see CIA World Factbook, Field Listing–Infant Mortality Rate. **www.cia.gov/cia/publications/factbook/fields/2091.html**.

Column 2 (Life Expectancy at Birth): UN Department of Economic and Social Affairs, Population Division, *2003. World Population Prospects 1950–2050: The 2002 Revision. Database*. **www.undp.org/hdr2003/pdf/ hdr03_HDI.pdf**.

Column 3 (Net Primary School Enrollment Rate): UNESCO Institute for Statistics, *Correspondence on Adult and Youth Literacy Rates. January. Montreal* (2003), *also available at UNDP, Basic Indicators for Other UN Member Countries* (2003), **http://pooh.undp.org/maindiv/hdr_dvpt/statistics/data/indic/indic_291_1_1.html**; Earth Trends, Country Profiles: Population, Health, and Human Well-Being–Singapore, **http://earthtrends.wri.org/pdf_library/country-profiles/Pop_cou_702.pdf** (displaying Singapore data from 1999). Taiwan data is based on statistics compiled by the Taiwan Statistics Bureau, **www.dghas.gov.tw/dgbas03/bs2/92chy/catalog.htm**.

Vietnam and China, which score poorly on civil and political rights, do well on primary school education, reaching levels comparable to that in the US. The Philippines and Indonesia, torn by domestic strife and affected by the Asian financial crisis that

Table 5. Public Spending Priorities (% GDP)

Country and Human Development Indicator Rank		Public Expenditure on Education 1998–2000	Public Expenditure on Health 2000	Military Expenditure 2001
145	Zimbabwe (LI)	10.4	3.1	3.2
58	Malaysia (M)	6.2	1.5	2.2
17	France (HI)	5.8	7.2	2.5
111	South Africa (UM)	5.5	3.7	1.6
29	Taiwan (UM)	5.5	0.4	1.5
74	Thailand (M)	5.4	2.1	1.4
35	Poland (UM)	5.0	4.2	1.9
121	Nicaragua (LI)	5.0	2.3	1.1
26	Hong Kong	4.9*	1.6	–
7	United States (HI)	4.8	5.8	3.1
65	Brazil (UM)	4.7	3.4	1.5
106	Iran (LM)	4.4	2.5	4.8
43	Chile (UM)	4.2	3.1	2.9
85	Philippines (LM)	4.2	1.6	1.0
127	India (LI)	4.1	0.9	2.5
30	South Korea (UM)	3.8	2.6	2.8
120	Egypt (LM)	3.7	1.8	2.6
28	Singapore (HI)	3.7	1.2	5.0
9	Japan (HI)	3.5	6.0	1.0
72	Romania (LM)	3.5	1.9	2.5
160	Tanzania (LI)	2.1	2.8	1.3
104	China (LM)	2.1	1.9	2.3
112	Indonesia (LI)	1.0	0.6	1.1
109	Vietnam (LI)	–	1.3	7.9

Sources: Column 1: United Nations Organization for Education, Science and Culture, UNESCO Institute for Statistics, RE–Public Expenditure on Education as % of GNI, GDP, and Government Expenditure Table, **www.uis.unesco.org/**. Hong Kong education figure from report to ICESCR Committee.
Column 2: The World Bank Group, World Development Indicators 2003 (World Development Indicators 2003 CD-ROM).
Column 3: Stockholm International Peace Research Institute, SIPRI Data on Military Expenditure, **http://web.sipri.org/contents/milap/milex/mex_data_index.html**.
Taiwan data is based on statistics compiled by the Taiwan Statistics Bureau. Taiwan Statistics Bureau, 2002 Social Indicators Contents, **www.dgbas.gov.tw/dgbas03/bs2/92chy/catalog.htm**.

increased poverty particularly in rural areas, suffer from relatively high rates of children who do not receive a primary school education. Thailand performs surprisingly poorly on this measure, reflecting to some extent the impact of the Asian financial crisis, although Thailand has historically underperformed on education relative to other Asian countries and to its level of wealth, particularly with respect to secondary enrollment rates.[57]

As Table 5 shows, Asian nations vary in the amount they spend on education, health, and the military as a percentage of GDP. On the whole, Asian states spend more on education than health, usually considerably more, with the exception of Japan. In contrast, France, the US, and Japan spend more on health than education, reflecting higher medical costs but also greater wealth. No OECD country spends less than 5% of GDP on health, whereas most developing countries spend only 2–3%. Given differences in the size of the economies, the actual amount spent varies widely. The WHO estimates that $30–40 per person is the bare minimum needed to provide basic health services. However, in 1997 the least developed countries spent on average $6/person and low income countries $13, compared to $125 in upper-middle income countries and $1,356 in high income countries. Making matters even worse in poor countries, rural residents and those in the bottom 20% of income usually receive a disproportionately small share of the medical services.[58]

EQUITABLE GROWTH: EQUALITY AND INEQUALITY IN ASIA

While wealth undoubtedly affects the ability of governments to provide education and health services to their citizens, how the government chooses to spend its money and how wealth is distributed among the members of society are also crucial factors in the quality of life of citizens, especially the most vulnerable in society. As Table 6 shows, Asian countries differ in terms of income distribution.[59] However, they all are more equitable than some of the worst offenders in Africa and Latin America. Indonesia, a low income country long associated with crony capitalism under Suharto, fares surprisingly well. Meanwhile Malaysia, a middle income country often linked with Indonesia in the Asian-values debates, fares rather poorly. The Philippines not only suffers from low income but also extreme income inequality. India, though poorer than China, distributes the wealth more equitably.

Among the high income countries, Hong Kong, with its laissez-faire economic policies and colonial past, is the least

Table 6. Income Inequality

Country and Human Development Indicator Rank		Share of Income or Consumption (%) 1990–2001		Richest 20% to Poorest 20% 1990–2001	Gini Index (%) 1990–2001
		Poorest 20%	Richest 20%		
9	Japan (HI)	10.6	35.7	3.4	24.9
72	Romania (LM)	8.2	38.4	4.7	30.3
112	Indonesia (LI)	8.4	43.3	5.2	30.3
30	South Korea (HI)	7.9	37.5	4.7	31.6
35	Poland (UM)	7.8	39.7	5.1	31.6
17	France (HI)	7.2	40.2	5.6	32.7
29	Taiwan (UM)	6.7	41.1	6.2	34.5
120	Egypt (LM)	8.6	43.6	5.1	34.5
109	Vietnam (LI)	8.0	44.5	5.6	36.1
127	India (LI)	8.1	46.1	5.7	37.8
160	Tanzania (LI)	6.8	45.5	6.7	38.2
104	China (LM)	4.7	46.6	7.9	40.3
7	United States (HI)	5.4	46.4	8.9	40.8
28	Singapore (HI)	5.0	49.0	9.8	42.5
106	Iran (LM)	5.1	49.9	9.8	43.0
74	Thailand (LM)	6.1	50.0	8.2	43.2
26	Hong Kong (HI)	5.3	50.7	9.6	43.4
85	Philippines (LM)	5.4	52.3	9.7	46.1
58	Malaysia (UM)	4.4	54.3	12.3	49.2
145	Zimbabwe (LI)	4.6	55.7	12.1	56.8
43	Chile (UM)	3.2	61.3	19.2	57.5
111	South Africa (LM)	2.0	66.5	33.3	59.3
121	Nicaragua (LI)	2.3	63.6	16.8	60.3
65	Brazil (LM)	2.2	64.1	31.5	60.7

Sources: World Bank, World Development Indicators (CD-ROM, current through 2003), also available at **http://hdr.undp.org/statistics/data/indic/indic_133_1_1.html** (Column 1), **http://hdr.undp.org/statistics/data/indic/indic_134_1_1.html** (Column 2), **http://hdr.undp.org/statistics/data/indic/indic_137_1_1.html** (Column 3), **http://hdr.undp.org/statistics/data/indic/indic_138_1_l.html** (Column 4). For Taiwan data see Report on The Survey of Family Income and Expenditure in Taiwan Area, Republic of China, www.129.tpg.gov.tw/mbas/doc4/eng/conte91.htm (last visited Dec. 30, 2004). Taiwan HDI rank is an estimate.

equitable, though Singapore and the US are not far behind. Conversely, Japan once again scores best, with South Korea and France also doing relatively well.

The numbers may be deceptive in that they do not indicate long-term trends. Malaysia, for example, reduced the spread in the 1980s only to see the gap widen rapidly in the 1990s.[60]

DIVERSITY WITHIN SUCCESSFUL EAST ASIAN COUNTRIES: TWO VARIANTS FOR INEQUALITY AND PUBLIC EXPENDITURES

There are two variants of the EAM, which differ with respect to inequality and public expenditures on health and education. Japan, South Korea, and Taiwan have paid more attention to equitable growth, whereas Singapore and Hong Kong have tolerated greater inequality. The World Bank made much of the EAM's growth with equality, noting that inequality even decreased in several countries during the boom years. However, the countries where there was a substantial decrease (.08 or more in the Gini coefficient) started off with high inequality. The average Gini coefficient for 1965–70 was approximately .48 in Hong Kong, .50 in Singapore, .43 in Thailand, .50 in Malaysia, and .40 in Indonesia. With the exception of Indonesia, they all had higher average Gini coefficients in the 1980s and 1990s—and still have considerably higher rates—than Japan, Taiwan, and Korea. These three countries had average Gini coefficients around .32 for 1965–70. In 2002, Taiwan had a Gini coefficient of .35 and Korea .32. Only Japan became significantly more egalitarian, at .25.

China began the reform era with one of the lowest Gini coefficients in the world—in the range of .15 to .22.[61] Obviously it was not going to be one of those countries where inequality declined as the economy grew. Its rates of .40 to .45 for the last several years are comparable to the rates of Hong Kong, Singapore, and Malaysia during their take-off periods of rapid growth from 1960 to 1980 and even to their rates today, although much higher than the rates for Japan, Taiwan, and Korea.[62] As discussed in Chapter 4, contrary to general perceptions, some recent studies have shown no significant increase, and indeed a decrease, in the Gini coefficient in China in recent years as a result of government policies to address concerns about inequality.

China's Gini coefficients are also in line with more general development patterns. The average Gini coefficient for countries with a real per capita income of less than $1,000 is .34. The average rises to .46 when per capita income is between $2,001 and $3,000, and falls to .33 when per capita income exceeds $6,000.[63] What is striking is that high income Hong Kong and Singapore, contrary to the popular image of egalitarian East Asian developmental states, continue to be much more inegalitarian than the world average.

Asian countries have also varied with respect to the allocation of spending on health and education. The general trend both in Asia and globally has been for increased spending on education as a percentage of GDP. The average rate of spending on education in Hong Kong, Korea, Singapore, and Malaysia was 2.5% of GDP in 1960, and 3.7% in 1989, with rates ranging from 2.8% to 5.6% in 1989. The average for all low and middle income countries was 1.3% in 1960, and 3.1% in 1989.[64] A decade later, most East Asian countries were spending between 3.5% and 6.2% on education, as indicated in Table 5.

China has spent less on public education as a percentage of GDP than other East Asian states. According to UNDP figures, China devoted on average 2.1% of GDP to education from 1998 to 2000, as Table 5 shows. However, according to official government sources, public expenditure has ranged from 2.5% in 1997 to 3.41% in 2002 to 2.79% in 2004, with the government committed to doubling spending to 6.6% by the year 2010.[65]

China's allocation of spending on basic and higher education has been generally consistent with the pattern in other East Asian countries. From 1998 to 2000, 37.4% of China's public expenditure on education was for primary education, 32.2% for secondary, and 15.6% for tertiary.[66] East Asian countries allocated on average roughly 15% to tertiary education and 60–80% to primary and secondary education during the period 1960–90.[67] The World Bank points out that although public expenditure on education as a percentage of GDP in East Asian countries was not significantly higher than in other developing countries, East Asian countries invested a greater share in primary and secondary education as opposed to tertiary education, with the allocation to tertiary education in Latin America and South Asia and Africa during similar periods averaging 24%. The Bank concludes that investing more in primary and secondary education contributes to greater and more equitable growth.

Disaggregating education spending in Asia suggests that there may not be a single most effective allocation of educational resources. There are significant differences among the East Asian states on spending for higher education. Singapore and Hong Kong, both high income countries with economies dependent on financial services and high technology rather than domestic manufacturing, allocated 31% and 25% of their educational budget to tertiary education in 1985. In contrast, Korea, Malaysia, and Thailand allocated between 10% and 15% to higher education. The growing importance of technological innovation in today's highly competitive global economy may justify higher investments in tertiary education. This may be all the more the case for China as its rising superpower status may restrict its ability to import certain technologies, highlighting the need for domestically driven innovation, particularly but not exclusively in the defense sector. In the last decade, spending on tertiary education has increased at a rapid rate in middle income countries, China included, with much of the increase coming from private spending in the form of higher tuitions.[68] Families are willing to invest more in higher education because of the high returns.

In China, the impact of education on income levels varies both by level of education and location. Yao found that urban family income levels rose as the education level of the head of household rose.[69] An urban worker with a university education earns 54–83% more than an urban worker with a secondary education, who in turn earns 38–58% more than someone with just a primary school education. In the countryside, the picture is more complicated. As in urban areas, the lack of a primary school education greatly increases the likelihood of poverty. However, while completing primary education had a strong effect on income, completing secondary education had little effect because rural production (agriculture and township village enterprises) requires few skills and relatively little education.

Educated rural youths generally must move to cities to find jobs that will pay a higher return on their education. This might suggest that the government policy, discussed in Chapter 4, of first ensuring everyone in the countryside is able to obtain a primary education before tackling the problem of ensuring universal secondary education is correct. On the other hand, reducing poverty in the countryside will require migration into cities of large numbers of rural youth who will need more than a primary education to compete.

As for health spending, South Korea and Japan have had higher public expenditure on health and a more balanced ratio of public spending on health to education than the others. Taiwan, Singapore, and Hong Kong (the greater China countries) have had reasonably high public spending on education but less public spending on health—relying on families and private spending to pick up the health tab. The differences should not be overstated however. Even South Korea and Japan rely heavily on families and social networks to provide care for the elderly, to cushion the shock of unemployment and to address poverty and other social welfare needs.[70]

China seems to be going the way of Singapore, Hong Kong, and Taiwan on public spending on education and health. While public spending on education has increased steadily to 3.41% in 2002, public expenditure on health was just 1.9% of GDP in 2000, in comparison to private health expenditure of 3.4%.[71] Although total health expenditure as a percentage of GDP rose slightly from 1991 to 2000, the government's share of total health costs dropped from 22% to 14%, with individual out-of-pocket spending increasing from 38% to 60%.[72]

Relying more on the private sector frees up money for other purposes. Where is the money going? One might think it is going to the military. With its pacifist constitution and military protection from the US, Japan can afford to spend more on health and education. Not surprisingly, Japan has the highest ratio of combined education and health to military spending at 9.5 to 1. Thailand and the Philippines spend more than five times as much on education and health as on the military, the US more than three times, South Korea more than two and half times, India twice as much, and China slightly less than twice as much. However, in terms of actual percentage of GDP,

China's expenditure on the military is low: 2.3% in 2000, although military budgets have been increasing by double figures every year. Moreover, there is considerable debate among analysts about the figures. The Pentagon's 2005 report estimated that China military spending might be as high as $90 billion, three times the official figure reported by Beijing. In response to criticism from the Pentagon and Defense Secretary Rumsfeld alleging China's military buildup is a threat to global security, Chinese officials have ridiculed the Pentagon's estimates of military spending.[73] They point out that in absolute terms the US spends almost eighteen times as much as China does on the military. Officials also claim that most of the money is earmarked for improving salaries and working conditions, and that some arms purchases are justifiable to modernize an antiquated defense system.

Whatever the differences in spending patterns, the bottom line is that China is still doing relatively well in addressing poverty, increasing longevity, and ensuring people are literate, although in recent years the rate of overall improvement in some areas has not kept pace with the high economic growth rate.[74] What accounts for this success despite relatively low rates of public spending?[75] One factor may be the size of the economy. While low as a percentage of GDP, absolute spending is high by the standards of developing countries. This explanation assumes that economies of scale are more important than per capita figures when it comes to poverty, literacy, and health—there may be some truth to that, but it doesn't seem like that could be the whole story.

The effectiveness of family and social networks is surely another factor. After all, other Asian countries have also relied heavily on family networks and private spending. As the Chinese economy has grown, many people have earned more, and built up considerable savings. They are able to draw on these funds in times of need to bail out family members facing a medical crisis or to send a relative to school. Civil society and NGOs have also played an increasing role in poverty reduction, both directly through financial donations and through training programs and the provision of services.

Another possible explanation is that local governments are playing a larger role than the numbers on public expenditure would suggest.[76] Given the emphasis on social order, local governments often find a way to appease protesting pensioners whose insolvent employers are unable to pay them their benefits. Local governments are also supposed to waive school fees for families that cannot afford them. The forgone revenue may not count as public expenditure, but the practice does help poor families get an education.

In any event, China has invested in human capital, more so in the form of poverty reduction and primary and secondary education than in health. Given the solid foundation, the government could afford to spend less and let inequality grow at least for a period—though that period now seems to be over. Longevity rates and other indicators of well-being are now declining for some segments of the population.[77]

The implications of the rising inequality for social stability and political reforms are however not clear. Many countries, developing and developed, have remained stable with much higher Gini coefficients. Arguably what may matter more is that people feel they have a fair shot at succeeding. One of the keys to the East Asian success has been the largely meritocratic nature of the system, often attributed to the influence of Confucianism. Access to government positions has been through a rigorous examination process. East Asian governments have provided education and the basic material conditions (housing, adequate food, and health services) to succeed. After that, it has been up to the individual to make the best of it.[78]

In that sense, the story in China is mixed. Clearly many people in China are getting rich and getting ahead because of corruption and guanxi. However, there is still extraordinary opportunity and social mobility. Peasants have gone on to own airlines; children whose parents are illiterate attend the most prestigious universities and become lawyers. Students must still pass a rigorous national examination to enter the best universities. As one might expect, a much higher percentage of Chinese are optimistic about the chances of their lives improving and of their children having a better life than in developed European countries or in failed developing states, as discussed in Chapter 7. Moreover, and somewhat surprisingly, even the vast majority of laid-off state-owned employees acknowledge that SOE reforms were required and in the national interest.[79]

But even if China's poor were discontent, there may be little they could do. As in other countries, those left behind by China's economic reforms are marginalized and lack effective channels to seek redress. That some people are much worse off may not lead to instability as long as the majority of citizens still feel their standard of living is improving. Fortunately, the government has repeatedly acknowledged the moral obligation to address rising inequality.

INSTITUTIONAL DEVELOPMENT: GOOD GOVERNANCE MEASURES

Asian governments that promoted Asian values often unapologetically defended their heavy-handed paternalistic ways by arguing that what mattered is the bottom line: economic growth, good governance, clean and effective civil servants. Table 2 shows that the Asia region on the whole scores relatively high on measures of good governance, including political stability, government effectiveness, regulatory quality, rule of law, and control of corruption, with the exception of voice and accountability where it ranked in the fiftieth percentile.

'Political stability and absence of violence' combines several indicators that measure the likelihood that the government will be overthrown or destabilized by unconstitutional or violent means, including terrorism. It is included as a good governance measure because political instability and violence not only affect the ability of the ruling regime to govern but deprive citizens of the ability to peacefully select and replace those in power. 'Government effectiveness' measures the provision of public services, the quality of the bureaucracy, the competence and independence of civil servants, and the credibility of the government's policy commitments. Whereas government effectiveness focuses on the institutional inputs required to implement policies effectively, 'regulatory quality' focuses on the policies themselves. It includes measures of market-unfriendly policies such as price controls or inadequate bank supervision, as well as perceptions of excessive regulation of foreign trade and business development, reflecting a bias toward neoliberal economic policies. 'Rule of law' measures the extent to which people have confidence in and abide by the rules of society, how fair and predictable the rules are, and how well property rights are protected. The indicators include perceptions of incidence of crime, the effectiveness and predictability of the judiciary, and the enforceability of contracts. 'Control of corruption' measures perceptions of corruption, the effects of corruption on business, and 'grand corruption' in the political arena.

Again, there is wide variation within the region, largely consistent with levels of economic development, as indicated in Table 7. In the high income weight class, Singapore wins the gold in the four main categories of good governance: government effectiveness, regulatory quality, rule of law, and control of corruption. It also outperforms the region in terms of voice and accountability and political stability, and the others in the high income category for the latter but not the former. The US takes the silver, with France and Hong Kong vying for the bronze. Although Japan scored well on infant mortality, life expectancy, income equality, and other quality of life measures, its scores on government effectiveness and regulatory quality leave something to be desired. While it ranks relatively high in rule of law, it fares relatively poorly on the corruption scale mainly because of grand political corruption.

While Taiwan outperformed the region on every measure, it underperformed relative to others in its income group on every measure. However, if classified as an upper-middle income country, as in the UNDP rankings, then it would do quite well relative to others in its income class. South Korea consistently outperforms the regional average. Moreover, relative to other countries in its upper-middle income bracket, it outperforms in the four main categories, although it lags behind in voice and accountability and political stability.[80] Malaysia outperforms the regional average on the four main indicators of good governance and political stability, though it underperforms on voice and accountability. It outperforms others in its group on government effectiveness and slightly on regulatory control, rule of law, and control of corruption, although it falls far short on voice and accountability.

Thailand, a middle income country according to UNDP standards but classified as lower middle by the World Bank, outperforms the region and the average in the lower-middle income class by a wide margin on every dimension.

China outperforms lower-middle income countries in political stability, government effectiveness, and rule of law; it does slightly better in control of corruption, and is about average in regulatory quality.[81] However, it scores much lower on voice and accountability. The Philippines, also in the lower-middle income category, scores high on voice and accountability, low on political stability, outperforms the income average on government effectiveness and regulatory quality, but lags slightly behind on rule of law and corruption.

Table 7. Quality of Governance (percentile rank, 2002)

Country and Human Development Indicator Rank		Voice and Accountability	Political Stability	Government Effectiveness	Regulatory Quality	Rule of Law	Control of Corruption
7	United States (HI)	90.9	56.2	91.2	91.2	91.8	92.3
9	Japan (HI)	79.3	90.3	84.5	78.9	88.7	85.1
17	France (HI)	88.4	70.8	90.7	85.6	87.6	89.2
26	Hong Kong (HI)	53.5	85.4	88.7	90.7	86.6	90.2
28	Singapore (HI)	65.7	91.9	100.0	99.5	93.3	99.5
29	Taiwan (UM)	74.2	70.3	82.5	80.9	80.9	77.3
30	South Korea (HI)	67.7	60.5	79.4	76.3	77.8	66.5
35	Poland (UM)	83.3	69.7	71.1	71.1	70.6	69.1
43	Chile (UM)	84.3	85.9	86.6	90.2	87.1	90.7
58	Malaysia (UM)	42.4	61.6	80.9	68.6	69.6	68.0
65	Brazil (LM)	58.1	48.1	50.0	63.4	50.0	56.7
74	Thailand (LM)	57.1	62.7	64.9	65.5	62.4	53.6
72	Romania (LM)	61.1	58.4	46.4	55.7	54.1	45.4
85	Philippines (LM)	54.0	29.7	55.7	57.7	38.1	37.6
104	China (LM)	10.1	51.4	63.4	40.2	51.5	42.3
106	Iran (LM)	18.2	25.9	39.2	8.2	33.5	44.3
109	Vietnam (LI)	10.6	61.1	48.5	25.3	44.8	33.0
111	South Africa (LM)	70.7	42.7	69.1	69.1	59.8	67.5
112	Indonesia (LI)	34.8	12.4	34.0	26.3	23.2	6.7
127	India (LI)	60.6	22.2	54.1	43.8	57.2	49.5
120	Egypt (LM)	22.2	34.1	46.9	38.1	57.7	47.9
121	Nicaragua (LI)	52.0	47.6	17.5	39.7	32.0	39.7
145	Zimbabwe (LI)	7.1	8.6	22.2	4.1	5.7	6.2
160	Tanzania (LI)	37.9	35.7	36.1	33.5	38.7	15.5

Source: World Bank, Governance Matters III: Governance Indicators for 1996–2002 (2003).

In the low income category, India outperforms others in all dimensions except political stability. Indonesia lags behind the regional averages and other low income countries on political stability, rule of law, and control of corruption, but outperforms others at its income level in voice and accountability, government effectiveness, and slightly in regulatory quality. Vietnam lags behind the region in all categories except political stability. However, it outperforms others in its income class in political stability, government effectiveness, rule of law, and control of corruption, though it lags far behind in voice and accountability.

PROVISIONAL SUMMARY: EAST ASIAN MODEL COUNTRIES VERSUS COUNTRIES IN OTHER REGIONS

Successful Asian states including Singapore, South Korea, Japan, Taiwan, and now Vietnam and China have implemented reforms, including institution-building measures and investment in education and human capital, which have benefited the broad populace. As Table 3 shows, the relationship between wealth and human rights performance in Asia and the Middle East is consistently strong except with respect to civil and political rights, suggesting that there is a culturally based antipathy to liberal values that explains the variance in those regions.

In contrast, the relationship between wealth and all types of rights is consistently weaker in Latin America and Africa, suggesting that the culprit is dysfunctional governments that serve the rich, if they serve anyone, at the expense of the general populace. Reform efforts have largely been undermined by patronage systems in which state leaders divert state assets into the hands of a few and the elite block reform efforts aimed at benefiting the majority of citizens.[82]

Legal reforms, economic growth, and democratization

Rule of law and democracy tend to be mutually reinforcing.[83] However, rule of law need not necessarily march in lockstep with democracy, and in Asia and the Mid East several of the legal systems that score highest in terms of rule of law are not democracies or are illiberal democracies. To be sure, what constitutes a democracy is subject to debate. In the UK, only 1.8% of the adult population was eligible to vote as of 1832, and only 12.1% as of 1884, with women receiving the right to vote only in 1930. In the US, only 5% of adults were eligible to vote in 1824, with blacks obtaining the right to vote only in 1870, and women following in 1920. Yet the US and the UK were still considered exemplars of rule of law.[84]

Singapore and even more clearly Hong Kong show that liberal democracy, or even a nonliberal version of democracy, is not a precondition for a legal system that generally complies with the requirements of a thin rule of law.

Contemporary Singapore has been described as a semi-democracy, pseudo-democracy, illiberal democracy, limited democracy, mandatory democracy, a 'decent, non-democratic regime,' a soft authoritarian state, and a despotic state controlled by Lee Kuan Yew (and now his son).[85] Critics note that elections are dominated by the People's Action Party (PAP) and opposition is tamed through the use of defamation suits against political opponents, manipulation of voting procedures, gerrymandering, and short campaign times. Given the dominance of the PAP, accountability in Singapore is achieved not so much through elections as through other means such as allocating limited participation rights to the opposition, inviting members of the public to comment on legislation, and the use of shadow cabinets where PAP members are asked to play an opposition role.

The primary role of law in Singapore is to strengthen the state, ensure stability, and facilitate economic growth.[86] Many decisions are left to the state and political actors, primarily the Cabinet headed by the Prime Minister. Civil society is limited, and characterized by corporatist relationships between the state, businesses, labor unions, and society. Administrative law tends to emphasize government efficiency rather than protection of individual rights. While individual rights are constitutionally guaranteed, they are not interpreted along liberal lines. Lee Kuan Yew and other government officials have invoked Asian values to emphasize group interests over individual interests, and to justify limitations on civil and political rights, including limits on free speech such that citizens are not allowed to attack the integrity of key institutions like the judiciary or the character of elected officials without attracting sanction in the form of contempt of court or libel proceedings. Labor rights are also limited in the name of social stability and economic growth. The paternalistic state promotes a substantive normative agenda and actively regulates private morality and conduct, with the government promoting social harmony and discouraging adversarial litigation. On the whole, the judiciary tends to follow the government's lead. Although the reason for that seems to be a genuine congruence of views on the part of most judges rather than overt political pressure on the courts, in some cases judges who have challenged the PAP have been reassigned.[87]

Despite the limitations on democracy,[88] the use of the legal system to suppress opposition, and a nonliberal interpretation on many rights issues, Singapore's legal system is regularly ranked as one of the best in the world. It was ranked in the top 99th percentile on the World Bank Rule of Law Index in 1996, and in the 93rd percentile in 2002. By way of broad comparison, the US and the average OECD rankings were in the 91st to 92nd percentiles for 1996 and 2002.

Like Singapore, Hong Kong has a well-developed legal system that is largely the product of British colonialism. Until the handover to the PRC in 1997, the system was widely considered to be an exemplar of rule of law, notwithstanding the lack of democracy and a restricted scope of individual rights under British rule. After the handover, the legal system continues to score high on the World Bank's Rule of Law Index, with only a slight drop from 90.4 in 1996 to 86.6 in 2002.

With the change of government, however, has come a somewhat different value orientation. Signs of the shift include pressure on the media to toe the government's line; limitations on free speech and assembly and in particular the requirement that demonstrators obtain prior approval from the authorities; consideration of a bill on religious sects, urged by Beijing, to control Falun Gong, along with the conviction of Falun Gong demonstrators; and the brouhaha over regulations required under Article 23 of the Basic Law dealing with a variety of potential treats to national security from sedition to disclosure of state secrets, which resulted in some 500,000 people taking to the streets.[89] The protesters, some of whom demanded faster democratization including election of the chief executive in 2007, were also upset by a downturn in the economy and the ineffective governance of Tung. Although the protests did result in the Article 23 legislation being postponed and Tung stepping down, the new government, backed by Beijing, rejected appeals to expedite democratization.

Among Arab countries, Oman, Qatar, Bahrain, Kuwait, and the United Arab Emirates are in the top quartile on the World Bank rule of law index but have a 0 ranking on the 0–10 point Polity IV Index.

Conversely, just as nondemocracies may have strong rule of law legal systems, democracies may have legal systems that fall far short of rule of law. Guatemala, Kenya, and Papua New Guinea, for example, all score highly on democracy (8–10 on the Polity IV Index) and yet poorly on rule of law (below the 25th percentile on World Bank rule of law index). Eight other countries receive an 8–10 score on the Polity IV index and yet score below the 50th percentile of countries on rule of law: Bolivia, Peru, Jamaica, Macedonia, the Philippines, Moldova, Nicaragua, and Argentina.

Moreover, both democracy and rule of law are clearly related to wealth. Empirical studies have yet to sort out the complicated causal ways in which democracy, rule of law, and wealth interact to support each other.[90] However, one of the striking features of the successful transition in Taiwan, South Korea, and more recently Thailand is that the transition to democratization has come only after economic growth reached relatively high levels.

In contrast, those countries that have attempted to democratize at lower levels have generally failed in the past, often times reverting to authoritarianism. Indonesia tried democracy just after independence from the Dutch between 1950 and 1957. The experiment ended when Sukarno declared martial law. Thailand went through numerous cycles of democratic elections followed by military-led coups—there have been some seventeen coup attempts since 1932. South Korea held elections in the 1960s and early 1970s before returning to authoritarian rule. The less-than-successful experiments with democracy in the Philippines from 1935 led to the declaration of martial law by Marcos in 1972. In Bangladesh, General Zia reclaimed power in 1975 when the democratically elected government was unable to make good on the promise of rapid development. Adopting neoliberal economic principles and promising rapid economic growth, Zia himself won elections in 1978 in a landslide. However, he was replaced by General Ershad in 1982.

Nowadays, those states that have attempted elections at low levels of wealth and with weak institutions continue to limp along with low levels of economic development, pressing social order problems, and massive discontent over the political system, as in the Philippines, Indonesia, India, Cambodia, Bangladesh, and now Timor-Leste, as we shall see in Chapter 7.

The experience of Asian countries is consistent with the experience of many countries elsewhere. As Pinkney points out, 'what is remarkable is that almost all third world countries have had at least nominally pluralist political systems at some time in their history, yet the majority did not (or could not) build on these to establish durable forms of democracy.'[91]

Empirical studies demonstrate that democracies are unstable at relatively low levels of wealth.[92] They have a life expectancy of just eight years when their per capita income is less than $1,000.[93] Of the twelve democracies established prior to 1950 with a per capita income below $2,000, eight failed.

Poor democracies are particularly vulnerable to economic downturns. As Przeworski et al. note, 'it is striking how fragile poor democracies are. In countries with incomes under $2000, of the 116 years during which declines in incomes occurred, twelve democracies fell the next year.'[94] The longer the economic decline, the more likely the regime is to fail. Economic difficulties also adversely effect authoritarian regimes, but to a lesser degree. Democracies are also more sensitive to overall income inequality. And whereas both democracies and authoritarian regimes are threatened when the rich get richer, in general only democracies are threatened when the poor get poorer.[95]

That wealth matters does not mean that there is a particular point at which countries necessarily become democratic. There have been and still are rich authoritarian or semi-democratic states, in Asia and elsewhere. Obviously, many countries have become democratic at very low levels of wealth.[96] And while per capita income is the best predictor of the survivability of democracies,[97] a few countries have managed to sustain democracy against the odds, including India, Costa Rica, Mauritius, Botswana, Jamaica, Trinidad, and Papua New Guinea. Other than India, these are all small countries with populations less than five million and several below one million. With some exceptions, they tend to be relatively wealthy by developing country standards, to have distributed wealth reasonably equitably, and to have invested in human capital and effective institutions.

Of course, not all authoritarian systems have succeeded in achieving economic growth, implementing rule of law, or in making progress on human rights and other indicators of human well-being. Whether cause or result, most very poor countries are authoritarian.[98] Since neither poor authoritarian regimes nor poor democratic ones are particularly good at ensuring growth, perhaps there is no need for a tradeoff between democracy and development.[99] If faced with a choice between a bad democratic government and a bad authoritarian one, most people would no doubt opt for a bad democratic one. Authoritarianism is certainly more risky. You are more likely to get miracles or disasters. Of the regimes that grew at an average rate of 7% per year for at least ten years between 1950 and 1990, all were authoritarian except for the Bahamas (where tourism, money laundering, and tax-haven revenues provided high per capita growth, albeit for a small population). On the other hand, eight of the ten countries with the lowest growth rates over a ten-year period were also authoritarian.[100]

Chinese and other Asians need not be reminded that authoritarian regimes may go badly astray. Laos, Myanmar, and North Korea are unfortunate reminders. Successful reforms require at minimum governments that are willing to invest in institutions and people, sound economic policies, and some luck. But we do not need to base our assessment of China on general empirical studies or a blind choice between an authoritarian regime likely to produce miraculous growth and one likely to fail miserably. There is a twenty-five-year track record for China, and an even longer track record for Japan and the other Asian tigers. Fortunately for Chinese citizens, China is following the path of Japan, South Korea, Taiwan, Hong Kong, and Singapore—not Laos, Myanmar, and North Korea, or for that matter the Philippines, Indonesia, Cambodia, Bangladesh, and India.

Constitutionalism and rights

Even during the authoritarian period in the successful Asian states, legal reforms began to empower legal institutions and give rise to constitutional norms, thus supporting nascent constitutionalism.[101] Judicial independence was limited prior to democratization, and in some cases even afterwards. The general pattern was for better performance in terms of social, economic, and cultural 'rights,' good governance, and law and order relative to civil and political rights.

Several caveats, qualifications, and disclaimers are in order. First, the broad category 'civil and political rights' needs to be disaggregated. As in Western countries in the eighteenth and nineteenth centuries during their take-off phase, the successful Asian states allowed certain sorts of freedoms, including some civil and political rights. In the West, as in East Asia, capitalism preceded democracy.[102] As noted, citizens in the successful East Asian countries enjoyed economic freedoms even during the authoritarian era—they were able to set up business and engage in trade and other economic transactions. Their property was protected by both formal and informal mechanisms, both vertically against takings by the state and horizontally in their dealing with other nonstate economic actors. In addition, their personal integrity was protected against arbitrary actions by the state through functional criminal and administrative law systems, provided they were not engaged in political activities that challenged the state. They were allowed for the most part to associate with whom they chose, to speak their minds, and to engage in religious practices, provided again that in so doing they did not challenge the state or threaten to disrupt social order. They were also able to participate in politics in various ways, even standing for office in local elections. But they were not given the right to stand for national elections or to elect their leaders—or if they were, the outcomes of the elections were highly controlled. In short, they enjoyed considerable freedoms, including some political freedom, but in the context of a nondemocratic or nonliberal system.

Second, South Korea and Taiwan fit the model in that after democratization the courts emerged as independent and authoritative forces capable of handling even politically sensitive issues involving controversial constitutional amendments and the criminal liability of past presidents impartially.[103] In contrast, other countries fit the model, but in a negative way in that democratization at lower levels of wealth has exacerbated or at least failed to resolve shortcomings in the legal system, including problems with the authority and independence of the judiciary. In Indonesia, corporatist ties between judges and the political, military, and business elite have undermined the authority and independence of the judiciary.[104] In the Philippines, the courts continue to be so heavily influenced by the politics of populist, people-power movements that basic rule of law principles are threatened.[105] Democratization alone is clearly not sufficient to ensure an independent and authoritative judiciary.

Third, the degree of judicial activism varies dramatically from country to country. The courts in South Korea, Taiwan, India, and the Philippines are among the most activist. In Taiwan and India, the courts have gone so far as to strike down constitutional amendments as unconstitutional. In contrast, the Supreme Court in Japan has rarely struck down laws. Courts in Singapore and Malaysia also continue to interpret rights narrowly, relying on a positivist rather than a purposive or natural law-based method of interpretation.

Fourth, activism is not the same as liberal. In Thailand, the courts have shown a conservative inclination to side with entrenched interest groups.[106] Similarly, although Indian courts have come to the aid of the disenfranchised in a variety of ways, the courts remain organs of the state, with judges inclined by personal circumstances and professional training toward moderate rather than radical solutions.[107] In Korea and the Philippines, court decisions are often more a reflection of populism than liberal principles.[108]

In general, Asian courts tend to be very deferential on matters of national security. National laws frequently prohibit or limit judicial review of many national security decisions. But even when judicial review is possible, Asian courts have been reluctant to challenge executive and parliamentary decisions involving national security.[109] They also tend to impose more restrictions than liberals would prefer on freedom of speech and the press, freedom of association, and the exercise of religion.[110]

The restrictions on free speech and the press are most apparent in North Korea and Myanmar, although Singapore, Malaysia, China, and Vietnam are also known for tight limits on the press. But even the more democratic countries in the region keep a short leash on the press and free speech by citizens.

South Korean President Roh has declared that the government will take legal action against any news organization that publishes editorials containing false information regarding government policy or personnel. In 2003, Roh personally brought a libel suit against four major newspapers that allegedly defamed him and his family by publishing falsehoods about his fund-raising activities and real estate transactions.[111]

In Indonesia, after a period of expansive freedom of speech and the press during the Habibe and Wahid years, the Megawati government, supported by a public increasingly wary of unfettered expression, pushed through a law that imposed several restrictions on freedom of expression, assembly, and the press. The former editor of a daily paper was found guilty of insulting the chairman of the Golkar party currently serving as speaker of legislature, while another editor was prosecuted for insulting Megawati.[112]

Meanwhile, in Thailand, the government or the army owns the main free-to-air television stations. The government has also used the leverage gained from licensing and advertisements to influence press coverage, resulting in self-censorship and the sacking of editors critical of the government.[113] Freedom House therefore demoted Thailand from 'free' to 'partly free' status.[114] The Philippines was also downgraded from 'free' to 'partly free' for failure to protect journalists and to prosecute those who murder journalists.

Despite a liberal press, India continues to prosecute people who criticize the judiciary, while libel cases remain common.[115] Even in Japan, a broad ban on incitement of illegal activities, permit requirements for demonstrations, and other restrictions allow the government considerable room to limit free speech in the name of public order.[116]

To some extent, these broad differences are attributable to different social and political philosophies, including majoritarian preferences for social stability.[117] To be sure, the Asian region boasts a wide diversity of religious systems and cultural practices, cautioning against simplistic conclusions based on stereotypes about Confucians or Muslims or Asian communitarians. Surely by now we are all aware of the need to avoid reifying, essentializing, and nationalizing culture—how could we not be, given how often this rather obvious point has been made? Nevertheless, numerous multiple-country quantitative studies have demonstrated significant regional effects with respect to democratization,[118] labor rights,[119] women's rights,[120] personal integrity rights,[121] freedom from government intrusions, rule of law and good governance,[122] and cultural values[123] that in turn affect rights performance.[124]

Fifth, cultural rights and personal integrity rights have varied depending on particular circumstances. Cultural rights have been influenced by the degree of ethnic diversity, the amount of religious conflict, and the extent to which ethnic or religious diversity has led to calls for autonomy and independence. Personal integrity rights have been affected by the degree of political stability, the need to wage civil war or battle insurgents, and most recently concerns over terrorism.[125]

Sixth, successful East Asian governments have taken seriously their obligations to provide the necessary minimal material conditions for human flourishing, subject to resource constraints largely in line with GDP levels, as the empirical studies indicate. However, Asian states have generally not treated economic and social 'rights' as justiciable. Rather, government policies reflect traditional paternalistic beliefs that rulers are obligated to ensure the material and spiritual well-being of the people. In East Asian countries, this belief derives largely from Confucianism; in other countries it may be supported by Buddhism, Islam, or other belief systems. While such traditions are grounded in a nonliberal worldview, they nonetheless provide a normative basis for social, economic, cultural, and collective rights claims today.

More recently, in response to the normative pressure of the human rights community to treat all rights as indivisible, several Asian countries have developed an active jurisprudence of economic and social rights. This is also in keeping with a redistributive, developmental model of rule of law in several Asian countries. This conception of rule of law emphasizes redistribution of wealth and social justice issues domestically, and the right of development, debt forgiveness, and the obligation of the North/developed countries to aid the South/developing countries internationally.[126] The Indonesian constitution contains a long list of social and economic rights, while Indian and Filipino courts have blurred or overcome the distinction between justiciable and nonjusticiable rights through interpretation of constitutional references to programmatic goals and directive principles. The involvement of the judiciary in these complex social and economic policy issues has naturally been controversial, and challenged both in terms of the merits of the decisions and judicial competence and the proper role for the courts.

A particularly pressing issue is whether well-intentioned reformers who push for the incorporation of such a broad array of positive rights in the constitutions of countries at relatively low levels of economic development are not setting the government up for failure by promising citizens more than the government can possibly deliver.[127] In India, the Bharatiya Janata Party government was voted out of office despite overseeing a period of rapid economic growth. The vote reflected a deep dissatisfaction with growing income disparities and widespread poverty amidst the growing wealth of some segments of society. The BJP's campaign slogan of India Shining only highlighted the discrepancies between the haves and the have-nots. By way of comparison, in wealthy South Korea, which has not made social rights justiciable, the government only made good on its promise to provide an equal education for all by providing nine years of compulsory education free of charge in 2003.[128]

Indonesia offers another cautionary tale. After the fall of Suharto, reformers, flush with optimism, wrote into the Indonesian constitution some of the most forward-leaning ideas of the human rights movement. Accordingly, the constitution now provides that each person has the right to physical and spiritual welfare, to have a home, to enjoy a good and healthy living environment, and to obtain health services. Reflecting the 'capabilities' approach, each person is entitled to assistance and special treatment to gain the same opportunities and benefits in the attainment of equality and justice.[129] The Megawati government in low income Indonesia was not able to live up to such broad commitments or even to effectively deal with terrorism and rising crime rates.

In contrast, Thailand under Thaksin seemed to be following a modified version of the EAM. Having democratized while still a middle income country and with relatively weak institutions, the government has struggled to improve the standards of living for citizens and maintain social and political order. Thaksin's ruling party acted in many ways like a traditional Asian government: a strong executive pushed through policies aimed at ensuring economic development and a better standard of living for the majority while cracking down on drugs, Islamic insurgents and other potential sources of disorder, including government critics. The government was elitist. Business leaders remained entwined in corporatist relations with the state. They, along with the middle class, emphasized economic growth and stability rather than radical reforms aimed at greater social justice.[130] However, Thaksin's administration also sought to address concerns over inequality, appealing to rural residents by promising—and delivering on—an agrarian debt moratorium, a revolving development fund for every village and inexpensive, state-subsidized medical care.[131] In recent years, the economy recovered from the Asian financial crisis, and the deterioration in quality of life as measured by the UNDP Human Development Index reversed.

However, human rights activists were critical of government policies, pointing out how problems remain with respect to disadvantaged hilltribe peoples and other socially vulnerable individuals, how development projects have resulted in displacement of farmers and destroyed their communities, how industrialization has resulted in the degradation of the environment, and how economic development has come at the expense of transparency and political participation and led to the growing dominance of the business community in the political arena.[132] In addition, the war on drugs led to more than 2,500 extrajudicial killings, while the crackdown on Islamic insurgents has resulted in many deaths. Thaksin's administration also took aim at human rights organizations. Not surprisingly, human rights groups cried wolf. Asia Director of Human Rights Watch Brad Adams claimed that 'Thailand has gone from being a beacon of freedom in the region to a country of high concern,' and that '[m]uch of the steady progress Thailand has made in the last decade has been rolled back under Thaksin's tenure.'[133]

On the other hand, the broad public seemed to appreciate that governments in middle income countries such as Thailand will inevitably have difficulty living up to the oftentimes idealistic standards of the critics. The overwhelming victory of Thaksin in the 2005 election suggested that most Thais supported government efforts to address pressing economic issues within the limits of available resources and to maintain social order. Despite strong support for democracy, half of Thais still rank economic development as more important than democracy.[134] As one Thai commentator on civil society observes, 'many of the NGOs and civic groups that challenge state power and address structural issues are routinely dubbed as too radical.'[135]

Thaksin resigned in April 2006, following months of protests over the sale of a family telecommunications business that led to a tax free profit of $1.9 billion for family members, returned to power and then was ousted in a military coup. At the time of his resignation, he still enjoyed strong support in rural areas, although he was unpopular with urbanites who opposed his strong-arm tactics. Despite the financial scandal, he received 16 million votes (60%) in a snap election boycotted by the opposition—down from the 19 million votes he received a year earlier but still a strong showing. To what extent the new rulers will continue to follow a modified version of the EAM remains to be seen.

China and the EAM of economic development

How does China measure up against the standards of the EAM so far? Economically, China has—like other East Asian states—adhered to some of the principles of the original and expanded Washington Consensus, rejected a few, and modified others. It has also benefited from very high domestic savings rates, a decrease in birth rates, and a reallocation of labor from agriculture to manufacturing, all significant factors contributing to growth in other Asian states.

Beijing generally followed the WC with respect to fiscal discipline. It has built up large surpluses of foreign exchange, which has allowed it to pump money into the economy at the first signs of a slowdown and to bail out banks burdened with non-performing loans. It has managed inflation reasonably well, despite brief periods of high inflation, and increased the authority and capacity of the PBOC as the central bank to manage macroeconomic policy. It has carried out significant reforms to the tax system and broadened the tax base, and used preferential tax policies to encourage foreign investment and promote exports. It has also taken steps to strengthen the collection of taxes, with collection rates rising from 11% of GDP in 1995 to 20% in 2004. While it has not reduced tax rates to any significant extent, it has attempted to limit the imposition of additional fees imposed by local government agencies and recently decreased taxes for low income earners and farmers.

China has been more circumspect when it comes to trade, foreign direct investment, and financial liberalization. China restricted imports through tariffs and quotas, and through limitations on the number of companies authorized to import and export. Particularly early in the reform process, the government sought to limit import of consumer goods both to protect domestic industries and build up foreign exchange reserves. Over time, the restrictions on trade have been relaxed. Fewer products are subject to quotas, tariffs have been reduced, companies have been given the right to import and export. Accession to the WTO continued, and may have accelerated, this trend, with China adopting some reforms not mandated by the WTO. China is now one of the most open developing economies in the world. Its average tariff rate of 10% is much lower than that of Argentina (32%), Brazil (31%), India (50%), and Indonesia (37%). Its ratio of imports to GDP is almost 35%, compared to 9% for Japan.[136]

As with trade, foreign direct investment has been slowly liberalized. At first, FDI was limited to certain sectors. The government encouraged the establishment of manufacturing companies and discouraged the establishment of companies in service sectors. Foreign companies were steered toward joint ventures rather than wholly foreign owned companies. They were limited to minority shares in key sectors. Restrictive clauses for the transfer of technology were intended to force foreign companies to make technology available to Chinese partners or companies on terms favorable to the Chinese parties; and foreign investors were encouraged to export through tax incentives. Over time, more sectors were opened to foreign investment. The restrictions on wholly foreign owned enterprises were relaxed, and then removed once China entered WTO in most industries. Technology transfer regulations were revised to be more transferor friendly, and more consistent with international commercial practices. China has also liberalized its service sectors to a greater extent than most developing and even most developed countries. To be sure, a number of restrictions remain, and will continue to remain, even after all of China's WTO commitments come into effect.[137] Nevertheless, China has been more open, and relied more heavily on foreign direct investment, than South Korea, Japan, or Taiwan.[138] In 2003, the ratio of the stock of foreign investment to GDP was 35% in China, compared to 8% in Korea, 5% in India, and 2% in Japan.[139]

The story is similar for deregulation and privatization. China has made it easier for both foreign and domestic companies to enter and, to a lesser degree, to exit. Registered capital requirements have been lowered. There are fewer restrictions on private companies. The State Council has sought to overhaul the approval process to reduce red tape, to make it more efficient and compatible with a market economy, and to reduce opportunities for rent seeking. Nevertheless, there is still considerable regulation. Given the fear of social unrest if too many insolvent SOEs go belly-up at once, the government has also imposed restrictions on bankruptcies. The government has sold off most small and medium-size SOEs as well some large ones, and allowed investors to obtain a minority share in others. However, it did so over time. It also continues to maintain the majority share in many companies. In addition, the government also attempted to improve corporate governance and the regulation of the securities markets. However, the dominance of state as the largest shareholder continues to undermine the effectiveness of the regulatory changes in both areas.

On the controversial issue of industrial policy, China has generally moved to break down state monopolies, allowing limited competition in key sectors such as telecommunication, insurance, and banking. Nevertheless, the government still controls or supports certain key sectors directly or indirectly. A fascination with size has fueled the establishment of group companies and a domestic merger and acquisition craze. Whether greater size will translate into higher profits remains to be seen, though past experiences suggest that larger state-directed firms are likely to show lower returns.[140]

The government has generally refrained from seizing the assets of companies, although many government agencies impose a variety of approved and unapproved fees that amount in some cases to an informal taking. In contrast, the rush to modernize and generate economic growth has resulted in widespread government taking of land and the relocation of citizens in both the countryside and in cities. As in other countries, property rights are protected both through the formal legal system and informal mechanisms. While the system is far from perfect, property rights may be enforced in court.[141]

China has moved more slowly on financial liberalization. Nevertheless, there have been financial sector reforms. Long ago, China abandoned the dual currencies for foreigners and PRC nationals in favor of a single currency. Foreign exchange regulations have oscillated, though the overall trend has been toward relaxation of control. At first, foreign companies were required to balance their own foreign exchange. Later they were able to exchange RMB for foreign currency at swap centers, and a few years later at banks. China then made current account expenses freely convertible. The Asian financial crisis slowed the push toward capital account convertibility. China has recently succumbed to pressure to revalue the RMB. The RMB is now tied to a basket of currencies rather than pegged to the dollar, and allowed to fluctuate within a range of 3% daily. On the whole, China's policies would seem to reflect 'the prudent liberalization of cross-border capital transactions' as required under the expanded WC.

The government has taken steps to hold banks to international standards and to improve their lending practices. Nevertheless, much remains to be done. The big four banks continue to engage in policy-based lending, mainly to prop up ailing SOEs. Despite various attempts to swap debt for equity or to recapitalize banks, the percentage of bad debts is still high. Foreign banks have been allowed into the market, albeit subject at first to geographical restrictions and other restrictions. By 2005, more than 200 foreign banks had established operational entities in China, in addition to 244 representative offices.[142] WTO commitments require opening of the banking sector to foreign competition, including allowing foreign banks to provide both foreign and local currency services to enterprises and individuals without geographical limitations and without approvals being subject to an economic needs test or quota. Foreign banks are also lining up to buy into Chinese banks, although the financial condition of the banks is worrisome.

China by and large has lived up to its WTO commitments. It has revised its laws to make them consistent with the principle of national treatment. It has reduced tariffs and quotas as required. It has opened up sectors to foreign investors. Although not all of these changes were completed exactly in accordance with the stipulated time schedule, some delays are to be expected given the enormity of the task and the size of China.

Nevertheless there are areas of concern. China has not always issued implementing regulations needed to clarify essential operational issues. It has also passed regulations opening certain sectors such as telecommunications and construction but then imposed high registered capital or eligibility requirements or imposed other non-tariff barriers.[143] Implementation of intellectual property rights remains a concern, although China has now bowed to pressure from the US and other developed countries to rely more heavily on criminal punishments to deter IP violators.

As noted, China has deviated from neoliberal economic principles but followed the expanded WC by attempting to tackle poverty and to shore up the social welfare system, particularly in recent years. Concerned with social stability, it has protected laborers by keeping inefficient SOEs afloat and preventing them from laying off employees.

However, it has simultaneously moved toward more flexible labor markets. The iron rice bowl of guaranteed employment for life is long since gone. Employees now sign labor contracts, although those with ten years or more are entitled to contracts without a fixed term. Part-time work is now more common. More generally, the government has for the most part relied until recently on growth to raise living standards. Government expenditures on employee relocation and training and social services however have increased under the Hu-Wen administration, as discussed in Chapter 4.

Conclusion

There are two competing versions of the affirmative view of modernization. The first emphasizes economic development as the motor for other reforms; the second puts freedom and democracy first. The policy implications of the two approaches are different. In light of the difficulties sustaining economic growth and the long time frames involved in reaching a high level of wealth, the economics- first approach tends to be more patient, and more tolerant of authoritarian regimes—at least the ones that are able to deliver the goods.

The freedom-first approach is less patient, and less willing to tolerate nondemocratic regimes—albeit subject to realpolitik compromises. The Bush administration's messianic promotion of democracy, for instance, entails applying political pressure on governments to democratize, rewarding those that do, and attaching conditionalities to aid and imposing economic sanctions on those that do not—despite the disingenuous claims that 'America will not impose our own style of government on the unwilling.'[144] At the extreme, this approach supports humanitarian intervention and even regime change, as in Iraq (although admittedly the desire to promote democracy only came to the fore after it was clear there were no weapons of mass destruction and no linkage between Iraq and Al Qaeda).

To many citizens in developing countries, and even to many Western liberals, this approach smacks of imperialism. While not opposed to the use of coercion to pursue America's interests, neoconservatives for their part find this normatively driven agenda excessively idealistic and at odds with the realism that has been the cornerstone of US foreign policy.

The second approach also tends to assume that individual freedom and neoliberal economic policies are enough, and that there is little need for the state. It is true there is no necessary connection between the view that freedom and democracy come first and a small state. Rather, this view reflects—or at least reflected—the dominant thinking among some of the leading Western economic powers. In contrast, the economics-first approach tends to favor a larger role for the state in setting economic policies, dealing with market failures and ensuring equitable growth, though again there is no necessary connection.

The economics-first view also tends to emphasize the need for developed countries to provide more aid and debt relief to developing countries, and to do more to address poverty. This poverty-reduction aspect tends to be supported by liberals (in the US political sense), labor parties, and progressives. In contrast, conservatives (in the US political sense) tend to be more dubious about poverty reduction.

> Conservatives argue that when it comes to poverty, societies are complex. The Bush folks, like most conservatives, tend to emphasize nonmaterial causes of poverty: corrupt governments, perverse incentives, institutions that crush freedom. Conservatives appreciate the crooked timber of humanity—that human beings are not simply organisms within systems, but have minds and inclinations of their own that usually defy planners. You can give people mosquito nets to prevent malaria, but they might use them instead to catch fish.[145]

Conservatives claim that the complexity of societies militates against a one-size-fits-all approach to poverty reduction. However, when it comes to democracy, societies are suddenly no longer hopelessly complex. Everyone loves freedom, and American-style freedom at that. As Bush declared in his second inaugural address: 'Some, I know, have questioned the global appeal of liberty—though this time in history, four decades defined by the swiftest advance of freedom ever seen, is an odd time for doubt. Americans, of all people, should never be surprised by the power of our ideals. Eventually, the call of freedom comes to every mind and every soul.' There is no need to worry about whether the conditions for the successful implementation and consolidation of democracy exist. Unfortunately, this optimistic view ignores the empirical record, which demonstrates that many of the factors that make societies complex and undermine efforts to reduce poverty—corrupt leaders, clientelist networks that benefit the elite at the expense of the masses, the lack of effective institutions—also undermine democracy.

Conversely, while some liberals and progressives worry about imposing freedom and democracy on other countries given the complexity of different societies, they see poverty reduction as universally desirable and feasible. Both sides appeal to fundamental values: freedom for one, the elimination of poverty and human suffering for the other. Both are right about one thing: societies are complex. As a consequence, exporting freedom and democracy does not always work; nor will increased aid, debt relief, and other such measures always succeed in reducing poverty. Reformers need to adopt a more pragmatic, less ideologically driven, approach to both poverty reduction and political reform in developing countries.

The experiences of Asian states tend to support the approach that emphasizes growth as the motor for reforms and to disconfirm the freedom and democracy first approach. However, several qualifications are necessary. First, economic growth has not led to democracy in all successful countries, and not to liberal democracy even in the countries that have democratized. Second, the state has played a larger role in the economy and in ensuring the basic material conditions to succeed in this era of globalization, or at least to survive, than envisioned by fans of neoliberal economic principles. Poverty has been addressed mainly through higher growth rates, with Japan, South Korea, and Taiwan redistributing wealth more equitably than Singapore and Hong Kong. Nevertheless, Singapore, Hong Kong, and China have adopted a number of specific measures to address poverty, despite greater reliance on private spending especially on health. Third, the reform process has been driven by elite decision-making rather than broad public participation. However, the elite have largely adopted policies that ensured reasonable investment in human capital and institutions. Above all, East Asian states have adopted a pragmatic approach to reforms. Governments experimented with different policies, promoted those that worked, and abandoned those that failed.[146]

The experiences of Asian countries shed light on three of the main points of contention in the many debates over neoliberalism, the WC and BC and the relationship between them: whether the WC requires neoliberalism's stripped-down minimalist state; whether the principles of the WC are to be applied without adaptation in all countries; and whether the BC entails a wholesale rejection of the WC.

As for the first issue, according to Williamson, the WC was never intended to minimize the role of the state in addressing poverty. Thus, WC proponents today need not and should not subscribe to populist interpretations that equate the WC with neoliberalism, market fundamentalism, Reagonomics, and Thatcherism—in short, 'let's bash the state, the markets will resolve everything.'[147] This may be an accurate reflection of Williamson's thinking at the time or an attempt to rewrite history. In any event, the view that states and the international community need to play a bigger role in alleviating poverty than suggested by neoliberals is now gaining ground, as reflected in the experiences of East Asian states, Rodrik's version of the augmented WC, the acceptance by the IMF and other international agencies of the need to consider the impact of their prescriptions on the least advantaged in society, and the renewed commitment by developed countries to address global injustice and the increasing gap between rich and poor countries.

As for the second issue, the various crises in Argentina, Mexico, Brazil, Russia, Indonesia, Thailand, and other countries that followed the WC most faithfully, in contrast to the success of East Asian countries that adopted a more pragmatic approach, have tilted the scales decidedly in favor of the view that one size does not fit all. To be sure, diehard supporters of neoliberalism and the WC continue to claim that countries failed largely because they deviated from neoliberal prescriptions and WC policies. Moreover, revisionists, including Williamson himself, claim that the basic approach is correct but may need to be modified somewhat in some cases.

This concession however narrows the gap between the supporters of the WC and the EAM, though much depends on the details of what may be modified and when.

Third, Beijing and other successful East Asian states have followed many of the basic WC principles in whole or in part. Thus, we need to avoid drawing too sharp a contrast between the 'BC' and 'WC.' There is some danger that in looking to China and other successful East Asian countries, developing countries may draw the wrong conclusion. Having shifted too far to the right in the past in adopting the neoliberal aspects of the WC, they may now shift too far to the left, rejecting basic market principles and giving in to populist pressures to provide more services and benefits than the state's limited resources will allow or in being overly protective of domestic companies. This risk seems highest in Latin American countries but can also be found in India, the Philippines, and Indonesia. Even in China, extreme populist and leftist anti-market voices do manage from time to time to make themselves heard above the steady drumbeat of rising GDP figures and high growth rates.

Nevertheless, China has largely followed the EAM on economic matters, and is likely to continue to do so in the future. As subsequent chapters will demonstrate, China has also followed the EAM in other regards as well. The next chapter shows that China is, for better or worse, following the EAM with respect to civil and political rights.

CHAPTER THREE

Taking rights seriously? Official policy and actual practice

This chapter begins with a brief overview of the governments' human rights policies. All too often, the governments' positions are simply dismissed as propaganda, rationalizations for a poor human rights record, or outright lies and distortions. There is some truth to these characterizations. Government reports do attempt to cast China's human rights record in its most positive light. At times, some officials issue blanket denials of abuses that simply cannot and should not be taken seriously. But then most governments' statements about their own human rights records tend to be selective, to emphasize positive aspects, and to gloss over problems.

While we should be cautious about taking all official statements at face value, we should not dismiss government statements and 'white papers' out of hand. These statements and reports present one side of the picture, and raise issues that may be overlooked or given short shrift from other perspectives. They provide valuable insights into how policy-makers in China perceive and frame the issues. Many of the concerns are legitimate ones, and shared by other governments in the world.

Nevertheless, I argue that there is a considerable gap between official policy and actual practice with respect to the protection of personal integrity rights and civil and political rights. However, even acknowledging serious problems with respect to torture, arbitrary detention, capital punishment, and the criminal law system more generally, China does not deserve as low a score as it gets on personal integrity rights. In contrast, despite improvements in the area of civil and political rights, China's low score on civil and political rights seems accurate, at least when it comes to the exercise of such rights in politically sensitive ways. The crucial question however is whether the tight limits are justified. While simply applying legal standards of wealthy liberal democracies to China is normatively problematic and unrealistic, in many cases the government incurs unnecessary reputational damage at home and abroad by cracking down too harshly on the exercise of rights and by failing to abide by legal procedures even when the restrictions are arguably justified.

China and the international human rights regime: engagement and resistance

China has ratified over twenty human rights treaties, including the International Covenant on Economic, Social, and Cultural Rights (ICESCR), the International Convention on the Elimination of All Forms of Racial Discrimination (ICERD), the Convention on the Elimination of All Forms of Discrimination Against Women (CEDAW), the Convention against Torture and Other Cruel, Inhuman or Degrading Treatment or Punishment (CAT), and the Convention on the Rights of the Child (CRC) along with its two optional protocols. It has signed but not ratified the International Covenant on Civil and Political Rights (ICCPR), and has opposed the International Criminal Court along with the United States, Israel, and a handful of other states.

China has actively participated in the international human rights regime in other ways as well, submitting reports, participating in the drafting of new instruments, engaging in numerous multilateral, regional, and bilateral dialogues on rights issues, and hosting a number of important regional and global human rights meetings.[1] Notwithstanding sovereignty concerns, China voted in favor of sanctions against apartheid in South Africa. China has also participated in

UN peacekeeping missions in East Timor, Bosnia, Liberia, Afghanistan, Kosovo, Haiti, and Sudan. Despite widespread criticisms of Chinese policing, Chinese police have participated in UN missions to train police in other countries. China has also allowed a limited number of visits from international rights monitors, including the special rapporteurs on torture, freedom of religion and the right to education, the Working Group on Arbitrary Detention, and even the US Commission on International Religious Freedom.

In participating in the international rights regime, China has, like other countries, sought to promote and protect its own national interests.[2] China, for instance, sought reforms of the Human Rights Commission, which Beijing saw—not without justification—as a biased 'court' for the trial of developing countries accused of violations of civil and political rights.[3] China supported the newly formed Human Rights Council, which replaced the Human Rights Commission. The reforms include an increase in the number of votes to become a member of the Council, making it more difficult for countries with poor human rights records to become members. Council members must also undergo a review of their human rights record. The US was one of four countries to vote against the Council.

Domestically, rights are now firmly entrenched in political and legal discourse. The 1982 constitution sets out the usual litany of civil and political rights as well as some social and economic rights such as free access to medical care. Although claims based directly on the constitution are generally not justiciable,[4] numerous laws and regulations have been passed to further specify and give legal effect to most rights. In 2004, the constitution was amended to provide expressly that 'the state respects and safeguards human rights,' indicating perhaps a greater commitment to effective realization of the rights provided by the constitution.

The 2003 White Paper announces the government's official position:

> China holds that the development of human rights is an important mark of the continuous progress of the civilization of human society, and an important part of the progressive current of world peace and development. Full realization of human rights is the common goal of countries throughout the world as well as an important target for China in her efforts to build a moderately prosperous society in an all-round way, as well as her 'peaceful

rise' in the world. China will, as always, devote herself to promoting the human rights cause, actively carry out exchanges and cooperation with the international community according to the provisions of the Constitution of China and the need for modernization of the country, and make her contributions to promoting the healthy development of the international human rights cause.[5]

More specifically, the government's official human rights policy consists of several main tenets. First, although some and perhaps most rights are universally valued at least to some extent when stated at a high level of abstraction, their interpretation and implementation depends on local circumstances, including the level of economic development, cultural practices, and fundamental values that are not the same in all countries: 'no country in its effort to realize and protect human rights can take a route that is divorced from its history and its economic, political and cultural realities.'[6] This is unimpeachable as a descriptive claim and as a legal claim. International law itself ties some rights to local levels of development. This is most notable in the ICESCR, which provides that economic rights may be achieved progressively consistent with a country's level of development. Limitation clauses that allow for restriction on rights in certain circumstances also inevitably introduce local factors. In addition, domestic legal doctrines 'localize' international law in various ways, including through the principle that international law and domestic laws should be interpreted harmoniously, and general jurisprudential principles that require judges to apply local customs and norms. While the moral relevance of local circumstances is often contested, the real issue is not *whether* local circumstances are normatively relevant, but *which* circumstances are relevant in which cases, as implied by the notion of a margin of appreciation afforded countries on rights issues.[7]

Second, while rights may be interdependent, they must be prioritized, and the international human rights community and Western countries privilege civil and political rights over other rights, including economic, social, and cultural rights, as well as collective rights such as the right of development. In China, given its current level of economic development and huge population, subsistence is the most fundamental right. Moreover, stability is a prerequisite for the enjoyment of all rights. The need to ensure economic development and stability justifies some limitations on the exercise of civil and political rights. This view is widely supported by Chinese citizens, and by the majority of citizens in poor developing countries around the world.[8]

The third main tenet of China's human rights policy is that the international human rights regime assumes a liberal democratic framework and emphasizes implicitly and in some cases explicitly individual autonomy to a degree not found in other traditions, including China's. Greater weight should be placed on the interests of groups within society, society as a whole, and the state. Moreover, the emphasis on rights should not obscure the importance of duties and the responsibilities of individuals toward others. While there is more truth to these points than often allowed by the regime's harshest critics, the question remains whether the limitations on civil and political rights are indeed necessary, proportional, or permitted under any reasonable interpretation of international law or even PRC law.

Fourth, international human rights, and the ability of individuals to raise claims based on such rights or the international community to pressure China to change its ways, are limited by sovereignty. Accordingly, China, like other countries, has made a number of reservations when ratifying rights treaties that prevent the submission of disputes to arbitration or the International Court of Justice, or that deny individuals standing to raise complaints under the treaties.[9] China also made a reservation to Article 20 of CAT that allows the committee to conduct investigations, including visits.[10]

China is by no means alone in objecting to the ever-increasing reach of the international human rights regime into domestic affairs.[11] Nor does China object to all attempts to monitor and improve the rights situation in China. Indeed, it would be hypocritical for China to participate in the condemnation and sanctioning of other states for violating human rights and yet assert that the UN and other countries are interfering in China's domestic affairs when they do the same. However, China continues to insist that dialogue on rights issues be carried out on the basis of equality and mutual respect, and that states refrain from coercive intervention except in cases of widespread and systematic violation of rights that characterize failed states torn by ethnic strife and genocide.[12]

China is in favor of strengthening international cooperation in the realm of human rights on the basis of mutual understanding and seeking a common ground while reserving differences. . . . Therefore, the purpose of international protection of human rights and related activities should be to promote normal cooperation in the international field of human rights and international harmony, mutual understanding and mutual respect. Consideration should be given to the differing views on human rights held by countries with different political, economic and social systems, as well as different historical, religious and cultural backgrounds. International human rights activities should be carried on in the spirit of seeking common ground while reserving differences, mutual respect, and the promotion of understanding and cooperation.

China has always held that to effect international protection of human rights, the international community should interfere with and stop acts that endanger world peace and security, such as gross human rights violations caused by colonialism, racism, foreign aggression and occupation, as well as apartheid, racial discrimination, genocide, slave trade and serious violation of human rights by international terrorist organizations. These are important aspects of international cooperation in the realm of human rights and an arduous task facing current international human rights protection activities.

Fifth, other states often use human rights as an excuse for strong-arm politics and to interfere in China's domestic affairs.[13]

China has firmly opposed to [*sic*] any country making use of the issue of human rights to sell its own values, ideology, political standards and mode of development, and to [*sic*] any country interfering in the internal affairs of other countries on the pretext of human rights, the internal affairs of developing countries in particular, and so hurting the sovereignty and dignity of many developing countries. Together with other developing countries, China has waged a resolute struggle against all such acts of interference, and upheld justice by speaking out from a sense of fairness. China has always maintained that human rights are essentially matters within the domestic jurisdiction of a country. Respect for each country's sovereignty and non-interference in internal affairs are universally recognized principles of international law, which are applicable to all fields of international relations, and of course applicable to the field of human rights as well. . . . Using the human rights issue for the political purpose of imposing the ideology of one country on another is no longer a question of human rights, but a manifestation of power politics in the form of interference in the internal affairs of other countries. Such abnormal practice in international human rights activities must be eliminated. . . .

Hegemonism and power politics continue to exist and endanger world peace and development. Interference in other countries' internal affairs and the pushing of power politics on the pretext of human rights are obstructing the realization of human rights and fundamental freedoms.

Again, the claim that human rights have been politicized and used to advance the interests of other states is undeniably true to some extent, as demonstrated by even a cursory glance at the dismal history of the United States' linkage of human rights to Most Favored Nation (MFN) status, access to the WTO, intellectual property rights, market access, and the revaluation of renminbi. Time and again the US threatened to deny China MFN status allegedly because of human rights violations, only to back off once China agreed to amend its intellectual property rules or to provide greater market access for foreign companies. In 2004, the US again sponsored a motion to censure China for human rights violations during an election year in which President George W. Bush was under severe pressure domestically to 'do something' about the rising trade deficit with China and the 'outsourcing' of jobs.[14] In contrast, there was no motion against China in 2002 and 2003, when the need for China's support in the US-led global 'war on terror' and in preventing North Korea's development of nuclear weapons overrode other concerns.[15] Nor was there a motion in 1998, when President Clinton was emphasizing constructive engagement in contrast to the Republican position of confrontation and containment, and China signed the ICCPR and ICESCR. The US has oscillated between confrontation and engagement depending on domestic politics and changing US interests.

The sixth main tenet is that many of the countries that criticize China for human rights violations have their own human rights problems. China and other Asian governments are right to point out that Western countries have committed atrocities in other countries in the past and have their own human rights problems. On the other hand, two wrongs do not make a right. That the US or any other country has problems of its own does not justify human rights violations in China or excuse China from meeting its obligations under PRC and international law. Each country must be held accountable for its human rights violations and take the necessary steps to stop such violations.

At the same time, the images of American soldiers abusing Iraqi prisoners played into the hands of PRC propagandists seeking to deflect attention from China's problems by highlighting the violations of others, while fueling a popular backlash against American hypocrisy. Already suspicious of American motives and tired of US moralizing, many Chinese, like others around the world, felt the US forfeited whatever little remaining moral authority it might have enjoyed to preach to other countries about human rights violations. As with the television evangelist whose flock deserts him after he turns up unexpectedly as the male lead in a homemade video of a drunken orgy in a shady brothel, US actions have led even some of the most ardent Chinese rights advocates to give up on the United States and look elsewhere for role models. Although some have praised the US for exposing the problems and promising to hold those responsible accountable, others ask how, in a country with a free press, widespread torture could have gone unreported by the mainstream media for so long despite several reports from human rights organizations and repeated complaints from Iraqis of abuse. Still others ask why Secretary of Defense Donald Rumsfeld and others in the chain of command are still in power, and wonder whether the US will hold senior leaders accountable under standards that US officials have claimed apply to other countries, including the newly developed command and responsibility theories developed by the International Criminal Tribunals for the Former Yugoslavia and Rwanda. Skeptics doubt that the US will apply the same standards to the US soldiers that it advocates for others, pointing out that prior to 9/11 the US criticized China for secret trials and other countries for military tribunals and yet has argued such methods are justified when it comes to US national security interests and the war on terror.[16] President Bush appears either disingenuous or to be living in a state of denial in claiming that those responsible were being systematically punished regardless of rank and the world would see the US investigation and handling of the abuses in Afghanistan, Iraq, and Guatanamo Bay as a model of transparency and accountability. In fact, his administration has done its best to keep a lid on the situation by withholding internal reports and obstructing external investigations.[17] Rightly or wrongly, these and other shortcomings in the US on human rights issues lead many Chinese to feel that China is the victim of a double standard.

Physical integrity rights and derogation of rights in times of emergency

Physical or personal integrity rights violations refer to political prisoners, extrajudicial killings, incidences of torture and arbitrary detentions. They are among the most basic of rights. They tend to be subject to wide variation by year in a particular country because wars and political crises may arise or end suddenly. For instance, despite thousands of complaints of torture and police brutality every year, the US had one of the best records in 1996, enjoying a level-1 ranking, indicating a country under a secure rule of law, where people are not imprisoned for their political views, and torture or political murders are rare or exceptional.[18] However, it has since been demoted to level 2 because of the detentions of suspected terrorists in Guatanamo Bay, Iraq, and Afghanistan and the secret arrests of thousands, including many Muslims, in the US,[19] which constitute arbitrary detention under the ICCPR.[20] Level 2 indicates a limited amount of imprisonment for nonviolent political activity. However, few persons are affected, and torture and beatings are exceptional. Political murder is rare.

Level 3 indicates extensive political imprisonment, or a recent history of such imprisonment. Execution or other political murders and brutality may be common. Unlimited detention, with or without a trial, for political views is accepted. At level 4 the practices of level 3 are expanded to larger numbers. Murders, disappearances, and torture are a common part of life. At level 5, the terrors of level 4 are expanded to the whole population. The leaders place no limits on the means or thoroughness with which they pursue personal or ideological goals.[21]

As expected, in the Asian region, there are more violations of personal integrity rights where there is political instability, rebel insurgencies, and terrorism, as Figure 4 shows.[22] At level 4, India remains a major trouble spot, due largely to ethnic and religious tensions. Also at level 4, Indonesia, even after democratization, continues to experience widespread personal integrity violations, consistent with the efforts to restore order in Aceh, Papua, and Maluku provinces and to prevent terrorism in the country.[23]

South Korea performed poorly in the mid-1990s, due apparently to violent protests by students and labor organizations. Although the number of persons arrested for violating the National Security Law has decreased in recent years, almost 80 people were arrested in the first year of the presidency of former human rights lawyer Roh Moo-hyun. Moreover, law enforcement agencies continue to emphasize confession and make use of 'special interrogation rooms' maintained in the prosecutors' office.[24] At level 3, South Korea is on a par with Malaysia, which was ranked higher in 1996 but which has suffered in recent years under the threat of terrorism and rising Islamic fundamentalism.

Vietnam scores higher than might be expected. Vietnam and Thailand both received a level-2 rating based on Amnesty International reports and a level-3 rating based on US State Department reports. Thailand, however, has recently experienced violent clashes between the government and Islamic groups in some Muslim-dominated southern provinces, leading to the imposition of martial law in the region.[25] Singapore merits a level-2 rating, reflecting the use of defamation laws to rein in high profile opposition figures and the reliance on tough national security laws and other nonliberal laws to crack down on terrorists, people inciting ethnic conflict, drug traffickers, and other criminals. Taiwan receives the highest level-1 score.

China received a level-4 ranking on the Political Terror Scale (PTS) based on both Amnesty International and State Department reports. This ranking puts China in the unsavory company of such notorious

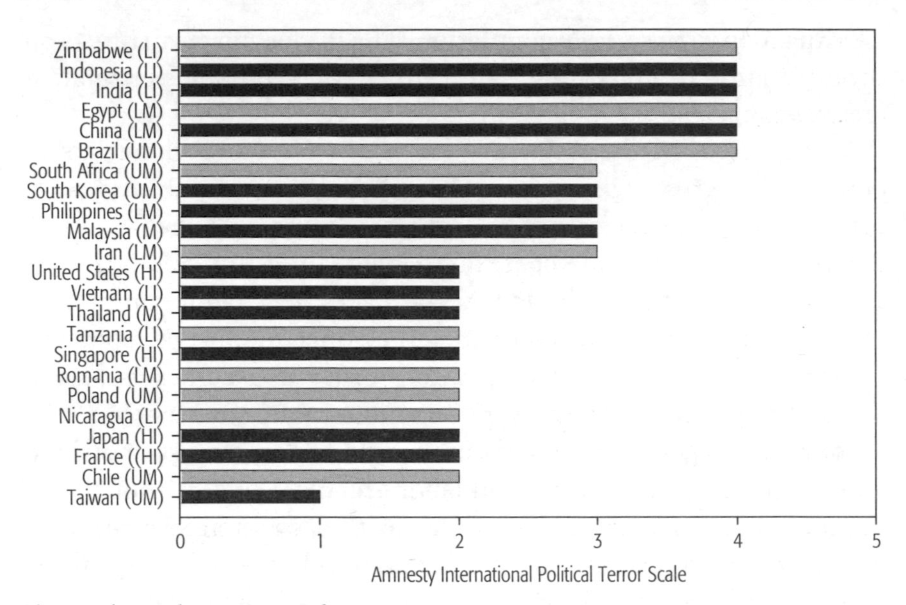

Fig. 4. Physical Integrity Rights 2002
Source: Gibney, *Political Science Terror Scale.*

rights violators as Kenya, Nigeria, Pakistan, Russia, and Sudan. Even North Korea and Cambodia received a better level-3 ranking based on Amnesty International reports. By way of comparison, few countries receive the worst level-5 rating. Examples include Afghanistan, Colombia, with its ongoing war against drug lords, and Nepal, where the government is currently fighting a civil war against Maoist rebels.[26]

Does China merit such a dismal rating? Unlike the situation in some of the other level-4 countries, there are few politically motivated extrajudicial killings or disappearances in the usual sense. The 2004 US State Department report did note that some dissidents without family members were detained or committed to psychiatric wards, which the report claimed amounted to disappearance.[27] However, commitment to psychiatric wards, while deplorable, is a far cry from the kind of widespread disappearances that plagued Latin American countries where large numbers of people were sent off to prisons to be tortured, many of them ending up dead in unmarked mass graves.

China also imposes more capital punishments than any other nation, and indeed more than the rest of the world combined. While

Amnesty International reported 1,639 confirmed death sentences in 2003,[28] one National People's Congress (NPC) delegate suggested the number may be as high as 10,000 per year.[29] Citing due process concerns, the US State Department suggests that the executions may in some cases border on extrajudicial killings.[30] Whatever the shortcomings in due process, a problem the government acknowledges and is seeking to address,[31] describing the executions as extrajudicial killing is a stretch of the normal application of that term as used in judging the rights performance of other countries. One wonders whether the State Department would describe the executions of criminals in the US as extrajudicial killings given the various due process failures that have contributed to numerous documented cases of innocent people being executed, and to a disproportionately high rate of executions of poor African American men, which have led the U.N. Special Rapporteur and even the US Supreme Court itself to describe the process as arbitrary and racially discriminatory.[32]

Torture remains a serious problem for a variety of reasons, despite being prohibited by PRC law and considerable efforts to stamp it out.[33] The scope of the problem is difficult to quantify however. The Supreme People's Procuracy has acknowledged about 400 cases per year during the 1990s.[34] Reports from human rights organizations and the overseas Falun Gong organization describe torture as widespread and systemic,[35] but Amnesty International also describes torture in the United States as widespread and systemic.[36] While relying on reports from the Falun Gong organization is likely to present a false impression of the scope of the problem,[37] official reports surely understate the amount of torture. In recent years, the government has adopted various measures to address the problem, including strengthening its anti-torture laws, increasing the penalties for abusing detainees, restructuring police departments, requiring prison guards to take professional exams every five years, appointing section-level officers based on open competition, limiting who can be taken to the police station for questioning and the length of the interrogations, firing incompetent police, and prosecuting more aggressively cases of abuse of police powers. The government's 2004 Human Rights White Paper notes that in 2003 the procuratorate prosecuted 259 cases of illegal detention, twenty-nine of illegal search, fifty-two of extorting confessions by torture, and thirty-two of abusing prisoners or detainees.[38] Nevertheless, despite the recent progress, much remains to be done.[39]

China's poor PTS score may also reflect concerns with arbitrary detention. Human rights organizations have criticized as arbitrary, and called for the elimination of, all forms of administrative detention.[40] In fact, China employs several different types of administrative detention, some of which exist in other countries. The various forms include: (i) administrative detention up to fifteen days under the Security Administrative Punishments Regulations; (ii) education through labor (ETL) (often referred to as 're-education through labor,' which has received most of the international media's attention); (iii) detention for education used to detain prostitutes and their clients; (iv) compulsory drug treatment; (v) forced detention in psychiatric hospitals; (vi) detention of juveniles who commit criminal offenses in juvenile centers, or of juveniles who commit lesser offenses in work-study schools; and (vii) 'stop and question' proceedings whereby suspects may be detained for questioning for up to forty-eight hours. Administrative detention is intended for minor offenses. Accordingly, it is meant to be a lighter form of intervention with a greater emphasis on rehabilitation than the more punitive formal criminal law system. Supporters, most of whom advocate significant reforms, argue that eliminating administrative detention will harm most of those the reformers are trying to help by pushing many marginal offenders into the harsh and decidedly unfriendly penal system, forcing them to live with hardened criminals, and causing them to be stigmatized as convicts.

One of the main criticisms of the various forms of administrative detention is that the failure to provide prompt judicial review of the detention decision violates international law. Article 9(4) of the ICCPR provides that '[a]nyone who is deprived of his liberty by arrest or detention shall be entitled to take proceedings before a court, in order that the court may decide without delay on the lawfulness of his detention and order his release if the detention is not lawful.'[41] Although China has not yet ratified the ICCPR, it has signed it, and is thus obligated not to act in ways that would defeat the object and purpose of the treaty. The UN Working Group on Arbitrary Detention has objected to ETL because only an independent judicial body can make the decision to deprive people of their personal liberty.[42] However, in some civil law countries, such as France and Switzerland, prosecutors rather than judges review the decision to arrest and detain. The European Court of Human Rights in the past found that this satisfies Article 5(3) of the European Convention, which requires that the authorities immediately bring an arrested or detained person before a tribunal empowered to exercise judicial functions.[43] Under PRC law, an Administrative Committee made up of civil affairs, public security, and labor officials decides whether to detain someone under ETL. In practice, however, public security officers dominate the decision-making process.

Although Chinese citizens do not have the right to challenge the initial detention decision immediately after being detained, they can challenge detention decisions later in the process through a number of channels, including administrative litigation in a court before a judge, and administrative reconsideration. They can also challenge detention decisions through administrative supervision, and a system of letters and visits whereby disgruntled citizens write letters to or visit judges, government officials, people's congress delegates, or virtually anyone else they think may assist them, including Party officials. Critics note that these channels are poor substitutes for prompt judicial review, are ineffective and expensive, and that detainees are often ignorant of their rights or lack the financial resources to exercise them. Furthermore, in some cases the authorities may abuse the detainees if they try to avail themselves of their legal rights. The government has attempted to respond to these concerns by strengthening administrative reconsideration of public security decisions. Regulations effective January 1, 2004 clarify the legal rights of detainees and others to challenge public security decisions.[44]

While providing detainees the right to challenge the detention decision shortly after detention is desirable and would bring the legal system more into line with international standards, whether it would result in much relief for those detained is highly questionable. Chinese judges do not want to coddle criminals. On the contrary, most judges share the prevailing society-wide belief in the need to be tough on criminals. Accordingly, the custodial judge's review in China may be nothing more than a rubber stamp, as it is in other countries.[45] Judicial approval of detention decisions is even more likely in China given the emphasis on social stability, rising crime rates, and the high proportion of crimes committed by nonresidents.

Human rights groups also object to long pretrial detention under both administrative detention procedures and the criminal law. In general, civil law systems tend to allow longer periods of detention while the investigation is being carried out. As a result, supporters of the inquisitorial system, with its emphasis on truth but long detention periods and limited role for defense counsel, complain about what they see as a bias toward the adversarial approach or even an American approach on the part of the ICCPR Committee and human rights organizations.[46] Nevertheless, the Supreme People's Procuracy has criticized public security officers for violating even the generous deadlines for detention in the PRC, citing more than 300,000 cases between 1998 and 2002. Accordingly, on November 12, 2003, the Supreme People's Court, the Supreme People's Procuracy, and the Ministry of Public Security jointly issued the Notice on the Strict Enforcement of the Criminal Procedure Law, and on the Conscientious Prevention and Correction of Excessive Detention.[47] The notice emphasized that procuratorates below the provincial level must obtain the next higher level's permission for any extension. The notice also warns against attempts to circumvent the law, such as changing jurisdictions, or withdrawing charges and then rearresting someone.

To facilitate implementation of the new rules, the Supreme People's Procuratorate has set up special telephone lines and email sites for filing reports on extended detention. More than 25,000 people subject to extended detention were released in 2003.[48] Notwithstanding such changes, detainees may still be legally detained for extended periods under the Criminal Procedure Law (CPL).

Another major complaint about both administrative detention and the formal criminal process is the lack of due process rights. Administrative detainees are entitled to some due process protections, though they do not enjoy all of those provided under the CPL.

However, in practice, many of the due process rights provided by the CPL to criminal defendants are not honored.[49]

One proposal for reform would do away with administrative detention as such, bringing offenses now subject to administrative detention into the formal criminal process. However, as this would result in a huge influx of cases into an already overburdened criminal justice system, most offenses would be subject to simplified and summary procedures recently introduced into the formal criminal system. Similar to plea bargaining in other countries, these procedures require a confession in exchange for leniency. Unfortunately, like plea-bargaining, the need to confess to obtain leniency diminishes significantly the value of the various rights and procedural protections afforded to the criminally accused, as the accused must forgo such rights in the rush to cut a deal with the police and prosecutors.

There are undeniably serious due process concerns both in administrative detention and formal criminal cases. However, it is important to distinguish between arbitrary detention in a procedural and in a substantive sense. Administrative and criminal detentions are rarely arbitrary in thc sense that substantive grounds are lacking for arrest and conviction. Nevertheless, human rights reports often depict the detentions as arbitrary because they allegedly involve persons engaging in political activities, usually peacefully, that many would claim are protected by domestic and international law. Such detainees then are characterized as political prisoners of conscience, another key component of the PTS index.

Although human rights organizations regularly highlight the use of administrative detention to detain political dissidents, academic experts have noted that the purpose of administrative detentions has changed over the last two decades, and that ETL and other forms of administrative detention are used primarily to deal with petty criminals.[50] In fact, less than 1% of those subject to ETL could be considered political prisoners, excluding Falun Gong disciples charged with violations under the generally applicable criminal laws. Including all Falun Gong cases, the percentage of political prisoners subject to ETL is around 2%.[51]

Similarly, there are by some estimates 500–600 prisoners serving sentences for the now repealed crime of counterrevolution.[52] While many rights organizations continue to press for their release, whether someone convicted under a valid law at the time should be released if the definition of the crime is changed or the crime is repealed is controversial. Such a person would not be released under US law.[53] In this case, most if not all of those convicted for the crime of counterrevolution would also be guilty under the new crime of endangering the state that replaced the old crime of counterrevolution. In fact, endangering the state may actually be easier to prove as there is no requirement to show subjective intent as in the case of counterrevolution. While counterrevolution was a frequently invoked charge in the politicized Mao era, accounting for almost 60% of the crimes in some years, today endangering the state accounts for less than 0.5% of crimes.[54]

In addition, Amnesty International claims 'scores of people' are still imprisoned for Tiananmen-related activities, although it has identified only fifty of them.[55] The head of Human Rights in China estimated that number to be about 130, while acknowledging the true number is unknown.[56] The US State Department Report, citing unspecified 'credible sources,' suggested the number of people still in prison 'for their activities during the June 1989 Tiananmen demonstrations' may be as high as 2000,[57] although that seems highly unlikely as few people were given sentences of fifteen years or more and of those, some would have been released on parole. Of course, the government claims that they are not imprisoned for their political views but for violating generally applicable criminal laws such as attempting to overthrow the state or disturbing public order.[58] Accepting their characterization as political prisoners and the highest of all the estimates of their numbers, they would constitute about 0.1% of the total prison population of 2 million, keeping in mind that China's incarceration rate is much lower than that of many other countries, particularly the United States (184 per 100,000 for China versus 701 for the United States).

Simply put, politics is generally not an issue in most criminal cases. I do not mean to trivialize Falun Gong or political dissident cases. These cases may severely harm individuals, may involve gross injustices, or may deter others from exercising their legitimate rights provided under PRC and international law.[59] However, we need to have some sense of the size of the problem. Taking China's population of 1.3 billion as the basis, and erring on the high side by assuming as correct the overseas Falun Gong organization's estimate of 20,000 prisoners of conscience, the total rate of detention would be 0.0015%.[60] Twenty thousand likely overstates the actual number, even accepting a liberal definition of 'political prisoner.' But even 20,000, while large in absolute terms, is relatively small given the size of the total population. It is difficult to see how China can be described as a country in which execution, political murders, disappearances, brutality, and torture 'are a common part of life,' as required for a level-4 PTS rating. To be sure, even a level 2 or 3 rating—while perhaps not making China exceptional among countries (including democracies) with a similar level of economic development and facing similar protests and challenges to the government—would still leave much to be desired.

MARTIAL LAW, STRIKE HARD AT CRIME CAMPAIGNS, AND TERRORISM

The ICCPR allows for the declaration of a state of emergency only when the life of the nation is threatened.[61] Principle 39 of the non-binding Siracusa Principles interprets 'threat to the life of the nation' to mean that a danger (i) is actual or imminent, (ii) is exceptional, (iii) concerns the entire population, (iv) threatens the whole or part of the state's territory, and (v) threatens the population's physical integrity, the state's political independence or territorial integrity, or the organized life of the community.[62] Even then, states cannot derogate from all human rights. Derogation is not allowed with respect to the right to life, the protection against torture and cruel and inhuman punishment, the right not to be held in servitude or slavery, recognition as a person before the law, or freedom of thought, conscience, and religion.[63]

Global practice, however, is considerably different. Countries generally react to threats to security by restricting rights. While some may take the current limitation on civil liberties in the US to be an anomalous response to September 11, it is entirely consistent with the response to previous perceived threats to national security.[64] Lincoln, for example, suspended habeas corpus during the Civil War. During the First World War, 2,200 people were prosecuted and more than 1,000 convicted under the Espionage and Sedition Acts. The right of habeas corpus was suspended and martial law imposed in Hawaii after Pearl Harbor, with many US citizens of Japanese descent interred in camps. And during the McCarthy era, the Supreme Court upheld a federal law that required labor union members to sign an oath swearing they were not members of the Communist Party and did not believe in the overthrow of the United States.[65]

The 'margin of appreciation' afforded countries is greatest when it comes to national security.[66] In upholding the British government's derogation of due process rights as necessary to control civil strife in Northern Ireland, the ECHR stated:

> It falls in the first place to each Contracting State, with its responsibility for 'the life of [its] nation', to determine whether that life is threatened by a 'public emergency' and, if so, how far it is necessary to go in attempting to overcome the emergency. By reason of their direct and continuous contact with the pressing needs of the moment, the national authorities are in principle in a better position than the international judge to decide both on the presence of such an emergency and on the nature and scope of derogations necessary to avert it. In this matter Article 15 § 1 [of the European Human Rights Convention] leaves those authorities a wide margin of appreciation. . . . It is certainly not the Court's function to substitute for the British Government's assessment any other assessment of what might be the most prudent or most expedient policy to combat terrorism.[67]

The Court also noted that it must not base its decision on twenty-twenty hindsight, but must consider the government's decisions and actions in light of the circumstances at the time.

A wide margin of appreciation does not mean unlimited discretion, of course, and a major concern of China's critics was the country's handling of the Tiananmen Square crisis. China declared martial law in parts of the country in 1989. Critics argue that the peaceful student demonstrations were not an adequate ground to declare martial law. But even if martial law was justified, critics argue that the decision to use force to clear the square in Tiananmen was not justified, and that excessive force was used. The disclosure of internal documents and discussions revealed differences of opinion among government leaders, although the final decision was made after lengthy discussion in which all sides had an opportunity to present their views.[68] The announcement was then made by Li Peng, as Premier and head of the State Council, in accordance with constitutional requirements. Today, public opinion remains divided in China about the government's policy regarding Tiananmen, in contrast to the nearly universal condemnation abroad. Some Chinese citizens see the government's response as excessively brutal but necessary to regain control and ensure an extended period of stability that has lasted until today, allowing China to progress economically while keeping the lid on social unrest from those who have lost out in the transition to a market economy.[69] They note that the students and other demonstrators had been repeatedly warned to leave the square and yet refused to do so despite being fully aware that martial law had been declared and military troops were prepared to clear the square by force if necessary. Others, led by those who participated in the demonstrations or lost loved ones, continue to call for justice and a reversal of the government's verdict on Tiananmen as political turmoil that disrupted social order and economic development. However, the government has refused to reconsider its official position.

A second area of concern for critics has been the cyclical campaigns to 'strike hard' at crime (*yanda*) which, although not involving a formal declaration of emergency, have led to human rights abuses and the curtailment of rights for the criminally accused. Government officials and court leaders consistently emphasize that the strike-hard campaign should be executed in accordance with the law. Nevertheless, the endless campaigns no doubt put pressure on police officers to make additional arrests, on prosecutors to prosecute more often and charge more serious crimes, and on judges to convict and issue heavier sentences within the range permitted by law. Goaded on by a public widely supportive of the war on crime, police, prosecutors, and judges, in their zeal to strike hard at crime, sometimes exceed the limits imposed by law.[70]

A third area of concern is that the 'war on terrorism' may be undermining progress on rights in China, as it has elsewhere. China beefed up its anti-terrorism laws by amending the Criminal Law in 2001.[71] Beijing has identified the East Turkestan Islamic Movement (ETIM) as a terrorist organization, citing more than 200 violent incidents in Xinjiang between 1990 and 2001, which resulted in 162 deaths and 440 injuries.[72] In a move that human rights groups have criticized, the United States supported the designation of ETIM as a terrorist organization, with the UN Security Council following suit.[73] In December 2003, Beijing added to the list the East Turkestan Liberation Organization (ETLO), the East Turkestan Information Center (ETIC), and the World Uighur Youth Congress (WUYC), as well as eleven individuals. ETIC and WUYC are based in Germany. All four groups openly advocate for East Turkestan's independence, although they generally do not endorse violence, at least publicly.[74] However, ETLO members have been involved in bombings and shootouts, according to the US State Department Counterterrorism Office.

Human rights groups have accused China of taking advantage of the recent global concern with terrorism to restrict the rights of Uighars and Tibetans. While it is clear that there have been a number of arrests in recent years, the details are often murky, with even the basic facts frequently contested.[75]

For instance, Uighar Shaheer Ali was sentenced to death in March 2003 for the 'illegal manufacture, trading and possession of weapons and explosives,' separatism, and 'organizing and leading a terrorist organization,' namely ETIM and the East Turkestan Islamic Party of Allah.[76] The court claimed Ali's organization took part in a beating, smashing, and looting incident in Yining on February 5, 1997. However, Amnesty International claims that independent eyewitnesses reported the incident was a peaceful demonstration calling for equal treatment for Uighars that became violent after security forces used tear gas and water cannons to disperse the protesters.[77] In an interview, Ali claimed he was a member of the Eastern Turkestan Islamic Reform Party, which he described as a nonmilitant organization. He also claimed he was repeatedly tortured while in custody.

Wang Bingzhang, a US based dissident, was sentenced to life imprisonment by a Shenzhen court after being convicted of espionage and leading a terrorist group. The Guangdong High Court upheld the judgment. The Shenzhen court's judgment and the official press reported in detail the evidence against Wang.[78] The judgment presented a lengthy review of the evidence, including witness testimony, documents from the National Security Bureau, and Wang's own publications and Internet writings, to show that Wang received payments for providing military secrets to Taiwanese intelligence organs, advocated terrorism through publications and on the Internet, plotted to blow up the PRC Embassy in Thailand, and planned an explosion in China on a national holiday.[79]

The case attracted the interest of the international community when Wang was apparently abducted from Vietnam along with Zhang Qi and Yue Wu, both of whom were later released by PRC authorities. Beijing claims PRC security officers rescued Wang after he was kidnapped. The UN Commissioner on Human Rights stated that his disappearance, arrest, and imprisonment violated international standards.[80] Wang went on a hunger strike to protest extended periods of solitary confinement and political education sessions three times a day.[81]

In a case that has led to considerable criticism abroad, Tibetan Lobsang Dondrub was executed for a series of bombings in Sichuan in 2002, while Buddhist teacher Tenzin Deleg was sentenced to death with a two-year reprieve.[82] The court found Lobsang Dondrub guilty of incitement to split the country and illegal possession of firearms and ammunition, and Tenzin Deleg guilty of incitement to separatism. PRC authorities claim that both defendants confessed to the crimes. However, Tenzin Deleg denies having confessed and reportedly shouted his innocence at trial before being silenced. Lobsang Dondrub reportedly also refused to confess. He was executed immediately after the Sichuan High Court upheld the Intermediate Court's verdict, even though Beijing officials had promised a US government delegation that the Supreme Court would review the case.[83] Other due process concerns included allegations that the defendants were not allowed to choose their own counsel and that they were tortured during the investigations. Critics of the decision note that Tenzin Deleg has a history of social activism, including renovating monasteries and establishing charitable organizations for orphans and the elderly, and is a staunch supporter of the Dalai Lama, but that he has no record of political protest. A government spokesperson responded to foreign criticism by claiming that the case was handled according to law and that courts in any other country would punish criminals who undermine state security and engage in terrorism.[84]

Civil and political rights

During the Mao era, Chinese citizens were afraid to discuss political issues with their family members, much less in public with foreigners. Today, political discussion is commonplace whenever friends and colleagues meet socially, while visitors are often surprised at how readily even first-time acquaintances are to criticize the government, disparage top leaders, or call for faster political reforms. Academics regularly publish works that criticize the government and call for greater democratization and political reforms. Legal scholars and government officials continue to press for constitutional reforms including greater judicial independence. The media, forced to respond to consumer interest as a result of market reforms, are ever more critical and free-wheeling.

At the same time, the government continues to impose—in some cases ruthlessly and with little regard for legal niceties or international opinion—severe limitations on civil and political freedoms when the exercise of such rights is deemed by the government to threaten the regime and social stability. The lines of what is permissible and what is not are clear and fixed in some areas, but vague and fluid in others. The time, place, and manner of expression are as important as the subject matter. What may be tolerated in some circumstances may be subject to greater restriction when there are certain aggravating factors present, such as attempts to organize across regions or to hook up with foreign organizations.

Accordingly, China receives a very low score on civil and political rights—ranking in the lowest 10% of all countries on the World Bank's voice and accountability index. As Figure 2 demonstrates, China scores poorly relative to many countries in Asia and elsewhere, and even does poorly relative to its level of economic development, as Figure 5 shows (see Chapter 6).

A closer examination of law and practice with respect to discrete civil and political rights reveals that the government is faced with difficult issues in several areas. First, however, a methodological note of caution: obtaining reliable, comprehensive information about many civil and political rights cases is difficult. Reports from human rights organizations and foreign government entities often provide a wealth of valuable information, frequently obtained under difficult circumstances that prevent more in-depth investigation. Nevertheless, the reports generally suffer from a cursory or one-sided presentation of facts, the lack of citation to sources for factual claims, reliance on hearsay evidence and unconfirmed information, and no or little legal analysis, with citations to relevant PRC or international law as rare as a snowman in the tropics. Most reports dismiss summarily the arguments of the government and prosecutors about violations of PRC law, underestimate the complexity of the legal issues involved, and assume an expansive and liberal interpretation of civil and political rights that is often contested as a matter of international law. They rarely attempt to place the individual cases selected within a broader comparative, historical, economic, or political context or include any statistical analysis that would give any indication of the representativeness of the cases. In short, many of the reports are more advocacy for a particular viewpoint than an impartial legal analysis of the merits of the decision.

On the other hand, although Supreme Court regulations require that most trials be open to the public and that courts publish judgments, politically sensitive cases are often closed to the public or are limited to a few observers, on the grounds that they involve state secrets and issues of national security. Nor are court judgments and documents submitted by the procuracy and defense counsel readily accessible, and in some cases they are not accessible at all. The facts as reported in those judgments that are available are often dramatically at odds with the facts as reported by human rights organizations or defense counsel, or subject to very different interpretations. Several cases involve serious due process concerns, including allegations of torture and forced confessions, which undermine the credibility of the prosecutors' claims and the courts' judgments. As a result, it is at times all but impossible to verify the facts and to assess the merits of the court's judgment as a matter of international and domestic law.

Nevertheless, by piecing together data from various sources on contested cases, and studying a number of cases with uncontested facts, there is sufficient information to obtain a reasonably accurate view of where the limits of freedom exist in practice. Given the size and diversity of China, reliance on a small number of select cases inevitably gives rise to questions about representativeness. Accordingly, I provide summary results of several cases for each type of right and for particular issues to establish the boundaries of individual freedom in practice today.

FREEDOM OF THOUGHT: STATE SPONSORSHIP OF IDEOLOGICAL ORTHODOXY AND RESTRICTIONS ON RELIGIOUS FREEDOM

The government unapologetically endorses socialism, including in the preamble to the constitution, which guarantees adherence to the four cardinal principles: the leading role of the Party, adherence to socialism, the dictatorship of the proletariat, and adherence to Marxism-Leninism-Mao Zedong thought, now buttressed by the 'Three Represents.' The Three Represents are Jiang Zemin's attempt to update socialism in accordance with today's market economy by shifting the focus away from the proletariat to the 'advanced productive forces,' including the private sector and entrepreneurs, in order to develop an 'advanced and modern culture' and serve the fundamental interests of the broad majority of citizens.[85] Whereas Jiang's formulation highlights that some will lose out in the transition to the market economy, the Hu and Wen regime, perhaps in an effort to distinguish itself from the Jiang regime, have paid more attention to social injustice and the needs of the least well-off in society. Significantly, however, the focus of both regimes is on the interests of the majority of the people, which the Party will continue to determine and serve, not on the rights of the individual interpreted as a countermajoritarian trump on the interests of society as a whole. Although the rhetorical commitment to socialism remains, socialist ideology is now less coherent, more widely contested, and much less of a factor in everyday life.

The government has also promoted the development of a socialist spiritual civilization, consisting of attacks on wholesale Westernization and bourgeois liberalism, combined with blatant appeals to nationalism, celebration of the importance of culture and art, praise for Confucianism, and exhortation of citizens to ask not what the nation can do for them but what they can do for the nation and their fellow citizens. Party efforts to bring about this new socialist spiritual civilization have been largely unsuccessful. While many Chinese respond to the nationalist component of the spiritual civilization plank, few take seriously the emphasis on socialism.

Appeals to Confucianism have also failed to take hold, in part because of the contested nature of Confucianism, which has been interpreted to support both liberal and authoritarian positions. Accordingly, the government is reluctant to appeal to Confucianism given efforts by some New Confucians to appeal to parts of the vast Confucian corpus to support democracy and human rights. Conversely, reformers are wary to make too much of Confucianism given that historically it was undeniably sexist, elitist, and inegalitarian, and failed to provide popular sovereignty or protect even the most fundamental civil and political liberties such as freedom of thought and speech.

China's educational policies continue to call for mandatory classes in politics and morals. When challenged by the Special Rapporteur on education, the government spokesperson replied that all governments inculcate political and moral values through the education system.[86] China is no different.

Mindful of a long history of religious movements toppling dynasties in the past, of growing problems with 'cults' around the world, and the rise of Islamic fundamentalism in recent years, China imposes content-based as well as time, place, and manner restrictions on religious beliefs and practices.[87] Freedom of religion is confined to five recognized religions—Buddhism, Taoism, Islam, Catholicism, and Protestantism—and registered places of worship.

All religious groups are required to register with the State Administration of Religious Affairs. Proselytizing by foreigners is not allowed, although in practice individual foreign citizens need not hide their faith, and foreigners may preach in registered churches or at the invitation of registered social groups.[88] Mormons and Jews are also allowed to practice.

The government claims that there are more than 100,000 venues for religious activities, and a 300,000 member clergy.[89] In addition, there are more than 3,000 national and local religious organizations, plus seventy-four religious colleges and schools.[90] Each religion is allowed to publish its own books and magazines, subject to various restrictions.[91] There are 30 million printed copies of the Bible.[92] The government provides funding to build and maintain places of worship, supports members of the clergy, offers preferential tax treatment to registered religious groups, and pays for trips to Mecca for some Muslims.

In addition to restricting belief to the five authorized religions, the government has imposed content-based restrictions on 'cults' and abnormal religious beliefs and practices. The crackdown on Falun Gong has received the most attention abroad, largely because of the tireless if one-sided efforts of the overseas Falun Gong organization.[93] The government has justified the ban by citing the sect's increasingly political agenda, organized demonstrations including one in which more than 10,000 people suddenly surrounded Zhongnanhai (the seat of the government), and the deaths of more than 1,600 adherents, including the self-immolation of five people, one of them a 12-year-old girl. Senior government leaders were apparently divided on how to deal with the sect, with some arguing for prosecution of particular individuals for violation of generally applicable criminal laws rather than an outright ban on the group. Whatever the merits on the substantive issue, the crackdown led to serious due process violations, including torture and deaths while in detention.[94]

The government has also outlawed a number of other sects, claiming their leaders lack theological training, preach the coming of the apocalypse or Holy War, exploit members for financial gain, or commit other violations of generally applicable laws such as rape, assault, and tax fraud.[95] The government has defended the policies by citing similar restrictions on cults in other countries. Unfortunately, international law provides little useful guidance in distinguishing normal from abnormal religious activities and legitimate groups from cults.[96]

The government's response to unapproved 'house churches' has not been uniform. Some have been closed, while others are allowed to operate, depending on their size, relationship to the official church, links to foreign organizations or other organizations, and their general capacity to foment social unrest.[97] Catholic priests aligned with Rome have run into problems because of conflicts over issues where the views of the Pope conflict with government policy, most notably with respect to family planning, birth control, and abortion. Authorities have also reportedly forced Catholics in Hebei, where more than half of China's Catholics are located, to follow the Patriotic Church or face fines, job losses, detention, or the removal of their children from school.[98] Leaders of Protestant house churches have also been detained.[99]

Buddhism is increasingly popular in China, and generally accepted by the government, although the government remains concerned that Buddhist beliefs and practices will support a movement for independence in Tibet. Buddhism and politics were fused historically in theocratic Tibet and remain closely aligned today. Tibetan Buddhists outside of the Tibetan Autonomous Region (TAR) enjoy greater freedom, and even in Tibet religious practices are generally accepted provided they do not serve as a base for political opposition.[100] Accordingly, the government continues to oversee the daily operations of major monasteries, and to insist that Party members and senior government employees adhere to atheism and not support the Dalai Lama. In addition, Tibetan monks and nuns have been sentenced on charges of endangering the state, separatism, and undermining the unity of nationalities.[101] Human rights groups protest that they are being detained for nonviolent political practices. The Tibet Information Network (TIN) estimated that the Chinese government has imprisoned approximately 150 Tibetans on political charges, 75% of whom are monks or nuns.[102] In a public relations disaster, the authorities replaced the boy recognized by the

Dalai Lama to be the eleventh reincarnation of the Panchen Lama with their own candidate.

The government has also taken steps to ensure that Islam does not become a source for political instability. The government has prohibited the teaching of Islam to children under 18, and prevented preaching by imams whose sermons are considered too fundamentalist. Furthermore, the government has limited the construction of mosques in areas of unrest, although it continues to support their building and renovation in other areas.[103] In a case that has come to symbolize government oppressiveness abroad, Rebiya Kadeer, a businesswoman and provincial delegate to the Chinese People's Political Consultative Committee whose social activist husband had sought political asylum in the United States, was sentenced to eight years in prison in March 2000 for providing state intelligence to foreigners. The state secrets were reportedly disclosed in local newspaper articles discussing the treatment of Uighars. She was subsequently released in response to international pressure from the US and others.

Another case that has caught the world's attention involves Uighar historian Tohti Tunyaz, who was sentenced to eleven years for inciting separatism and illegally acquiring state secrets after returning from Ph.D. studies at the University of Tokyo.[104] The state secrets appear to be fifty-year-old documents obtained for research purposes from a librarian in Xinjiang. Tohti is also accused of writing and publishing *The Inside Story of the Silk Road*, which allegedly advocates 'ethnic separatism.' However, Japanese scholars have denied that Tohti ever published such a book. In 2001, the UN Human Rights Committee declared that Tohti was arbitrarily detained, and that the sentence violated the right to freedom of thought and speech.[105]

FREEDOM OF SPEECH: CRITICISM OF THE GOVERNMENT

The 1991 Human Rights White Paper noted that according to the constitution, citizens have the right to criticize and make suggestions regarding any government entity or official and the right to expose any government entity or official for violation of law or dereliction of duty.[106] In practice, however, there are limits.

One clear line in the sand is advocating the overthrow of the CCP or the government, whether by violent or nonviolent means, even if the actual threat is minimal or nonexistent, although again aggravating circumstances are usually required. For instance, Luo Yongzhong was sentenced for three years for inciting subversion for publishing on the Internet articles calling for the overthrow of the Party and criticizing the Three Represents and the government's handling of the Tiananmen incident.[107] Similarly, Wang Zechen was sentenced to six years for subversion for attempting to establish a Liaoning branch of the banned China Democratic Party, attacking the Party as a dictatorship, and advocating the end of the single party system and the establishment of a multiparty system with separation of powers.[108] In court, Wang did not contest the facts but argued the acts were legal. In another case, He Depu was sentenced to eight years in prison for collaborating with the banned China Democracy Party, posting essays on the Internet that incite subversion, and signing an open letter calling for political reforms.[109] According to his wife, he shouted calls for democracy and criticisms of the one-party system at his hearing.[110]

Another controversial case raises the issue of how clear and present the danger to the state must be before triggering the state's criminal justice machinery, and shows that the government, wary of student activism, closely monitors attempts to establish student organizations for political purposes. In 2003, Yang Zili, Xu Wei, Jin Haike, and Zhang Honghai, four of the eight members of an unregistered group of students and recent graduates called the New Youth Study Group, received eight to ten years for subversion.[111] According to the judgment of the Beijing Intermediate Court, the purpose of the group was to 'actively explore ways of improving society.' The articles of the group and related documents included ideas for expanding the size and influence of the group through publications and Internet postings, as well as rules on membership and dues. Apparently, the group planned on setting up branches in Xian and Tianjin, though there does not appear to be any evidence that branches were actually set up. The court judgment relied heavily on the testimony of other members of the group, one of whom was cooperating with the Ministry of National Security, and two others who, under repeated questioning from security officers and the threat of criminal prosecution for their own involvement, signed damaging statements claiming that the group opposed socialism and sought to overthrow the Party and establish a liberal democracy. The reports accused Zhang Honghai of wholesale rejection of the Party, Yang Zili of advocating liberalism and opposing single party socialism, Xu Wei of advocating an uprising by farmers and the use of violence if necessary to change the system, and Jin Haike of describing the political system as authoritarian and advocating the overthrow of the Party. The court also cited articles written by the defendants, some posted on the web and others not published, which showed that they were not happy with the current political situation and allegedly demonstrated their intent to overthrow the government. However, the court did not discuss in detail the content of the publications or cite passages to support these conclusions, other than to note that publications by Yang Zili described democracy in China as fake democracy, and called for an end to 'old man politics.'

On appeal, defense counsel for Xu Wei pointed out that four of the founders were Party members, and that the members voluntarily terminated the group.[112] He portrayed the members as patriotic citizens whose only goal was to improve society. He also noted that the group raised just a couple hundred RMB in dues, and lacked the wherewithal to overthrow the state. The defendants and their lawyers also contested the evidence by the procuracy, claiming statements were taken out of context and the meaning twisted, and that the witness testimony was given under pressure, inconsistent, and inaccurate. The defendants further objected that the court refused to consider exculpatory evidence. Two of those who wrote reports along with other members of the group were not allowed to testify on appeal. Citing inconsistency with other evidence, the Beijing High Court also refused to recognize letters from the three members who had written reports, two of which were in the possession of the Intermediate Court during the first trial, denying that the group ever sought to overthrow the Party or the government.[113] After repeating the Intermediate Court's evidence and findings in full, the

High Court summarily dismissed the defendants' arguments that there was insufficient evidence of subjective intent to overthrow the government as well as insufficient evidence of inculpatory objective acts. The courts did not expressly address the issue of advocacy of violent versus nonviolent proposals to change the government. Nor did the courts address the issue of the likelihood that the defendants' acts would lead to the overthrow of the government.

Agitating for a reversal of the Tiananmen verdict may also land one in trouble. The government detained the leader of the Tiananmen Mothers, Ding Zilin, along with two other members of the group, although they were subsequently released.[114] Apparently they were sent T-shirts from Hong Kong with the logo 'Tiananmen Mothers.' More seriously from the government's perspective, the Human Rights Commission had received a videotape of their testimony regarding their efforts to have the government reassess Tiananmen. Social activist Hu Jia was also temporarily detained for planning a demonstration to commemorate Tiananmen.[115] In some cases, however, the punishment may be more serious, particularly if there are other allegations or aggravating circumstances. A petition signed by 192 people calling for political reforms and a reassessment of Tiananmen led to the arrest on subversion charges of at least six of the signatories.[116]

Three years after being detained, Huang Qi was finally sentenced to five years for inciting subversion for managing a website where he posted articles on Tiananmen, Falun Gong, and the banned China Democratic Party.[117] The Intermediate Court decision is interesting for two reasons. First, it expressly rejects the argument raised by Huang Qi that his actions were protected by the right of free speech, arguing that the right does not extend to defamation or spreading rumors to incite subversion and undermine state interests or national security. Second, the court rejected the prosecutor's charge that Huang was trying to 'split the nation' by posting articles calling for Xinjiang independence on the ground that the articles were posted by others on Huang's site.

Although the media regularly carry exposés on corruption, the government has imposed limits on stories involving high-level officials, for which approval must be obtained. Li Zhi, a government official in Sichuan, was sentenced to eight years for subversion after posting an article on the Internet and in chatroom discussions exposing corruption at high levels of the government, and for contacting foreign dissidents.[118] An Jun, who founded an anti-corruption NGO that attracted more than 300 people, was also sentenced to four years for exposing corruption.[119]

Individuals who have reported classified information about SARS and AIDS have also been detained for revealing state secrets, among other charges. The government detained Wan Yanhai, head of the Beijing-based AIDS Institute, for one month for revealing state secrets when he posted information about HIV deaths on his website.[120] Henan health official Ma Shiwen was also detained for revealing state secrets, though he too was subsequently released without standing trial.[121] Acknowledging the scope of the AIDS problem, the government in 2003 adopted new policies on AIDS, devised a long-term plan for treatment and prevention, and began to provide free medical treatment and testing.[122] AIDS victims may also be able to use the legal system to fight discrimination in employment and elsewhere. In a related case, a person infected with Hepatitis B recently won an administrative litigation suit when he was denied a post as a civil servant because of his disease.[123]

FREEDOM OF THE PRESS

Chinese citizens now have greater access to a wider variety of information and cultural products due to changes in technology including the Internet and satellite television; market reforms that have forced newspapers, television stations, and book publishers to respond to consumer demands; and the rise of a small number of independent publishers and an even smaller underground press. Nevertheless, the government continues to maintain tight controls on what gets published.

The list of sensitive topics that are off limits or require prior approval varies from time to time, and is enforced with varying degrees of strictness. Topics have included the government's handling of SARS; the prosecution on corruption charges of successful business people like Zhou Zhengyi and Yang Bin; financial information such as speculation about the appreciation of the Renminbi or the selling of stocks by government agencies; exposés about former government officials who go into business or become lobbyists; and reports on land seizures and mass demonstrations.[124] Oftentimes, the media will be allowed to discuss a topic until the government or the courts have taken a final position, as in the 'BMW case,' where a rich and well-connected woman crashed into a crowd after a dispute; the Liu Yong case, where a former NPC delegate depicted as a mafia boss was sentenced to death; and the Sun Zhigang case, where a college student was beaten to death while in administrative detention. All three cases were widely debated on the Internet and covered in the press, leading to a central level investigation in the BMW case, a highly unusual retrial by the Supreme Court in the Liu Yong case, and the elimination of detention and repatriation in the Sun case.

Discussion of popular books may also be restricted, such as *The Chinese Peasant Report*, detailing the plight of farmers today, or the *Heart of Girls*, which described the sexual awakening of a teenager and was considered pornographic. Other books and magazines may also be subject to censorship, removal from shelves, or confiscation at customs. However, the widespread if illegal practice of selling 'book numbers' and leasing out publication numbers for magazines allows many publications to slip past the censor. Banning books now often simply results in increased demand, with books reportedly banned still readily available even in major Beijing bookstores or in small street stalls. In one interesting case that shows how efforts to implement rule of law are paying dividends even in politically sensitive cases, a lawyer won an administrative litigation suit challenging Customs' confiscation of a book on the Yanan period published by Chinese University of Hong Kong.[125]

However, in other cases, exceeding the bounds of permissible coverage has resulted in confiscation of publications, closure of the paper, sacking of editors, or arrests. In 2001, authorities confiscated an edition of the *Securities Market Weekly* containing an article about Li Peng getting rich.[126] In 2004, editors of the widely popular muckraking *Southern Metropolis News* were arrested on embezzlement and bribery charges.[127] The editor of the progressive *Beijing*

News was fired, while several other papers have been closed down or come under pressure to curtail critical reporting. In 2005, thirty-two journalists were imprisoned, fifteen for writings published on the Internet. Foreign reporters have also been harassed or detained for covering sensitive stories such as the plight of North Korean refugees or allegedly revealing state secrets.

The government has clearly struggled over how to manage the potential risks caused by the increasing numbers of Internet users. The government regularly blocks sites, regulates Internet cafés, holds servers and Internet companies responsible for content published on their sites, and prosecutes individuals who post articles that the authorities find go too far in criticizing the government or that reveal information deemed to be state secrets. All of the top ten sites for the topics 'Tibet,' 'Taiwan China,' and 'Equality' were blocked, as were eight of the top-ten sites for 'Democracy' and 'Chinese Dissidents,' and six of the top-ten sites for 'Freedom China' and 'Justice China.'[128] Similarly, 20–25% of the top 100 URLs were blocked for 'Hunger China,' 'Famine China,' and 'AIDS China.'

Several foreign news URLs are also regularly blocked, although other foreign news sites are available. The government has issued regulations that limit access to chatrooms. The rules only permit websites to run news forums about a subject if the mainstream state-run media has already covered the story.[129]

The arrests of Liu Di, Du Daobin, and others for Internet postings have been the subject of much public debate. Liu Di, the 'Stainless Steel Mouse,' was a student at Beijing Normal University. She was detained and then released months later for operating a popular website and posting satirical articles about the Party, as well as articles calling for the release of Huang Qi.[130] Her arrest led to two online petitions signed by over 3,000 people.

Du Daobin was arrested for posting twenty-eight articles on the Internet, including some that opposed limitations on democracy and civil liberties in Hong Kong, and for receiving funding from foreign organizations.[131] His arrest led to a petition, signed by over 100 writers, editors, lawyers, philosophers, liberal economists and activists, calling for a judicial interpretation to clarify the crime of subversion.[132] Citing the nonbinding and decidedly liberal

Johannesburg Principles, the petition argued that seeking change through peaceful means should not constitute incitement of subversion, and that the government should not rely on subversion charges to restrict critical discussion of government shortcomings, maintain the reputation of the ruling regime, enforce ideological controls, or even prevent instability.[133] After the petition, Du was convicted of inciting subversion, but his three-year sentence was commuted to four years of probation.[134]

Although China has passed a number of regulations regarding Internet activities, convictions for posting articles on the Internet are usually based on generally applicable criminal law provisions. Posting on the Internet, which reaches a diffused and unidentified audience, serves therefore as a triggering or aggravating factor: the same speech that would be tolerated in a different forum even though in violation of the criminal law results in arrest and detention when posted on the Internet. Sentences are usually in the two- to four-year range.

Despite limitations, the media has emerged as a powerful source of government supervision, to the point where some commentators have questioned whether the media is becoming a demagogue.[135] Citizens have effectively used the media and Internet to hold the government and even the judiciary accountable. The media's job is being made easier by local freedom of information acts. Shanghai, Guangzhou, Shenzhen, and Beijing have all passed or are reviewing open government information acts. The State Council is also contemplating a national open government information act, and the National People's Congress has included a freedom of information law on the legislative agenda.[136]

A letters and visits system provides citizens with another channel to challenge government actions.[137] Most governments, people's congresses, and courts have a letter and visits section to handle citizen complaints. Every year millions of disgruntled citizens write letters to senior government leaders or make a pilgrimage to provincial capitals or even to Beijing to seek an audience with government officials. The Supreme Court alone received 152,557 letters and visits in 2002, including 1,140 inquiries from the people's congress, of which 500 petitions were received during the national people's congress session alone. Some courts devote more personnel to responding to letters and visits and supervision issues than to actually hearing civil cases. Obtaining the support of the media greatly enhances the chances that one's petitions will be taken seriously.

PORNOGRAPHY

Although the government periodically supports campaigns against pornography, it is readily available in books, magazines, DVDs, and on the Internet. Suggesting a less than wholehearted commitment, China blocks just 13% of the 752 sites generated by a search for 'free adult sex,' whereas commercial filters used by Saudi Arabia and other countries block 70–90%.[138] The government's approach is to focus on producers and distributor rather than users. Thus, a court fined and sentenced to three years defendants who operated a website containing pornographic pictures, novels, and movies. The defendants had set up web advertisements for foreign advertisers and received commission payments. The court found that posting pornographic material online was criminal and that obtaining income from foreign advertisers was considered 'spreading pornography for profit.'

In contrast, the government has tolerated watching pornographic movies in one's own home. In a much publicized case, a Shanxi couple was awarded damages after police stormed into their bedroom while they were watching an adult movie, and a scuffle broke out between the husband and police, resulting in injuries to the husband.[139]

FREEDOM OF ASSEMBLY

As of 2002, there were more than 133,000 social organizations, including 111,000 private nonprofit corporations.[140] Although all social groups are legally required to register, there are also reportedly as many as one to two million unregistered 'NGOs.'[141] Social organizations are subject to various degrees of supervision and control, with the government again imposing both content-based and time, place, and manner restrictions. Some groups are not allowed to register, including the China Democratic Party and Falun Gong. The founders of the China Democratic Party Xu Wenli, Wang Youcai, and Qin Yongmin were sentenced on subversion charges in 1998 to thirteen, twelve, and eleven years respectively.[142] Wang and Xu have since been released on medical parole and are in the United States.[143]

The government requires prior approval of all demonstrations. Approval is not possible in some cases, such as Falun Gong protests, and virtually impossible to obtain in other cases, such as for protests of government takings and relocations, treatment of HIV patients, and labor disputes. China ratified the ICESCR with a reservation that provisions regarding unions and strikes be interpreted consistently with PRC laws. Labor unions remain tightly controlled and marginally effective, often serving as a bridge between workers and the state or management. Many foreign investors have opposed the formation of strong unions within their companies. PRC law does not recognize the right to strike, although work slowdowns and strikes do occur.[144]

Despite the restrictions, demonstrations are a regular event. In 2005 alone there were almost 87,000 demonstrations, most of them not approved.[145] Demonstrations are growing in size, and increasingly cross industrial and geographical lines. Tactics have also changed, with a marked rise in violence. According to the Public Security Ministry, 13% of the demonstrations in 2005 involved mob violence, resulting in the deaths of 23 police and injuries to over 1,800 more in the first nine months alone.[146]

In most cases, the protesters are allowed to demonstrate provided the demonstration is peaceful, orderly, and limited in size and duration. The government frequently responds to demonstrations by pumping in funds to buy off the protestors. However, authorities also frequently arrest the leaders of the demonstration. In addition, thugs, often hired by companies with an economic interest in the dispute or with ties to the local government, have sought to intimidate protesters.[147] And while the authorities generally use non-lethal means to deal with protesters, police shot and killed several people involved in a protest over inadequate compensation for land taken by the government to build a powerplant. Police claimed the protesters were killed by warning shots that went astray, and that they had fired tear gas to disperse the protesters, who had thrown gasoline bombs at them.[148] In other cases, government officials have been removed from their posts when excessive force was used to quash protests.[149]

ASSESSING RESTRICTIONS ON CIVIL AND POLITICAL RIGHTS

The government does not tolerate much dissent in public and imposes numerous restrictions on the exercise of civil and political rights. Are such restrictions consistent with international law? More importantly, are they justified? Unfortunately, international law is less determinative on many more issues than often assumed. Human rights groups and activists within China often invoke liberal principles or interpretations that are not accepted as a matter of international law.[150] For instance, the Johannesburg Principles cited by the petitioners in the Du case have not been adopted in whole by any country. Incorporating the contemporary US standard,[151] Principle 6 states that expression may be punished as a threat to national security or public order only if a government can demonstrate that: (i) the expression is intended to incite imminent violence; (ii) it is likely to incite such violence; and (iii) there is a direct and immediate connection between the expression and the likelihood or occurrence of such violence.[152] However, in general, national security restrictions require a showing of a serious potential harm but a lesser degree of imminence and likelihood than restrictions for public order. Although the distinction between violence and nonviolence is an important factor to consider, clearly nonviolent acts, such as injecting a virus into a country's national defense computer system, may endanger the state. Similarly, while a clear and present danger is more threatening than a vague and distant danger, a state need not wait until the last minute to take steps to protect national security or public order.[153] Countries differ over whether violence must be likely and imminent even for public order restrictions. Some countries require only that the speech will likely lead to a violation of law or breach of the peace, while others (often former British colonies) require an even lesser showing that the comments are likely to incite ill-will or contempt for the government.[154]

Rather than a bright line test based on the distinction between violence and nonviolence, restrictions on rights are subject to a balancing test. The ICCPR Human Rights Committee, the ECHR, and other bodies apply a three-part test. To be valid, the restriction must (i) be prescribed by law; (ii) serve a legitimate purpose; and (iii) be necessary. While this analysis is intended to be conducted on a case-by-case basis in light of the particular circumstances at the time, it is useful to apply this test generally to the restrictions on civil and political rights in China. A case-by-case approach tends to 'skew' the results toward greater civil and political rights, as it is always difficult to see how the actions or words of a particular individual could possibly constitute a threat to the more powerful state or have much of an impact on a society of 1.4 billion people. Conversely, a wider perspective that considers the range of threats from a variety of different sources tends to support more conservative solutions. A broader approach will usually reflect a more utilitarian concern for aggregate social benefits whereas a case-by-case approach fits more easily with a moral absolutist or deontological approach that sees rights as trumps of social interests.

Not surprisingly, China and other East Asian countries that have adopted a more restrictive interpretation of civil and political rights generally defend their positions not by arguing the specifics of individual cases but by pointing to larger empirical trends, and in particular the records of other developing countries that have adopted a restrictive approach to civil and political rights, as opposed to those that have adopted a more liberal approach. Thus, they point out that the East Asian countries that have succeeded in maintaining stability and social order, achieving economic growth, reducing poverty, and improving people's living standards, have adopted a restrictive approach to civil and political rights, whereas other countries in Asia and elsewhere that have adopted a more liberal approach, at least during their period of rapid economic development, have generally not managed to achieve political stability, economic growth, or the same level of achievement on other measures of rights and human well-being. On the other hand, rights activists rely heavily on particular cases, often involving egregious violations or especially vulnerable or sympathetic defendants.

Neither approach is entirely satisfactory. The latter tends to underestimate the importance of stability and social order to economic growth and the protection of human rights. The former runs the danger of justifying any and all restrictions in the name of political stability, social order, and economic growth. Many people believe, for instance, that democracy is not appropriate for China at this stage and that given the potential for instability, the government is justified in limiting certain civil and political rights in the name of social order (and, because social chaos would undermine economic growth, in the name of development). Yet, they also believe that the government unduly restricts civil and political rights. A more balanced approach is needed, one that moves beyond these general arguments to consider specific instances of restrictions, while at the same time bearing in mind that developing countries such as China face a number of threats to social order and political stability that wealthy, politically stable countries do not face. Thus, China is likely to reach a different balance given the horrific consequences for everyone were China to become unstable or were Cultural Revolution-like social chaos to reoccur.

The first prong of the three-part balancing test requires that the government actions be prescribed by law. In China's case, the constitution, laws, and administrative regulations provide ample grounds to restrict pornography, religious practices, demonstrations, criticism of the government and the Party, and to justify the confiscation of property, the assessment of fines, administrative detention, and criminal punishments. Whether the laws are clear enough to prevent citizens from unexpectedly running afoul of them is however an issue in some cases, given the broad and vaguely stated provisions on state secrets, subversion, and endangering the state. Yet it is unlikely that most people convicted in the cases discussed earlier were unaware that they were crossing the line given previous convictions for similar behavior, though many clearly felt that their actions should not have been considered illegal. Still, a judicial interpretation of subversion and related charges, and a narrower definition of 'state secrets,' would go a long way toward clarifying the scope of impermissible activities and expanding the range of legitimate activities without detriment to state interests.

A separate but related issue is whether the procuratorate in these cases laid out with sufficient detail the alleged acts constituting the offense or the precise threat to national security. The danger of relying on broad allegations of subversion or endangering the state is readily apparent in this era of heightened sensitivity to terrorism. Yet in several of the cases, there was little analysis of specific statements in the articles alleged to be evidence of subversion.

As for the second prong, the restrictions generally serve a legitimate purpose on their face, such as national security, public order, and morality. However, in cases critical of government AIDS policies or involving exposure of corruption, the restrictions appear only to serve the interests of the ruling party or to protect the reputation of particular officials rather than to protect national security or the interests of the nation. The tendency of governments around the world to rely on broad state secret laws and vague references to national security to cover up government mistakes has been exacerbated after 9/11, and should be resisted in China and elsewhere.[155] Moreover, by invoking a broad state secret law, the government prevents defendants from relying on the truth of their criticisms to establish a defense: the mere disclosure of damaging information is sufficient to find wrongdoing.

The final prong is usually the most crucial in evaluating the legitimacy of restrictive policies. The requirement of 'necessity' as interpreted by the ECHR and other bodies does not mean the restriction is 'indispensable,' although it must be more than merely 'reasonable' or 'desirable.'[156] As noted, the ECHR affords countries a margin of appreciation in deciding what is necessary, with the widest margin in the areas of national security and morality. In addition to being necessary, the restriction must also be proportionate, while some jurisdictions such as the United States apply a higher 'least restrictive' standard for limitations of fundamental rights.

The Universal Declaration of Human Rights and other international documents require the restrictions to be necessary *for democratic order*, even though democracy is not required under the ICCPR. Some of the arguments for free speech in a democracy may not apply in a socialist state, although many of the same arguments would apply at least to some degree. For example, the argument that political speech, including criticism of the government, deserves special protection in a democracy given the need for citizens to elect their leaders may be weakened, whether in the context of prior restraints on free speech or post-speech regulations.

In most cases, however, the difference will be between liberal and nonliberal positions. Thus, the liberal emphasis in other countries on autonomy, individualism, and self-development will lead to different outcomes than in China. Not everyone assigns the same value to civil and political freedoms relative to social order. Social order ranks much higher in the normative hierarchy of most Chinese than it does in the normative hierarchy of many Westerners, in part because stability is more precarious in China.

But even accepting such differences, are the restrictions imposed by China necessary? To some extent, the response turns on assessments of China's stability. Ironically, the argument of many liberal critics that China is very unstable tends to undercut their opposition to restrictions on civil and political rights. China clearly faces a number of threats to stability, including increasing rural poverty, rising urban unemployment, a weak social security system, and a rapidly ageing population that has pushed the elderly into the streets to protest for retirement benefits. In addition, China has a looming banking crisis that could put an end to the economic miracle, leading to further unemployment and more unrest. The desire for greater autonomy if not independence among many Tibetans and Xinjiangese, the rise of Islamic fundamentalism in the region, and the difficulty of separating Buddhism and politics in Tibet also present risks that cannot be dismissed, even if they should not be exaggerated.

More generally, authoritarian regimes are particularly stable in the $3,000 to $4,000 per capita (PPP) range.[157] However, the likelihood of a transition to democracy increases when per capita income is between $4,000 and $6,000, with the tipping point at which a regime is more likely to be democratic than authoritarian being $4,115.[158] In 2001, China's per capita income was $4,020.[159] Thus, China is just beginning to outgrow a highly stable period for authoritarian regimes, and likely will become increasingly unstable as pressure grows for political reforms, as evidenced in the rapidly rising number of large-scale and increasingly violent demonstrations.

Another test applied by some courts to assess the justifiability of restrictions on rights is to multiply the probability or likelihood by the degree of harm to calculate the expected danger or threat.[160] With one-fifth of the world's population, almost half of whom are living on less than $2/day, and a history of chaos as recent as the Cultural Revolution, the consequences of instability for China, the region, and the world would be severe. Adopting this measure virtually assures a wide margin of deference to restrictions in the name of public order.

In practice, the balance reached by the government seems to be that individuals are generally free to pursue their own interests, engage in religious beliefs, or criticize the government as they like, provided their acts are not combined with any of the aggravating circumstances discussed above that increase the likelihood of unrest. While acknowledging the possibility of instability, many of the decisions fail to provide any discussion of how the particular acts in question will lead to instability or endanger the state. A more considered analysis of the nexus between the acts and disruptions of the public order or harm to the state would expand greatly the range of civil and political rights without harming national security or state interests. It is difficult to see how either a broader categorical approach or a narrower case-specific analysis could justify the tight limitations on discussion of issues of legitimate public concern such as constitutional reform, medical crises, corruption, government takings, and rising income gaps. After all, these issues are widely discussed anyway.

Moreover, whatever the outcomes on the substantive merits, the many due process violations even under China's own laws—including incidents of torture, the lack of transparency and a public trial, and excessively long periods of detention—violate both international and domestic laws. Nor should lawyers be harassed and prosecuted for trying to protect the legitimate rights of their clients, or environmental organizations and human rights groups unable to register or closed simply for raising issues of genuine public concern.[161] Conversely, officials and police who rely on excessive force in dealing with demonstrators, or who turn a blind eye to local thugs who beat and intimidate protesters, should be held liable and given stiff punishments as a deterrent to others.

Conclusion: narrowing the gap

Regrettably, Chinese authorities at times impose unnecessary and unjustified limitations, even allowing that there may be legitimate differences in normative values and in views on the need to restrict civil and political rights to ensure social stability and economic growth. Citizens and their representatives are denied access to legal and political channels provided in laws and regulations for protecting their rights, or harassed for seeking to hold the government to commitments it itself has undertaken. With other avenues choked off, citizens are taking to the streets in massive, ever more violent, protests. It is in the government's own interest to rectify these problems, as they tarnish the government's reputation at home and abroad, undermine the legitimacy of the Party, and run counter to the government's efforts to promote rule of law and maintain social stability.

Whether the future is likely to see more repression or greater protection of the exercise of civil and political rights depends in part on the outcome of deeply contested debates about how to respond to the increasing social tensions, the sharp rise in demonstrations, and the specter of a popular uprising such as the color revolutions in the former Soviet republics.[162] Among the three dominant competing perspectives, one extreme emphasizes repression of dissent and tight limits on social organizations and the exercise of civil and political rights that threaten political stability, combined with an ideological battle to win the hearts and minds of Chinese citizens, government officials, and Party members by revamping socialism and explaining the reasonableness of the current reform agenda.[163] Signs of this approach include the increased restrictions on the press and the Internet, the arrest of lawyers and human rights activists, the closure or close monitoring of social organizations, the crackdown on public intellectuals, the cancellation of academic conferences on constitutionalism and political reform, and the extended old-school campaign to 'maintain the vanguard' (*baoxian*) that has forced officials and academics to spend so much time in political meetings.[164]

At the other end of the spectrum are those who argue that rapid and broad-ranging reforms are necessary to prevent the reform process from stalling, to meet the rising demands from the citizenry, and to avoid a political crisis. Rather than tightening restrictions on civil society and the exercise of civil and political rights, the government should relax restraints.

A third, moderate perspective acknowledges that the country is confronting a variety of serious challenges to social stability, as is typical for middle income countries. Hence, there is a need to maintain restrictions on civil and political rights. However, at the same time, there is an equally pressing need to continue to invest in human capital, to strengthen institutions, to pay more attention to social justice and the wealth effects of economic reforms, and to gradually expand civil and political liberties. In short, stick to the East Asian Model. Repression alone does not provide a long-term solution. It simply increases the likelihood that at some point there will be some sort of political crisis or that China will end up like other stable but dysfunctional middle income countries.

At the moment, the moderate approach appears dominant. Despite the tightening in some areas, reforms have continued in other areas. The State Council's 2005 democracy white paper is generally reflective of this approach, with its invocation of classical ideas such as democratic-centralism resting somewhat uncomfortably with calls for greater public participation and description of new institutions such as social consultative committees.[165]

The moderate approach inevitably will give rise to criticisms from both those who think the government is being too repressive and moving too slowly on reforms, and from those who take the opposite view. Almost everyone will object to some specific policies or the results in particular cases. The renewed emphasis on democratic centralism seems to be an attempt to manage diverse views without allowing conflicting views or discontent to undermine political stability. Citizens are allowed to express their views on controversial issues, and thus to blow off steam, but only up to a point. Once the various viewpoints are debated, and the authorities reach a decision, public discussion is curtailed.

Maintaining a balance will be difficult. The short term is likely to be rocky. However, Bueno de Mesquita and Downs have shown that authoritarian regimes are able to achieve economic growth and postpone democracy by providing standard public goods—such as public transport, public health, and primary and secondary education—while controlling public goods necessary for political coordination, such as civil and political rights and a free press.[166] An authoritarian regime that ensures economic growth and restricts coordination goods has a substantially higher chance of survival, whereas allowing freedom of the press and civil liberties decreases the regime's chance of survival by 15–20%. The experiences of Asian countries suggest that, at least up to a point, this strategy produces better results than democratization at low levels of wealth. Of course, in some cases authoritarian regimes may unjustifiably delay the transition to democracy or be too restrictive in particular cases.

Whereas China clearly falls far short on civil and political rights even when judged against other countries in its income class, China does much better on most other major human rights measures and indicators of human well-being, as we shall see in the next chapter. Both the tighter constraints on civil and political rights when the exercise of such rights threatens social or political stability and the better performance on other measures are typical of the EAM.

CHAPTER FOUR

Social and economic rights, law and order, women's rights, and cultural rights

After analyzing China's performance with respect to social and economic rights, law and order, women's rights and cultural or minority rights, I summarize the factors that explain China's rights performance and discuss obstacles to better performance.

Social and economic rights: poverty, health, and education

China defends its human rights record by pointing to a stunning rise in wealth that has lifted over 150 million people out of poverty in less than a decade and improved the quality of life of hundreds of millions more. From 1978 to 2001, the real income per capita increased more than five times for rural residents and more than four times for urban residents.[1] An official average annual growth rate of 8.2% from 1975 to 2001 and 8.8% from 1999 to 2001 has resulted in steady progress in the (UNDP) Human Development Index (HDI), from 0.52 in 1975 to 0.72 in 2001.[2] The HDI measures life expectancy at birth, adult literacy, school enrollments, and standard of living. As Figure 3 indicates, China does much better relative to other countries on the HDI than it does on the index for civil and political rights. As expected given the high correlation between wealth and social and economic rights ($r = .92$), China outperforms low income India on all measures, including infant mortality, life expectancy, and primary school enrollment, as indicated in Table 4.

To be sure, economic growth in China has not benefited everyone equally. The eastern coastal region is much wealthier than the rest of the country, rural areas are poorer than cities, and lay-offs from SOEs and collectives in education have created a pool of urban poor most of whom lack the education or skills to compete in the market.[3] According to the UNDP, in 1998, the richest 20% consumed 47%, while the poorest 20% consumed just 6%.[4] By 2003, the share of the top 20% had risen to 51%.[5] Some 4.6% live below the national poverty line, although nongovernmental sources suggest the number might be much higher.[6] One-fourth of the population, or over 300 million people, lacks sustained access to an adequate water source.[7] In addition, 9% of the population is undernourished, and 10% of children under 5 are underweight for their age. The rapid growth has also taken its toll on the environment.

Even with increases in the income gap during the reform era, China is still roughly on a par with the United States and other Asian countries such as Hong Kong, Singapore, the Philippines, and Malaysia, and considerably more egalitarian than Zimbabwe, South Africa, Chile, or Nicaragua, as indicated in Table 6 (p. 50). Moreover, the process of modernization inevitably involves a period of urbanization where rural residents are moved into cities and rural incomes lag behind urban incomes. As noted in Chapter 2, the general pattern is for inequality to increase during the development phase and then usually, although not always, to decrease. In a country as large as China, the process will take several generations to reach a stable equilibrium.

In the meantime, the government has responded to growing inequality both in the countryside and cities by issuing a steady stream of legislation to improve social welfare, strengthen job training and creation programs, reduce the tax burden on farmers, increase rural productivity, ease restrictions on migrant workers and enhance their rights to education and medical treatment, and stimulate growth in western and central regions. Perhaps more importantly, the government has given substance to the commitments and promise of these new regulations by increasing spending. For instance, the government spent some 70 billion yuan in 2003, an increase of almost 20% over 2002, on the 'three-stage guarantee' for laid-off workers that provides a basic living allowance, unemployment insurance, and then a subsistence allowance if the person still cannot find employment.[8] The government also allocated an additional 4.6 billion yuan to subsidize job creation.[9] There were 29 million retirees from enterprises covered by welfare, an increase of 41% over 2002. Nearly sixty million people have been covered by the rural old-age insurance scheme, and almost 1.4 million farmers received pensions.[10] Although these increased expenditures will by no means put an end to the problems, and will benefit different groups disproportionately, with former state-owned enterprise (SOE) employees better taken care of than others, they do demonstrate some level of commitment of the new leadership to pay attention to social justice issues.

These measures appear to be having some effect. Despite frequent claims of rising inequality, inequality for China as a whole remained virtually constant from 1995 to 2002.[11] When broken down further, both urban and rural inequality decreased, although inequality *between* rural and urban areas increased.[12] However, one study found that prior estimates of rural–urban inequality, and hence their impact on the national Gini coefficient, have also usually been overstated because they failed to take into consideration the higher cost of living in urban areas and did not include migrant workers, who earn less on average than other urban residents, thus decreasing the difference between average rural and urban income.[13] Others argue the opposite—the gap is even larger than reported if one considers systemic factors such as access to health and education, which are biased in favor of urban residents. In any event, all agree the gap in rural–urban incomes remains high in comparison to most other countries in Asia and elsewhere. In response, the Hu administration recently eliminated the agricultural tax, reiterated the promise of free schooling for rural children, and proposed subsidized medical care in the countryside.[14]

Despite the inequality, the overall number of rural and urban residents living in poverty has been significantly reduced. One study found that between 1995 and 2002, rural residents in broad poverty declined from 246 million to 96 million, a 61% decline, while the number in ultra poverty declined from 104 million to 34 million, a 67% decline.[15] Similarly, the number of urban poor living below the higher threshold also decreased significantly, by 17%.[16]

According to the WHO, Chinese citizens in general are living longer and healthier lives, with China largely on track to meet the Millennium Development Goals by 2015.[17] From 1949 to 2001, life expectancy doubled, reaching 70.6 years.[18] The population with access to essential drugs reached 80–94%; 77–9% of 1-year olds are immunized against tuberculosis, measles, and other illnesses. In 2000, 86% of pregnant women had access to health care, and maternal mortality dropped from 62 per 100,000 in 1995 to 53 per 100,000 in 2001, although in some rural areas the rate can be as high as 400 per 100,000.[19] The percentage of women giving birth in hospitals was 72.9%, up 15% from 1995.[20] Efforts to encourage breastfeeding also paid dividends, with 54% of urban mothers and 72% of rural mothers breastfeeding for four months. All are significant improvements.

However, there are many areas of concern. There are still problems with Hepatitis-B, tuberculosis, and lack of potable water, as well as new medical issues such as an upsurge in AIDS, sexually transmitted diseases, obesity, death by traffic accidents, and mental illness. Moreover, with longer life spans and demographic changes due to its one-child policy, China is facing the problems associated with ageing, including more people suffering from chronic ailments, a lengthening of the course of diseases, and constant increases in medical and pharmaceutical costs. All of these issues have an enormous impact on health care facilities, services, and costs.

While spending on health lags far behind spending in rich countries, as expected, the government has aggravated the problem by relying heavily on households to bear the rising costs of medical treatment. As noted, government spending as a share of total costs has decreased rapidly in the reform era as the state has sought to marketize health services. As a result, access to medical care has deteriorated for those without personal or family resources, and adequate facilities are not available in some areas even for those who could afford to pay for treatment. Medical treatment in the countryside in particular leaves much to be desired. The government has set up a number of pilot projects to test out a Rural Cooperative Medical System, but the results so far are not promising. Even in urban areas, where the Urban Employee Basic Medical Insurance System now covers well over 100 million people, many residents lack access to affordable medical care.[21] Underpaid doctors whose bonuses are tied to the revenues they generate demand side-payments from patients, and overprescribe expensive drugs or order unnecessary tests to boost profits and their own salaries. Hospitals are rushing to purchase expensive medical equipment in the hope of generating higher rates of return rather than focusing on the basic provision of public health services. As in many countries, there is a deep division among those that prefer to rely on market forces and privatize the health care system, and those that believe the government should be primarily responsible for health care. The government appears to be treading a middle course, relying both on market forces and government provision or subsidization of basic services for the urban and rural poor.

The government has done better with respect to education, though again problems remain. PRC law provides for nine years of compulsory education. In 2001, adult literacy was 85.8%, up from 78.3% in 1990. Youth literacy is even higher, at 97.9%.[22] In comparison, the average youth illiteracy rate in low income countries is 32%, and 5% in middle income countries.[23] The government has proudly noted that according to UNESCO in 2003, China made the most progress in eliminating illiteracy in the past decade among the forty countries surveyed.[24]

However, illiteracy rates are higher among women, minorities, and in rural areas. As recently as 1999, nearly 100 million mostly rural women were illiterate.[25] In response, the government initiated Project Hope to assist children in poor districts and the Spring Buds Scheme to promote girls' enrollment or return to school to complete their primary education. According to the Ministry of Education, the proportion of females receiving education at all levels has risen and the overall educational level of women has improved. From 1990 to 2000, the illiteracy rate among women has decreased from 32% to 13.5%, and the total population of female illiteracy has decreased from 159 million to 62 million. Less than 5% of young and middle-aged women are illiterate, despite higher overall rates of female illiteracy.[26] In 2000 the primary school enrollment rate of female students reached 99.1%. Even in the economically less developed western regions, the rate of school enrollment of female students reached 95%. At present, the proportion of female students in China's primary schools is 47.2% and that in colleges and universities is 43.95%.[27]

Despite such achievements, the UN Special Rapporteur (SR) on the Right to Education issued a critical report that challenged some of the data and offered a number of recommendations for improvement.[28] The SR noted that many public schools had begun to charge tuition and impose other fees, which the poor are not able to afford. She recommended that all fees be eliminated and that the budgetary allocation for education be increased to the 'internationally recommended' minimum of 6% of GDP, though few countries actually meet that level.[29] She also noted ongoing problems with gender equality and with education for minorities, including the lack of bilingual education. In addition, she recommended a clarification of the rights of young unmarried people to sex education and family-planning services and to self-protection against sexually transmitted diseases and AIDS.

The government responded with a scathing critique, accusing the SR of being politically biased, distorting the facts, and discounting China's achievements.[30] Beijing complained that the SR ignored information provided by the government, relying instead on materials from overseas sources and organizations. The government pointedly observed that although the SR did not visit Tibet, she nevertheless made 'biased and irresponsible comments' on education in Tibet.

To some extent, the divergence in perception of China's educational progress lies in the difference between the government's approach, which relies on regulations and general statistics, and the approach of the SR and other human rights organizations, which highlights individual cases or relies on accounts of oftentimes disgruntled parties about how the laws are implemented in practice. For instance, on the issue of school fees, the government noted that the State Council has issued regulations requiring that schools charge only a single fee and that fees be waived for indigent students. However, as with other types of laws, local governments often ignore or modify central regulations.

In other cases, the difference seems to be more one of spin or interpretation, or due to the tendency of human rights advocates to hold up idealistic standards that cannot be achieved given China's current level of development and regional variations. The SR, for example, accused China of backing away from its commitment to universal nine-year compulsory education.[31] The government acknowledges that nearly 10% of the population lives in regions where universal education can only be provided at the primary level or even only up to the third or fourth year of primary school. In light of significant regional disparities, the government has adopted a pragmatic approach that involves different plans in different regions and seeks to promote compulsory education progressively by realizing six-year universal compulsory education first. However, the government adamantly denied that it was backing away from universal nine-year compulsory education as a long-term goal.[32]

The rise of a middle class has also led to what may develop into the type of two-tier educational system found in many developing and developed countries. A number of elite private schools have arisen catering to the affluent. In the public sector, the difference in the quality of education between key schools and ordinary schools is also large. Access to key public schools and elite private schools often depends on the wealth and social connections of the parents. As education becomes increasingly important as a means of upward social mobility in the increasingly competitive global economy, the differences between those with wealth and thus able to obtain a better education and those without it will likely grow and become entrenched unless the government adopts measures to equal the playing field.

The rights of migrant workers have also been a source of contention.[33] The influx of migrant workers and the rise of laid-off urban workers have led to concerns about social order, aggressive begging, the rise of slum towns, and increased crime in urban areas. Until June 2003, authorities relied on a system of administrative detention known as 'detention and repatriation.' The system served humanitarian purposes and protected social order in urban areas by providing relief, education, and resettlement to migrants and urban poor. According to one report, upwards of two million people were subject to detention and repatriation each year, including a 'substantial proportion' of children.[34] In June 2003, the State Council repealed the 1982 regulation and issued new regulations that continued to provide social welfare to vagrants, but removed the compulsory detention component.[35] The new provisional rules require relief centers to provide food and shelter to those in need, send them to hospitals for medical treatment, contact their relatives, and arrange for transportation to their homes.

Another issue is the legal enforceability of rights. The constitution provides for citizens' rights to work, rest, education, scientific research and cultural activities, material assistance from the state for aged, ill, or disabled citizens, and ownership of lawfully obtained property. As is also true elsewhere, many economic rights because of their inspirational nature, vagueness, or policy implications with respect to distribution of resources are not considered to be justiciable. Nevertheless, a number of cases have arisen in relation to some of these rights, particularly the right to education. In fact, the first case to directly invoke the constitution as a basis for a claim absent implementing legislation involved the right to education.[36] One subsequent case involved a student who successfully sued her school for damages for failing to inform her about her college entrance exam scores in time to apply to university, while in another education case a student sued the school and various individuals for allowing someone else to use her name and exam score to enter university.[37]

In still another case that combined the right to education with a discrimination claim, three students from Qingdao sued the Ministry of Education for its admissions policy that allowed Beijing residents to enter universities in Beijing with lower scores than applicants from outside Beijing.[38] The plaintiffs filed the suit directly with the Supreme Court. Although the Supreme Court has the discretionary power to hear important cases in the first instance, it opted not to exercise the power, rejecting the case on jurisdictional grounds and advising the plaintiffs to file suit in Intermediate Court. Facing a number of serious legal obstacles, including that the Administrative Litigation Law permits challenges to the legality of specific administrative acts but not generally applicable administrative regulations, the students withdrew the case. The students claimed a moral victory in that their suit called attention to the unfairness of the current policy, and led the Ministry of Education to reconsider, although not yet change, the policy.

Law and order

Chinese leaders as well as leaders of other Asian states, such as Lee Kuan Yew, Singapore's Prime Minister from 1959–90, have often been critical of the high crime rates, rampant drug use, and social disorder in economically advanced Western liberal democracies. Rather, they champion family and communitarian values, social stability, and law and order. Tables 8 and 9 demonstrate that there are significant differences between Asian and Western countries in terms of crime rates and other indicators of social order.

Table 8. Crime Statistics (rate per 100,000) 1997–2002

Country and Human Development Indicator Rank		Total Crime	Murder	Rape
7	United States (HI)	4160.51	5.61	31.77
9	Japan (HI)	2300.77	1.1	1.85
17	France (HI)	6932.26	4.07	17.63
26	Hong Kong (HI)	1085.64	1.03	1.41
28	Singapore (HI)	703.84	0.8	2.81
29	Taiwan (UM)	2179.03	5.13	10.16
30	South Korea (UM)	1664.06	2.18	4.29
35	Poland (UM)	3634.84	3.15	6.09
43	Chile (UM)	1496.92	4.54	9.97
58	Malaysia (M)	729.71	2.1	5.78
65	Brazil (UM)	927.41	22.98	8.5
72	Romania (LM)	2207.05	7.44	8.34
74	Thailand (M)	245.53	8.07	6.17
85	Philippines (LM)	–	7.85	4.21
104	China (LM)	133.82	2.16	–
106	Iran (LM)	–	–	–
109	Vietnam (LI)	83.56	1.08	–

Table 8. *(contd.)*

Country and Human Development Indicator Rank		Total Crime	Murder	Rape
111	South Africa (UM)	8176.04	114.84	121.13
112	Indonesia (LI)	63.48	0.8	0.73
120	Egypt (LM)	–	–	–
121	Nicaragua (LI)	1372.27	24.03	26.03
127	India (LI)	671.2	3.93	1.6
145	Zimbabwe (LI)	6560.61	10.15	38.38
160	Tanzania (LI)	1647.98	7.95	10.05

Country and Human Development Indicator Rank		Theft	Drug Offense	Incarceration
7	United States (HI)	3804.58	539.92	701
9	Japan (HI)	1871.13	21.68	54
17	France (HI)	4224.57	182.19	93
26	Hong Kong (HI)	623.16	36.77	184
28	Singapore (HI)	415.5	85.08	388
29	Taiwan (UM)	1473.03	111.13	250
30	South Korea (UM)	386.31	8.97	125
35	Poland (UM)	1727.46	93.65	211
43	Chile (UM)	705.66	16.68	204
58	Malaysia (M)	581.43	78.95	161
65	Brazil (UM)	–	46.29	160
72	Romania (LM)	1028.33	2.04	199
74	Thailand (M)	90	438.13	401
85	Philippines (LM)	10.21	14.53	94
104	China (LM)	87.75	3.92	184
106	Iran (LM)	–	–	226
109	Vietnam (LI)	31.41	11.26	71
111	South Africa (UM)	3565.81	111.85	402
112	Indonesia (LI)	45.26	3.77	38
120	Egypt (LM)	–	–	121
121	Nicaragua (LI)	579.97	22.79	143
127	India (LI)	44.01	2.25	29
145	Zimbabwe (LI)	1958.11	57.03	160
160	Tanzania (LI)	194.11	13.39	120

Sources: Columns 1–5: Interpol, International Crime Statistics: Country Report, at **www.interpol.int/Public/Statistics/ICS/**.
Column 6: International Centre for Prison Studies, School of Law at King's College of the University of London, World Prison Brief. **www.prisonstudies.org/**. Some Taiwan, US, and Singapore data came from compilations by national statistic offices. Taiwan HDI rank is an estimate.

Crime rates must be used with caution because of differences in definitions of crimes, the willingness of rape victims to report rapes, broad yearly fluctuations, and differences in the level of economic development. In addition, demographic differences such as the percentage of rural population and youths also affect crime rates. Notwithstanding such qualifications, the results are striking: East Asian countries, especially in the higher income brackets, tend to have much lower crime rates relative to their level of economic development, industrialization, and urbanization. For instance, the total crime rates for high income countries France and the United States are two to ten times the rates in Japan, Singapore, and Hong Kong. The much higher crime rates hold across the board for property offenses such as theft and burglary, violent crimes such as murder (which are generally considered to suffer from fewer problems in reporting and data collection), and drug offenses. The United States suffers from particularly high levels of violent crime, especially rape.

The lower income countries such as China, the Philippines, Indonesia, India, and Vietnam have lower crime rates than the wealthier countries. Data collection is particularly problematic in low income countries, making comparisons more difficult. However, it would appear that crime is a greater problem in India than in China, Vietnam, and Thailand. In short, despite a rising crime rate, China still maintains a relatively stable social order. Walking the streets of Beijing alone late at night does not fill one with the sense of trepidation that comes from a similar stroll through the streets of New York or Los Angeles. A 2002 nationwide survey of 100,000 people found that 80% felt safe due to the strike-hard campaign.[39]

Countries vary widely in how they deal with criminals. The US has the dubious distinction of the highest rate of incarceration in the world, as well as some of the most severe punishments. In contrast, France and Japan have low rates of incarceration relative to their crime rates, and tend to place more emphasis on noncustodial sanctions, and in Japan's case on rehabilitation as well. In general, however, Asian states with the exception of Japan rely on heavy punishments. China is no exception. In 2001, 25% of verdicts in criminal cases resulted in a sentence greater than five years (including life imprisonment and the death penalty). This number is already down from the high thirties and low forties in previous years.[40] China also carried out more capital punishments in a three-month period in 2001 than were carried out globally in three years.[41]

Other indicators of social order such as suicide, divorce, and young mother rates are less clearly tied to a country's level of wealth. As indicated in Table 9, suicide rates are highest in Japan, followed by France, and then a cluster of countries including China, South Korea, and Hong Kong, followed by the US and India. Thailand and the Philippines, perhaps because of religious influences, have very low rates. However, other reports have indicated a much higher rate for China, particularly among rural women.[42] The high rate of suicide among Chinese women reflects their low economic and social status, the high incidence of violence, and limits on their ability to escape and pursue a more desirable life.[43]

Divorce rates have been growing in China, more than doubling in fifteen years from 0.9% in 1985 to 1.9% in 1999.[44] Nevertheless, China still has a much lower rate than other countries, including the United States and South Korea. Again, there is wide regional variation, with coastal and more developed areas experiencing a higher rate of divorce. According to the *People's Court Daily*, nearly a quarter of marriages in the coastal provinces end in divorce.[45]

Births to young mothers is not a serious problem in China due to family planning regulations that encourage later marriages and limit births. Of course, China's one-child policies, relaxed recently, have been much criticized both for violating the right to procreate and the coercive manner in which they have been carried out.

Women's rights

China, proud of its record on women's rights relative to other countries, hosted the Fourth World Conference on Women in 1995. Judged by the standards of the UNDP Gender-related Development Index,[46] China does reasonably well relative to its income. Again, as

Table 9. Social Order: Divorce Rates, Suicide Rates, Young Mothers

Country and Human Development Indicator Rank		Divorce Rate (per 1,000) 1996–2000	Suicide Rates (per 100,000) 1991–2002	Births by Mothers Between Age 15–19 (per 1,000 population 1995–2000)
7	United States (HI)	4.19	10.85	9.14
9	Japan (HI)	1.98	25.3	0.70
17	France (HI)	1.98	17.75	1.58
26	Hong Kong (HI)	1.95	13.25	1.08
28	Singapore (HI)	1.20	9.45	1.07
29	Taiwan (UM)	–	13.59	0.50
30	South Korea (UM)	2.52	13.55	0.63
35	Poland (UM)	1.09	15.4	4.12
43	Chile (UM)	0.42	5.8	10.19
58	Malaysia (M)	–	–	4.06
65	Brazil (UM)	0.60	4.2	19.05
72	Romania (LM)	1.40	12.35	7.93
74	Thailand (M)	–	4	12.41
85	Philippines (LM)	–	2.1	11.80
104	China (LM)	–	13.9	0.97
106	Iran (LM)	0.81	0.2	13.86
109	Vietnam (LI)	–	–	6.52
111	South Africa (UM)	0.83	–	21.34
112	Indonesia (LI)	–	–	15.10
120	Egypt (LM)	1.17	0.05	14.36
121	Nicaragua (LI)	–	3.45	45.06
127	India (LI)	–	10.65	12.52
145	Zimbabwe (LI)	–	7.9	31.34
160	Tanzania (LI)	–	–	39.37

Sources: Column 1: United Nations, Demographic Yearbook 2000, Table 25—Divorces and Crude Divorce Rates: 1996–2000. **http://unstats.un.org/unsd/demographic/products/dyb/DYB2000/Table25.xls**.
Column 2: World Health Organization, Suicide Rates per 100,000 by country, year and gender (Table). **www.who.int/mental_health/prevention/suicide/suiciderates/en/**.
Column 3: United Nations Department of Economic and Social Affairs, Population Division, World Population Prospects: The 2002 Revision Population Database, **http://esa.un.org/unpp/**. Taiwan HDI rank is an estimate.

the index is highly correlated with wealth ($r = .93$), a country's performance should be judged in comparison to other countries in its income class. As Table 10 indicates, while China scores much lower on the GDI than high income countries such as the United States, Japan, and Singapore, and much higher than low income countries such as India, Zimbabwe, and Egypt, it is comparable to other lower-middle income countries such as Iran, the Philippines, and Romania.

Table 10. Women's Rights and Well-being

HDI Rank	Country	Gender-related Development Index	Female Literacy (2001)			Earned Income Estimates (PPP US$) (2001)			Political Participation by Women (as % of total) (2000)	
			Female	Male	Female to Male Ratio	Female	Male	Female to Male %	Ministerial Level	Seats in Single or Lower House
7	United States	0.94	N/A	N/A	N/A	26,389	42,540	62	31.8	14.3
9	Japan	0.93	N/A	N/A	N/A	15,617	35,061	45	5.7	7.3
17	France	0.93	N/A	N/A	N/A	18,607	29,657	63	37.9	12.2
28	Singapore	0.88	88.7	96.4	0.92	14,992	30,262	50	5.7	11.8
30	South Korea	0.88	96.6	99.2	0.97	9,529	20,578	46	6.5	5.9
35	Poland	0.85	99.7	99.8	1.00	7,253	11,777	62	18.7	20.2
43	Chile	0.83	95.7	96.1	1.00	5,055	13,409	38	25.6	12.5
58	Malaysia	0.79	84.0	91.7	0.92	5,557	11,845	47	N/A	10.4
65	Brazil	0.77	87.2	87.4	1.00	4,391	10,410	42	0	8.6
72	Romania	0.77	97.4	99.1	0.98	4,313	7,416	58	20.0	10.7
74	Thailand	0.77	94.1	97.3	0.97	4,875	7,975	61	5.7	9.2
85	Philippines	0.75	95.0	95.3	1.00	2,838	4,829	59	N/A	17.8
104	China	0.74	78.7	92.5	0.85	3,169	4,825	66	5.1	21.8
106	Iran	0.71	70.2	83.8	0.84	2,599	9,301	28	9.4	4.1
109	Vietnam	0.69	90.9	94.5	0.96	1,696	2,447	69	N/A	27.3
111	South Africa	0.66	85.0	86.3	0.99	7,047	15,712	45	38.1	29.8
112	Indonesia	0.69	82.6	92.1	0.90	1,987	3,893	51	5.9	8.0
120	Egypt	0.63	44.8	67.2	0.67	1,970	5,075	39	6.1	2.4
121	Nicaragua	0.66	67.1	66.5	1.01	1,494	3,415	44	23.1	20.7
127	India	0.57	46.4	69.0	0.67	1,531	4,070	38	10.1	8.8
145	Zimbabwe	0.48	85.5	93.3	0.92	1,667	2,905	57	36.0	10.0
160	Tanzania	0.40	67.9	84.5	0.80	432	610	71	N/A	22.3

Source: UNDP *Human Development Indicators* (2003). Because of the lack of gender- disaggregated income data, female and male earned income are crudely estimated on the basis of data on the ratio of the female non-agricultural wage to the male non-agricultural wage, the female and male shares of the economically active population, the total female and male population and GDP per capita (PPP US$) (see technical note 1). Unless otherwise specified, estimates are based on data for the most recent year available during 1991–2000.

Despite steady and significant progress in improving women's lives, the government acknowledges that a number of serious problems remain. Violence against women is a major issue, including domestic violence and marital rape, sexual violence while in custody, sexual harassment in the workplace, trafficking of women, and forced prostitution. A 2000 survey by the All China Women's Federation (ACWF) found violence occurs in 30% of Chinese households, of which 80% involves spousal abuse.[47] Although more common in rural areas, domestic violence occurs throughout China and at all socioeconomic levels.

China's population policies have been criticized for their effects on women, including forced abortions and sterilization, and female infanticide.[48] Although genetic testing that determines the sex of the fetus is prohibited, it has become a lucrative underground business that contributes to abortions of female fetuses and an unusually high ratio of males to females. The male/female imbalance may contribute to kidnapping and trafficking of women, many of whom end up forced into marriage with males in poor villages.

Although economic reforms have greatly improved the lives of many women, the transition from a centrally planned economy to a market economy has increased poverty for some citizens, including a disproportionate number of women. Women have been laid off in greater numbers than men and have more difficulty finding new jobs.[49] They also suffer from gender segregation of the labor market, with an overconcentration in the low-paying service sector. Nevertheless, compared to other countries, including many other wealthy countries, Chinese women enjoy higher rates of employment, better jobs, and a higher ratio of female to male income earned.[50] Indeed, as indicated in Table 10, the female to male income ratio in China is higher than in the US, and much higher than in India, Iran, Chile, and Singapore.

While the problems are clear, the solutions are either not clear or difficult to implement. Several factors complicate the task of devising and implementing effective solutions. As the CEDAW Committee recognized, China's size and diversity pose special challenges to the realization of gender equality. Differences in the experiences of urban and rural women require different solutions.

The general conflict in the international human rights movement between women's rights, often interpreted in light of the experiences of women in Western developed countries, and the cultural and religious beliefs and practices of minority groups in non-Western developing countries, further complicates policy-making and undermines efforts to implement state policies aimed at promoting the rights of women. As is true elsewhere, progress on promoting women's rights is hindered by deeply embedded traditional views about the proper role of women in the family, in society, and in relation to men. The CEDAW Committee has observed that 'the persistence of prejudice and stereotypical attitudes concerning the role of women and men in the family and in society, based on views of male superiority and the subordination of women, constitutes a serious impediment to the full implementation of the Convention.'[51] The Committee also noted that the government has focused on protecting women through numerous labor regulations that protect women rather than empowering them.

The Committee suggested the government should adopt a more empowerment-oriented approach, encourage a national dialogue on attitudes toward women, and campaign publicly to change traditional attitudes.[52] A number of more targeted reforms have also been proposed for each of the specific issues.

For example, in response to lower female literacy rates, the CEDAW Committee recommended that the government abolish school fees and allocate adequate resources to ensure universal literacy and primary education, something easier said than done in most developing countries. The Committee also recommended revision of textbooks and the curriculum to eliminate gender stereotypes and to include the achievement of gender equality as a societal goal, reflecting the importance of consciousness raising and the rather optimistic belief that if only those responsible for the problems understood the negative consequences for women they would change their behavior. The Committee on the Rights of the Child suggested that local leaders be invited to take a more active role in supporting the efforts to prevent and eliminate discrimination against girls and to provide guidance to communities, although it is not clear to what extent the mostly male leaders support the goals of reform.[53]

With women holding just 5% of ministerial positions in 2000 and constituting 22% of the NPC, the proportion of women in political positions is low. However, while the numbers of women in ministerial positions is low relative to other countries, the number of female legislators is high. In response to the low levels of women in top positions of government, the CEDAW Committee recommended affirmative action and reservation of a specified number of seats for women delegates in people's congresses.[54] The Committee also called for more gender balance in the composition of village committees. However, the Committee ducked the controversial issue of whether to impose affirmative action quotas on the open, competitive process of democratic elections at the village level. Nor is it clear that China is legally or morally obligated to support the long-term prospects of women by sacrificing the short-term interests of villagers, both male and female, by potentially forcing them to settle for less qualified village leaders.

Concerned about the consequences of women's loss of employment, or of interrupted employment, on women's rights to housing, health care, and social security, the CEDAW Committee urged the government 'to analyse, from a gender perspective, the effects of its economic policies, and to take steps to mitigate and counteract their negative effects on women.'[55] In addition to enforcing existing labor laws, the Committee encouraged the government to increase women's redress against discrimination and inequality at work by promoting the recognition of women's right to participate in workers' organizations and their right to strike. The Committee also recommended more participation of women in government policy-making for rural areas and for small businesses and other income-generating projects.[56]

The CEDAW Committee responded to the high rate of suicide by recommending that the government pay urgent attention to the issue, research the causes of the high rates, provide better mental health services, and ensure that women have equal enjoyment of land rights independent of their marital status. However, as most of the problems occur in poor rural areas, adequate mental health services are not likely to be available for some time. Adequate health care of any type will only be available when China reaches a much higher stage of wealth, at which point women will have more options and be less inclined to commit suicide in the first place. Attempts to address the land rights of women through the amended Marriage Law and other regulations have run into resistance at the local level, where the rules conflict with social norms.

Efforts to combat violence against women have included public campaigns aimed at changing traditional values, the establishment of government and nongovernment bodies devoted to domestic violence and related issues, the tightening of provisions in the criminal law relating to various forms of violence against women, amendment of the Marriage Law to make reference to domestic violence, and the passage of local regulations addressing in greater detail domestic violence issues.[57] Nevertheless, a great deal remains to be done to change deeply entrenched attitudes, particularly in rural areas. Further efforts are needed to establish hotlines, shelters, and support networks for battered women, and to improve the legal framework. Future legal reforms are expected to include a stand-alone law on domestic violence that clarifies the issues of spousal rape and psychological abuse and strengthens remedies for victims of spousal abuse, sexual harassment in the workplace, and human trafficking.[58] Unfortunately, as demonstrated by the experiences of many other countries, having laws against domestic violence, sexual harassment, and human trafficking on the books does not ensure that the police and the judiciary will enforce them if the laws are radically at odds with social norms and practices.

Prostitution has become widespread with the transition to a market economy. The CEDAW Committee recommended that prostitution be decriminalized,[59] although prostitution itself is technically not a crime under the current PRC criminal law. Only pimps and brothel owners are subject to criminal sanctions. Prostitutes are subject to administrative detention and fines. Imposing fines however usually results in the women going back to work as prostitutes to earn the money needed to pay the fines. Ironically, many human rights organizations and advocates, including former Human Rights Commissioner Mary Robinson, have called for the elimination of administrative detention.[60] The most likely result of eliminating Detention and Education, the form of administrative detention used to detain prostitutes, would be that the criminal law would be amended to include prostitution, thus subjecting prostitutes to criminal punishments.

The Committee is on more solid ground in calling for greater attention to health services for prostitutes and for measures to facilitate rehabilitation and reintegration of prostitutes into society. At present, the recidivism rate for prostitutes is extremely high. Some PRC scholars claim that a 30% recidivism rate for prostitutes subject to Detention and Education would be a success.[61] It is difficult to rehabilitate those who do not believe they have done anything wrong. According to one study, 88% of women detained in Jiangsu in 1985 to 1986 on charges of prostitution did not regard their behavior as criminal.[62] While lengthy detentions likely will fail to effectively achieve the goal of education and rehabilitation, as the currently high recidivism rates indicate, short-term administrative detention to conduct health checks could curb the exploding rate of sexually transmitted diseases and HIV/AIDS. In the long run, economic growth will result in greater economic opportunities for women, although prostitution is likely to remain a permanent part of society, as it is elsewhere.

The CEDAW committee recognized 'that population growth is a genuine and severe problem and legitimate concern and that considerable progress has been made in providing family planning services.'[63] Nevertheless, the manner in which population growth is controlled leaves much to be desired. Despite laws that prohibit forced abortions and sterilization, local officials whose career prospects hinge on meeting family planning targets often turn a blind eye or encourage the practices. However, changing demographics have resulted in a relaxation of the one-child policy, and market reforms and greater wealth have decreased the impact of economic disincentives for those who want more than one child.

The failure to use adequate birth control leads to many abortions. The CEDAW Committee has noted 'with concern that only 14 per cent of men use contraceptives, thus making contraception and family planning overwhelmingly a woman's responsibility. In the light of the fact that vasectomy is far less intrusive and costly than tubal ligation, targeting mainly women for sterilization may amount to discrimination.'[64] The Committee recommended consciousness raising and education to encourage more men to take responsibility for birth control.

The Committee also recognized that male children are still expected to support the elderly, particularly in the countryside, contributing to the preference for boys. The Committee encouraged the government to address the linkages between economic security in old age and family planning, and to expand educational and employment opportunities for rural women in order to eliminate son preference. The Committee further suggested that the government improve its enforcement of laws against sex-selective abortion, female infanticide, and the abandonment of children. However, as a developing country, China is hard-pressed to provide an adequate welfare net for urban residents, much less for the many hundreds of millions more living in rural areas.

The Committee further noted that current laws provide insufficient legal safeguards for women's rights and insufficient remedies for rights violations. Since the first round of recommendations from the Committee in 1999, the government has carried out extensive publicity campaigns to increase awareness among women of their legal rights and to educate government officials and the general public about women's issues. The government has also passed a number of laws and amended others to clarify issues and improve legal remedies, has enhanced access to the justice system by expanding legal aid, and has overseen the buildup of a network of governmental and nongovernmental entities devoted to the promotion of women's rights. However, legal aid centers remain underfunded, the legal system remains relatively weak and ineffective in the face of opposing social norms, and women's groups have had little impact on changing deeply held attitudes, particularly in rural areas.

Cultural and minority rights

The study of cultural rights is complicated by the fact that China is a large country, with fifty-five different ethnic groups constituting approximately 8–9% of the population. The legal regime is complex, with numerous autonomous zones,[65] preferential policies, and a wide range of local regulations. Accordingly, different minority groups or even members of the same minority group are subject to different rules depending on where they are located. In addition, international law and domestic law are not clear on many points relating to the rights of minorities. Moreover, many issues are not resolved through the formal legal system.[66] There are also different values at stake, and sharply divergent views among Hans and ethnic groups on many issues, including empirical issues.

The government claims that it has greatly improved the living standards of minorities, affords them considerable political autonomy and opportunities to participate in national and local governments, offers them preferential treatment in education, employment, and family practices, and protects cultural sites and practices, including religious practices so long as they are nonpolitical. On the other hand, the SR on Racism and Racial Discrimination expressed concerns in his 2002 report that Tibetans in the TAR suffer various forms of systematic and institutional discrimination in the fields of employment, health care, education, housing, and public representation.[67] The Congressional-Executive Committee on China found that minorities that are willing to accept state controls have been able to preserve their culture and join Party and government ranks. Minorities that demand greater autonomy are subject to more restrictions, including government policies and actions that are sometimes inconsistent with Chinese laws and regulations.[68]

There is no doubt that China's minority regions are wealthier than in the past, and that the standard of living has improved for the vast majority of individuals. However, minority regions are often remote and predominantly rural and generally still poorer than the Han-dominated eastern, more urbanized, region. In response, the government listed poverty relief for relatively small ethnic minorities as a focus of the state's development-oriented poverty reduction program, adopting special policies to help members of twenty-two ethnic-minority groups each with a population less than 100,000.[69] In 2003, the government channeled 400 million yuan in development funds to ethnic minorities, and spent another 600 million yuan to develop trade and local businesses as part of preferential policies.[70]

Critics claim that economic policies have disproportionately benefited Hans living and working in minority areas, that some projects favored Hans, especially for technical and senior positions, and that minorities have less access to credit and financing.[71] The government counters that minorities hold the majority of positions in local governments, that all fifty-five ethnic groups are represented in the NPC, with minority candidates constituting 14% of NPC delegates even though they represent only 8–9% of the population, and that minorities hold key Party posts. Nevertheless, minorities tend to have more positions in government, whereas Hans continue to hold relatively more positions in the Party, which remains the ultimate authority. In addition, there are relatively few minority persons in the most powerful positions of government or the Party.[72]

Critics also allege that development has upset traditional living patterns and led to relocation. Such complaints are perhaps inevitable in the march toward economic development and modernization. However, allegations of genocide based on an influx of Hans into Tibet and Xinjiang and the destruction of cultural practices are overstated. Cultural genocide and ethnocide are not crimes defined by and grounded in international law. Not even the Dalai Lama claims that the conflict in Tibet is genocide as defined in international law. Sautman argues 'the concept of "cultural genocide" as a stock in trade of Tibetan émigré ideology is meant to be provocative and incitory, rather than an intellectually appropriate conceptual framework for assessing PRC state policy as it affects culture in Tibet. Designed to bolster the legitimacy of the émigré ethno-territorial movement, much of the émigré discourse on cultural genocide is a systematic misreading of the effects of the cultural transformation that attends social and economic change in Tibet.'[73]

Hans tend to congregate in the large cities, which generally tend to be better off than rural areas.[74] Being on average more educated, Hans also tend to have higher paying jobs, and thus can afford better housing. However, government policies have encouraged Hans to migrate to Xinjiang and Tibet, while encouraging educated minorities to leave.[75] Nevertheless, higher educated Tibetans are able to take advantage of expanding opportunities, with Tibetans claiming over 70% of staff and worker positions in state-owned units, including cadres, in the TAR. Tibetans with at least a secondary school education level are generally able to compete with Hans. But at the lower end of the economic spectrum, Hans in urban areas, attracted by subsidies, outcompete Tibetans.

Illiteracy has been greatly reduced among minorities, but remains significantly higher than the national average in some minority areas. According to government statistics, 32.5% of the population in the TAR was illiterate in 2000,[76] although the rate for young and middle-aged people is less than 3%.[77] Enrollment for children in the TAR is 86% (compared to 93% nationally). Illiteracy among young and middle-aged Uighars in Xinjiang is less than 2%.[78]

Native language and bilingual education have also been a concern of rights groups, with the Committee on the Elimination of Racial Discrimination recommending that children in all minority regions should have the right to develop their own language and culture.[79] However, this goal is difficult to achieve given that there are over twenty-five different languages used in China, with many minorities dispersed throughout the country or living in predominantly Han areas. The Education Law and other laws provide that schools with a majority of ethnic students may use the oral and written languages of the ethnic group. Tibetan is the main language in 60% of middle schools in Tibet.[80] There are also Tibetan curriculum high schools, although most offer classes in Chinese as well. Minority students, who benefit from affirmative action in entering colleges, are able to take the national entrance exam in their own language. On the other hand, while Tibetan and other minority languages may be used in courts and official business within the particular minority region, Chinese is often a requirement for economic and social advancement both within the region and the rest of the country. Thus the desire to promote Tibetan culture by emphasizing Tibetan language in schools is at odds with the need to learn Chinese to succeed in the broader society. Accordingly, Tibetan parents favor bilingual education for their children even at the primary school level, as is also true for Tibetans living in India. Nevertheless, the government's efforts to increase use of Mandarin in Tibet and Xinjiang have increased concerns over loss of cultural identity.

In a controversial move, the SR on Education recommended that China allow religious education. This drew a sharp retort from Beijing, which claimed that while people enjoy freedom of religion, and parents are free to instruct their children in religious beliefs at home during non-school hours, China adopts a general policy of separating education from religion. Accordingly, the Compulsory Education Law provides that no organizations or individuals may use religion to interfere with public education. In keeping with this policy, authorities closed down the Ngaba Kirti Monastic School in Sichuan, which was built with private funds, and provided traditional monastic education to rural Tibetans.[81] Anyone below the age of 18 is also not allowed into mosques or other places of worship, although in practice this policy may be relaxed in areas where unrest is not an issue. Similarly, non-religious schools run by religious organizations are allowed in some areas, and there are religious schools and colleges for students over 18 years old.[82]

International practice varies widely with respect to religious education, with states divided on whether religious education should be allowed at all, whether the government should fund religious schools, whether religious schools must meet minimal curricular requirements and when limitations are justified on the teaching of religious beliefs that may incite demands for self-determination, challenge the ruling regime, or upset public order.

Causes of rights problems and general constraints on improved performance

Empirical studies have demonstrated the importance of a number of factors on human rights performance, including wealth, war, politics, culture, population size, and institutional development. China is no exception.

Economic factors go a long way toward explaining both the improvements in rights performance in recent decades and the continuing problems, many of which are directly or indirectly related to poverty and lack of resources. Ongoing deficiencies in access to food, clean water, medical care, and education are most directly related to China's relatively low level of economic development, although a weak tax system and policies that fail to redistribute resources from China's increasingly wealthy high income earners exacerbate the problems. Economic growth is therefore necessary but not sufficient to sustain improvements in social and economic rights and other indicators of human well-being. Wealth, or the lack thereof, also contributes to ethnic tensions and even a higher incidence of violations of personal integrity and civil and political rights: economically well-off people generally do not take to the streets to protest, favoring less confrontational channels for advancing their interests that do not threaten social stability or challenge the state to the same degree. Indeed, China's nouveau riche tend to be politically conservative and supportive of the regime, if only out of fear that demands for faster political reforms will lead to political instability and social chaos, thus undermining their steady incomes and threatening their comfortable lifestyles. In contrast, most protests result from economic injustices, often by people who have little to lose. Many other main areas of conflict are also fundamentally economic in nature, including the problems associated with laid-off workers and labor activism, government land takings and relocation, migrant workers, and urban crime—the majority of which is committed by migrant workers with little money in their pockets.

Population size is relevant in several ways. First, China's huge population is directly tied to quality of life as reflected in social and economic measures because limited resources are spread thin over large numbers. China has the world's fourth largest economy but is a lower-middle income country on a per capita basis. Second, as elsewhere, population size is a proxy for ethnic diversity, which leads to conflicts between minority groups and the government, between minorities and the majority Hans, and among minorities. Such conflicts result in restrictions on civil and political rights, especially in Xinjiang and Tibet, and complicate the issue of cultural rights. Third, the sheer size of the population results in a 'large' number of violations of physical integrity rights and civil and political rights, though proportionally the number is small. Fourth, and more substantively, the size of the population makes control more difficult and instability more likely; thus, the expected danger value, calculated by multiplying the likelihood of instability by the consequences of chaos, is also higher. In a country the size of China, even the most radical anti-government movements and bizarre cults attract significant followings, especially now that the Internet has facilitated long-distance communications.

Political, ideological, and *cultural* factors also explain some of the results, particularly with respect to the tight restraints on civil and political rights.[83] China's leaders do not apologize for not being liberals. Clearly statist socialism influences the government's general position on human rights and as well as the outcome in particular cases. The Party in its role as vanguard sets the normative agenda for society. In addition, there is a smaller private sphere and a correspondingly larger role for the state in supervising and guiding social activities.

Political views in China are not limited to either support for statist socialism or liberal democracy. There is also considerable support for neo- or soft authoritarianism, and for various forms of communitarianism. Neo-authoritarians prefer single-party rule to genuine democracy. They would either do away with elections, or were that not politically feasible, limit elections to lower levels of government. If forced by domestic or international pressure to hold national elections, they would attempt to control the outcome by imposing limits on the opposition party or through their monopoly on major media channels. Like the statist socialists, they favor a large role for the government in controlling social activities. Nevertheless, they would tolerate a somewhat smaller role for the government and a correspondingly larger civil society, albeit one still subject to restrictions and characterized by corporatism.

In contrast, communitarians support genuine, though not necessarily immediate, multiparty democratic elections at all levels of government. Urban communitarians fear chaos, and distrust the rural population. Consequently, many are willing to postpone national elections in favor of a more gradual process where elections are permitted at successively higher levels of government. Like the statist socialists and neo-authoritarians, they believe state leaders should determine the normative agenda for society, and hence allow a larger role for the state in managing social activities than in a liberal democratic state. However, they prefer a somewhat more expansive civil society. Although some groups, particularly commercial associations, might find close relationships with the government helpful, other more social or spiritual groups might not. Communitarians would permit these spiritual groups to operate without state involvement, provided they are not seen as challenging public order or morality.

In terms of rights, liberal democrats tend to emphasize civil and political rights over economic, social, and cultural rights. Rights are often conceived of in deontological terms as distinct from and normatively superior to interests.[84] Rights are considered to be prior to the good (and interests) both in the sense that rights 'trump' the good/interests and in that rights are based not on utility, interests, or consequences but on moral principles whose justification is derived independently of the good. To protect individuals and minorities against the tyranny of the majority, rights impose limits on the interests of others, the good of society, and the will of the majority. Substantively, freedom is privileged over order, individual autonomy takes precedence over social solidarity and harmony, and freedom of thought and the right to think win out over the need for common ground and right thinking on important social issues.[85] In addition, rights are emphasized rather than duties or virtues.

In contrast, communitarians endorse an interpretation of human rights that emphasizes the indivisibility of rights. Greater emphasis is placed on collective rights and the need for economic growth, even if at the expense of individual civil and political rights. Rather than a deontological conception of rights as antimajoritarian trumps on the social good, rights are more often conceived of in utilitarian or pragmatic terms as another type of interest to be weighed against other interests, including the interests of groups and society as a whole. Accordingly, stability is privileged over freedom; social solidarity and harmony are as important, if not more so, than autonomy and freedom of thought; and the right to think and express dissenting views is limited by the need for common ground and consensus on important social issues. Communitarians, neo-authoritarians, and statist socialists also pay more attention than liberal democrats to the development of moral character and virtues and the need to be aware of one's duties to other individuals, one's family, members of the community, and the nation.

As with communitarians, neo-authoritarians and statist socialists view rights in utilitarian or pragmatic terms. However, unlike communitarians, they favor a more central role for the state. Statist socialists are especially likely to view rights as useful tools for strengthening the nation and the ruling regime. Consequently, they are more likely than neo-authoritarians to invoke state sovereignty, Asian values, and the threat of cultural imperialism to prevent other countries from interfering in their internal affairs while overseeing the destruction of the communities and traditional cultures and value systems that they were allegedly defending. Nevertheless, communitarians and neo-authoritarians in China are also likely to object to strong-arm politics and the use of rights to impose culture-specific values on China or to extract trade concessions in the form of greater access to Chinese markets. Moreover, like communitarians, neo-authoritarians and statist socialists favor order over freedom. They go even farther than communitarians, however, in tilting the scales toward social solidarity and harmony rather than autonomy, and are willing to impose more limits on freedom of thought and speech. While neo-authoritarians prefer to restrict the right of citizens to criticize the government, statist socialists prefer broader restrictions, drawing a clear line at public attacks on the ruling party or challenges to single party socialism. Despite recent societal changes that have reduced the effectiveness of 'thought work,' statist socialists continue to emphasize its role in ensuring a common consensus on important social issues.

On some issues, there are clear preferences among the majority of citizens, notwithstanding the general differences among the various camps. There is for example a clear preference for stability and economic growth, even if that means postponing democracy and tolerating for the time being greater restrictions on civil and political rights. At the same time, there is little support for political dissidents or for those who push for liberal interpretations on many rights issues or for immediate democratization.

Similarly, there is wide support for the war on crime. Polls in 1995, 1996, and 1997 found that social stability and crime topped the concerns of urban residents.[86] The public has strongly supported the government's periodic strike-hard campaigns. One poll of 1,000 residents in Guangzhou found that 81% felt social order had improved in 2001, and that 73% believed the strike-hard campaign contributed significantly to the improvement.[87] The *People's Daily* reported that 90% of Beijing citizens believed that the campaign in December 2001 improved their safety.[88]

There clearly is widespread public support for heavy punishments, including the death penalty. In a 1995 survey of 5,006 citizens, less than 1% believed that the death penalty should be abolished.[89] In fact, more than 22% believed that there were too few death sentences.[90] Although public opinion polls about crime may sometimes be misleading in that the questions fail to distinguish between serious crime and petty crime, in China the public's support for heavy punishments runs the gamut from violent crimes to property and economic crimes to drug use and morality crimes.[91] In the Guangzhou poll, almost two-thirds remained seriously concerned about theft and robbery and hoped that the government would take additional steps to deal with these crimes. Meanwhile, a 1997 survey of 1,200 Beijing residents found that 90% believed drugs would become a major menace to morality and the nation if effective measures were not taken, and urged the government to impose heavier punishments.[92] Where there is such a clear majority preference, reforms that go against the tide are not likely to be passed into law. Even if they do become law, there is a good chance that the laws will not be implemented in practice.

Institutional factors also inhibit the protection and advancement of rights. Although China has various official and quasi-official human rights research centers, there is no national human rights commission or ombudsmen for the promotion of human rights. Nor is there an Asian regional system comparable to that in Europe, the Americas, or Africa that could serve as a source for rights promotion or the development of jurisprudence. Of course, given its sovereignty concerns, China is not likely to accept the jurisdiction of a regional court adjudicating issues arising in China or between China and other member states.

China's domestic legal system remains relatively weak in some areas, although it has greatly improved in many ways over the last twenty years. Courts are able to handle most cases competently and independently. Party organs rarely intervene in individual cases.[93] Nevertheless, the judiciary still lacks the authority to decide many controversial political and social cases independently, as suggested by the long delays before issuing verdicts in some of the civil and political rights cases discussed previously. Similarly, the courts often fail to provide adequate protection in many land confiscation cases and other administrative litigation cases.

Even when courts do decide cases independently, they are obligated to apply nonliberal laws, such as those that recognize only registered social organizations and require prior authorization to demonstrate, while giving the authorities broad grounds to deny applicants permits and wide discretion in interpreting vague laws on state secrets, endangering the state, and disturbing the public order. The lack of a constitutional review body arguably also impedes the protection of rights, although such a body would most likely not be all that liberal or effective given the current circumstances based on the experiences of other East Asian countries at a similar stage of development.

Conclusion: relative success in most areas within limits of resources and other constraints

Chinese citizens enjoy greater rights to participate in governance and more freedoms than ever before, although the authorities continue to impose severe limitations on civil and political rights whenever the expression of such rights is perceived to threaten the regime or social stability. In terms of *subject matter*, calls for democracy and the overthrow of the Party or government; advocacy of independence and greater autonomy for Xinjiang, Tibet, and Taiwan; religious practice outside officially sanctioned bounds by 'cults' or in-house churches; labor activism; and exposés of corruption at high levels are subject to restraints depending on the circumstances. The authorities are particularly likely to intervene when *the manner* of exercising such rights involves social organization across regions, large-scale and well-coordinated demonstrations, exposure to a wide and unidentified audience through the mass media and Internet, and links to foreign entities. In contrast, individuals, academics, and government officials can generally express their views in private or even publicly to a limited and defined audience, although some liberal academics have been fired from their university posts or harassed in other ways. Despite the restrictions, China's level-4 PTS rating overstates the degree of 'political terror.'

Assessing the performance of any criminal justice system is a problematic exercise. People attach different weights to competing values, such as the rights of individual suspects and the importance of assuring that no innocent person is wrongly convicted on the one hand, and social order and the freedom and interests of individuals who may be victims of crime, even violent crime, if suspects are not detained or are acquitted on 'technicalities' such as the exclusion of tainted evidence, on the other. People also disagree about the purposes of the criminal justice system and the relative weights assigned to deterrence, rehabilitation, retribution, vengeance, education, and incapacitation. And they disagree about the causes of crime and hence the relative effectiveness of different ways to confront it. Nevertheless, there is some evidence that China's policies have been successful in curtailing crime.

Despite the recent increase in crime rates, China still has much lower murder, rape, and burglary rates than the United States, France, and Germany, though the murder and rape rates are now higher than in Singapore and Japan. China also has lower murder, rape, and burglary rates than other lower-middle income countries like the Philippines and Romania.

While the legal system serves social order reasonably well, it fails to provide individuals with the protections and remedies owed them under PRC laws. There are still numerous serious shortcomings in the criminal justice and administrative detention systems, and many possible reforms that would strengthen the protection of the rights of the accused and offer citizens recourse against abusive officials without imperiling social order or the authority of the government.

Analysis of social and economic rights is hindered by the basic problem encountered in most legal systems: social and economic rights are generally not justiciable. Accordingly, we must rely on general laws, policies, and statistics, supplemented by a few cases on rather narrow issues. Unfortunately, the statistics and facts are often unreliable or contested. Even the proper standards for measurement are heavily contested: scholars disagree over the utility and significance of different measures of poverty, for instance. There is also a conflict between the idealism of human rights activists who expect wonders despite the reality of limited resources, and those who would set more realistic standards consistent with China's level of development and priorities for government spending.

Notwithstanding such qualifications, China does well both absolutely and relative to its income level in housing, feeding, and clothing its vast population. It also does well relative to its income level in education and on many health indicators despite limited public spending. However, China is a relatively poor country, with wide regional disparities and considerable inequality. The new leadership of Hu and Wen has shown sensitivity to issues of social justice, implementing a number of policies to ease the hardships of those who have lost out in the transition to a more competitive capitalist economic system. In so doing, they are able to draw on a rich tradition of 'people as the basis,' stretching back to Mencius, that requires leaders to ensure the material and spiritual well-being of the people. While such traditions are grounded in a nonliberal paternalistic worldview, they nonetheless provide a normative basis for social, economic, cultural, and collective rights claims today.

Women's rights also present a mixed picture, as is generally true everywhere. China has made undeniable progress in improving women's lives. Nevertheless, the government's representative acknowledged in his report to the CEDAW Committee in 1999 that despite the government's efforts to include women in the nation's development, many rural women are still poor, many are still illiterate, and many women workers have been laid off during the economic transition.[94] The participation of women in political life is still low, especially at higher levels of government; domestic violence still occurs frequently; and social ills such as female trafficking and infanticide remain problems. Globalization and the turn to a market economy have created new opportunities and benefited some women while giving rise to new challenges and harming other women. The spokesperson emphasized, however, that the government is determined to continue its efforts to address the issues women face, and welcomed the support of the international community. Yet further progress is likely to be slow. Gender issues are deeply embedded in a society's traditions and life forms, and thus require a holistic approach involving fundamental changes in social norms and structural changes in the economic, political, and legal orders.

Religion is a contentious area—again, as it often is elsewhere. Religion was a significant factor in twenty-five regional or civil wars during the 1980s.[95] The potential for religion to challenge state authority and undermine social stability has led to a wavering doctrine regarding the separation of church and state around the world. Within Asia alone, freedom of religion exists side by side with state-endorsed atheism in China and Vietnam, and Islam as the official state religion in Malaysia. Meanwhile, in the Philippines, Catholicism is privileged in numerous ways, including constitutional provisions on abortion and divorce that reflect Catholic religious principles.[96] In Japan, Shinto remains favored, with courts reluctant to hold visits by state leaders to Shinto shrines to be a violation of the principle of separation of state and church.[97] And in Thailand, Buddhism is so dominant as to constitute implicitly the official religion.[98] Despite the official endorsement of atheism, China tolerates religious practice subject to concerns about social stability.

China has sought to improve the lives of its many ethnic minorities through a series of policies to stimulate economic growth and a complicated regulatory framework that establishes special autonomous zones for Tibet, Xinjiang, and other ethnic regions, and provides preferential treatment in employment, education, and family planning to minorities. Nevertheless, as in other countries, ethnic divisions, often based on religious identities, have led to tensions between the Hans and other ethnic groups and have precipitated calls for greater autonomy and even secession. Conflicting views about the effects of government policies, conflicting interpretations of the facts, and normative differences have resulted in widely different assessments of China's record on cultural rights between Hans and members of the various minority groups. Due in part to efforts to improve the living conditions of minorities and in part to the implementation of tight controls, China has managed for the most part to avoid large-scale ethnic conflicts. However, sporadic bombings and other acts of violence have occurred. The government has responded with force, and by tightening control on possible sources of dissent.

In short, China is by and large following the EAM on rights issues. Citizens enjoy a range of freedoms. They are generally free to engage in economic activities. They are free to join most social organizations. Citizens have wider access to information and increasing channels for public participation. Nevertheless, as in other East Asian states when they were at a similar level of development, such freedoms are subject to restraints when social and political stability is threatened, or perceived by the authorities to be threatened.

Despite a variety of problems, China does well relative to its level of development on most measures of human rights and well-being. Yet China is among a handful of the countries most frequently targeted for systematic government violations, supporting the view that China is subject to a double standard.[99] The next chapter examines why that might be.

CHAPTER FIVE

Of rights and wrongs: why China is subject to a double standard on rights

Since 1990, there have been eleven attempts to censure China before the UN Commission on Human Rights in Geneva, although each has failed. Human rights groups regularly issue scathing reports condemning China for widespread human rights violations.[1] Every year, the US State Department claims serious abuses, frequently describing the situation as deteriorating. UN bodies and officials, including the special rapporteurs on the rights to education, religious freedom, and torture, have also issued critical reports.

On the other hand, as we have seen, the Chinese government regularly counters with reports chock-full of statistics showing considerable progress on a wide variety of fronts. While acknowledging much remains to be done, the government maintains its critics are biased, human rights are being misused for political purposes, and China is being held to a double standard.[2]

Many Chinese citizens feel the same way. They too see the human rights policies of Western countries, particularly the US, as hypocritical and hegemonic power politics.[3] In a survey of 547 students from thirteen universities in China, 82% claimed that for other countries to initiate anti-China motions before the UN Commission on Human Rights constituted interference in China's internal affairs; 71% believed that the true aim of the United States and other countries in censuring China was to use the human rights issue to attack China and impose sanctions on it, with 69% maintaining that this constituted a form of power politics.

Chinese citizens are particularly sensitive about infringements on China's national sovereignty in part because of decades of bullying by foreign imperial powers. But many also feel that China today is being held to a different standard than other countries. The US and other Western powers sit idly by while gross violations of human rights occur in Burundi, Colombia, Nigeria, Uganda, India, Saudi Arabia, and countless other countries, and yet are quick to criticize China even though most Chinese enjoy more extensive freedoms and a better standard of living than ever before. Behind the double standard, they suspect, lies the desire of the US and other developed countries to contain China and prevent it from emerging as a rival superpower.

The very fact that government leaders and Chinese citizens feel China is being held to a double standard, whether or not it is true, has several negative consequences for human rights. The steady stream of criticism leveled at Beijing has led to testy relations between China and UN rights bodies, the US and other countries, and international human rights NGOs. The government is often quick to assume a defensive posture, stonewalling or defending its record at length in the face of criticism rather than exploring constructive ways to improve the current situation. Beijing has also been reluctant to allow visits by inspectors from the UN or other countries, and has imposed restrictions on those visits it does authorize. At times, the reaction has been even more hostile and antithetical to progress on rights issues. In response to the annual US State Department report, which the State Council has denounced as 'an amateurish collection of distortions and rumors' driven by 'anti-China forces who don't want to see the existence of an increasingly wealthy and developed socialist state,'[4] China now issues its own critical report on the rights situation in the United States.[5] In addition, China has canceled bilateral dialogues on human rights as well as programs on rule of law in response to the attempts to censure it in Geneva.

Apart from the negative government reaction, the public's support for international reform efforts has also been weakened. Many citizens are suspicious about the motives of NGOs. Even reform-minded academics often find that NGOs lack an adequate understanding of the situation in China, and that their proposals for reform are out of touch with the existing norms or simply infeasible given China's current conditions. Public opinion about America, seen as the leader of Western critics, has undergone a dramatic shift in the last twenty years, from wildly supportive to highly critical.[6] Sometime in this century China will likely emerge as a major economic, political, and ultimately military power capable of challenging US hegemony. Instilling a feeling of resentment and hostility in Chinese citizens who believe China is being treated unfairly diminishes the likelihood of a peaceful and cooperative relationship between the superpowers.

The feeling that China is subject to a double standard has led to a growing nationalism.[7] While nationalism may take the form of pride in one's culture and country, in China nationalism is often based on a more negative feeling of resentment. The resentment stems from a general sense that China, this once great civilization, is being denied its rightful place in the world. Ironically, applying a double standard to China feeds a trend to emphasize the distinctiveness of China, and of Asian countries more generally, as evidenced in the debate over Asian values.[8]

China has been subject to considerably more censure than many other countries with a worse record across a range of indicators. Why is this?[9]

Why China is held to a double standard

BANG FOR THE BUCK: CHINA'S LARGE SIZE JUSTIFIES ALL THE ATTENTION

Critics claim that improving the rights situation in China would benefit one-fifth of the world's people, and thus focusing resources on China is justified. However, India also received a level-4 PTS rating, and suffers from much more severe poverty than China, with twice as many people living on less than $1/day, twice the rate of infant mortality, and more than double the illiteracy rate. Its good governance rankings, with the exception of voice and accountability, are similar to those of China.[10]

Moreover, while India and China both received level-4 PTS ratings, violations of physical integrity rights in India appear to be more severe.[11] In 2001 and 2002, security forces killed an average of 1,600 militants per year. Some of those killings occurred in 'fake encounters,' where the security forces summarily executed suspected militants and other civilians offering no resistance. The bodies of many of those killed showed signs of torture and bore multiple bullet wounds. Estimates of unexplained disappearances in Kashmir and Jammu alone since 1990 range from nearly 4,000 according to government sources up to 8,000 according to NGOs. Security forces reportedly used civilians as human shields while patrolling and in searching for landmines. Military and paramilitary troops also engaged in abduction, torture, rape, and arbitrary detention. Death in custody is common for both suspected militants and ordinary criminals. In 2001, there were over 1,300 such deaths nationwide. The UN Special Rapporteur on Torture has claimed that security forces systematically tortured suspected militants to coerce confessions and to obtain information. The authorities also tortured detainees to extort money or as summary punishment. Rape while in custody is also common. In addition, prison officials reportedly use prisoners as personal servants and have sold female prisoners to brothels. Yet few members of the security forces are ever held accountable. Antiterrorism and national security laws have been used to detain people for long periods of time, without judicial review, while permitting the use of testimony obtained under duress.[12] In addition, thousands of ordinary criminal suspects remain in detention without charge, in violation of Indian law. India's legal system, plagued by corruption and a lack of resources, is overburdened and unable to try civil or criminal cases in a timely manner. As of July 2002, there were 13 million cases pending in lower courts, and 3.5 million cases in high courts. Some 75% of detainees were unconvicted prisoners awaiting completion of trial. In Jammu and Kashmir, the judicial system barely functions due to threats against judges and witnesses and tolerance of the government's heavy-handed crackdown on terrorists.

The US State Department also notes 'occasional' limits on freedom of the press and freedom of movement, as well as

> harassment and arrest of human rights monitors; extensive societal violence against women; legal and societal discrimination against women; forced prostitution; child prostitution and female infanticide; discrimination against persons with disabilities; serious discrimination and violence against indigenous people and scheduled castes and tribes; widespread intercaste and communal violence; religiously motivated violence against Muslims and Christians; widespread exploitation of indentured, bonded, and child labor; and trafficking in women and children.

To be more specific, restrictions on freedom of speech and the press in India include the use of criminal defamation laws against journalists and occasional beatings, detentions, and harassment of journalists, which has resulted in some self-censorship. The government has also sought to influence the media by threatening to revoke state advertising. In addition, the government bans books, including Salman Rushdie's *The Satanic Verses*, and prohibits objectionable content on satellite channels, notably morally inappropriate tobacco and alcohol advertisements. The government also limits access to the Internet, and has arrested people on conspiracy charges for posting articles.

The government restricts academic freedom, most notably by regulating academic partnerships between Indian and Western universities in line with Hindutva philosophy, which advocates an emphasis on Hindu cultural norms in public education. Some advocates of Hindutva oppose conversion from Hinduism and believe all Indian citizens should adhere to Hindu values, including resisting changes to the caste system.

Religious tension between Hindus, Muslims, and Christians threatens the secular foundation of the state, and has led to bombings, rioting, and murders. Accordingly, the Religious Institutions (Prevention of Misuse) Act prohibits the use of any religious site for political purposes. Foreign Christian missionaries, who must obtain permits, have not been allowed access to northeastern states because of concerns about political stability.

Although freedom of assembly is generally respected, permits are required to demonstrate, and separatist groups are routinely denied permits. Furthermore, the police have used force to maintain control. Human rights organizations were not allowed to move about freely in Jammu and Kashmir due to fear of attacks by security forces and militants. Several individuals have documented abuses in these areas, including lawyers and journalists, and have subsequently been attacked or killed. The government's investigation of the 2002 killing of human rights lawyer Naveleen Kumar has yet to produce any results.

The government also refused a visa to the Secretary General of Amnesty International after Amnesty International issued a critical report regarding the government handling of the religious-based violence in Gujarat. The government refused to allow the UN Special Rapporteurs on Torture and Extrajudicial Killings to visit in 2002.

Shockingly, even 56% of women claim that domestic violence is justified. Upper caste gangs engaged in mass rapes of lower caste women as part of a strategy of intimidation, and gang rapes were used as punishment for adultery or as coercion or revenge in rural property disputes. However, police routinely refuse to arrest rapists, while the courts fully adjudicate only 10% of rape cases, creating a culture of impunity for rapists. Dowry disputes remain common. Although banned, Sati—the burning of widows on their husbands' funeral pyre—continues in some areas.

Dalits or 'untouchables,' the lowest caste, make up the majority of bonded labor, face segregation in housing and marriage, and tend to be malnourished, poor, and illiterate. Brahmins, the highest caste, make up 78% of the judiciary and 50% of the parliament, even though they constitute just 3.5% of the population.

Despite such problems—which taken together are at least as serious as the problems in China without even considering China's better performance at reducing poverty and improving people's living standards—the US and its Western allies never once sponsored a motion to censure India for rights violations during the period 1990–2004, when China was subject to eleven motions. Nor has the US State Department cited India as a country of political concern, despite condemning China for 'egregious, systematic ongoing abuses of right of religious freedom,' even though the Commission on International Religious Freedom, an independent nine-member advisory body established by Congress, urged it to do so. The Commission cited among other serious problems fatal attacks against Muslims and Hindus and the government's failure to address adequately the killing of as many as 2,000 people in Gujarat in 2002.

Population size may matter, but apparently not when it comes to even-handed treatment of rights violations. Even if, as critics allege, China merits additional attention because of its size, there is no excuse for distortions of the factual record or for failures to provide a balanced view that presents China's rights performance within a comparative context. If anything, the extra attention and resources spent on China should lead to more careful study, a better understanding of the local context and the issues, and ultimately more nuanced and higher quality reports.

EMPHASIS ON CIVIL AND POLITICAL RIGHTS VIOLATIONS AND BIAS AGAINST NONDEMOCRACIES

A more likely explanation than pure size for all the attention paid to China is that there is some truth to Beijing's complaint that the human rights regime is biased toward liberal democracy and does not want to see a nonliberal democratic regime succeed. Nondemocratic countries are held to higher standards than democracies. As a result, China is judged more harshly, while India and other democracies with poor rights records tend to be given the benefit of the doubt, receiving the equivalent of a 'get-out-of-jail-free' pass.

The bias of the human rights regime and the media against nonliberal democratic regimes is longstanding.[13] UN resolutions for systematic government violations of human rights have overwhelmingly been meted out against a handful of nondemocratic developing countries with poor civil and political rights records, even though they may do relatively better on other human rights measures and indicators of well-being, including physical integrity violations.

In 2002, China, which received a 4 on the PTS scale, was targeted for criticism for systematic human rights violations in Geneva, while only Afghanistan among the eight countries with the worst PTS rating of 5, was targeted. The democratic or semi-democratic states of

Israel, Liberia, and Colombia, all of which had a PTS rating of 5, were not targeted for systematic violations, although Israel was subject to criticism with respect to the human rights situation in occupied Palestine. Indeed, China was one of only four countries with a level-4 rating to be targeted for systematic violations. Even though there were twenty-two countries with a level-4 rating, almost half of them democracies or semi-democracies, all four targeted countries were nondemocracies, with the possible exception of Iran, which arguably might be classified as a semi-democracy. Furthermore, three out of the four countries with a PTS rating of 3 or 2 that were subject to a motion for systematic violations were nondemocracies, the exception being semi-democratic Cambodia. If Iran and Cambodia are considered nondemocracies, then all of the motions for systematic violations in 2002 were against nondemocracies, even though many democracies or semi-democracies had worse or equally poor records with respect to personal integrity violations.

A study of the UN Human Rights Commission from 1982 to 1997 found that 'most draft resolutions which target governments for systematic human rights violations are introduced by Western states and place a heavy emphasis on civil and political rights which are lacking in many Third World states.'[14] Observing that only twenty-two governments have been the subject of resolutions for systematic rights violations, the report pointed out that 'only a few offenders have been designated in resolutions for any type of human rights violations, generally those states with insufficient political clout to mobilize regional opposition to their passage . . . '[15] Among the notable absentees on the list of countries targeted by resolutions for systematic rights violations is US ally Saudi Arabia. Even the ardent promoter of universal rights Jack Donnelly acknowledges that 'certain countries are singled out, for partisan purposes, to the exclusion of other, no less reprehensible regimes.'[16]

The report acknowledged the legitimacy of complaints of bias on the part of China and other developing countries:

It is true, as some Third World states complain, that Western states are seldom targeted in Commission resolutions and that none has been targeted for domestic human rights violations of any kind. That the Commission has been unable to pass even a single resolution addressing human rights conditions in a Western state reduces its credibility as a representative of human rights for the entire international community and gives rise to criticisms, such as China's, that developed states 'have made every effort to attack developing countries with so-called human rights abuses while turning a blind eye to their own inglorious human rights record. In fact, they have turned the Commission into a "court" where they put developing countries on trial.'[17]

A related reason for the double standard is that much of the reporting on China by the general media and human rights monitors tends to focus on particular horrific cases of human rights violations. The emphasis on individual cases, especially heart-wrenching cases that are not representative of the system as a whole, creates a misleading impression of how serious the problems are and a distorted image abroad.[18] First-time visitors to China are often bewildered when they don't see machine-gun toting soldiers in military fatigues on every corner or find ominous-looking public security agents in black trench coats lurking suspiciously in alleyways and Internet cafes. The power of horrific, individual cases to drive human rights policies toward China should not be understated.

Reporting on China frequently suffers from a number of other shortcomings that provide fodder to those seeking to portray China as an evil empire. Much of the reporting on China continues to be framed by the narrative of 'good dissidents' battling the 'oppressive authoritarian state' in a noble quest for democracy and social justice—an image constantly reinforced by the repeated playing of the now-graying footage of an individual citizen blocking the path of a tank more than fifteen years ago in Tiananmen. Indeed, the Western press still treats each passing of June 4th as a major event, while within China the broad public has already moved on, and the day is often passed without notice. Moreover, in reporting on the annual roundup of dissidents and Tiananmen Mothers, the Western press usually applies the same distorting lens of a broad-based struggle for democracy as in the first round. In 1989, the press, reflecting its own concerns rather than the actual concerns of the demonstrators, managed to take the incoherent and conflicting demands of students, which merged with popular dissatisfaction over inflation and corruption, and transform the hodgepodge into a movement for democracy. Today, the calls for reversal of the government's verdict on Tiananmen and justice for those who lost relatives are portrayed as a popular uprising for democracy. However, supporters of a reversal on Tiananmen do not necessarily support democracy. In any event, whatever the views about democracy among those who believe Tiananmen should be revisited, support for dissidents, liberals, and democracy in the form of general elections is limited among the broader public. Most people continue to focus mainly on improving their standard of living, which is entirely understandable in a country in which much of the populace lives on less than $2/day.

Human rights NGOs have historically targeted civil and political rights violations, and continue to devote most resources to such issues.[19] Reports of dissidents being arrested, newspaper editors being sacked, prisoners being tortured—these might seem to be the kind of stories one can sink one's teeth into, as opposed to dry statistics about increases in Gini coefficients and the wage differentials between men and women sorted by industrial sector. But one should just as easily be able to relate to stories of children living in shacks without water, of families so poor that they cannot afford to take dear-old granny to the hospital, or of gray-haired pensioners forced to take to the streets in protest over not being paid their paltry retirements benefits.[20] The emotive appeal of the issue alone cannot explain the difference in coverage.

Perhaps part of the fascination with civil and political rights is that they seem to be real rights—legal entitlements enforceable in courts. There is the drama of a court case, where the lone individual goes up David-like against the all-powerful state, aided only by his sidekick, the high-minded lawyer out to ensure justice despite the odds. Since most countries, including China, continue to treat most social and economic rights as nonjusticiable, advocates are forced to fall back on statistics and to make policy arguments about how resources are to be allocated. They must work through the legislative and administrative channels, a process that requires more consensus building than social activist litigation and is at odds with the confrontational and accusatory style of many human rights NGOs.

Civil and political rights issues might also seem easier to solve. While the distinction between civil and political rights as negative rights, and social and economic rights as positive rights, is easily overstated, the distinction is still significant. The latter generally do require more resources and involve larger-scale resource allocation decisions, even allowing that it is not cheap to run a democracy and establish a functional judiciary that meets the requirements of rule of law, as evidenced by the empirical studies that show a high correlation between wealth, democracy, civil and political rights, and rule of law.

Moreover, emphasizing social and economic rights leads directly to questions about globalization, global inequality, and who benefits from free trade policies and neoliberal capitalism. Perhaps citizens in developed countries simply prefer to blame evil governments for depriving people of civil and political rights rather than consider their own responsibility for global poverty, how protectionist trade measures and subsidies for domestic industries in rich countries dwarf the petty amounts of aid provided to poor countries, or how developed countries exploit technological advantages for profit through an intellectual property regime that keeps life-saving medicines out of the hands of the sick and dying in developing countries.

Whatever the reasons for the greater attention paid to civil and political rights and democracy, the nature of the reports regarding rights issues tends to skew the picture. The US State Department reports for China as well as other countries invariably start with a description of the nature of the political regime, as if that were the most significant determinant for rights in the country. To be sure, the reports only discuss civil and political rights, in itself a clear indicator of bias. The 2004 report on China begins: 'The People's Republic China . . . is an authoritarian state in which . . . the Chinese Communist Party . . . is the paramount source of power.'[21] Imagine it began instead: 'Human rights and other indicators of well-being across the board are highly correlated with wealth. China outperforms the average country in its lower-middle income category on every major indicator except civil and political rights (as is generally true for other East Asian countries).'

Since empirical studies have repeatedly demonstrated that wealth is a more important factor than regime type even with respect to civil and political rights, beginning with a statement of China's income level and a comparison to the average country in its income class would go a long way toward placing China's performance within a more meaningful comparative context, and presumably better serve the legislative intent behind the reports by allowing members of the US congress to better assess China's rights performance. It might also diminish the feeling among Chinese that China is being singled out for particularly harsh criticism because of its nondemocratic nature.

Notwithstanding China's overall steady progress across a range of human rights indicators, State Department reports in 1999, 2000, and 2001 claimed that the human rights situation deteriorated or worsened.[22] Every year the reports have painted a dismal picture, with reports from 1995 to 2001 claiming 'widespread' violations, and reports from 2002 to 2004 claiming 'numerous' and 'serious' abuses. In 1998, when the Clinton administration decided to forgo a motion to censure in favor of constructive engagement, the report began with a positive statement that progress had been made, but then immediately qualified that claim by noting that serious problems remained and China continued to commit widespread human rights abuses.[23] The only other year to begin with a positive statement was 1994.[24] In addition, brief positive statements are sometimes included in the introductory section, including praise for legal reforms, rising living standards, public sector reforms, expansion of the private sector, or government decisions to release dissidents and allow visits from the Dalai Lama and UN rights monitors. The 2001 State Department report even noted that many Chinese now have more individual choice, greater access to information, and expanded economic opportunity. However, the few clipped phrases of faint praise are buried in a long and much more detailed litany of problems and violations.

The bias against nonliberal democratic regimes is also evident in discussions of rule of law and good governance. Mentioning rule of law in relation to China often meets with wide-eyed disbelief and derision, even though China outperforms many countries, including many democracies, at its level of wealth on the World Bank's rule of law index. Some knowledgeable legal commentators even argue that China lacks a legal system.[25] One of the main reasons China's efforts to implement rule of law are so summarily dismissed is that commentators conflate rule of law with liberal democracy. For the same reason, many liberal human rights critics claim that Singapore lacks rule of law, even though Singapore's legal system is routinely ranked among the best in the world. To be sure, the US has long enjoyed a reputation as a country in which the rule of law reigns supreme despite the upholding of slavery laws, regulations that discriminated against women and denied them the right to vote, sedition laws that imposed severe limitations on free speech, and rulings that led to the internment behind barbed wire of American citizens of Japanese descent. However, the rise of the human rights movement, the preference for democracy, and a liberal interpretation of rights obscure the historical lesson that rule of law and liberal democracy need not go hand in hand.

The application of double standards is also reflected in intellectual property-related trade sanctions. Throughout the 1990s and still today, China and Russia have been guilty of widespread and roughly comparable intellectual property violations.[26] Yet while China was designated a Priority Foreign Country four times, Russia never made the list.[27] Members of the US Congress defended the differential treatment on the ground that the US needed to cut the fledgling democracy in Russia some slack.[28] Now that Putin has brushed aside the Bush administration's instructions on how to run his country, the US is taking a tougher stance.

Nowhere is the double standard more evident than with respect to military affairs. Defense Secretary Rumsfeld has criticized China for wanting to upgrade its military given that it allegedly is not threatened, and chided China for wanting to develop a military capability that extends beyond the region. At the same time, the US has established numerous security alliances in Asia, recently added Taiwan as a security concern to its treaty with Japan, sought to strengthen its strategic partnership with India in part by providing civilian nuclear technology despite India's failure to comply with the Nuclear Nonproliferation Treaty, and then sent four aircraft carriers to engage in 'war games' in the Pacific for the first time since the Vietnam war after a Quadrennial Defense Review identified China as the greatest threat to the US military. Nor did Rumsfeld explain why the US is justified in spending ten to twenty times more than China on maintaining a military capable of striking anywhere in the world while China is supposed to be content with the bare minimum necessary for self-defense.

Human rights as power politics: a grand strategy of containment?

A popular view among Chinese citizens is that other countries are holding China to a double standard as part of a grand strategy of containment. China's status as a member of the Security Council and its increasing economic clout distinguish China from other poorer, less politically powerful countries with weak human rights records, making it a special target.

There is no doubt that in some cases concerns about China's growing power leads to the demonization of China as a godless regime that brutally oppresses its people. For some critics, China has now taken over for the Soviet Union as the evil empire whose opposition helps define and affirm their own identity. The opposition to China may be particularly intense because China is both the Soviet Union, the rising military power, and Japan, the rising economic power engaging in unfair trade practices and threatening to 'buy up America,' rolled into one. For these new post-Cold War warriors, China must be prevented from becoming so powerful as to challenge American supremacy. China's ascendancy must therefore be fought at every juncture: economically, politically, and militarily. Chinese citizens' concerns about containment are not then purely a figment of their collective imagination.

Nevertheless, the underlying logic of the popular view that criticism on human rights issues is part of a grand strategy of containment is not immediately apparent: how will criticizing China on rights issues serve the purpose of containing China and prevent China from emerging as a superpower?

The direct effect on China of criticism of its record on rights seems to be minimal. To be sure, the US has linked trade benefits such as

MFN status and access to WTO to human rights violations. However, concerns over human rights violations did not prevent China from obtaining MFN status or from joining the WTO. In addition, some people, in objecting to the sale of US or Canadian companies to Chinese entities, have raised human rights issues, although the main concerns seem to be a combination of xenophobic and realpolitik worries. Little objection is made when other countries with poor human rights records purchase US or Canadian assets. Chinese companies have been thwarted in their efforts to buy some companies, and may be paying a human rights (or rising superpower) premium when they are successful. However, in general, economic sanctions have been too limited to have much of an impact on China's economy, and thus to have much of a long-term effect in slowing down China's rise to power. Furthermore, attempts to impose sanctions are offset by other efforts to assist China in revamping its economic system and achieving growth, which after all is also good for US companies and the global economy.

The US and EU have also supported an arms embargo and limitations on sale of dual use technology in part by citing China's poor record on human rights. Such limitations fit more easily with a containment strategy, and it is true that some politicians use human rights violations as an excuse to justify the embargo. However, the EU was prepared to terminate the embargo until the Bush regime pressured Tony Blair to reverse course and oppose the change on the ground that such arms could be used against the US if it ever found itself defending Taiwan against a PRC attack. But by themselves, the limitations do not seem sufficient to support a strong link between human rights criticisms and a strategy to keep China in its place.

One theory is that the criticism of China for civil and political rights violations will lead to significant policy changes, which will in turn lead to chaos or at least a much weaker state as China prematurely rushes to democratize, thus setting China back for years. Proponents of this view point out that the advocacy of human rights have led to people power movements that brought down the government in the Philippines, Indonesia, and now Ukraine and Georgia. The Bush administration reportedly also sought $85 million to promote 'political change'—which is to say regime change—in Iran by subsdizing dissidents, labor unions, and human rights activists.

Advocates of containment may believe that a democratic China would pose less of a threat, and might believe the economic growth will lead to a demand for civil and political rights, which will in turn lead to a demand for democracy and regime change. However, China is not Iran, and the Hu administration is not Hamas. Gambling that democracy would weaken China without plunging it into chaos would be an extremely high risk strategy. Few if any of China's harshest critics would wish for chaos to stall China's march toward power given the negative consequences for everyone if China becomes unstable.

Another possibility is that criticizing China on human rights deprives China of legitimacy and 'soft power,' thus making it more difficult for China to persuade others to join it in pursuing policies that serve China's interests. China has spent time and political resources fending off motions to censure. However, China has also managed to pursue a number of bilateral and multilateral relationships, including a stronger alliance with Russia and a stronger ASEAN. Indeed, the charm offensive of the Hu and Wen regime is widely perceived to be more effective in winning over allies in Asia than Bush's war on terror-driven, 'either you are with me or against me,' policies. Notwithstanding such diplomatic successes, the demonization of China may have impeded China's international influence to some extent.

Generally, countries gain little by making a major issue of human rights violations in other countries—which is why they rarely do it. Why then do the United States and to a lesser extent European countries risk upsetting economic relations with China by constantly raising human rights issues? The most likely explanation is that most Americans and Europeans genuinely believe democracy and liberal rights are best for everyone, including Chinese. The spread of democracy and freedom has been part of American political culture for a long time, and central aspects of the foreign policies of presidents from Wilson to Carter to Reagan and now to Bush.

President Bush, who has undertaken the mission of spreading the US's way of life around the globe with all of the fervor of a religious zealot, has proudly declared: 'Our nation's cause has always been larger than our nation's defense. We fight, as we always fight, for a just peace—a peace that favors human liberty . . . Building this just peace is America's opportunity and America's duty.'[29] The administration's statement on America's National Security Strategy is equally adamant about the benefits of following the American way:[30]

> In pursuit of our goals, our first imperative is to clarify what we stand for: the United States must defend liberty and justice because these principles are right and true for all people everywhere. No nation owns these aspirations, and no nation is exempt from them. . . . America must stand firmly for the nonnegotiable demands of human dignity: the rule of law; limits on the absolute power of the state; free speech; freedom of worship; equal justice; respect for women; religious and ethnic tolerance; and respect for private property.

To be sure, not everyone shares 'the American' conception—as if there were one unified American view—or more particularly the Bush regime's conception of justice, liberty or rule of law, or of what constitutes proper restrictions on free speech, or how the principles of religious and ethnic tolerance are to be squared with the need to preserve order in the face of ethnic violence and secession movements.

Even when the criticisms of China are motivated by good intentions, those in China who do not share the same ideals or who do not believe they are appropriate for China now may still perceive the efforts to promote such values as a form of hegemony. Persaud helpfully distinguishes between three forms of American hegemony.[31] *Primitive hegemony*, closely associated with neoconservative thinking and containment theories, maintains that it is natural and appropriate for the US to pursue its own interests at the expense of other countries or the international order. If necessary, the US should set aside international law and rely on the threat or use of coercive force to achieve American goals. *Enlightened hegemony*, which makes more concessions to liberal thought, emphasizes that America does not have the power to achieve its interests alone in this increasingly interdependent world, and thus attaches more importance to peace, cooperation, and multilateralism. *Benevolent hegemony* is more cultural and based on the missionary zeal to do good in the world by bringing American values and way of life to everyone. Americans, reconstructed as a single harmonious people with common values, are the chosen people whose mission, should they accept it, is to save the world. Whatever the difference in methods and motives, all three share a conviction that American-style capital markets, democracy, rule of law, and liberal rights are superior and universally desirable. They all assume Americans know what is best for other people.

The hubris is astounding, and all too often lethal. The First Gulf War was estimated to have resulted in 100,000 civilian deaths.[32] In response to the criticism that 4,000–5,000 children were dying every month in Iraq as a result of US intervention, Secretary of State Madeleine Albright blithely declared that 'we think the price is worth it.'[33]

According to US human rights reports, a ruler who claims the right to decide what is best for the people is considered a dictator. A country where citizens are not allowed to participate in the decision-making process over life and death matters is considered authoritarian. Paradoxically, the US, the leader of the free world, decides for others what is in their best interests and imposes the costs of its decisions on them in the name of democracy.

To be sure, the zeal of some American politicians for exporting liberal democracy is not necessarily shared to the same degree by the broad public. Despite a moral streak in American political culture, there is little public support for a moral crusade abroad in the name of human rights. For most Americans, promoting democracy and human rights trails far behind such practical and realpolitik concerns as protecting US jobs, safeguarding the interests of US businesses abroad, securing adequate supplies of energy, and defending the security of our allies.[34] The commitment to democracy and rights for everyone is broad but shallow. As a result, American human rights policy is inconsistent and incoherent. Notwithstanding all of the political grandstanding, harsh criticisms of China's record and calls for sanctions cannot obtain the support of the majority when confronted with the costs in terms of US business interests and other foreign policy objectives. In the end, US actions fall short of the high-minded rhetoric, and human rights concerns take a back seat to the war on terrorism, the need to secure China's cooperation in resolving the Korean peninsula crisis, and increased opportunities for American companies to do business in China. But linking human rights criticisms with issues of outsourcing, the value of the RMB and the budget deficit appears to many Chinese as nothing more than a cynical manipulation of human rights to further US economic and geopolitical interests.

THE GOVERNMENT'S OWN SHORTCOMINGS

Although reporting on China reflects a bias against nonliberal democratic regimes, the PRC government has itself to blame for much of the bad press. The government has largely ceded the public relations battlefield to international NGOs by failing to hold public trials or restricting access to trials, by failing to publish judgments in controversial cases, and by refusing to allow independent monitors access to prisons and other sites to investigate allegations of abuses. The lack of transparency, combined with the egregious nature of some violations, leads people to suspect the worst, feeding the stereotypical image of China as a repressive totalitarian state.

While the government has acknowledged and been reasonably open with respect to problems in areas other than civil and political rights, it continues to hide behind broad claims of state secrets and national security to prevent public debate in many politically sensitive civil and political rights cases. If government leaders believe that their administration's general positions on human rights issues as well as the outcomes in specific cases are defensible, then they should permit all but the rare politically sensitive cases that genuinely involve state secrets to be tried in public, with the defendants afforded all of the due process protection promised by PRC and international law. The government should also disclose as much information as possible and hold parts of the trial open even when state secrets and national security issues are involved. The international community would then have a better sense of the facts and the relevant issues, legal and otherwise.

Given the potential for instability and other circumstances such as majoritarian value preferences that fall within a reasonable margin of appreciation, the government in all likelihood will impose more restrictions on civil and political rights than do economically advanced, politically stable Western liberal democracies. Undoubtedly, there would still be disagreements over the outcomes of particular cases, the wisdom of particular policies, and the legality under international law of certain acts, just as there are debates over these issues in other countries. The government could then address these concerns through its white papers on human rights. Academics and citizens could also debate the issues. As heads of an emerging superpower and responsible member of the international community, Chinese leaders should have the courage of their convictions, be willing to subject their decisions and actions to international and domestic scrutiny, and revise their policies as appropriate.

Conclusion: the benefits of avoiding a double standard

To recognize that China is being held to a double standard is not to excuse human rights violations or to diminish the urgency of addressing the problems. On the contrary, acknowledging that China is subject to a double standard clears the way for a more effective engagement with China on human rights issues. Apart from the inherent desirability of greater fairness, a more even-handed and accurate assessment of China's human rights situation within a broader comparative perspective will soften the aggressive defensiveness of the government. So doing will allow all sides to work together in a more cooperative fashion to achieve feasible solutions consistent with China's level of economic development and contingent circumstances.

Acknowledging the areas in which China has made considerable progress also highlights the areas where progress has been slower. Government leaders have reached out to the foreign community for assistance on many rights issues. Government leaders might be more willing to revisit sensitive issues regarding free speech, religious freedoms, and the rights of minorities if they felt their concerns were taken more seriously, and the difficulties that many countries face on these issues were acknowledged. Even if the balance drawn between individual liberties and stability, national security, and state interests remains contested, a more balanced approach would help clarify the areas of genuine disagreement.

A more balanced approach on human rights issues would facilitate cooperation on other issues from nuclear proliferation to international terrorism to environmental degradation. It would also soften a growing politics of resentment and nationalism, and thus may contribute to a less confrontational relationship between China and Western powers as they attempt to negotiate a new balance of power in keeping with China's growing economic, political, and military influence.

CHAPTER SIX

Institutional reform: rule of law and good governance

Critics are often quick to attribute any failure in governance—whether the belated response to SARS, AIDS, or natural disasters, shortcomings in the implementation of rule of law, or widespread corruption—to China's political system, while downplaying similar problems in democratic states.[1] Yet the government has managed to maintain political stability and steady growth despite such unexpected and potentially disruptive events as the Asian financial crisis, SARS, increases in oil prices after September 11th and the war in Iraq, and rising trade protectionism and hostility toward China in Europe and America. In that regard, China is like other East Asian states that reacted quickly and effectively to macroeconomic shocks from the oil crises in the 1970s and 80s, sudden decreases in world demand for exports, the Asian financial crisis, and the devastating tsunami in 2004. Insulated to some extent from the political pressures facing government officials in democratic states, East Asian governments have relied on technocratic administrators and a flexible, pragmatic approach to respond quickly and effectively to pressing events.

The quality of governance is reflected in the World Bank good governance indicators, with China outperforming or at least doing as well as the average country in its income class, including many democracies, on the core indicators.

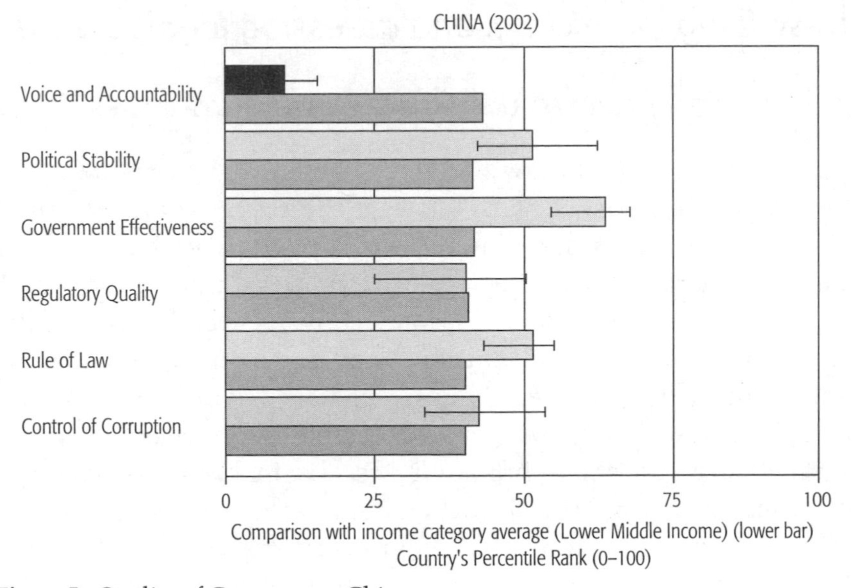

Figure 5. Quality of Governance: China
Source: World Bank Governance Indicators (2003).

This chapter applies and evaluates existing conceptual tools for describing, predicting, and assessing legal reforms in China, in the process shedding light on the various pathways and methodologies of reform to facilitate assessment of competing strategies. While drawing on China for concrete examples, the discussion involves issues that are generally applicable to comparative law and the efforts to implement rule of law in other developing countries, and thus addresses the broader issue of what we know and don't know about law and development. The case studies of particular reforms demonstrate the complexity of the reform process, its path-dependent nature and the political nature of reforms. China's relative success to date supports a more pragmatic, less ideologically driven, approach to reforms. The examples also illustrate the difficulties of China's legal reform project and why reforms in developing countries all too often fail. After considering what lessons China's experiences provide for the law and development movement, I discuss the challenges reformers in China face at this critical juncture.

Describing, predicting, and assessing legal reforms

DESCRIBING REFORMS: HORIZONTAL METAPHORS

The dominant trope in law and development has been the 'legal transplant.'[2] Dissatisfied with some of the connotations of transplants, commentators have offered a host of alternative metaphors and catchy phrases, including legal irritant,[3] legal translation,[4] legal transformation,[5] legal transposition,[6] convergence/divergence/differentiation,[7] selective adaptation,[8] and institutional monocropping.[9] Not to be outdone, Chinese scholars have their own rich metaphorical lexicon: *bentu ziyuan* (native resources),[10] the ever-popular X (e.g. rule of law, human rights, criminal law, judicial independence, discovery rules) with Chinese characteristics, which echoes the turn of the century motto of 'Chinese as substance, Western as means' (*zhongti, xiyong*) itself a distant echo of the Confucian notion of harmony but not identity (*he er bu tong*).[11]

Each has advantages and disadvantages. In general, they differ primarily with respect to the degree of change in the target country's legal system, the amount of target country agency, and the open-endedness of the reform process as compared to a steady procession toward a predetermined end.

Taken as a botanical metaphor, *legal transplant* suggests a teleological development toward a fixed endpoint—legal systems will mature into a robust liberal democratic rule of law just as Aristotle's tiny acorn will one day become a sturdy oak tree. Of course, some transplants may not survive, given the different soil and weather conditions. Similarly, some legal systems may fail to grow into a full-fledged liberal democratic rule of law. The risk of incompatibility is even clearer when 'legal transplant' is understood as a medical rather than botanical metaphor. Just as some recipients of organ transplants may reject incompatible tissue, so may some systems reject liberal democratic rule of law or more particular institutional reforms or practices.

The medical interpretation suggests that the transplant may lead to discrete changes without any overall systemic change: although an organ is replaced, the recipient is still the same person. The botanical reading suggests the possibility of fundamental system change, although more discrete changes are also possible: a change in the rules for mortgaging property that is based on common law practices need not lead to the replacement of a civil law tradition with common law, much less to a fundamental change in the conception of rule of law. In contrast, '*legal irritant*' captures the way a new rule or practice may disrupt the existing legal culture and current legal practices, sometimes in unexpected and far-reaching ways.

The *legal translation* metaphor highlights how donors and recipients may understand and interpret a rule in diverse ways. Broad principles such as 'presumption of innocence' or 'due process' have been construed very differently in different legal systems, and even quite differently over time within the same legal system. Even seemingly specific legal terms are often indeterminate in important ways. This may result in different interpretations and applications, as critical legal scholars and postmodern devotees have labored to point out. Simply copying legal codes, without any understanding of how subsequent interpretations may have twisted 'the plain meaning' beyond all recognition for laypeople, suggests that much will be left out in translation, unless the translator is deeply familiar with the actual practice in the source country. Conversely, on the recipient side, deeply ingrained beliefs may lead to misunderstandings or creative misinterpretations, much as when key Buddhist concepts were given a Taoist flavor in the transmission of Buddhism to China.[12]

Whereas the processes of legal transplantation and translation are primarily unidirectional, the triad of *convergence/divergence/differentiation* opens up the possibility that all legal systems may be changing, and that change may occur in multiple directions. For instance, globalization has caused changes to legal systems in traditional exporter states in Euro-America as well as in the developing countries that are normally the importers. Moreover, the process can be interactive, as in the 'race to the bottom' as countries continually change their tax codes, labor rules, and social security policies to compete for foreign investment.

Legal transformation, *legal transposition*, and *selective adaptation* also call attention to the fact that institutions, rules, and practices may be changed in the process of adoption. However, selective adaptation places more emphasis on target-country agency. Rather than being merely passive recipients, legal actors in the target state actively choose elements and reject others, interpret terms consistent with local perceptions and understandings, and modify or rework institutions, rules, or practices in light of domestic circumstances.

X with Chinese characteristics also suggests agency adaptation, while *Chinese as substance, Western as means* suggests that the degree of localization will be significant, with legal reforms driven mainly by domestic concerns.[13] The latter also suggests (incorrectly in my view) that China's leaders may view legal reforms as an instrumental fix for some technical problems but that the transition to rule of law will not fundamentally change the nature of the political order.

While useful in some respects, all of these metaphors share three common shortcomings.[14] First, as illustrated below, they tend to oversimplify the reform process.

Second, all allow for some degree of change in the process of transmission, but do not specify or quantify the amount of change beyond which the original becomes something new and different. Take, for instance, the triad of convergence/divergence/differentiation. These distinctions are always a matter of degree, particularly in a country as large as China. Depending on one's focus, one can describe the overall trajectory of change in China's legal system as well as changes in particular institutions, rules, or practices in terms of all three. There has been some movement in the direction of rule of law, even a liberal democratic rule of law, and constitutionalism,[15] and yet at the same time one could find evidence of divergence and differentiation. Similarly, there seems no way in principle to distinguish between a transplant that has been selectively adapted and a new hybrid, or between a new interpretation of a translated rule and a new and different rule. At some point of specificity, every system is unique: X with Chinese characteristics is banal unless one specifies the meaningful differences between X and its counterparts in other countries.[16] Whether the differences are meaningful will depend on one's purpose in comparing the systems. As there are many reasons to compare legal systems, there will be no single standard.

Third, and perhaps most importantly, these metaphors, while useful in describing legal reforms, do not help predict or explain which foreign models are likely to be adopted and why, which transplanted institutions, rules, or practices will take hold and which will be rejected, or which native resources or Chinese characteristics will become part of the legal system in China. The explanatory or predictive project requires further specification and testing of a range of variables, as will be discussed shortly. First, however, a few words on vertical metaphors.

DESCRIBING REFORMS: VERTICAL METAPHORS

While the previous metaphors emphasized a horizontal relationship between a source country and recipient, metaphors such as *top-down* versus *bottom-up* or *deductive* versus *inductive* invoke a vertical dimension. Many commentators have argued that legal reforms in China have been 'top-down'—orchestrated by the central government and Party leaders—with some commentators praising this approach and others criticizing it. Central authorities clearly have played a key role in setting the direction for reform and approving major policy changes such as the shift to a more law-based order. However, in practice, many, if not most, specific reform initiatives originate at lower levels as judges, prosecutors, lawyers, and officials working in the system attempt to solve problems encountered in carrying out their duties.[17]

Whereas a deductive approach to regulation attempts to derive appropriate rules, practices, or institutions from a pre-given set of general principles or models, an inductive approach identifies a problem, examines the various solutions to the problem to identify patterns and general principles, and then tests the principles by applying them in different contexts and observing the results or consequences. Thus, in one version of the inductive model, the first step is to identify the problem. The next task is benchmarking, which entails surveying promising ways of solving the problem that are superior to those currently used, yet within the existing (local) system's capacity to emulate and eventually surpass. After that comes simultaneous engineering, where interested parties propose changes to the provisional design or solution based on their own experiences and needs. The final component is error correction and learning by monitoring: participants and independent actors monitor progress by pooling information from their own experiments with information from other localities about the results of their approach to similar problems.[18]

In general, deduction is associated with foreign models transplanted to China and implemented in a top-down fashion. In this approach, foreign governments, foreign legal experts, and international development agencies are likely to play a significant role in the reform process, as they are most familiar with the foreign model. One example would be the attempts of international actors to promote a highly particularistic liberal democratic conception of rule of law in China based on the legal systems of Western Europe and America. A more specific example would be calls by UN organs and international NGOs to eliminate all forms of administrative detention, based on assumptions about criminal law and the protection of individual rights derived from the experiences of other countries, which are then applied to China without further consideration of the actual costs and benefits of eliminating detention.

In contrast, induction shares greater affinities with a bottom-up approach that gives a more prominent role to local actors in recognizing problems and devising solutions. As we shall see, China has developed a number of institutions and practices to overcome the problems of judicial corruption and the lack of competence of some judges, including reliance on an adjudicative committee of senior judges to review cases and individual case supervision by the procuracy, people's congress, and the judiciary itself.

It is possible to mix and match some of these elements and thus produce different strategies for reform (and most likely considerable confusion in terminology in the absence of concrete examples). The reform agenda of some countries might be dictated largely if not exclusively by domestic concerns, and it might be top-down or bottom-up, deductive or inductive (or both). Similarly, foreign actors might advocate an inductive approach by emphasizing local knowledge and local participation in agenda setting and implementation.

PREDICTION

While descriptive metaphors continue to proliferate, there has been less progress in identifying the factors that lead to successful transplants or to convergence rather than divergence, or in testing the factors that might favor deductive approaches rather than inductive approaches or vice versa.[19] Nevertheless, empirical studies in other areas have made some progress in sorting out key components behind social, legal, and political change.[20] These studies as well as past experience suggest several important factors.

One factor in the adoption of a model is the *prestige, power, and normative appeal of the exporter* or promoter. The US, EU, and individual European countries often advocate their own models for capital markets, corporate governance, criminal law, and so on. Although the EU has dedicated more funds to rule of law programs in China than the US government has, US-based models have an advantage in that many Chinese legal scholars study in the US and hence are most familiar with the US system. Moreover, the literature on the US is easily accessible and in English. The US also exercises influence indirectly through the international development agencies such as the IMF and World Bank, through international legal regimes such as WTO and the UN human rights system, and through NGOs.

Domestically, the *prestige, power, and normative appeal of the local promoters* who back the import or a local alternative also plays a role, especially when there is division among the ruling elite as to which path to take. More generally, the lack of local ownership is one of the main reasons for the failure of legal reform projects sponsored by the international community.

Interest group politics—who will benefit and who will be harmed—also explains why some reforms are adopted and others are not, and why some foreign models are adapted in particular ways in China. Opposition may come from actors within the legal system such as the bar association or senior members of the judiciary who benefit from the current system, however inefficient or corrupt.

The nature and relative robustness of *civil society* is another factor. In some cases, reformers will be able to mobilize civil society to overcome the lack of political will at the state level or elite opposition to reforms. In other cases, civil society may be weak, or divided about the merits of legal reform in general or particular legal reforms. Bottom-up approaches often rely on greater participation by citizens, NGOs, and civil society. Part of the problem with exporting bottom-up approaches based on deliberative democracy is that they assume civil society in developing countries will be equally robust and play the same role as in Western liberal democracies. This will often not be the case.[21]

Economic factors (GDP per capita, growth rates, amounts of foreign direct investment) affect the demand for rule of law and the ability of a country to afford reforms and operate an efficient legal system staffed by well-trained and well-paid professionals immune from corruption. Apart from GDP levels, the distribution of wealth, the degree of marketization, and whether the money was earned through broad-based market activities or is 'easy' money derived from the sale of oil or other natural resources may also be factors.[22]

The *nature of the political regime* is another factor, as is the level of development of political institutions. Some institutions and practices that work well in a liberal democracy may not work so well or may not be feasible in China; conversely, some institutions or practices that work well in China would not be acceptable in a liberal democracy.

Even when there is no ideological barrier to transplantation, local institutions may lack the *institutional capacity* to implement reforms. China has had to rebuild virtually from scratch key institutions such as the courts, procuracy, law schools, and the legal profession, all of which were weakened or destroyed during the Cultural Revolution. Nevertheless, legal reformers in China still enjoyed the benefit of a relatively strong state and political stability. Reformers in failed states or transitional states undergoing regime change as a result of war face even greater challenges. As in Iraq, leaders of the new government have their hands full simply restoring law and order, and thus may be diverted from focusing on economic, political, and legal reforms.

A related issue is *institutional culture* and the *compatibility of reforms* with institutional norms and practices. China's civil and criminal law systems were based on an amalgam of civil, socialist, and traditional law. Efforts to introduce elements of a common law system have challenged the theoretical underpinning and normative assumptions of the existing system, and required judges, prosecutors, and lawyers to adopt different roles. Similarity in legal systems facilitates understanding between external and internal actors, reduces system friction, and decreases the likelihood of unexpected consequences arising. At minimum, reforms are likely to be more effective when relevant actors are familiar with the laws, practices, or institutions being adopted. Fortunately, in this era of mixed legal systems, many key actors will be aware of the general features of other systems.

As the case studies below illustrate, many other factors could be added to the list depending on the particular issue at stake, including population size, ethnic diversity, cultural traditions, and religious beliefs, and unforeseeable events like a particularly egregious case of injustice that results in a public clamor for change.

APPRAISAL AND EVALUATION: THE NORMATIVE DIMENSION

In the end, how we describe reforms or whether the process is one of induction or deduction—i.e.—'how we get there'—may not matter as much as the results. While in some cases the results may be clearly preferable, in other cases they may be more difficult to assess. Is it enough that people comply with the new regulations or institutions? Of course, people could comply with bad rules or bad systems.

To be sure, compliance is not always a minimal accomplishment—surely government leaders in China would appreciate greater compliance with tax payment rules and less tax avoidance. On the other hand, low compliance does not necessarily mean a law is not effective. There is very little compliance with speed limits on US highways. However, the laws are still effective in that most people do not exceed the speed limit by more than 5 m.p.h. (depending on how strict enforcement is). Conversely, a high level of compliance may not mean a law is effective because compliance may have been obtained by setting a low standard that did not require change in behavior.[23]

The passing of a law may also serve a variety of functions, some of which may have little to do with either compliance or effectiveness in the sense of behavioral change. For instance, many countries sign human rights treaties with no intention of complying or changing behavior. Rather, they do so because the costs of ratifying human rights treaties have been low, and they may be able to avoid censure or send a signal that they are on their way to becoming good members of the international community. The annual vote in Geneva to censure China for human rights violations (more accurately, civil and political rights violations) and China's bid to hold the Olympics influenced the timing of China's signature of the ICESCR. Similarly, in 2004, China passed a redundant regulation against soccer hooliganism presumably to assure foreign critics, upset by the anti-Japanese behavior of Chinese during the final of the Asia Cup in Beijing, that China was capable of holding the Olympics in 2008.

Legal reforms may also be assessed in terms of economic efficiency and wealth maximization. But should reforms be judged against a Pareto or Kaldor–Hicks efficiency standard,[24] or against a standard of equity or justice, perhaps one that reflects current human rights standards? If assessed against current human rights standards, should all rights in the ever-expanding corpus of rights treaties be treated equally? Using justice as the standard raises the issue of 'whose justice?'

A second concern in assessing reforms is whether the standard should be an absolute or relative one that takes into consideration levels of wealth and other contingent circumstances.

Moreover, regulatory reforms may take time to take hold. What may seem like a terrible mistake may turn out to be a success with the passing of time. Some reforms may also set the stage for future reforms. Intermediate benchmarks are necessary to avoid unduly dismissive assessments because of disappointing progress on long-term goals.

Case studies of legal reforms

RULE OF LAW

One of the biggest regulatory innovations in China in the last twenty-five years has been the transition to rule of law (the only other comparable change being the transition to a market economy). Some may doubt the transition to rule of law is an innovation, even allowing that the move toward a more law-based regulatory system represents a drastic change from Mao-era governance. China's efforts to implement rule of law are typically described in terms of a transplant deduced from a pre-given foreign model and implemented in top-down fashion by the central government. The assumption is often that China is moving toward a liberal democratic conception of rule of law. This assumption is unfounded, at least for the short term (and I have argued for the medium and long terms as well), and misses what is innovative about rule of law in China. China has not attempted to mimic some ideal Western legal order, much less to import wholesale a liberal democratic rule of law.[25] The first hint that something might be awry with the standard assumption/description should be the government's declaration, now incorporated into the constitution, that China is in the process of establishing a *socialist rule of law state*. To be sure, there are competing conceptions of rule of law in China, as there are elsewhere.[26]

The complexity of the process of implementing rule of law in China illustrates the previously discussed shortcomings in commonly used metaphors. The process has involved much more innovation from the bottom than usually suggested. At minimum, it is fair to say the process has been both top-down and bottom-up. Nor is the deductive/inductive distinction very useful when applied to the question of why Chinese leaders endorsed rule of law after Mao. Chinese leaders faced a lack of economic growth, a history of arbitrary rule with power often in the hands of a single person, and flagging legitimacy, among other problems. They may have induced from the examples of other states that rule of law might be a solution to these problems. Or perhaps they deduced this conclusion from the general principle (itself derived from empirical studies and case studies) that rule of law contributes to economic growth, limits government arbitrariness, and enhances legitimacy.

Horizontal metaphors are equally problematic. Most horizontal metaphors highlight the Western origin of rule of law and the transmission to China. Yet China embarked on legal reforms for its own purposes, and the reform agenda has been driven primarily by domestic concerns. Even allowing that reformers have looked to foreign legal systems for guidance, the conception and implementation of rule of law in China as reflected in current institutions, rules, and practices are significantly different from any existing legal system in the West or any paradigmatic 'Western rule of law ideal.' Describing China's rule of law as a transplant or translation of an original Western prototype fails to capture the significant indigenous contribution to a new and unique model of rule of law: statist socialist rule of law.

Of course, many will question whether a socialist rule of law is really rule of law, especially given the many imperfections in the legal system and well-documented human rights abuses.[27] This concern reflects a second shortcoming with horizontal metaphors mentioned earlier: horizontal metaphors offer little guidance in telling us whether the changes are so significant that we are dealing with a funny-looking transplant, a hybrid or a new species altogether.

Nor do the horizontal metaphors shed much light on why some features are adopted and others rejected. Defenders of rule of law with Chinese characteristics or native resources provide precious little guidance regarding which characteristics will or should become part of rule of law. In the end, these slogans serve mainly as a caution that imported ideas, rules, and practices will be adapted in light of local circumstances. This is of course true. But which factors will determine which foreign or indigenous elements survive and which die out? What will determine whether the attempts to implement rule of law will fail or succeed?

The nature of *the political system* has received most attention in China, with many commentators arguing that rule of law is incompatible with single party socialism. However, as we have seen, democracy is neither necessary nor sufficient for rule of law.

In short, regime type will influence the contours of rule of law in China and may place some constraints on its implementation, particularly with respect to cases involving political issues that threaten the rule of the Party. On the other hand, China clearly has made great strides toward implementing a legal system that meets the requirements of a thin rule of law in recent years, and may continue to do so for years to come before reaching its potential within the current political structure. China's political regime has made possible some institutions and practices such as review by adjudicative committees and individual case supervision by the procuracy and people's congress that would be difficult to reconcile with conceptions of judicial independence and separation of power principles in liberal democracies.

Cultural factors have also been cited for many of China's problems, with some commentators arguing that China's Confucian heritage, authoritarian past, and reliance on social networks may prevent or at least make more difficult the implementation of rule of law. When starkly stated, this view verges on Orientalism.[28] Clearly other Asian states have implemented legal systems that score highly on rule of law indices. Nevertheless, cultural factors may play a role in implementation of rule of law and in the adoption and operation of particular institutions or the application of particular rules.[29] For instance, administrative litigation remains under-utilized in part because people are still getting used to the idea that citizens may sue officials. Differences in local customs and national laws may lead to deviations in implementation from law on the books, especially in criminal law and family law issues. Similarly, traditional attitudes toward substantive justice sometimes lead to inflated expectations from the legal system, and frivolous or excessive litigation where parties ask the court to make up for shortcomings in the welfare system or the lack of unemployment insurance, even if that entails setting aside the law and acting illegally in the name of equity or social justice.

Culture is not however the main obstacle to realization of rule of law in China. Many of the most serious impediments are *institutional*. Twenty-five years of reforms have greatly strengthened the courts, procuracy, police, legal profession, administrative law, and legislative systems. Nevertheless, these institutions are still weak by developed country standards. It takes decades to create efficient, professional, and clean institutions. It also takes time to change institutional culture.

China's institutional problems are however also a function of *wealth*, as is generally true elsewhere. At very low levels of development, the formal legal system may not play a great role in the economy. However, the demand for an efficient and fair legal system rises as the economy develops. This leads to more investment in institutions, including higher salaries and more training. Mechanisms of accountability to ensure efficient and fair outcomes are also developed, including anti-corruption commissions, internal review processes, and in China channels for individual case supervision by the procuracy and people's congress. The result is more professionalism and better performance. But such changes take time and resources. Developing countries simply cannot afford some of the 'solutions' to institutional problems available to richer countries. For example, judges in many of the legal systems that score the highest on rule of law indices tend to be highly paid, at least by PRC standards. But increasing salaries to the point where judges need not rely on corruption to live a decent life may not be possible in China given all the other pressing financial demands on the government.[30] In response to the comment from a German lawyer at an international conference in Beijing that judicial corruption is not a major problem in Germany because judges are highly paid, a member of the PRC judiciary noted that some poor counties in Western China often owe judges several months back pay.

How then do we assess efforts to implement rule of law in China to date? The assessment will differ depending on one's time frame. If one takes a snapshot view, there are still many problems. Individuals living and working in the system are likely to be frustrated by ongoing problems, and highly critical. However, if one considers that rule of law took centuries to establish in Western states, the progress in China in less than thirty years is remarkable.

Similarly, if one compares China against the standards of legal systems in the US or Europe, or against the idealized version of how those legal systems function or the utopian, perfectionist requirements of human rights activists, then one will be bitterly disappointed about 'the lack of rule of law in China.' But given the importance of wealth, comparing poor countries to rich countries is like comparing a piano to a duck. If on the other hand, one compares China's legal system against the standard of other developing countries, then one cannot help but be more positive about the accomplishments to date and prospects for the future.

The outcome of the assessment will also depend on which aspect of the legal system one focuses on. Different areas of law are also progressing at different rates, with the commercial law area among the strongest. The quality of the judiciary varies by level of the court, the region, the type of case, and the division within the court. Most of the worst problems with judicial corruption and competence are in basic level courts. On the whole, courts in the more developed eastern region and in larger cities are more advanced than courts in the western or middle region and in small towns. Of course, a professional, competent, and honest judiciary is only one of the institutions required for a functional legal system: the legislature, police, procuracy, as well as the legal, notary, and accounting professions are all progressing at different rates and confronting their own set of sometimes overlapping issues.

Many of the reforms have increased the efficiency and the fairness of the legal system as a whole, as indicated in the higher scores on the World Bank rule of law index, which largely reflects the elements of a thin or procedural rule of law. Evaluating the system in terms of broader standards such as justice or human rights is more controversial because justice means different things to different people, and human rights are much contested, especially once one moves beyond the broad wish-list of oftentimes abstract rights in international treaties to how those broad provisions are to be interpreted and implemented in practice.

CRIMINAL LAW: A ROCKY ROAD TO AN ADVERSARIAL SYSTEM

One of the most significant reforms in criminal law was the transition from an inquisitorial system to a more adversarial system in the mid-1990s. In an inquisitorial system, a judge or prosecutor conducts the pretrial investigation; detention periods tend to be long, with little role for the lawyer, who is often limited to brief visits with the accused after initial questioning; at trial, the judge actively pursues the truth by questioning witnesses and overseeing the production of evidence. The process is structured as a search for truth conducted by impartial officers of the state. In contrast, in an adversarial system, the process is structured as a contest between the parties. Judges are not involved in pretrial investigation; lawyers play a much larger role both before and during the trial; and the judge serves as a passive umpire at trial.[31] Thus, the move to an adversarial system radically altered the role of procuratorates, judges, and lawyers. The 1996 amendments also provided a number of rights to protect the accused, including earlier access to a lawyer, the right to review documents and call witnesses, the right to post bail, and limits on the length of detention.

The extent to which the changes were attributable to foreign pressure as opposed to domestic demands is difficult to determine as China's criminal system was under attack both abroad and at home by those working within the legal system. Again, China did not simply attempt to import wholesale a particular foreign model—much to the dismay of foreign critics.[32] Nevertheless, the changes clearly reflected a shift from an inquisitorial system toward an adversarial one, and thus could be considered more of an import than a homegrown product (although the inquisitorial model itself was an earlier import from Germany and Japan). The change reflected the increased familiarity of Chinese reformers with US law and the prestige and power of the US that arguably has led to the Americanization of criminal law, as reflected in the trend to interpret the rights provided in the ICCPR and other international treaties in terms of an adversarial model.[33]

The central authorities hailed the changes as a milestone on the road to rule of law, and issued the usual notices to the relevant state actors urgently encouraging them to faithfully implement the reforms. Unfortunately, implementation has proven disappointing: lawyers have been routinely denied access to their clients, the prosecutors have refused to turn over exculpatory evidence or provide defense counsel access to all the information in the dossier, defense counsel have been unable to question key witnesses who often do not show up at court to testify, the high rate of confessions has reduced the role of lawyers to one of seeking leniency, and allegations of torture remain common.[34]

What accounts for these difficulties? Are they the result of political ideology—the repressive authoritarian state is out to persecute criminal defendants and repress political dissidents, as commonly suggested in Western news accounts? Political ideology is at best only a small factor. Most cases are just run-of-the-mill criminal cases involving theft, murder, rape, drugs, and the like. While crime disrupts social order, criminals do not directly challenge the Party's right to rule. To be sure, the government has an interest in maintaining law and order, as do all governments. But what makes criminal cases special, and distinguishes criminal law from other areas of law, is that there is little support for criminal law reforms on the part of the public; most citizens see such reforms as harming, rather than furthering, their interests. The government has responded to the fears of the public by acceding to citizens' demands to crack down on crime. Thus, interest group politics explains much of the harsh crackdown on crime, much as they explain the war on crime in other countries.

The harsh treatment of criminals is also the result of cultural factors, including majoritarian preferences for social stability; a tendency to favor the interest of the group over the individual; and the lack of a strong tradition of individual rights. The traditional emphasis on substantive justice also makes it harder to take the procedural rights of criminals seriously.

Economic factors and social change also play an important role in undermining efforts at criminal reform. Industrialization, urbanization, and a transition to a market economy generally lead to rising crime rates, particularly when combined, as they usually are, with increased social and economic inequality. Similarly, in China, market reforms have led to higher crime rates, reflecting the re-emergence of criminal activity such as violent crime, organized crime, drug-related crime, prostitution, and gambling.

The rise in crime from economic transition has undermined efforts to implement liberal criminal law reforms in many countries. Immediately after the fall of socialism, many of the former Soviet republics, often with the advice of human rights groups, enacted liberal criminal laws that afforded suspected criminals the procedural safeguards lacking during the Soviet period. However, the rising crime rates that followed in the wake of the transition to a market economy resulted in a popular backlash that led to a rollback in the recently enacted rights for the accused.[35]

Institutional factors again play a significant role. China's weak legal institutions have been unable to stand up to the combined pressure from an angry public demanding heavy punishments to deter criminals and a political regime seeking to shore up its legitimacy by pandering to the public's appetite for vengeance. Indeed, key institutions have not been fully committed to reforms. Not surprisingly perhaps given their law and order orientation, the police and procuracy in particular have resisted many of the changes. However, even the judiciary has seemed at best lukewarm about the changes.

Moreover, the amendments fundamentally altered the roles of the police, prosecutors, judges, and defense bar, upsetting the balance of power among them and challenging longstanding institutional norms. The police and prosecutors, who stood to lose the most, have resisted yielding power to the courts and defense bar. The police and procuracy are in a difficult position. On the one hand, crime rates are inevitably going to rise given the larger trends of marketization, urbanization, and modernization. On the other, as institutions, the police and procuracy have lost, and will inevitably continue to lose, power to the courts, defense bar, and the people's congresses as China moves toward a more law-based order. Accordingly, they will bear much of the blame for failing to curb crimes while at the same time suffering diminished powers to fight the war. The result has been a series of petty but highly symbolic skirmishes, such as over whether prosecutors are required to stand up when judges enter the room and whether judges may sit at elevated podiums. More seriously, the procuracy has sought increased powers of supervision over individual court decisions and issued a series of interpretations that restrict the rights of criminals provided by the amendments. The interpretations are at odds with SPC interpretations or the even more expansive interpretations of the defense bar and some legal academics. The police have also opposed legislative changes that would restrict the Ministry of Public Security's rule-making capacity and impose more procedural and substantive restraints on the exercise of police power.

Some of these problems are due to institutional inertia. For example, the system has long emphasized confessions. Similarly, long periods of detention; lengthy interrogations; limited participation by legal counsel in the pre-trial; less reliance on oral evidence at trial; brief trials before a judge without a jury; less concern for evidentiary rules, including greater reliance on hearsay evidence; and narrower exclusions of tainted evidence are all deeply embedded features of the civil law tradition.

In sum, notwithstanding the relatively short time frame and some marginal improvement for some criminal suspects, the criminal reforms must be seen as largely a failure at the basic level of compliance. Perhaps they were just too drastic, requiring a shift in power toward the courts and the defense bar when the courts were relatively weak and the defense bar even weaker. Moreover, the reforms—although widely supported by legal academics, the defense bar, and foreign commentators—did not receive support from the general public. Indeed, it would be odd were the legal system to actually provide criminal suspects all of the rights granted them under the laws. Given the shortcomings in the legal system as a whole in delivering on rights protection, criminals would then receive more protection than ordinary law-abiding citizens! One would not expect criminal law to be the leading force of legal reform or the cutting edge for taking rights seriously.

A useful thought experiment is to consider whether reformers would have been better off trying to build on and improve the inquisitorial system, and whether it would be better at this stage to revert back to an inquisitorial system. Most likely any attempt to improve on the inquisitorial system would also have met, and would still meet, with limited success. An inquisitorial system requires impartial and professional prosecutors and judges committed to discovering the truth. At the time, there was little differentiation between the criminal system and the political system, and the level of professionalism was relatively low. Today, there is somewhat greater differentiation and a higher level of professionalism, although the feasibility of an impartial quest for the truth is debatable given the emphasis on striking hard at crime.

Nevertheless, the inquisitorial system, with its longer detention periods that reduce the threats to society even if at the expense of individual liberty, fits more readily with the public's desire for social stability. With its emphasis on truth, it also conforms more closely to traditional emphasis on substantive justice than does the adversarial system, which emphasizes procedural justice and a fair fight between the parties. Skillful lawyers who get their clients off on a technicality are even less likely to be celebrated in China than elsewhere. An inquisitorial system might then reduce the conflicts between the defense bar and the police, procuracy, and courts—conflicts which have resulted in the arrests of lawyers for allegedly obstructing justice, inducing false testimony, or fabricating evidence. It is perhaps worth noting that some of the more successful criminal law systems in Asia and indeed the world are primarily inquisitorial, including in Japan.[36] Although Japan, Taiwan, and other states are under pressure from human rights critics to adopt a more liberal rights based approach, whether such an approach would be successful given public attitudes is doubtful.[37] While all criminal justice systems suffer from serious flaws, an inquisitorial system might better suit China's current circumstances.[38]

SUMMARY AND SIMPLIFIED PROCEDURES: BALANCING JUSTICE AND EFFICIENCY

In response to the rising number of criminal cases and the heavy burden imposed on criminal law judges, the Supreme Court, Supreme Procuratorate, and the Ministry of Justice jointly issued regulations in early 2003 that provide for summary procedures and streamline the process in regular criminal cases.[39] Summary procedures may be used in criminal cases in which the facts are clear, the defendant admits guilt, and the maximum potential punishment is less than three years in prison. A single judge oversees the trial, as opposed to the usual panel of three judges. In keeping with the traditional emphasis on rehabilitation, judges are instructed to treat leniently those who voluntarily admit guilt. At the same time, the Supreme Court, Supreme Procuratorate, and Ministry of Justice jointly issue regulations that streamline the procedures in ordinary criminal cases.[40] In contrast to summary procedures, the case is still tried by a panel of three judges rather than a single judge.

The move toward simplified procedures began as an unapproved local experiment, and thus is another example of a bottom-up innovation. Indeed, at the time, critics pointed out that the simplified procedures were at odds with the Criminal Procedure Law. The procedures resemble plea bargaining, which inquisitorial systems have traditionally shunned because it is inconsistent with the emphasis on impartial discovery of the truth. However, in recent years, Italy, France, Argentina, and other inquisitorial systems have adopted plea-bargaining mechanisms, although they differ in important ways from the US model.[41] Whether PRC advocates of summary and simplified procedures deduced or induced the new procedures in light of plea-bargaining models in other countries—and thus whether the changes are to some extent a foreign transplant—is hard to say. Surely judges in China all have some familiarity with plea bargaining—how can they not given all of the US cop shows and movies? Yet they were also responding to local circumstances.

Again, the reforms are not simply a matter of blindly copying a particular foreign model. The two regulations attempt to address efficiency problems without going so far as to accept a US-style plea-bargaining system. The summary procedures are limited to cases with a maximum potential sentence of three years, and the simplified ordinary procedures cannot be used in cases in which the death penalty is possible. In contrast, in the US, offenders charged even with crimes subject to capital punishment may plea bargain. Both the summary and simplified procedures also differ from US-style plea bargaining in that the defendant and procuratorate do not agree in advance to a (recommended) sentence or in the case of charge-bargaining to the charges. Rather, the judge or judicial panel has the final authority to set the sentence, subject to the proviso that those who voluntarily confess should be treated leniently. Given the wide range of possible sentences, and the inevitable vagueness in determining in some cases what counts as serious or aggravating circumstances, judges still retain considerable discretion in determining the sentence. On the other hand, the system is more oriented toward substantive justice and ascertaining the truth than American plea bargaining. The judge must confirm that the defendant's acts do in fact constitute a crime and that the evidence is sufficient to support the charge. Thus, it is not possible, at least in theory, for someone to plead guilty to a lesser charge that clearly does not fit the facts in exchange for a lighter sentence, as happens in the American system. The court must also verify that the defendant has voluntarily admitted guilt, thus giving defendants who wish to repudiate their confessions an opportunity to do so and to raise any claims of torture or coercion. Moreover, rather than giving up the right to trial completely, the defendant has the right to make a statement and present 'a defense' in order to explain the situation and persuade the court to be lenient.

Although the new rules are at odds with traditional inquisitorial processes, they are consistent with the longstanding tradition in China of emphasizing rehabilitation and confessions in exchange for leniency, which may explain their quick adoption. The procedures may also have benefited from the championing of the Haidian court in Beijing, which is known for its progressive nature and highly qualified judges (since many judges are willing to take lower positions than they might get elsewhere to stay in Beijing). Perhaps more importantly, the changes enjoyed widespread support among key institutional players. Judges, prosecutors, and lawyers all benefit from a quick process to end cases. Judges don't have to make tough calls and run the risk of being overturned on appeal. Prosecutors can meet their quotas for cases handled without as much effort, and ensure a conviction. Lawyers, who can rarely charge high fees given the low economic status of most criminals, can rely on volume to generate income, and still claim success in that they are able to obtain a lenient sentence. The main opponents are likely to be human rights groups who fear people will be coerced into pleading guilty despite all the various procedural safeguards.

Even though the new procedures are too recent to assess empirically, the advantages and disadvantages of plea bargaining in general are well known.[42] While some scholars debate the need for plea bargaining, most concede that legal systems could not function without it, at least without devoting considerably more resources to criminal cases than the public is likely to approve. The main disadvantages are normative. Even supporters acknowledge that plea bargaining deviates from the image of a criminal justice system that protects the rights of the accused through elaborate procedures culminating in a trial by a jury of one's peers:

> The criminal process that law students study and television shows celebrate is formal, elaborate, and expensive. It involves detailed examination of witnesses and physical evidence, tough adversarial argument from attorneys for the government and defense, and fair-minded decision-making from an impartial judge and jury. For the vast majority of cases in the real world, the criminal process includes none of these things. Trials occur only occasionally—in some jurisdictions [in the US], they amount to only one-fiftieth of total dispositions. Most cases are by means that seem scandalously casual: a quick conversation in a prosecutor's office or a courthouse hallway between attorneys familiar with only the basics of the case, with no witnesses present, leading to a proposed resolution that is then 'sold' to both the defendant and the judge. To a large extent, this kind of horse trading determines who goes to jail and for how long. That is what plea bargaining is. It is not some adjunct to the criminal justice system; it *is* the criminal justice system.[43]

Most significantly, the accused often have little choice but to accept whatever is offered, and some innocent people, particularly risk-averse ones, will accept a plea bargain and admit guilt to avoid a much heavier punishment. In China's case, the accused will likely feel even more constrained given the high conviction rates, the threat of a heavier punishment, and the practical obstacles to mounting an effective defense.

Although a judge will then review the plea, in most cases the review will be formalistic and perfunctory, as it is in other countries. At the hearing, the accused will repeat the magical words prescripted by his lawyer or told to him by the police regarding his guilt and the voluntariness of his plea. Nevertheless, in some cases the judge may examine the dossier and acquit if the facts or legal basis for conviction were obviously lacking. The hearing also provides an opportunity for the accused to allege torture or other police misconduct and to change his plea.

ADMINISTRATIVE DETENTION: CHINA'S SECOND LINE OF DEFENSE

The various forms of administrative detention and some of the problems with it were discussed in Chapter 3. For present purposes, the first salient point is that the mix of types of administration detention has changed over time. Revisions to the Criminal Procedure Law in 1996 eliminated one of the more well-known forms, shelter and investigation (*shourong shencha*), while incorporating its central aspects. In 2003, the State Council repealed the 1982 regulation regarding detention for repatriation (*shourong qiansong* or DR), which was mainly aimed at migrant workers. Administrative detention of prostitutes and drug users, relied in the early years after elimination, was eliminated and then reinstated when prostitution and drug use arose again in the reform era.

The second important point is that the purpose and application of administrative detention has changed over the years. Whereas in the past administrative detention was a way of dealing with political offenses, administrative detention nowadays mainly deals with petty criminals. The main purpose is still to rehabilitate, retrain, and find employment for minor offenders, encourage prostitutes to look for other ways to earn a living, and treat drug addicts. Although administrative detention now also serves more punitive and deterrent ends, it is meant to be a lesser form of punishment than the decidedly harsh criminal law system, which historically was reserved for enemies of the state and hard-core recidivists who resist efforts to transform them into productive members of society. In recent decades, the nature of crime has changed. Financially desperate migrants unable to find a job or to obtain payment of their salaries, and youths with too much time on their hands and an increasing taste for the material offerings available as a result of economic reforms, are the biggest offenders. Administrative detention is therefore an intermediate line of defense between persuasion by family, friends, and neighbors and hard time in prisons.

Administrative detention is clearly not a transplant from contemporary Western liberal democracies. As we have seen, human rights organizations have demanded elimination of all forms of administrative detention, particularly Education through Labor. However, the government has resisted international and domestic pressure to eliminate administrative detention. Reforms to the system have largely been the result of changing internal conditions. The State Council, for example, had been considering reform of detention and repatriation for some time, in part because of widespread abuses of migrant workers while in custody. What ultimately tipped the scales, however, was the public uproar over the tragic death of college graduate Sun Zhigang while in detention. His death led to large demonstrations in Guangdong and unprecedented petitions by legal scholars challenging the legality of DR and calling for its abolishment. The conversion of detention and repatriation from a coercive mechanism for addressing surging crime and social problems caused by the influx of over 100 million migrant workers into a means of humanitarian relief was also the result of a change in leadership. The new Hu-Wen government was seeking to garner public support by presenting a humane face, and to differentiate itself from the Jiang regime by assigning a higher priority to social justice issues and to the protection of those left behind by China's economic reforms.

The future of administrative detention is difficult to predict. There are three main schools of thought. One group, consisting primarily of liberal academics and rights activists, believes that at least Education through Labor and perhaps all forms of administrative detention should be eliminated. Some in this group would incorporate some or all of the current minor offenses handled through administrative means into the criminal law, but then decrease the possible punishments and rely more heavily on noncustodial sanctions such as fines, community service, and probation. Still others would completely depenalize some offenses.

The second group, consisting mainly of government officials from the Ministry of Justice, the Ministry of Public Security, and the police, favor maintaining ETL and other forms of administrative detention, albeit with minor reforms. They insist administrative detention is necessary to maintain law and order given the increase in crime and its changing nature. They resist attempts to subject administrative detention to further judicial review.

The third, and by far the largest, group would retain ETL and other forms of detention but subject them to major reforms, including passing national-level legislation (an NPC law) to shore up their legal basis, clarify the scope of offenses, and provide additional procedural constraints and safeguards. Some in this camp may prefer more drastic reforms or even the elimination of administrative detention, particularly ETL, but believe that abolishment is not possible at this time given strong resistance among the general public and the lack of political will from the top, where the central leaders repeatedly emphasize the need to strike hard at crime. Thus, they see major reform as a politically necessary compromise. Others in this group, including even some liberal, reform-minded legal scholars, believe the rise of crime and the need to ensure social stability create a legitimate need for ETL and other forms of administrative detention while China negotiates its way through a difficult period of economic, political, and social transition.

In terms of assessment, administrative detention is no doubt often subject to abuse, and in need of reforms. However, the formal criminal system is no better and in many ways would be worse. Eliminating all forms of detention will likely hurt the vast majority of those the reformers are seeking to help by pushing them into the formal criminal system, where they will receive longer sentences.[44]

Noncustodial sanctions will not be appropriate for many of the migrant workers, prostitutes, drug users, or youths that make up the majority of detainees. For instance, fines only work if people have the money to pay them or at least have a job so that they can earn the money to pay them. But the unemployed youths or migrant workers who do not find a job or do not make enough to live on as it is do not have the means to pay fines. Not surprisingly, fines are used more often in economically developed countries than in poor countries. Nor would fines necessarily be desirable in the case of prostitutes and drug addicts. Presumably, prostitutes would have to go back to prostituting, and drug addicts may have to steal or sell drugs, to pay the fines.

A much more likely result than greater reliance on noncustodial sanctions or depenalization is that the authorities will devise other ways to criminalize the behavior. This is in effect what happened when detention and investigation was eliminated as a form of administrative detention but largely incorporated into the criminal law and then supplemented by greater reliance on detention and repatriation. Similarly, the elimination of detention and repatriation is beginning to give rise to new ways of handling social problems caused by the influx of migrant workers. Claiming that the repeal has led to increased crime and abuse of the relief centers by people who were not in fact indigent, the Ministry of Public Security issued the 'Notice Regarding the Strengthening of Current Social Order Management in Accordance with Law.' The Notice calls on public security to redouble efforts in attacking a variety of deviant behavior, including interfering with traffic when begging, disturbing the public order by aggressive begging in public places, soliciting for prostitution in public places, and interfering with government activities when petitioning officials for relief.[45] Concerned about the financial and social order impact of the national regulations, several local governments have rushed to pass regulations that attempt to shift some of the financial burden to others and to clarify many of the difficult operational issues resulting from the new policy.[46]

Finally, the elimination of administrative detention will inevitably result in greater reliance on summary and simplified procedures, with all the shortcomings for the protection of the rights of accused when cases are disposed of through plea bargaining. Summary procedures were the response to an increase in criminal caseloads. There are 500,000 criminal cases each year. There are however more than three million minor cases handled by the police every year.

The complexity of the issues thus complicates the task of predicting the path of reforms. Determining whether administrative detention should be eliminated, or if retained how the various types should be reformed, involves numerous judgments about contested empirical and normative issues, as well as competing institutional interests. These are at once both technical and political issues. The same is true for the next two innovations: adjudicative committees and individual case supervision.

JUDICIAL INDEPENDENCE: ADJUDICATIVE COMMITTEES

The adjudicative committee consists of senior judges within each court. The committee decides cases that are difficult, controversial, or important for social, economic, or political reasons. PRC legal scholars have debated the advantages and disadvantages of the system for more than a decade.

Supporters argue that review by more senior judges is necessary in light of the low level of competence of some judges. They also suggest the system reduces corruption. Some claim the system enhances the independence of the judiciary in that the adjudicative committee, which includes the president and other high-ranking Party members within the court, may be better able to resist outside influences than more junior judges. Zhu Suli, Dean of Peking Law School, has supported the adjudicative committee as an example of a native resource that contributes to rule of law with Chinese characteristics.

On the other hand, the vast majority of PRC legal scholars and most international commentators oppose the system and advocate its abolishment. Under the current system, the judges who decide the case are not the ones who hear it. Accordingly, the judges who do hear the case feel they have no power. Thus, they have little incentive to pay attention to the arguments during trial. Nor do they feel responsible for the judgment, even when it is issued in their names. Further, critics claim judges hearing the cases become timid, and are quick to hand over tough cases to the adjudicative committee rather than working through the issues themselves, even though doing so may result in delays. The system may also increase the opportunities for corruption as disgruntled parties may persuade senior judges to intervene on their behalf. At minimum, these scholars conclude, it has not been an effective means of reducing judicial corruption.

Objections of legal scholars notwithstanding, the likelihood of abolishing the adjudicative committee in the near future is low. Thus, some scholars argue that rather than tilting at windmills, reformers should focus their energies on reducing the role of the adjudicative committee and implementing procedural reforms to the way the committee operates.

Consistent with this strategy, the SPC's reforms to the presiding judge system gave individual judges and the collegiate panel more power to decide cases without the need to obtain the approval of the division chief, president, or the adjudicative committee. The SPC's second five-year agenda announced further reforms. The adjudicative committee is now to hear directly major or difficult cases or those with general applicability. The SPC also proposed that the court president or head of the division join the collegial panel. Still another change is to create separate committees for civil and criminal cases to avoid the problem of criminal law judges hearing civil cases and vice versa.

Foreign advisers who insist on elimination of adjudicative supervision committees to bring the PRC legal system more into line with the image of an independent judiciary in their own countries are likely to miss the opportunities for marginal improvement. On the other hand, few foreign advisers will have enough knowledge of the way the adjudicative committee actually operates to provide feasible reform recommendations. Even fewer will be aware of the ebb and flow of internal debates and thus which way the political wind is blowing. But even when they are, their ability to influence the outcome of this inherently domestic political process is usually limited.

INDIVIDUAL CASE SUPERVISION: BALANCING JUDICIAL INDEPENDENCE AND JUDICIAL ACCOUNTABILITY

In China, legally effective 'final' judicial decisions may be challenged through a process known as 'individual case supervision' (*gean jiandu*, ICS). This additional review procedure may be initiated by interested parties who petition the court, procuracy, or the people's congress to challenge a legally effective decision on their behalf, or initiated by people's congresses, the procuracy or the court acting on their own, in criminal, civil, and administrative cases.[47]

ICS is certainly innovative. Indeed, this type of review of individual cases by the legislature may be unique to China, and would run afoul of separation of power principles in most legal systems.[48] Procuracy review of civil cases is also highly unusual, as is review by adjudicative committees after the appeal process has run its course.

ICS began locally, and is thus another example of a bottom-up reform. Although an attempt to pass a national law in 1996 died in committee, local governments have continued to experiment with ICS. The Supreme People's Court and Supreme People's Procuracy have issued notices and interpretations regarding various issues arising in conjunction with ICS, and local governments have passed many more regulations since 1996. In terms of the inductive innovative process described previously, there has been problem identification, benchmarking, simultaneous engineering, and some attempts at monitoring and assessment.

Assessing ICS is difficult because there is some truth to both sides of the argument. Supporters argue ICS is necessary because of the low level of professional competence of some judges, the existence of judicial corruption, and the adverse influence of local and departmental protectionism. They claim supervision helps to correct injustices, promotes the rule of law, and serves a deterrent function.

Opponents argue ICS impedes judicial independence, hinders the emergence of a more authoritative court, and leads to conflicts between the courts and other state organs. In addition, ICS undermines the fundamental rule of law principles of certainty and finality: cases drag on for years, without any procedural or time limits. As ICS often occurs before appeal, supervision also distorts the normal appeal process. Moreover, critics argue ICS is inefficient: a large amount of judicial resources are devoted to requests for retrial, while the number of cases in which the judgment actually changes on review is small. And while intended to cure the evils of corruption and local protectionism, ICS is not an effective way of doing so because corruption and local protectionism are systemic problems and thus require systemic solutions. Indeed, ICS itself may lead to outside influence, corruption, and local protectionism, raising the eternal question of who will supervise the supervisors.

In general, people's views of supervision are largely a function of their experiences and position in the system. The people's congress, as the representative of the people, cannot ignore the requests of their constituents to address what are often legitimate complaints of horrible injustice. Procuratorates generally favor supervision because it provides another opportunity to prosecute the case and correct their own mistakes in the first trial. Certainly one can understand that prosecutors, who tend to be more law and order oriented than judges everywhere, would be upset when judges acquit people they think are guilty or impose much lighter sentences than they think the criminals deserve. No doubt prosecutors feel that the court should accept their interpretations of the laws and view of the facts. As an institution, the procuracy is not likely to cede power easily and accept the elimination or limitation of supervision.

Conversely, the courts are likely to resist supervision. Surely it must be frustrating for judges to be called before a panel of people's congress delegates to explain a decision, especially when many on the panel have not studied law and based their interpretation of the case on a one-sided presentation of the law and facts by one of the parties.

On the whole, parties support supervision when they win as a result of it and oppose it when they lose. As for the public more generally, it is doubtful that many citizens have an accurate view of the costs and benefits of supervision, the number of cases supervised, the percentage of reversal, and so on. Supervision is not likely to be an effective way to restore confidence and trust in the court. On the contrary, supervision may hurt in that the media tends to report cases in which there has been some wrongdoing rather than those cases where the verdict was upheld. Thus, the public is likely to obtain a false impression of how many cases are reversed after supervision, and to draw the conclusion that additional ICS would reveal a similarly high percentage of mistaken cases.

The Party and central government have no obvious stake in either side of the argument. From their perspective, the goal is a legal system that can issue fair and impartial judgments in most cases, and thus satisfy the needs of economic actors for efficient and predictable results and of citizens for equity and just outcomes. ICS is one way to overcome incompetence and corruption, even if at the cost of efficiency.

Very few cases are supervised, and even fewer result in a changed verdict.[49] The number of supervised cases resulting in a change of verdict on retrial would seem to suggest the courts decide incorrectly only a small percentage of cases, whether because of judicial incompetence, corruption, local protectionism, or other reasons. On the other hand, the relatively high rate of reversals, remands, and mediated settlements of the cases actually supervised might suggest that more cases should be supervised.[50] At minimum, it means that eliminating ICS would result in thousands of parties every year being forced to live with unjust decisions. Elimination of ICS on efficiency grounds therefore runs directly up against support of ICS on justice grounds, raising the perennial question about the value of justice.

In my view, ICS is necessary at present. There are still too many cases in which individuals are denied justice to do away with ICS now. While some may disagree about the wisdom of retaining ICS, all will agree that significant reforms are necessary to make the process more transparent, fair, and efficient. Moreover, as the issues of judicial competence and corruption are addressed, the costs and benefits of ICS, and the balance between judicial independence and judicial accountability, equity and efficiency, substantive justice and procedural justice, will change. Thus, the desirability of ICS and the manner in which it is carried out will need to be revisited in light of changing circumstances.

Law and development lessons from China

What then does this selective survey of legal reforms tell us? First, our descriptive metaphors are of limited utility. In some cases it is possible to describe a particular institution, rule, or practice as a foreign transplant or the result of a top-down/deductive or bottom-up/inductive process. However, most reforms will involve a mixture of foreign and domestic inputs that interact in complicated ways, as well as attempts to deduce what will work from both general principles and local circumstances, and to induce possible solutions from experiments, pilot studies, and experiences both in China and abroad.[51] Metaphors such as selective adaptation or X with Chinese characteristics are better suited to capturing the complexity of reforms, but they fail to provide much guidance in predicting the outcome of reforms.

Second, efforts to explain or predict which reforms will be successful are just beginning. Political ideology, level of economic development, position in the global economy, institutional capacity, cultural differences, colonial history, and interest group politics are all key factors. The relevance of the factors will vary in different regions, different countries within the region, different types of legal systems, and different areas of law within a given legal system, and be more or less significant at different stages in the reform process.

Studies relying on current abstract variables such as rule of law must be complemented by more specific studies that break rule of law down into more discrete institutions and practices. Separate studies should focus on each of the major institutions: judiciary, prosecutor, police and correctional officers, and legal professions. The development of other actors and institutions that perform law-related services should also be taken into account. Similarly, scholars should pay more attention to the different pace and trajectory of development in different areas of law, and explore the mechanisms by which reforms in one area may have spillover effects in other areas.

Additional multi-country empirical studies are likely to shed further light on some of the main factors that determine success or failure in legal reforms.[52] While useful, such studies will never explain all of the institutional variation or the results in particular countries. The outcome of specific reforms such as individual case supervision or administrative detention is the result of a complex interplay of factors and a highly contested domestic political process. Broad empirical studies must be complemented by in-depth qualitative studies that shed light on the local political process and other local factors.

While most commentators portray political ideology as the main obstacle to establishing rule of law in China, the more pressing obstacles at present involve the lack of institutional capacity. In the future, economic factors, the interests of key institutional and social actors, and ultimately political ideology if China remains a single-party socialist state, are likely to exert the most influence on legal reforms and the likelihood of their succeeding. This suggests that when political will for reform is present, reforms aimed at improving institutional capacity are likely to be beneficial. Reforms however must be sequenced to avoid overtaxing the existing institutions.

China's relative success in carrying out reforms to date is attributable in part to strong domestic support for the reforms, which in many cases have deviated from the models proposed by the international community. Although the reform process in China falls far short of the deliberative democracy ideal (or even the highly compromised version that exists in advanced Western liberal democracies), it generally involves a lengthy deliberative process that brings together legislators, academic experts, representatives from key sectors affected by the changes, and foreign consultants. With the passage of the Law on Legislation and experiments in administrative rule-making, the public has a greater opportunity to participate in law-making and rule-making processes through public hearings and other avenues for comment. Nevertheless, the reform process has been primarily a technocratic one driven by experts and elites inside and outside the government.

The nondemocratic nature of China and other Asian countries that followed the EAM may facilitate effective policy formation. In democracies, the public good nature of legal reforms is a barrier to reforms in that even though reforms would be welfare enhancing overall, the benefits may be widely dispersed, leading to collective action problems.[53] Individual beneficiaries of reforms may not have the incentive to become politically active, while those with a vested interest in maintaining the status quo inside or outside the government will be motivated to block reforms or to undermine reforms at the implementation stage.

In China, the ruling party has been able to push through welfare-enhancing legal reforms despite opposition from certain sectors. To be sure, even in China, the policy-making process is contested, and compromises are frequently required to pass reforms. Nevertheless, the Party generally retains the authority to resolve disputes between different state organs when necessary.

When there is considerable political opposition to reforms among key actors, the options are more limited. Reformers may try to persuade opponents as to the merits of reforms or cajole them into accepting changes that may be at odds with their immediate or long-term interests. Alternatively, they may try to circumvent the opposition by building broad-based support. When the opposition comes from the elite factions seeking to protect their entrenched interests, reformers may turn toward bottom-up approaches. However, in many cases, such efforts will not be sufficient. Reformers may need to co-opt or buy out opponents, sometimes by packaging controversial measures with other reforms desired by the opposition.

Compromises—the nitty-gritty of everyday politics—are often necessary. But a compromise acceptable to all parties is not always possible. In such cases, major reforms may have to be put in the 'too hard' basket, to be addressed later when conditions change.

In the meantime, reformers should focus on smaller, more technical changes. Although they should not waste resources on projects that cannot be implemented, they should resist the temptation to walk away when the political will for fundamental change is not present.

That said, there may be very little that can be done in failed states until the regime is changed and political stability restored. Currently, three views appear to be emerging regarding how to handle failed regimes. The first, more aggressive approach, advocates an imposed trusteeship, preceded by regime change, if necessary through military force, as in Iraq. The second position advocates walking away from failed states until the conditions for reform are ripe. Rather than wasting valuable resources in places where there is little hope for effective change, the international community should apply its limited resources to those countries where there is a reasonable prospect of improvement.[54] The citizens of these states are left to suffer their own fate and to struggle to overcome problems on their own. A third, middle approach, advocates a range of arrangements between international actors and states that would limit to various degrees the sovereignty of the target state in exchange for development assistance.[55]

This survey also demonstrates some of the difficulties with evaluating legal reforms. In particular, evaluation raises issues about the proper time-frame and standard. Too often foreign commentators jump to negative conclusions about legal reforms in China and elsewhere because they have not produced miraculous changes overnight. We need more time to see how some reforms will play out.

In some cases, things may have to get worse before they can get better. Some of the changes to the legal system in recent years have resulted in China being caught halfway between a civil system and a common law system both for criminal and civil law. However, the changes were not accompanied by changes to the rules regarding discovery, thus resulting in lawyers having to go to court with inadequate information to effectively argue their case. Once the problems became apparent, the SPC issued rules to strengthen discovery rights.

Many reforms are meant to be second-best solutions to short-term problems of weak institutions, corruption, and lack of sufficient legal training for some judges. Once these problems are addressed, there will be less need for an adjudicative committee to review cases or for individual supervision by the legislature or procuracy. The need to pace reforms will require accepting second-best solutions that will inevitably be criticized by significant political factions.

Legal reforms may be evaluated according to a range of very different standards, producing very different conclusions about whether reforms were successful or not. Comparisons of the legal system in poor countries to that of rich countries will lead to the preordained and all too often condescending conclusion that the legal system in developing countries is primitive. This patronizing conclusion then leads to the well-intentioned effort to export models that are not appropriate for the context, or less well-intentioned neo-imperialistic attempts to impose one's own contested normative values on others and to force them to adopt institutions that serve one's own economic and political interests.

Assessment of legal reforms will involve controversial normative issues about the proper distribution of resources and the proper balance between efficiency and justice, social stability and individual rights, and substantive and procedural justice. The majority of citizens in different societies may come to different conclusions on such issues. As is true elsewhere, conflicting ethical views and competing conceptions of justice and rule of law within China ensure that there will continue to be disagreement about the normative merits of specific reforms.

The task of balancing the costs and benefits of reforms is usually best left to the domestic political process. While the political process will be flawed to one degree or another, the lack of local ownership of reforms, and in particular the opposition of key state and social actors, is likely to undermine reform efforts. Moreover, there are benefits to allowing states to make their own decisions, learn from their mistakes, and make adjustments accordingly. The resulting rules are likely to enjoy greater legitimacy, and the process itself is likely to contribute to democratic learning and the maturation of political institutions and civil society.

Finally, and related, what this survey demonstrates most of all is the need to be pragmatic about legal reforms. We should avoid the Arthurian quest for the Holy Grail: a single, comprehensive, unified theory able to predict both macro and micro legal system reforms in all countries. Attempting to impose too specific a model is likely to fail, as the repeated attempts to force a liberal democratic model of rule of law on other countries have shown. Similarly, attempting to transplant institutions or practices that may work in wealthy countries to poor countries is likely to fail. Greater appreciation of differences in local circumstances, including levels of wealth, popular attitudes, and existing political institutions and cultures, is required if reforms are to succeed.

Critics complain that the general lessons allegedly learned about law and development are superficial and abstract.[56] Yet in many cases reports by practitioners include a plethora of more specific proposals and suggestions derived from in-depth case studies. The problem is that these context-specific suggestions shift the focus away from generalist foreign advisors toward those with greater local knowledge.

Although many international participants in the new law and development movement claim to have learned the lesson that there is no single blueprint, they often react negatively to any attempt by local governments to deviate from model laws or to experiment with innovative institutional arrangements. The international community has been extremely hostile to several regulatory innovations in China, including administrative detention, adjudicative supervision committees, and individual case supervision. The knee-jerk proposals to simply eliminate these institutions typically fail to consider the negative consequences that would likely result from their elimination. A European human rights commissioner once acknowledged that eliminating administrative detention would most likely make things worse for most of those now subject to such detention, but then noted that it would be politically impossible for him given his position and constituency back home to support a more nuanced approach for China that would allow for the continuation of some form of administrative detention. Doing so would undermine the apparent universality of the right of habeas corpus and the seeming yet ultimately illusory consensus on the right to be free from 'arbitrary detention.'

A pragmatic approach will also require that states be afforded a wider margin of appreciation on contested rights issues and given greater leeway to deviate from neoliberal economic policies to reduce social tensions.

The conflict between neoliberal prescriptions and social stability arose in the context of China's Bankruptcy Law. Worried about the social unrest that could result from massive lay-offs of employees, the drafters struggled over the treatment of state-owned enterprises and whether funds should be set aside for the retraining and resettlement of workers before being used to offset the claims of secured creditors. The political compromise was to carve out an exception for certain, presumably large, state-owned enterprises, with the exception to be phased out over time. In addition, the draft law requires payment of employee salaries, social insurance fees, and other compensations as provided by laws and regulations, including arguably retraining and resettlement costs, prior to payment to secured creditors. Foreign commentators and representatives from international financial organizations, as expected, dutifully expressed concerns about these deviations from international norms and best practices, all the while repeating the mantra that there is no single approach or universal solution to bankruptcy issues. Some even acknowledged, when commenting in their personal capacity rather than as a representative of international financial organizations or their foreign investor clients, that these compromises did seem to be reasonable adjustments to local circumstances. In any event, given the complexity of the issues and the less than stellar results of relying on foreign experts in other countries, China should be allowed to experiment on what are essentially domestic political issues, albeit with an international economic component, and to make its own mistakes.[57] One can hardly imagine the leaders from the G-7 countries deferentially acceding to instructions from the IMF on such contested domestic political issues as bankruptcy reforms, tax rules, or social welfare policies, although the political uproar that would surely ensue is easy to imagine.

China has for the most part been able to resist international pressure to conform to a particular legal paradigm, in part because of its size and geopolitical importance, and in part because the leadership remains fundamentally pragmatic. While the scientific background of state leaders is often cited as a negative, such a background fosters a pragmatic, problem-solving outlook that gives greater weight to consequences than ideology, the latest theory of development, or the latest version of the WC.[58] Much as China's leaders resisted the advice of international experts to go for 'big bang' economic reforms in favor of a more gradual approach, so have they resisted efforts to blindly ape a liberal democratic rule of law. And just as the slower approach to economic reforms resulted in impressive economic growth without many of the severe negative consequences of following the big bang strategy, so has the contextualized approach to legal reforms resulted in steady progress.

To be sure, critics argue that the slow pace of reforms has delayed the day of reckoning, and increased the ultimate costs of more fundamental reforms. Which side will have the better of the argument remains to be seen, and hinges on the ability of Chinese reformers to continue to improve the legal system and ultimately to address the political obstacles that are currently barriers to the full realization of rule of law and likely to become even more serious barriers in the future. There is a real danger that government leaders will move too slowly on political reforms and fail to implement in a timely way deep institutional reforms of the legal system, including greater independence and authority for the judiciary as the level of competence of judges increases.

Conclusion: whither reforms in China? Overcoming the middle income blues

Although China has made rapid progress in improving the legal system and good governance, progress appears to be slowing, if not reversing. As Figure 6 indicates, China's rule of law and good governance rankings are all lower in 2004 than in 1998. While the lower rankings may be a statistical anomaly or due to subjective biases, there are signs of reform fatigue and diminishing returns.[59]

After twenty-five years, China is now embarking on a new—and critical—phase in the reform process. A variety of factors have contributed to the need for deeper reforms at this particular juncture, and yet complicate the efforts to implement such reforms.

First and foremost, economic reforms had led to a much more pluralistic society, with citizens deeply divided in their interests and normative views. Second, state organs also have different interests, and support or oppose reforms based on whether they serve their institutional interests.

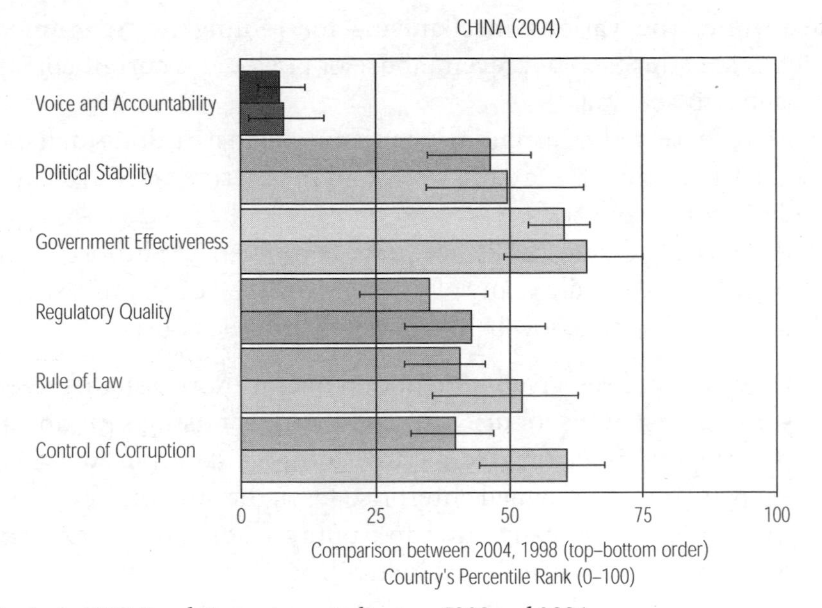

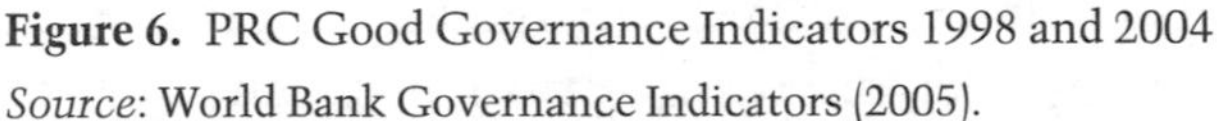

Figure 6. PRC Good Governance Indicators 1998 and 2004
Source: World Bank Governance Indicators (2005).

Third, economic reforms and the government's efforts to promote rule of law and rights consciousness among citizens have led to greater demands on the legal system. All state actors—people's congresses, administrative agencies, the procuracy, the police, the courts—are under pressure to reform to meet the demands of a more diversified market economy and an increasingly pluralistic citizenry with greater consciousness of their rights. People's congresses are supposed to provide a means for balancing different social interests. Administrative agencies are supposed to reduce red tape and facilitate business. The social welfare system is supposed to ensure retirees are able to collect their pensions and laid-off workers are provided with unemployment benefits and job retraining. Administrative reconsideration bodies and the courts are supposed to provide mechanisms for resolving conflicts fairly and efficiently, thus providing the necessary predictability and certainty for businesses to operate and citizens to plan their personal affairs.

Meanwhile, the various mechanisms for reining in government officials are supposed to prevent abuse of power and curtail corruption and rent seeking.

Unfortunately, the current mechanisms and institutions for handling the rising tensions are too weak and ineffective, as is typical in middle income countries.

Fourth, the judiciary lacks adequate competence, authority, and independence to handle many of the controversial economic, social, and political disputes now being funneled into the courts.

- Courts have been given jurisdiction over minority shareholders suits against SOEs for disclosure violations, raising a number of complicated issues regarding how to prove damages and what happens if a state-owned enterprise loses the suit and the liabilities force the company into bankruptcy, leading to massive layoffs and an increase in social instability.
- The courts are also being inundated with labor disputes from factory workers suing over unlawful termination and unsafe working conditions, and migrant workers seeking unpaid wages and protesting compulsory overtime in excess of the number of hours stipulated in the Labor Law. Retirees are suing their former employees or the local government for failure to pay pensions, raising important social policy issues in the absence of an effective welfare system.
- Courts are hearing an expanding range of discrimination claims brought with respect to the rights of migrant workers, education, the retirement age for female workers, hepatitis, and AIDS.
- The new propertied class is turning to the courts to protect their main asset—their homes. Disputes between newly created homeowner associations and developers and their affiliated management companies often involve allegations of corruption and collusion between the defendants and local government officials. They pit one powerful group, real estate developers, against increasingly powerful private citizens who are themselves often government officials or members of the nouveau riche with strong government connections.

- Land disputes are exploding both in urban and rural areas as governments in pursuit of economic growth requisition land for developers, again raising issues of corruption and collusion.[60]
- Social activists have sought to bring suits against the local government for forced abortions and other violations of family planning policies and regulations.
- Citizens, often aided by newly formed (and sometimes not licensed) environmental groups, are seeking to close down polluting enterprises in their area.
- Courts are also handling cases that touch on sensitive national security issues or affect social stability, including cases involving very broadly defined state secrets regulations that are used against whistleblowers who reveal government corruption or malfeasance.
- In addition, many cases raise the issue of social justice as those who have lost out in the course of economic reforms look to the courts for protection: what are people entitled to given the government's goal of establishing a harmonious society (*hexie shehui*) or at least a *xiaokang* society?[61]

Whether courts have the competence to decide many of these issues is a much-debated topic everywhere. There has been a global trend to funnel social and political conflicts into the courts. The results in some countries have been positive. In other cases, the result has been overreaching, ideologically driven decisions that have negative social, economic, and political consequences.[62] In comparison to their counterparts in other systems, Chinese judges may be somewhat less well positioned to handle these types of cases given the lower education levels for some judges and the heavy emphasis on theory and formalism in Chinese law schools.

Whether or not Chinese or other courts are competent to decide such matters, the Chinese judiciary in some cases lacks adequate authority and independence to handle these controversial issues, especially when they involve conflicts with other state organs. Funneling these divisive issues into a court system that lacks the independence and authority to handle them undermines the reputation of the judiciary and in turn the government's efforts to promote rule of law. Lacking effective channels for resolving the conflicts generated by economic, social, and political reforms, citizens are increasingly taking to the streets to seek justice—or at least to vent their anger.

Fifth, the government lacks the resources to prevent many of the conflicts from arising in the first place by throwing money at the problems. As a lower-middle income country, China is hard-pressed to meet the demands for greater public spending on education, health care, social security, and pollution control, much less to address the large regional differences in levels of wealth and the rural–urban gap. To be sure, as in any country there are debates about whether the government should be allocating so many resources to military spending, space missions, or high-profile projects such as the Olympics given the pressing needs in other areas.

THE NEED FOR DEEPER REFORMS

The reform process in China is at a crossroads. As reforms have continued, tensions and conflicts in the political system between the ruling party and state organs, among state actors, between state and society, and among different interest groups in society have increased. At this stage, there are few if any Pareto improvement reforms: few if any reforms will benefit everyone, even if they increase the efficiency of the system as a whole or contribute to greater wealth. Even seemingly highly technical reforms have a political dimension because reforms will produce winners and losers, whether in terms of distribution of economic resources, distribution of power among state organs, or the strengthening of some legal actors such as the criminal and the defense bar at the expense of others such as the members of the general public who assign a higher priority to social order. Now that the 'easy' reforms for which there has been a broad consensus have been completed, the politics of reforms have become more pressing. Although deeper reforms are required, they are controversial, and hotly contested.

As the legal reform process in China has entered into this extremely complicated and intensely political phase, differences have surfaced over fundamental issues such as the nature and purpose of rule of law, administrative law, and the judiciary. No longer is it sufficient to fall back on broad generalizations such as the purpose of rule of law is to facilitate economic development, provide a peaceful mechanism for resolving conflicts, promote social stability, and enhance the legitimacy of the government. Nor is it sufficient to claim that administrative law serves the dual purpose of enhancing—or balancing—government efficiency and the protection of rights; or that China needs a court system that is independent and strong, just and efficient, authoritative and trusted by citizens. These generalizations are no doubt true, but they do not resolve the practical issues at hand. It is not clear how these broad goals are to be translated into particular institutional reforms given the tensions between efficiency and justice; between a more independent and authoritative court and the desire of other institutions to increase their powers of supervision over the courts; and between a more open and transparent political system with a greater role for the public, and the efficiency of the reform process that has largely been led by a technocratic elite.

The resolution of these issues inevitably implicates highly contentious social and political issues. In that sense, they go beyond the bounds of a thin or procedural rule of law to the differences that define competing thick or substantive conceptions of rule of law. Most of the reforms to date have been of the more limited technical type required to implement a thin rule of law—that is to meet the basic requirements that any legal system must meet to be a legal system regardless of whether the broader political-normative framework is liberal democratic or socialist. However, unless these fundamental issues are addressed, legal reforms will remain at an impasse. The more limited technical changes to date and any such further changes, as contemplated for example in the SPC's second five-year agenda, will be at best only partially effective. The legal system will not be able to achieve the government's broad goals of facilitating economic development, social justice, and a harmonious society. Citizens will continue to be dissatisfied with the legal system, and seek alternative means to pursue their interests and obtain justice, including demonstrations.

To be effective, future reforms to the political-legal system must encompass at least six major aspects. First is *prevention*. Given the growing social tensions, the increasing pluralism of society, and the inadequacy of current mechanisms for dealing with such tensions, there is a need to prevent disputes from arising in the first place. This entails addressing some of the major social cleavages, including the rural–urban income gap, the regional income gap, and the intra-urban gap between those who have benefited from economic reforms and those who have lost out.

Second, the current mechanisms for handling conflicts must be strengthened. This will require sorting out some of the institutional conflicts preventing a realignment of powers among state organs. It will require deciding what the policy should be on key issues and then translating those policies into clear laws and regulations that allow citizens to plan their lives accordingly and dispute resolution mechanisms to resolve disputes consistently based on clear legal authority. And it will require recognition of the right of citizens to challenge government acts and lawyers to represent their clients in controversial economic, criminal, or political cases. While they will frequently lose under the restrictive and nonliberal laws typical of the EAM, they will win in some cases, and the government will have to defend its policies to the public.

Third, and related, there is a need for macro-level planning regarding which institutes will handle what type of disputes. While there are perfectly good reasons to provide various mechanisms for handling certain conflicts, at present the many overlapping mechanisms for handling disputes often leads to inconsistencies, inefficiencies, and turf-battles among state organs.

Fourth, the increasing pluralism of society means that there will be a growing number of issues over which reasonable people may disagree.[63] Procedural mechanisms must be developed and strengthened to handle the increasingly diverse views in society. In particular, there needs to be greater political participation in the decision-making processes, whether through public hearings, consultative committees, or participation in the nomination or election of officials. Empirical studies have found that procedural justice, including a sense of having had a say in the outcome, is frequently more important to determining perceptions of legitimacy than the substantive outcome.[64] This is borne out by village elections in China, which have demonstrated that people generally are more willing to compromise or accept decisions that are not in their interest when they believe they had a fair opportunity to be heard and participate in the decision-making process. This approach is also consistent with the efforts to expand public participation as reflected in the Law on Legislation, the drafting of an Administrative Procedural Law, the experiment with access to information acts and the increasing reliance on social consultative committees.

Fifth, and a corollary, greater attention must be paid to procedural justice in mechanisms for resolving disputes, whether through mediation, the letter and visits system, court cases, or other means. Participants must perceive the mechanisms to be fair, regardless of the outcome in the particular case. This will require addressing corruption, local protectionism, and other factors that unfairly influence the outcome. It will also increase trust in the courts.

Sixth, greater efforts should be made to explain the proper role *and the limits* of the legal system and rule of law. The legal system is not the proper forum for resolving all contentious issues. Moreover, the traditional emphasis on substantive justice—expressed through the rapidly growing reliance on letters and visits—leads to unrealistic expectations from the legal system. The unrealistic expectations undermine trust in the judiciary when the legal system then fails to resolve each and every social problem, to ensure social justice, or to provide a substantively just outcome in the eyes of all parties to a conflict.

Although China is now entering a difficult phase in the reform process, it is much too early to conclude that China is 'trapped in transition.'[65] Other East Asian states would also have appeared to be trapped in transition at a similar level of development. However, the success of other East Asian states suggests that China may be able to overcome the obstacles. Their success, combined with the failure of so many other states, suggests that the most likely way for China to overcome the middle income blues is to continue to follow the EAM, including with respect to democratization. The next chapter considers the lessons Chinese leaders and citizens are likely to derive from the experiences of developing countries in Asia and elsewhere with democratization.

CHAPTER SEVEN

Debating democracy

Foreign leaders, including President Bush and James Leach, chairman of the House International Relations Subcommittee on Asia and the Pacific and co-chairman of the Congressional-Executive Commission on China, have suggested that the successful democracies in Asia such as Taiwan may provide inspiration for China. On the contrary, Chinese leaders and citizens are not likely to be inspired by what they see elsewhere in Asia or other regions. Rather, they are more likely to conclude that the best approach is to continue to follow the EAM, and postpone democratization until the country is richer and more stable.

Democracy in Asia: inspiration or warning?

'MESSY' ELECTIONS

The affirmative view of democracy places a great deal of faith in elections as a means of holding government officials accountable, resolving social conflicts, and addressing social justice through the empowerment of the least well off. Anyone who believes most Chinese citizens are likely to see elections as the answer to their problems based on the experiences of Asian countries should think again. Elections, while providing scandal for the media, hardly inspire confidence or match the inflated rhetoric about the ability of democracy to hold government officials accountable or allow citizens to pursue their own personal version of human flourishing. Recent presidential elections in Asia have been particularly disheartening.

In the 2004 elections in Taiwan, Chen Shuibian seemed willing to risk confrontation with China just to stay in office, continually challenging Beijing and Washington with calls for a national referendum and constitutional changes, despite stern warnings from Beijing and Washington to avoid further provocation. Even close observers of Taiwanese politics—used to, as they are, fisticuffs and chair-throwing by members of the legislature—were shocked by the dirty politics in which the KMT compared Chen to Hitler, and then the bizarre shooting of the president and vice-president by a slow-moving bullet on the day before elections.[1] Capitalizing on the sympathy vote from the shooting, Chen claimed victory by less than 30,000 votes out of a total of 13.3 million. After weeks of protests and demonstrations both peaceful and otherwise by supporters of the LDP, Chen was finally sworn into office, where he presided over a deeply divided public. With his poll numbers plummeting as the economy faltered, Chen continued to test the waters and the patience of Washington and Beijing by taking a series of small steps toward independence, including scrapping the largely symbolic National Unification Council. With his party plagued by corruption scandals, Chen faced widespread pressure to resign.

In the Philippines, where former actor Joseph Estrada was impeached and forced out of office after being linked to illegal pay-offs from gambling lords, President Arroyo squared off against another leading film actor, Fernando Poe, a high school drop-out who had never held public office, although he did once play a town mayor in the movies. Poe studiously avoided the issues in a campaign long on symbol and short on substance on the part of both candidates.[2] Just over one year later, President Arroyo herself faced impeachment over alleged election fraud and corruption. Former President and estranged ally Corazon Aquino led the demonstrations in the streets. Although Arroyo's control of the House of Representatives allowed her to survive the impeachment vote, polls showed eight out of ten Filipinos no longer trusted her and seven out of ten wanted her impeached. A few months later, Arroyo declared a state of emergency after she survived the third coup attempt of her five years in office.

Meanwhile, in South Korea, President Roh was impeached on charges of illegal campaigning, corruption among his aides, and mismanagement of the economy, then acquitted and reinstated. However, his subsequent attempt to replace several cabinet members without following constitutional procedures gave rise to complaints of amateurism and unflattering comparisons to the heavy-handed ways of former dictators.[3]

The presidential elections in Indonesia featured two former military men. One of them, General Wiranto, the head of Suharto's former Golkar Party, is accused of being a war criminal for his role in East Timor. Far from being disqualifying, the accusations seem to have caused some Indonesians to support him in a show of nationalist resistance to foreign pressure. In the final runoff, former General Susilo Bambang Yodhoyono won in a landslide over the incumbent Megawati, who failed during her tenure to resolve domestic security issues, reduce corruption or meet heightened expectations for social justice.

In India, the voters threw out the BJP despite a growth rate of 8%, opting instead for the Congress Party, led by the Italian born Sonia Ghandi, widow of the assassinated former Prime Minister Rajiv Ghandi—who then promptly decided not to take office. The turmoil caused the single biggest one-day drop in the stock markets ever, although the markets recovered when Ghandi named an economist known for his market orientation to head her party. The elections—marred by the deaths of over twenty women and children in a stampede to secure sarees, a bomb that killed eleven people attending a political rally in Kashmir followed by boycotts of the polls by separatist militants, the murder of twenty-six policemen by Maoist guerillas in Jharkhand, the shooting deaths of three political party members in Bihar, and the usual charges of rampant vote buying—were described as relatively clean and successful by Indian standards.[4]

In Nepal, the problems go beyond mere messy elections. A Maoist insurgency, one of the lowest levels of economic development in Asia and an unstable monarchy are all undermining democracy. Real life events, as reported by the CIA, read like the desperate attempts of Hollywood screenwriters to come up with novel plot lines in this jaded age of weary worldliness:

In 2001, the crown prince massacred ten members of the royal family, including the king and queen, and then took his own life. In October 2002, the new king dismissed the prime minister and his cabinet for 'incompetence' after they dissolved the parliament and were subsequently unable to hold elections because of the ongoing insurgency. While stopping short of reestablishing parliament, the king in June 2004 reinstated the most recently elected prime minister who formed a four-party coalition government, which the king subsequently tasked with paving the way for elections to be held in spring of 2005. Citing dissatisfaction with the government's lack of progress in addressing the Maoist insurgency, the king in February 2005 dissolved the government and assumed power in the Kingdom.[5]

Democracy proponents often argue in the face of poor economic performance, massive demonstrations, calls for regime change, and elections marred by violence and vote buying, that democracy is 'messy.'[6] However, the same apologists for democracy are quick to criticize every shortcoming under an authoritarian regime, and to call for immediate elections as a solution. One can only imagine the scorn that would be heaped on anyone so bold as to offer in response to political violence, widespread corruption, and other social maladies in authoritarian states, the limp excuse that 'authoritarianism is messy.' At minimum, the performance of both democratic and nondemocratic regimes should be scrutinized and evaluated objectively and without bias.

DISAPPOINTING RESULTS, ESPECIALLY IN COUNTRIES THAT DEMOCRATIZED AT LOW LEVELS OF WEALTH

In turning from the periodic sideshow of elections to the actual performance of Asian democracies, Chinese leaders and citizens are likely to draw three conclusions. First, based on the dismal performance of countries that have attempted to democratize at low levels of wealth both in the past and more recently, for China to democratize now would be folly given the current level of wealth and the lack of other conditions generally associated with successful consolidation.

Far from an inspiration, India is generally seen as a warning of what happens when countries democratize prematurely. Compared to China, India is poorer, less politically stable, and generally perceived as more corrupt, chaotic, and poorly governed. Fairly or not, many Chinese attribute the differences largely to democracy. *The Economist* summarized the ills besetting Indian democracy as 'not just . . . constituencies handed down like family heirlooms; but also . . . venal, sometimes thuggish and often outright criminal candidates; . . . parties appealing not on the basis of policies but of narrow regional or caste interests; . . . coalitions formed not out of like-minded ideologies but out of naked power-seeking.'[7]

Scholars often wonder how India has managed to sustain democracy. Part of the explanation seems to be that the state is too weak to overcome the various centers of power and no single group is sufficiently powerful to dominate the others. However, as Lele and Quadir note: 'The literature on democracy and development . . . rarely mentions the most obvious and perhaps the only necessary condition for the survival of formal democracy. It can survive and thrive anywhere as long as it protects the interests of the entrenched and dominant classes and as long as they can hold economic, political and ideological sway over the subaltern classes.'[8] Whatever the explanation, democracy has not addressed pressing issues of extreme poverty for many citizens, led to a just and efficient legal system, or put an end to ethnic conflicts, religious tensions, or caste-based discrimination. If anything, the emergence of right-wing Hindutva as a political force has exacerbated the ethnic and religious conflicts.

Nor are Chinese likely to be inspired by the Philippines. The government is notoriously weak, corrupt, and inept. The country is politically unstable. Democracy remains elitist. Effective participation by citizens is limited:[9]

At both the levels of policy-making and implementation, the avenues for citizen participation are limited by lack of transparency, poor dissemination of information, lack of consultation, lack of financial resources and over-centralization of decision-making on the part of the state. On the part of civil society, the weaknesses are under-utilization of existing avenues, the lack of technical expertise, poor organization capacities, fear of co-optation by and general distrust of the state and ideological differences that hamper coordination, collaboration and taking a unified position toward government.[10]

Political parties are weak and lack a coherent ideology, with members jumping ship as their fortunes change: 'Political parties are therefore nothing more than the tools used by the elites in a personalistic system of political contests. The elites themselves do not form stable or exclusive blocs or factions. Their boundaries are provisional and porous at any point in time. They revolve around political stars rather than around ideologies. They nurture networks of followers or supporters who are dependent on them for money, jobs, favors or political access, not party members loyal to party principles . . .'[11] As Rocamora points out, 'Without effective political parties, families and clans have become the effective political units in local politics. Since victory and defeat in election determines the economic fate and honour of the clan, the use of all available means to gain victory including violence and fraud is understandable.'[12]

Nor has democracy resolved vital socioeconomic problems. As we have seen, the Philippines is a lower-middle income country in terms of per capita income like China, with scores roughly similar to China's in terms of poverty, infant mortality, and longevity. There are also similar problems with the education system as in China: the government is unable to meet its commitment to free compulsory education for all; local schools charge fees that the poor can't afford; drop-out rates are high as children must work to contribute to family income; there is a growing gap between those who can afford education in better schools, many of them private, and those who cannot. If anything, the problems in the Philippines are more severe than in China.[13]

In Indonesia, the nature of democracy is contested, with the debates fragmented and confused.[14] There is no consensus on what the purpose or purposes of the state should be. Significant differences separate Islamicists (with a wide range of views within the Muslim community), labor, liberal democratic supporters of the IMF vision, and nationalists who see legal reforms and good governance as forms of neo-imperialism.[15]

In comparison to China, Indonesia remains very poor and very poorly governed. Since democratization, there has been a general deterioration in social order, a rise in crime, an upsurge in vigilante groups, and widespread unrest among Muslims in several provinces. Democracy has not resolved the critical problems of deeply entrenched corruption and clientelism, which are undermining the independence of the judiciary and efforts to implement rule of law. Transitional justice issues remain unresolved. The government has refused to extradite those accused of war crimes to the special tribunal in Dili. Indonesian courts have acquitted or imposed light sentences on senior officers in charge of East Timor. The US State Department described the trials as seriously flawed and lacking credibility. The legal system as a whole is extremely weak.[16] Judges are incompetent, corruption is widespread, the litigation process is slow and inefficient, with cases often taking as long as seven years to complete. Senior judges stubbornly resist reforms that would decrease their power and opportunities for rent seeking. The public prosecutor is seen as highly corrupt, incompetent, and militaristic. The police force suffers from lack of competence and corruption. The Ombudsmen Commission has received considerable foreign donor support, even though it has been relatively ineffective, because donors think it serves the purposes of transparency and provides the kinds of checks on government that are important in a liberal democracy. The bar association is deeply divided, and has not been a source for reforms.

The state is simply too weak to carry out significant institutional reforms. Civil society, for its part, remains ineffectual in challenging longstanding systems of patronage. Robinson points out that, '[a]s in Russia, the rapid unraveling of state power left reformers exposed to the full force of oligarchic power and gangsters—this was the sort of civil society unleashed in Indonesia.'[17] Cynical about the possibilities for reform given entrenched elite interests, many local NGOs with younger members are focusing on smaller, grassroots institutional reforms, and just biding their time until their generation is in power and can carry out more radical reforms.

Linnan observes that the international donor community has assumed a similar conception of the state and civil society as in developed Western states—an independent and liberal civil society in opposition to a largely secular and limited neutral state.

He suggests that donors may be unwilling to accept non-Western conceptions of the state and civil society, as in socialist China or in Indonesia where Islam, communitarianism, and a post-colonial concern with nationalism play a more important role. The combination of communitarianism and nationalism leads to a more corporatist relationship between social organizations and the state that challenges the typical if somewhat overstated emphasis on civil society as independent from and in opposition to the state. It also leads to a greater emphasis on collective goals. As he notes, 'communitarianism is not the pallid conceptual variety of Anglo-American jurisprudence. Instead, it reflects two factors: first, how society works differently under circumstances when average per capita GDP is less than US$1,000; and second, the fact that the vast majority of Indonesia's population is not further removed than one generation from a rural village setting in which cooperation-intensive rice agriculture shaped society.'[18]

Indonesia might eventually prove successful in consolidating liberal democracy. However, other possible scenarios include: the emergence of a hardline Islamic regime; the rise of a military regime that might use the specter of Islamic fundamentalism, the failure of the government to achieve economic growth, or the breakdown of law and order to grab power; a turn toward more authoritarian methods by the democratically elected president to deal with the growing insurgency and the breakdown in law and order; or the emergence of a nonliberal, more communitarian or collectivist regime of the type found in Singapore, Taiwan, South Korea, and Japan.

In Cambodia, economic growth lags far behind that of China. The economy is heavily dependent on tourism, textiles, and foreign aid. Growth slowed dramatically in 1997 and 1998 due to the regional economic crisis, civil violence, and political infighting. However, growth picked up in 1999, the first full year of peace in thirty years.[19] The economy grew at a 5% clip from 2000 to 2004, aided in part by a bilateral textile agreement with the US that gave Cambodia a guaranteed quota of US textile imports and tied further imports to improved working conditions and enforcement of labor laws in compliance with international standards. Longer-term prospects for the economy are less promising. The bilateral agreement with the US ended in 2005. Cambodia must now compete head-on with China, India, and other developing countries. The failure to invest in human capital and institutions has left Cambodians ill-prepared for the ruthless competition of the marketplace:

The long-term development of the economy after decades of war remains a daunting challenge. The population lacks education and productive skills, particularly in the poverty-ridden countryside, which suffers from an almost total lack of basic infrastructure. Fully 75% of the population remains engaged in subsistence farming. Fear of renewed political instability and a dysfunctional legal system coupled with extensive government corruption discourage foreign investment.[20]

Bangladesh remains poor, overpopulated, and poorly governed. Political infighting and corruption at all levels of government have hampered economic and political reforms. While most of the elite and middle class favor economic liberalization, many of the poor oppose it. The ruling party has the parliamentary strength to push through needed reforms but lacks the political will to do so. The failure of market reforms to benefit all has led to violent protests and a marked decrease in political stability, as indicated in the drop from the 27th percentile in 1998 to the 12th percentile in 2004. The government's reaction has been harsh, as reflected in the worsening civil and political rights record, with Bangladesh dropping from the 45th percentile in 1998 to the 29th percentile in 2004 on the World Bank voice and accountability index. Other indicators are also significantly lower. Bangladesh plummeted from the 43rd percentile to the 11th percentile on control of corruption, from the 41st percentile to 13th percentile on regulatory quality, from the 39th percentile to the 26th percentile on government effectiveness, while its legal system remained stuck in the bottom quartile on the rule of law index.[21]

In Nepal, more than 40% of the population lives below the poverty line. While the annual per capita income in Nepal is less than $200, the government has spent *ten million dollars a week* on fighting the Maoists. Tourism revenues have all but disappeared and foreign investment and exports are down by 90%. The long-term prognosis is bleak, due to 'the small size of the economy, its technological backwardness, its remoteness, its landlocked geographic location, its civil strife, and its susceptibility to natural disaster.'[22]

One of the main arguments in favor of democracy is that democracies generally better protect human rights. It is true that many empirical studies show that democracy is one of the factors generally associated with better rights protection. However, at lower levels of wealth, democracy frequently does not produce the desired results. The transition to democracy often leads to chaos and repression.

A number of quantitative studies demonstrate that the third wave has not led to a decrease in political repression, with some studies showing that political terror and violations of personal integrity rights actually increased in the 1980s.[23] Other studies have found that there are nonlinear effects to democratization: transitional or illiberal democracies increase repressive action. Fein described this phenomenon as 'more murder in the middle'—as political space opens, the ruling regime is subject to greater threats to its power and so resorts to violence.[24]

More recent studies have also concluded that the level of democracy matters: below a certain level democratic regimes oppress as much as non-democratic regimes.[25] Bueno de Mesquita et al. found 'that improvements in a state's level of democracy short of full democracy do not promote greater respect for integrity rights. Only those states with the highest levels of democracy, not simply those conventionally defined as democratic, are correlated with better human rights practices.'[26]

Democracy consists of different elements or dimensions. The Polity IV measure increasingly favored by researchers is a 21-point scale made up of five components: competitiveness of executive recruitment, competitiveness of participation, executive constraints, openness of executive recruitment, and regulation of participation. Describing their conclusions as 'somewhat melancholy ones from the standpoint of state building and human rights,' de Mesquita et al. dispel the notion that rushing to hold elections will lead to a marked improvement in human rights:

States cannot rapidly improve human rights conditions by focusing on particular aspects of the democratization process at the expense of other aspects that appear less strongly related to the protection of personal integrity rights. These more weakly associated reforms must be in place before other reforms yield improvements. Still more disconcerting is the finding that the process of democratization does not consistently produce human rights benefits until it is virtually complete. The early progress in democratization likely to be achieved during the initial years of state-building has little, if any, impact. Elections, for instance, can be held at the earliest stages of nation building, but elections without multiparty competition and constrained executives . . . can make matters worse rather than better [cite omitted]. Multiparty competition and executive constraints take considerably longer to institutionalize than does an electoral process.[27]

The experiences of Asian countries are largely consistent with the findings of these multi-country studies. As noted, unlike China, India appears to deserve its level-4 PTS rating. In Indonesia, there have been numerous human rights violations after the fall of Suharto, most notably with respect to ethnic violence, the tragedy in East Timor, and the violence that marred the 1999 elections. Although Cambodia held elections in 1993 and 1998, thc period was marked by battles between government armed forces and the Khmer Rouge, resulting in continued human rights violations. The government offered amnesty to key leaders and supporters of the Khmer Rouge, much to the dismay of many rights advocates. Nevertheless, stability remained an issue with a preemptive coup by Hun Sen in 1997 in which more than fifty people were killed, many of them shot in the back of the head after arrest.

In the Philippines, there have been numerous rights violations, including disappearances, extrajudicial killings, arbitrary arrests, and prolonged detention, as the government struggles to defeat insurgents. Consistent with popular views in other countries threatened by political instability, most Filipino citizens apparently do not consider the government's tough treatment of insurgents and terrorists to be human rights violations.

Amnesty International has reported massive human rights violations in Nepal by both the military and Maoist guerrillas, including the killing and kidnapping of civilians, torture of prisoners, and destruction of property. In defense of the government's suspension of constitutional freedoms and harsh actions, Nepal's

Prime Minister declared: 'You can't make an omelette without breaking eggs. We don't want human rights abuses but we are fighting terrorists and we have to be tough.'[28]

Of course, not all of the news is bad. Asian democracies generally have fewer political prisoners than in authoritarian regimes; citizens enjoy greater freedom of speech, association, and assembly; and the media is subject to fewer restrictions, although it is generally still considerably less free than in Euro-America. Nor are all of the problems in these countries due to democracy, any more than all of the problems in authoritarian states are due to authoritarianism. There is also a danger of comparing the performance of Asian democracies against some Western ideal, or failing to account for the general negative impact of low levels of wealth on political stability, good governance, and the protection of rights.

At higher levels of wealth, democracy has certain economic advantages. While the average growth rate of authoritarian regimes is slightly higher than for democracies above $3,000 per capita, growth is labor extensive and labor exploitive. The labor force grows faster, but the marginal worker is less productive and the average worker much less productive than in democracies. In short, 'wealthier dictatorships grow by using a lot of labor and paying it little.'[29] In contrast, democracies take better advantage of technology and get more out of their workers. China of course has plenty of labor. Nevertheless, the various advantages of democracies once a higher level of wealth is obtained suggest that at some point China will be better off democratizing.

A second lesson, however, is that China is likely to develop its own variety of democracy, which will most likely be closer to the nonliberal elitist democracy found in other Asian countries than to the liberal democracy found in Euro-America.[30] As former Singaporean Ambassador Chan Heng Chee has observed, 'developing countries may benefit from a "postponement" of democracy and when it eventually does arrive, Asian democracy must be expected to look different from the Western type: it will be less permissive, more authoritarian, stressing the common good rather than individual rights, often with a single dominant party and nearly always with a centralized bureaucracy and "strong state."'[31]

What kind of democracy?

There are significant differences in East Asian democracies. Nevertheless, some of the more common features may be relevant for the future of democracy in China. One such feature is that East Asian democracy emphasizes a strong state rather than the more limited liberal state. Weakened by colonialism, war, and internal strife, Asian states have turned to democracy as a way of strengthening the state. In China, the call for democracy was first raised in response to the weakness of the Qing. Today many nationalists continue to see democracy as the means for China to once again claim its rightful place as a leading power. National security, state sovereignty, and the dignity of the people remain key concerns throughout Asia, and especially in China.

State legitimacy is largely performance based. The priority is on economic growth. The government is obligated to provide for the material well-being of citizens. At the same time, in contrast to the liberal state, the state is more involved in setting a moral agenda and creating the conditions for a harmonious society. There is less emphasis on individual rights and more on collective interests, including social stability.

The majority of citizens want strong leaders who can deliver the goods, and are willing to give them great leeway in pursuing their goals.[32] There is less concern with formal checks and balances. Citizens elect imperial presidents with wide discretionary powers whom they can trust to exercise sound judgment because of their moral character—the modern day equivalent of the sagely and virtuous Confucian *junzi*. Four of five Koreans, for instance, agree that the 'moral and human qualities of a political leader are more important than his ideas,' with nearly two-thirds agreeing that 'if we have political leaders who are morally upright, we can let them decide everything.'[33] Not surprisingly, few Koreans opposed at the time President Kim Young Sam's extralegal measures to attack corruption.[34] Showing a similar disregard for rule of law principles, President Kim Dae-jung used a general tax audit of all the major news media companies as a cover for persecution of his political opponents and encouraged, in the name of popular sovereignty, civic groups to violate laws preventing unregistered political groups from engaging in political campaigns.[35]

L. H. M. Ling and Chih-Yu Shih have argued that democracy in Taiwan is a way of installing a virtuous and benevolent ruling elite.[36] They point out that once Lee Teng-hui was elected and had consolidated power, he sought to forge a moral consensus that would lead to social harmony and strengthen the state. Rather than being constrained by law, he sought to change the law and legal institutions to reflect and better serve his moral agenda.

Meanwhile, in Thailand, the commitment to rule of law and separation of powers remains weak. A majority would accept government control over the judiciary or even parliament to promote the well-being of the nation.[37] In a bow to popular opinion, Thaksin was narrowly acquitted on corruption charges, clearing the way to take office in 2001. Once in power, he repeatedly invoked popular support to oppose the power of unelected judges. Promising the people happiness and prosperity, he remarked that it was 'strange that the leader who was voted by 11 million people had to bow to the ruling of the NCCC and the verdict of the Constitutional Court, two organizations composed of only appointed commissioners and judges . . .'[38] Not one to beat around the bush, he also defiantly stated: 'Democracy is a good and beautiful thing, but it's not the ultimate goal as far as administering the country is concerned . . . Democracy is just a tool, not our goal. The goal is to give people a good lifestyle, happiness and national progress.'[39] Despite such views, he won in a landslide victory to gain a second term in 2005, before being forced to resign just months later in the wake of allegations of corruption and abuse of power.

In contrast to broad-based forms of participatory or deliberative democracy, democracy in East Asia relies more heavily on good governance by a technocratic elite.[40] There may be a robust civil society, but it is not very politically involved. In post-democratic Korea, for instance, a flourishing civil society has not led citizens to actively engage in public deliberation. Korean citizens increasingly suffer from political apathy, social diffidence, and moral anomie.[41] Many Asian citizens have not internalized democratic values required for deliberative democracy, including toleration of diverse viewpoints. Two-thirds of Koreans believe that too many competing groups will destroy social harmony, while almost half believe that 'if people have too many different ways of thinking, society will be chaotic.'[42] Some 40% believe that 'the government should decide whether certain ideas should be allowed to be discussed in society.'[43] Three out of four Thais view a diversity of political and social views as threatening, while almost half are unwilling to tolerate minority viewpoints.[44]

The willingness to defer to government leaders leads to the tyranny of the elite and grand political corruption. Yet the public is quick to turn on leaders who abuse the people's trust or whose morally upright image is tarnished by corruption scandals. The high-handed ways of strong executives also leads to conflicts between the president and members of his own party and conflicts with other elite. The president then goes from imperial to imperiled in short order, and is subject to impeachment or a vote of no confidence, or limps along as a lame duck with little public support.

In short, democracy in East Asia is often a story of grand political corruption, of clientelism and the dominance of the elite and business interests, and of imperial presidents with little regard for rule of law. Thus, a third lesson likely to be drawn from the experiences of East Asian democracies is that democracy is no panacea even in those countries typically cited as success stories, and won't be in China either.

Conclusion: a critical appraisal of democracy

Advocates of the affirmative view of modernity continue to tout democracy as appropriate for all countries. Yet despite the vast amount of resources spent on promoting democracy around the world and the initial excitement surrounding the most recent wave of democratization, most third-wave democracies have turned out to be stunningly disappointing. The empirical reality—studiously ignored by those who confuse the slogan 'democracy and freedom for all' with a sound foreign policy and development strategy—has simply not lived up to the hype. It is true that many countries have democratized in the sense of holding some form of national elections from time to time. But the number of cases of successful consolidation of liberal democracy is small, and dwarfed by the number of failures. In his revised 2003 edition of *Democracy in the Third World*, Pinkney strikes a decidedly more pessimistic note than in the 1994 edition: 'While virtually all of Latin America and the vast majority of countries in Africa and Asia are now living under elected governments, breadth has been achieved but not depth, quantity but not quality, transition but not consolidation.'[45]

As in the previous waves of democratization, several third-wave democracies have reverted back to various forms of authoritarianism or have become mired in highly dysfunctional states of formal democracy. Many if not most democracies today are illiberal democracies. It is often difficult to tell them apart from authoritarian regimes except for the holding of periodic elections where the outcome is tightly controlled. The vast majority of democratic governments remain corrupt and inefficient. Few have managed to achieve sustained economic growth.

One of the cardinal principles of democratic transition theory is that successful transitions to democracy must not attempt to radically alter the property rights of the bourgeoisie or go too far in limiting the power of the military.[46] As a result, most transitions to democracy do not result in significant reallocation of political and economic resources. In many countries elites from the previous regime continue to control political power and key state resources.

Even when a new elite takes over, the avenues for public participation generally remain restricted and ineffectual. In many Latin America countries, strong clientelist and paternalistic states dominate civil society. In Africa and parts of Asia, the state is frequently weak, but so is civil society, often divided as it is along ethnic lines. Social groups generally lack the resources and skills to participate effectively in the policy-making processes. Internal disagreements and a general distrust of the state also undermine effective coordination. After democratization, civil society, once united in opposition to the authoritarian state, becomes fragmented. Entrenched conservative interests quickly organize and challenge more progressive groups in the public sphere. A variety of single-interest social groups compete for financing and to be heard on a range of issues from women's rights to public schooling to environmental degradation. When former opposition leaders become government leaders, they typically lose patience with human rights activists and other critical voices constantly reminding the government how far short it falls of inspirational ideals for a progressive society.[47] Political parties are frequently fractured, and dominated by personalities rather than substantive policy platforms. Elections do nothing to address the abject poverty, obscene inequality, and horrific human suffering so often found in developing democracies. The bottom line is a hollowing out of democracy, which all too often benefits a few, who become increasingly rich, at the expense of the many.

The political dominance of the business elite and the rise of money politics in newly established democracies undermine the democratic potential of elections, making a mockery of equality and fair competition inherent in the slogan of 'one person, one vote,' just as they do in longstanding democracies where the reality is often closer to 'one dollar, one vote.' Democracy then serves a legitimating function for an entrenched hierarchical order in which government officials and business leaders have a closer and more mutually rewarding relationship to foreign business interests than to their own constituents and fellow citizens.[48] Many poor people internalize arguments that they as individuals are responsible for their dire straits, undermining efforts to create a movement to address larger structural reforms needed to address poverty, including the need to pay greater heed to global injustice. NGOs do their best to put out fires here and there, but do not or cannot address the larger structural issues of globalization and unequal economic development among and within states. By taking on some of the welfare functions abandoned by the state, they may actually be aiding the neoliberal project and undermining the possibility of a critical revaluation of the politics of development. In those few newly established democracies fortunate enough to enjoy sustained growth, the middle class facilitates political stability, but often at the expense of more radical popular movements.[49]

Critics decry the large gap between *formal or electoral* democracy, where elections are controlled by and serve the interests of elites, and *substantive or progressive* democracy, which gives equal voice to the marginalized and addresses the disparities in resources, power, and opportunities.

In sharp contrast to the mainstream literature, critical authors do not see democratic consolidation as just a process of allowing the elites to settle their disputes through the use of prevailing political institutions. Nor do they contend that a polity becomes democratic only by holding periodic national or local elections. . . . [T]hey claim that the main purpose of creating a democratic political culture is to develop a new structure of governance designed to expand human capabilities. A system such as this not only allows people to participate in decision-making, it also ensures that people hold governments accountable for all of their actions.[50]

Yet the commonly offered solution to the twin problems of democracy and inequality—more democracy, and in particular more 'empowerment' of the disenfranchised—is inadequate. Allowing greater voice to the poor, while desirable, is no magic cure:

Participation by the poor in civil society and governance bodies, by and in itself, does not necessarily lead to effective poverty reduction results. Prescriptions of participation by the poor to alleviate poverty seems to be based on the faulty assumption that, if only the poor were participating more actively in programs designed to improve their conditions, then they would be on the road to redemption. Not only is this view patronizing, it is also ignorant of the complexities surrounding the human experience and causes of poverty. States often lack the political will and resource commitments to implement community-based poverty reduction programs.[51]

Given the harsh reality in most developing democracies, it is hardly surprising that the majority of citizens have little faith in their governments and are fed up with politics. Between 1996 and 2000, only 27–37% of Latin Americans expressed satisfaction with democracy.[52] Support for democracy in 2002 was lower than in 1996 in all but four countries. Few place much hope in democratic institutions, with only 19% trusting political parties, 22% trusting parliament, and 26% trusting the judiciary. Citizens are registering their disgust and indifference by refusing to exercise their hard-won right to vote in ever-increasing numbers. Latin Americans have lost confidence in democracy because of the lack of economic growth, the deterioration of public services, the rise of crime, and the persistence of widespread corruption. In such an environment, politics and elections become a side issue. Instead, people have turned in increasing numbers toward religion and ethnic issues, often with dire consequences for the stability of the newfound democratic regime. When they do vote, they increasingly are opting for populist candidates who reject much—sometimes too much—of the Washington Consensus.

It is tempting to attribute the problems of developing democracies to growing pains: surely over time these troubles will be overcome. There are however two serious problems with this pollyannish view. First, describing these dysfunctional, oftentimes failed states, as in 'transition to democracy' is simply no longer credible, and fails to capture the depth of the problems or the depressing reality that many countries are caught in a stable but bleak cycle of poverty, government malfeasance, and despair.[53]

The odd state in which many 'democracies' find themselves is so confusing that scholars cannot even agree on what would constitute consolidation or whether consolidation is a meaningful way to approach the issue. Scholars with a minimal definition of democracy as procedural or electoral democracy often dispense with the notion of consolidation entirely. Those who define democracy substantively in terms of equality and social justice find precious few examples of consolidated democracy. Even those in the middle with more modest definitions of democracy that emphasize political culture, citizen participation, government accountability, and institutions such as rule of law find few examples of consolidation among third-wave democracies.[54]

So dire is the situation that scholars have now turned their creative energies to classifying dysfunctional democracies, in hopes of being able to formulate better policies for turning them around. Thomas Carothers, for instance, distinguishes between two types of dysfunctional democracies, one suffering from 'fleckless pluralism' and the other hindered by a 'dominant-power.' The former is more common in Latin America, the latter more common in Africa, with examples of both in the former Soviet republics.[55]

In light of the poor empirical record of democracies, the dominant view through the 1960s, 70s and early 80s that there are preconditions to successful democratization is now making a comeback—although no one is sure what the necessary preconditions are or how to satisfy them. At minimum, no one is saying that economic wealth is the only relevant factor, or that it is a necessary or sufficient condition. An institutionalized market economy; a reasonably high level of wealth; a robust and democratically oriented civil society; cultural values that promote tolerance, civility, and compromise; ethnic and religious harmony; elites willing to compromise and to distribute resources and opportunities more equally; political stability; and functional institutions, including a legal system that meets the requirement of rule of law and government institutions that practice good governance—all may be desirable, and may facilitate democratic consolidation. But what happens when those conditions are not present?[56]

The second problem with the view that fledgling democracies will work out the kinks over time and then all will be well is that the crisis with democracy is not limited to developing countries. Developed countries have their own share of problems. According to the Eurobarometer, the majority of EU citizens do not have much trust in the parliament, national government, judiciary, or the press. A mere 17% trust political parties. The overwhelming majority of citizens in the newer EU countries are dissatisfied with the way democracy works in their countries, while a full 40% of all EU citizens are not satisfied.[57]

In Asia, between 75% and 92% of citizens are dissatisfied with the government in democratic Japan, South Korea, India, Indonesia, and the Philippines.[58] Taiwan and South Korea have generally been considered success stories in that they have achieved relatively mature democracies, although the violence and allegations of impropriety in the 2004 presidential election in Taiwan have tarnished Taiwan's image. With a 2.0 ranking on Freedom House's political rights and civil liberties scale, they are categorized as 'liberal democracies,' despite shortcomings in rule of law and restraints on executive power.[59] Nevertheless, a large number of citizens in Taiwan and South Korea continue to harbor serious doubts about democracy. One survey found that 'support for democracy lags well behind the levels detected in other emerging and established democracies. And on some dimensions of belief, the two publics exhibit a residual preference for authoritarian or non-democratic principles, akin to the portrait of traditional or "Asian values."'[60] Support for democracy declined in South Korea after the financial crisis and the scandals in the Kim Young Sam presidency, including one involving his son. Whereas almost 60% of Koreans believed that the political system was working well in 1994, only 36% felt so by 1999.[61]

In the US, where the Bush administration has staked its claim to a place in history on the killing of terrorists and the exporting of 'freedom and democracy,' the list of complaints is long. Leading many people's lists is the dominance of money in elections. Parties are dependent on interest groups for financing—groups that take advantage of numerous loopholes in porous campaign finance regulations to funnel money to their preferred candidates, often in the guise of nonpartisan infomercials that conceal the group's true identity and party affiliation. Incumbents are perpetually raising funds for the next election. They are rewarded for diverting attention from their duty to serve the public by victory in the next round, with members of the House enjoying an unconscionably high victory rate in excess of 90% and senators a slightly less but still hefty 75% margin. They are also aided by blatant gerrymandering and partisan redistricting schemes.

Many potential candidates simply give up in the face of the overwhelming odds created by the incumbent advantage in fund-raising and gerrymandering. An editorial in the New York Times entitled *Elections with no meaning* pointed out that in 2002:

> 80 of the 435 House races did not even include candidates from both major parties. Congressional races whose outcomes were in real doubt were a rarity: nearly 90 percent had a margin of victory of 10 percentage points or more. It is much the same at the state level, only worse. In New York, more than 98 percent of the state legislators who run for re-election win, usually overwhelmingly. Anyone who knows anything about New York's state government knows that's not because the populace is thrilled with the job they're doing.[62]

Also high on many people's list of complaints is the diminishment in the quality of civil discourse. Rather than the Habermasian utopia where citizens meet on equal terms to reason out their differences in a spirit of compromise, the public sphere is now dominated by demagogues competing to see who can shout the loudest and ideologues spouting prepackaged sound bites. Privately funded think tanks organized along party lines prepare these carefully crafted vignettes, often on the basis of public opinion polls that allow them to target highly specific swing groups. These think tanks contribute to the vulgarization of scholarship, luring academics with grant money tailored to a particular ideological agenda, the promise of being able to 'make a difference' and research positions where autonomy over one's research agenda is given up in exchange for never having to set foot in a classroom again.[63]

The media, increasingly dominated by a few major conglomerates, treats the audience as consumer. It contributes to the decrease in the quality of public discourse by 'manufacturing consent' for a particular ideological view, often by seeking out the most extreme spokespersons for a mock debate.[64] News has become partisan entertainment: watch the Fox channel, and see the mighty conservatives gang up on the token liberals; or read the *New York Times* and see how cosmopolitan liberals view the rest of the world.

The result is an increase in apathy among voters, especially among the poor and marginalized, who, like their counterparts in developing countries, suffer from growing inequality and the lack of social justice. The index of voting equality dropped from .644 in 1964 to .546 in 2000. Whereas in 1964, 54% of eligible voters in the bottom income quintile in the US voted (as compared to 84% in the top quintile), only 39% voted in 2000 (as compared to 72% in the top quintile).[65]

Many people around the world, in rich and poor countries, are deeply dissatisfied with democracy, but they see few viable alternatives. Democracy seems to be 'the only game in town,' even if a losing one for most.

Large majorities in many developing countries would readily trade their political freedom for social stability and sustained economic growth. Twice as many Latin Americans—some 56%—would choose development over democracy, with 50% agreeing or strongly agreeing with the statement that they would not mind having a nondemocratic government if it could solve economic problems.[66] In response to a similar question, over twice as many Chinese felt that economic development was more important than democracy.[67] Similar results in other developing countries in Asia are not surprising given that 60–84% of Indonesians, Indians, Filipinos, Vietnamese, and Chinese identify economic difficulties as their number one concern, with 37% of Indonesians, 44% of Indians, 57% of Filipinos, 31% of Vietnamese, and 18% of Chinese claiming difficulties in affording adequate food.[68] Somewhat more surprising is that a 1998 survey in wealthy Korea found that two-thirds of Koreans claimed economic development was more important than democracy, while in a 1999 survey only one out of seven chose democracy.[69]

To be sure, few people in developing democracies long for the return of military dictatorships and oppressive authoritarian regimes that often were no better at sustaining growth or distributing what wealth was generated. No one wants to live in a failed state dominated by rival army factions or torn by religious or ethnic violence. But the choice is not either dysfunctional democracy or dysfunctional *and* brutal authoritarian regimes. Several authoritarian regimes in Asia have been successful in stimulating growth, improving public services, ensuring stability, and curtailing corruption. Thus, whereas the majority of Latin Americans see no alternative to democracy, many Asians see some form of soft authoritarianism or nonliberal democracy as viable options.

Most Chinese citizens are happy with their lives, optimistic about the future, and relatively satisfied with the government on the whole, largely because the government has been successful at maintaining stability and improving the living standards of most people. In 2002, two-thirds of Chinese thought their lives would improve in the next five years, compared to only 8% who anticipated being worse off. A 2005 survey of seventeen countries found that 50% of Chinese felt they had in fact made personal progress in the last five years, the highest percentage of any country. In addition, 51% are satisfied with their household income, 82% are satisfied with their family life, and 63% are satisfied with their job. More than 70% expressed satisfaction with national conditions. In contrast to the vast majority of citizens who are dissatisfied with the government in Asian democracies, almost half of Chinese, and almost 70% of Vietnamese, are satisfied with the government.[70]

For Chinese and Vietnamese, and increasingly for others trapped in dead-end democracies in Asia and elsewhere, the markets before democracy approach of China and other East Asian countries understandably holds some attraction. This does not mean that Chinese and Vietnamese citizens would not some day prefer democracy to the current political system. It simply means that democracy is not the main issue at present for most people. However, China may democratize at some point in the future, just as other East Asian states have. Thus, the next chapter considers the implications of China democratizing or not.

CHAPTER EIGHT

What if China democratizes? What if it doesn't?

Gazing into a crystal ball to predict when a country will democratize and what the consequences will be is a risky business. Seemingly solid regimes can crumble suddenly, sometimes due to unforeseen events. Nevertheless, given the firmly held belief among some that China should democratize, we need to consider the likely consequences. No one wants to see China democratize only to descend into chaos. What then are the consequences of democratizing or not democratizing likely to be? I begin with the domestic consequences and then turn to the implications for other countries and the world order.

Domestic economic, political, legal, and social development implications

The consequences of democratizing depend of course on how and when China democratizes.[1] Sudden regime collapse, perhaps precipitated by an economic crisis followed by massive social unrest, would have extremely negative repercussions both domestically and internationally. However, democracy is most likely to be the result of evolution rather than revolution. China will most likely democratize when there is a broad consensus among state leaders and citizens alike that soft authoritarianism has outlived its purposes. The transition is likely to involve a pact among the elite. There is a reasonably good chance that the CCP, or a sizeable faction within it, would be able to reconstitute itself as a social democratic party or some other reformist party and then retain power. There may be single-party dominance for a considerable period, as in Japan, Singapore, and Malaysia. Whoever becomes the leader would most likely enjoy broad powers. The opposition may be split among factionalized parties who draw support from the charisma of particular persons rather than established political positions, as in South Korea, Thailand, and the Philippines. As a result, the real contest may be over who emerges as head of the reconstituted CCP. This battle may be largely an internal party matter, and not much more transparent or subject to public influence than the current process to choose the leader of the CCP.

If the transition is the result of evolution and consensus that soft-authoritarianism has outlived its purpose, then the transition is likely to occur at a relatively high level of wealth. If so, democratization will be supported by, and not threaten the vested interests of, the middle class or big business. Civil servants are also likely to favor moderate change, and to retain their positions after democratization. The existing corporatist ties between the state, technocratic elites, and the business community will remain largely intact. The government may be more open and transparent, and subject to scrutiny by a somewhat more liberated and aggressive media. But citizen participation in political affairs will still be limited. Civil society will be divided between groups with a political or economic agenda that are closely aligned with the state, and groups that are nonpolitical or have turned away from politics toward religion, cultural activities, or other private pursuits.

The ruling technocratic elite will still enjoy considerable powers. Rulers will be expected to get the job done. If democratization occurs in the near future, the legal system will still be relatively weak. The institutions and mechanisms for checking state power in particular will be unable to restrain a strong executive led by a charismatic ruler that enjoys, at least for the first few years after election, a popular mandate to protect China's national interests, attack corruption, and put an end to what will inevitably be rising crime and more social disorder.

Even if democratization is postponed for decades, China will have a lower per capita income than the US or other high income countries. The government will be under tremendous pressure to maintain high growth rates and to shelter segments of the population from the adverse effects of economic globalization. If anything, a democratic government may be more vulnerable to popular pressure and thus more likely to engage in protectionist trade practices. Trade deficits, and hence economic tensions, will continue for years to come whether or not China democratizes given lower wages in China and a much lower per capita income.

Intellectual property violations will continue regardless of the nature of the regime until the costs to the domestic political economy exceed the benefits, just as they did in the West and in the other successful Asian countries. Already, domestic businesses are the main victims of IP violations. However, domestic companies face the same issues as foreign companies, including an unwillingness on the part of local governments dependent on economic growth to put a stop to IP violations that would increase unemployment; institutional weaknesses in the legal system and agencies for enforcing IP violations, combined with insufficient resources; and strong economic incentives for IP violators to risk punishment, even criminal sanctions, given the lack of alternatives in a developing country such as China where many people are unemployed or underemployed. Although the US adopted a more tolerant approach toward IP violations once Russia democratized, China is another story. It is highly unlikely that China will receive the same benefit of the doubt given the large trade deficits and the general fear that a rising China, whether democratic or not, threatens US hegemony. It is much easier to be gracious toward the vanquished than the next up and coming challenger.

Foreign investment in China might also go south, figuratively and literally, if democratization led to political or social instability. Foreign investors may also be put off by more aggressive unions and increased pressure to comply with environmental standards. In general, foreign investors do not mind authoritarian regimes provided the government is able to ensure stability, avoid excessive rent seeking, and provide the necessary economic freedoms and infrastructure to facilitate business transactions.

The economic challenges for the short term are to continue to push through changes that will make China more competitive in the long term, including structural reforms needed to improve efficiency and increase the flow of information as well as further legal reforms. Premature democratization may make institutional reforms more difficult. Civil war, social disorder, and political infighting weaken states and undermine the government's capacity to carry out necessary reforms. Powerful interest groups, especially big business, are more likely to dominate the political process, blocking reforms that benefit the broader public.

Implementation of rule of law is a long-term process. Democratization might lead to greater judicial independence and a more authoritative court, but it need not, as we have seen in some other countries in Asia and elsewhere. It will not magically solve the substantive problems that plague the legal system. Unlike the magician who pulls a rabbit out of a hat, Chinese leaders—whether democratically elected or not—cannot simply click their heels three times, mumble a few words and presto, out pops a competent core of judges to staff thousands of basic level courts. Nor will democratization suddenly put an end to judicial corruption, transform institutional culture, or reduce the tensions between the courts, procuracy, and legislature. If anything, it may become more difficult to force the courts, legislature, and procuracy to accept compromises when they are struggling to assert themselves in the new political order. On the other hand, the nature and purpose of the legal system would change. As a result, the legal system would produce different outcomes on some issues depending on whether China implements a communitarian or liberal variant of rule of law or some other variant.

The implications for the protection of rights are also mixed. Democratization at low levels could lead to political instability, chaos, and state repression, and hence an increase in personal integrity violations, as it has in so many other countries. There would most likely be fewer political dissidents, although again weak democratic regimes generally do not tolerate much criticism. Even if democratization occurs at a higher level of wealth, China—like other East Asian states—may invoke tough state security laws to crack down on anyone perceived to threaten political stability. The war on terrorism has legitimated reliance on these rules, or led to further abuse, depending on your political position. Many of those arrested may consider themselves to be engaging in the lawful exercise of their rights to criticize the government or advocate political reforms, and thus might still be characterized as political dissidents.

Most Chinese citizens however would enjoy broader civil and political rights under a democratic regime, even though civil and political rights would still be restricted, as in other Asian countries, and in countries at lower levels of development more generally. The media would be subject to restrictions in part because the public tends to be less liberal and less tolerant of dissenting opinions. In addition, the Chinese media is likely to continue to suffer from a lack of professionalism, to be subject to corruption and pay-offs, and to be prone to abusing its power and acting more as a demagogue than a watchdog.

Religious and ethnic issues will continue to be a problem under either type of regime. Rural minority regions will be poorer than other areas for a long time to come. The influx of better-educated and more highly skilled Hans will exacerbate ethnic tensions. Democratization might lead to greater demands for self-determination, even independence, for Tibet and Xinjiang. However, no administration is going to permit independence in the foreseeable future. As we have seen, democracies are fully capable of brutal repression of insurgencies and ethnic groups demanding greater autonomy and independence.

Crime is going to increase regardless of the type of regime as China becomes more industrialized and urbanized. However, democracy may exacerbate the increase in crime and social disorder if democratically elected leaders feel compelled to allow rural residents to move to urban areas without any restrictions, as might be necessary given that the majority of citizens live in rural areas and are no doubt tired of the discriminatory policies that have benefited urbanites at their expense. Indeed, underlying the common complaint among intellectuals and urbanites that China is not ready for democracy because the masses are ignorant and uncivilized (*suzhi tai di*) is the fear that rural peasants know all too well what is in their interest. Moreover, a democratic government would most likely also feel compelled to bow to international pressure and adopt more liberal laws to protect the rights of criminals, at least initially. If so, this might decrease the deterrent effect of the current harsh laws, resulting in more crime.

To be sure, democracies are perfectly capable of waging war on criminals. In the face of widespread calls to crack down on crime, developing democracies tend to cut back on the protections afforded criminals. It is unlikely that any Chinese government would abolish capital punishment or spend valuable political capital on defending the criminally accused in the face of public opposition. The problems of institutional culture and conflicts among the various branches involved in criminal justice are also largely regime independent. These problems will take time to resolve, and will be part of a larger process of legal reforms and professionalization. While progress in reforming the criminal law system is possible, it will be an uphill battle under any type of regime.

Democratization is not likely to have much of an impact on women's rights either. Women's rights are adversely affected by traditional attitudes, which are no more easily changed in a democracy. The transition to a market economy and economic globalization would still create problems for women in a democratic China, as they have elsewhere. The political impact of women in the informal sector, who are most likely to have suffered from economic globalization, is limited by their inability to organize. In general, women in other countries have not been successful in using the vote to resolve pressing issues because women don't vote as a block or solely on the basis of which candidate will better advance women's rights.

Labor groups are likely to benefit from democratization, although some Asian democracies have kept a tight leash on unions. While workers may be free to form unions, they will be gaining that right at a time when economic globalization has largely eroded its value. In the US, where only one out of thirteen private workers belong to a union, membership has decreased by two-thirds over the last fifty years. China has not suffered deindustrialization like many other countries. However, the work unit is less important than in the past, there is greater reliance on flexible labor markets, and many people work in rural areas or service industries, all of which make organization difficult.

Nor would freer unions necessarily emerge as a strong force for workers or the underclass. In many other Asian democracies, including Japan, unions have maintained close ties with government and management. Unions in Asia and elsewhere have also sought to protect their own, rather than worrying about the claims of non-union members for social justice.[2] In the US, the AFL-CIO is now split over the issue of whether to reach out to non-union members of the working class poor. Supporters argue that the union must broaden its political base by involving the growing number of marginalized people who have not benefited from economic globalization but who lack the capacity to organize large-scale social movements. It is not at all clear that Chinese workers in the manufacturing sector would have much desire to align themselves with workers in the informal sector or that unions would join political cause with the least advantaged members of society.

For the poor to be taken seriously generally requires paternalistic intervention by the elite plus the support of the middle class. It is possible that a charismatic leader could be elected on a platform that emphasizes social justice and the need to redistribute resources to the poor. The Hu and Wen administration initially enjoyed considerable popular support for what seemed to be more humane policies concerned with the plight of the least well off. However, the least well off continue to suffer. China is an increasingly pluralistic society, and it will be difficult for a party campaigning for office to appeal to everyone. Democracies are prone to elite domination because the elite have more resources, stronger social networks, and more organizational skills. The result, as we have seen, tends to be a lack of social justice, and political apathy, particularly among the least well off.

The debate over social justice in China rages today among 'the right' and 'the left.' While each of these broad categories contain many different, and even incompatible, positions on various issues, the left generally attributes poverty to structural causes rather than individual failure, and favors a larger and more direct state role in addressing the needs of the poor. In contrast, the right generally holds that the best approach is to maintain high levels of growth, to invest in human capital and institutions, and to provide citizens with the necessary tools and opportunities to compete successfully. The outcome of these debates will determine whether China develops more along the lines of Singapore and Hong Kong, or Japan and South Korea. To be sure, 'radical social justice' of the type envisioned by proponents of progressive democracy is likely to prove as elusive in China as it has everywhere else.

Would a democratic China be more nationalistic? Nationalism is a controversial subject. There is general agreement that nationalism is on the rise in China, and that nationalism is both a product of manipulation by the state and also a heartfelt and autonomous bottom-up movement. There is also a general consensus that the government so far has had the authority to ensure that nationalism does not get out of hand, but that it is playing with fire in stirring up nationalist sentiments. The government managed, albeit with difficulty, to put an end to weeks of violent protests in spring 2005 over Japan's attempt to become a permanent member of the Security Council and textbook changes that many Chinese felt glossed over Japan's actions in China during the Second World War.

There is not much agreement on anything else, including whether nationalism is likely to facilitate or hinder democratization, whether democratization would increase or mitigate the negative affects of nationalism, and whether a democratic but nationalistic China would be outwardly aggressive.

Some commentators believe that stirring up anti-Japanese or anti-American sentiments hinders democratization by directing attention away from domestic political reforms. However, others believe protestors are also frustrated with the government and the slow pace of political reforms, and just looking for ways to vent their pent-up frustrations. Thus, anti-foreign protests could easily turn into anti-government protests and calls for democratization.

While some worry that democratization will make nationalism more difficult to control, democracy proponents counter that the government would have less need to promote nationalism since it could rely on consent as the basis for its legitimacy. The latter view assumes that nationalism is largely a product of government manipulation rather than the result of a heartfelt bottom-up movement largely beyond the power of the government to control. Experience elsewhere suggests that nationalism cannot be turned on and off like a faucet.[3] Although democracy advocates often argue that open discussion will defuse nationalism, clearly many demagogues have risen to power in democracies by playing the nationalist card.

Views are also divided on whether Chinese nationalism is likely to lead to external aggression. One view portrays nationalism as harmless. Nationalism is just the healthy desire to see China restored to its rightful place as a great civilization after centuries of occupation and bullying by foreign powers. On this view, China has never or rarely been outwardly aggressive or expansionist. Foreign policy in the imperial era favored harmonious relations with others; today foreign policy is based on the Five Principles of Peaceful Co-existence. China's rise to superpower status will be peaceful—other countries have nothing to fear. The contrary perspective challenges this rosy view of Chinese history, and suggests that nationalism may lead to a much more aggressive foreign policy.

Nationalism to the point of xenophobia is of course not limited to China. Witness the recent hysteria over the attempts of Chinese companies to purchase IBM, Maytag, and most significantly the oil supplier Unocal—even though the US government has continually pressed China to privatize state-owned assets to make it easier for US companies to purchase major SOEs at fire-sale prices, and to relax its foreign investment rules so that American companies can more readily dominate key sectors of the Chinese economy from telecommunications to securities to banking. Witness also the worries in developed countries about outsourcing and the loss of jobs to China, India, and other developing countries—even though the loss of one job in Europe or America means employment for thirty-five people in poor countries.[4] And witness the political grandstanding of US politicians over the growing US trade deficit with China and their attempts to pressure China to free its currency—even though Federal Reserve Chairman Alan Greenspan concluded that there was no credible evidence that a higher valued yuan would help US manufacturers or lead to more US jobs, and warned that imposing punitive trade sanctions would most likely have the counterproductive effect of actually slowing China's move toward a flexible currency.[5]

Conflict is more likely when two nationalistic countries come into contact with each other. Will China's arising then threaten the international human rights regime, undermine democracy, lead to the support of dictators, and result in clashes with the US or China's neighbors? What type of world power will China be?

A clash of civilizations? Human rights and Chinese values

China, whether democratic or not, might adopt a more aggressive human rights policy based on differing ideologies and competing interpretations of rights as part of a cultural war with the US, and a larger struggle for the hearts and minds of the international community as China and the US compete for dominance. Yet this is unlikely. Although China has criticized the human rights movement for being biased toward liberalism and has begun to strike back at the US by issuing its own critical report of human rights in the US, it has done so mainly as a defensive measure, on the theory that the best defense is a good offense. It did not, for example, rush to join Singapore and Malaysia at the forefront of the debates over Asian values, even though many of its positions were compatible with the Asian values platform. Rather, China has sought to portray itself as a responsible member of the international community through increased participation in the international human rights regime. If anything, China is generally perceived as being surprisingly passive in not formulating new proposals or participating actively in international organizations except with respect to Taiwan and issues that bear directly on its own national security.[6]

As a strategic matter, the government will most likely conclude that there is not much point in a frontal assault on liberal democracy or in persuading others that liberalism is morally inferior to communitarianism or some other view. There is strong support for liberal democracy among the elite in international organizations, despite the poor empirical record of democracies and the many existing critiques of liberalism and democracy from Western and Asian scholars.[7] Most people tend to stick with what they believe—which is generally what they grew up believing. Philosophical arguments are unlikely to persuade most people to change their fundamental moral beliefs. Indeed, firmly held moral views are stubbornly impervious to contrary evidence regarding the actual consequences of such views or arguments in support of opposing viewpoints.

Even were government leaders so inclined, China lacks a coherent, normatively attractive positive ideology to export. Attempts to advocate Asian values, New Confucianism, and communitarian alternatives to liberalism have suffered from the lack of a systematic coherent theory.[8] In contrast, despite significant points of contention among liberals, there is a general sense that liberalism has some proper intellectual foundations—although liberalism also benefits from the halo effect where people assume there must be something to it since the richest and most successful countries are liberal democracies. Whether in the West or in Asia, communitarianism always seems less reputable, less solid, because of the lack of a systematic theoretical exposition. It seems more like a marginal critique of liberalism than a credible, full-fledged alternative able to stand on its own. We are still waiting for an Asian (Chinese, Korean, Thai, Buddhist, Confucian, Islamic) Rawls to synthesize values, beliefs, practices, and institutions into a normatively attractive systematic alternative to liberalism that is compatible with modernity and yet sufficiently distinctive to be more than just a variant of liberalism.[9] At present, Chinese citizens are much too divided about the future of China to produce such a consensus. It will be decades before China reaches a point of relative social, economic, and political stability to produce the kind of thick consensus needed to articulate a credible alternative, and to benefit from its own halo effect. By that time, China is likely to have democratized and become more like the other Asian countries on contested rights issues. If so, any normatively attractive alternative to liberalism will contain enough common ground with liberalism to avoid a 'clash of civilizations.' The debates will be more similar to the debates between liberals and communitarians or conservatives than to the conflict between communism and capitalism, or between Islamic fundamentalism and liberal democracy.

For the near future then, China is likely to keep a low profile while it consolidates power—so long as it is allowed to. China first articulated its rights policy when forced to respond to the criticisms of the international community in the wake of Tiananmen. The repeated attempts to censure China for human rights violations in Geneva resulted in China refining its critique of the human rights regime, becoming more active in counterattacking other countries, becoming more adept at manipulating procedural mechanisms in the UN human rights system, learning how to use its growing economic clout to lobby other countries more effectively for support, and investing more resources to influence the operation and restructuring of human rights bodies. Similarly, China's response to increased pressure from the Bush administration and the international community to democratize was to issue its own white paper on democracy.[10]

The next major challenge for China is how to respond to the increasing international and domestic pressure to ratify the ICCPR. On the one hand, China will continue to be criticized unless it ratifies the treaty. On the other hand, ratification will inevitably lead to greater confrontation with the international rights community by forcing China to defend more explicitly its interpretation on a whole series of contested rights issues. Some reform-minded Chinese scholars have argued that China could ratify the ICCPR without attaching many reservations or qualifying declarations on the basis that the PRC constitution and other laws provide for virtually all of the rights set out in the ICCPR. Apart from deliberately downplaying the gap between formal laws and actual practice, this view ignores the politics of interpretation. The rights in the ICCPR are stated at a fairly high level of abstraction, and thus are subject to a wide range of interpretation. The ICCPR Human Rights Committee is charged with interpreting the ICCPR. The committee's interpretations tend to be decidedly more liberal than the interpretation of the Chinese government. Although the committee's interpretations are nonbinding, they do carry weight in the international community, and can and will be used to 'shame' China. Were China to ratify the ICCPR, it would most likely do so with either a blanket reservation that the ICCPR has no domestic effect, as the US has done, or with a series of reservations and statements that greatly limit the domestic impact of the treaty. Either approach is fraught with risk. The US has been widely criticized for its reservations. China is sure to be subject to considerably greater criticism.

To be sure, Chinese citizens take tremendous pride in Chinese culture and civilization. Once China has consolidated power, Chinese citizens, led perhaps by charismatic nationalists demanding that China stand up to the US and its allies,[11] may push their government to champion a rights policy that reflects 'Chinese values.' Of course, not all 1.4 billion Chinese share the same values, and people's values will change as China becomes wealthier and more urbanized.[12] Nevertheless, fundamental beliefs tend to change slowly. If so, then China would most likely promote human rights policies that are less liberal and more collectivist or communitarian, that offer states a wider margin of appreciation on contested issues, and that reject a neo-Kantian deontic justification for rights in favor of a more pragmatic approach. While not constituting an all-out clash of civilizations, the different approach would produce different outcomes in particular cases across a range of issues. Ironically, pragmatic Chinese are more likely to be genuinely tolerant of different life forms than allegedly tolerant liberals.

LEADER OF DEVELOPING STATES? THE RIGHT TO DEVELOPMENT AND GLOBAL JUSTICE

Developing states see China as their natural ally in the struggle for global justice. Given China's geopolitical importance and rising economic clout, China is expected to play a leading role in the struggle to persuade wealthy countries to take the right to development seriously. China's support is also pivotal in the fight for fairer trade policies that do not result in increased impoverishment of developing countries while the rich get richer. Poorer countries want China to take a strong stand on issues such as access to patented drugs, protection of cultural artifacts, and local know-how not recognized under TRIPS, restrictions on the use of anti-dumping and safeguard mechanisms to limit imports of textiles and other products from developing countries, increased aid, and perhaps most importantly the elimination of agricultural subsidies and tariffs in developed countries. China, for its part, has been cautious about assuming the role of representative of developing countries, doing so on a case-by-case basis when the particular policy position favorable to developing countries is consistent with China's general national interests.

Nevertheless, China's human rights policies would likely emphasize the need to ensure the material well-being of all humans and to provide them with the tools and conditions to succeed, in keeping with the principles of the EAM. There is at least some hope that an increasingly powerful China, even after it becomes a benefactor rather than a beneficiary, will continue to pressure the international community to take seriously the right to development, to address global inequality, and to ensure that the poorest countries have adequate resources to develop and maintain political and social stability. China has for example canceled over $1 billion in debt from African countries. It has also emphasized the need to provide preferential treatment to Cambodia, Laos, Myanmar, and Vietnam in the framework agreement to establish a free trade zone with the Association of Southeast Asian Nations (ASEAN). And it has made a number of pledges to the UN to assist developing countries, including eliminating all tariffs on certain products and offering over US$10 billion in concessional loans and preferential export buyer's credit to developing countries over a three-year period, increasing aid and providing anti-malaria drugs and medical assistance, and contributing to the development of human capital by training professionals from developing countries.

While optimists hope that China will emerge as a champion of developing states, the more cautious simply hope that China avoids manipulating and exploiting the international trade regime for its own economic benefit, or at least does so to a lesser degree than other superpowers in the past. Most likely China, whether democratic or not, will do what is necessary to solidify power and protect its own economic interests, just like the US and other powerful countries, although it may be more generous and even-handed toward developing states.

China so far has adopted a cooperative attitude on economic issues. During the Asian financial crisis, it maintained a stable RMB at the expense of China's own exports in order to mitigate the impact of the crisis on its Asian neighbors. In the free trade agreement with ASEAN, China offered unilateral concessions on over 130 agricultural and manufacturing products, granted WTO benefits to countries that are not WTO members, and allowed countries to reap the benefits immediately under an Early Harvest Programme.[13] China has also imposed voluntary export controls on textiles, thereby effectively relinquishing the lower end of the market to Bangladesh and other developing countries. In addition, China allowed the RMB to float within a limited range in response to US pressure, and sought a broad-ranging compromise with the US and the EU over textiles.

All of these actions are arguably explicable in terms of China's larger interests. Maintaining a stable RMB during the Asian crisis and entering into a free trade agreement with ASEAN solidified relations with neighbors worried about a rising China. Strengthening regional ties both diminishes the likelihood of conflict within the region and provides an offsetting balance to US dominance globally and in the region. With increasingly higher production costs, China may lose the lower end of the market anyway to Bangladesh and other poorer countries. Apart from avoiding the imposition of US tariffs on Chinese goods, China's adoption of a more flexible exchange rate defuses inflationary pressures and fosters economic stability. A comprehensive textiles agreement allows all sides to avoid a series of WTO skirmishes that could lead to a trade war.

There can be little doubt that China has already begun to flex its economic muscles, for better or worse. It joined with other Asian countries in raising a WTO challenge to the US over steel imports. It has used its economic leverage to prevent countries from supporting Taiwan independence and membership in certain international organizations. It has also sought to establish a number of bilateral treaties and various forms of strategic partnerships with countries from Australia to Brazil for both political and economic reasons. A richer and more powerful China will be all the more likely to use its growing economic resources to persuade others to support its policies.

HUMANITARIAN INTERVENTION

China's rising may also have an impact on the developing area of humanitarian intervention. A nondemocratic China will remain cautious about infringements on sovereignty, sanctioning humanitarian intervention only when there is widespread and systematic abuse of rights, most likely subject to approval by the UN. It may also support governments that deal harshly with threats to social order, in keeping with the EAM.[14] A democratic China might be more likely to intervene and less likely to condone violent crackdowns to maintain order, but it is doubtful that policies would be significantly different based on the views of other East Asian states that have still taken a relatively conservative position on intervention.

Failed regimes present an interesting case. A stronger, more powerful China, whether democratic or not, is likely to perceive failed states as a threat to geopolitical stability, and a source of terrorism that could embolden separatist movements in China. The initial response may be to address the problems created by global inequality and a discriminatory trade system, and to provide material and technical assistance to developing states. The government has for example emphasized a 'new security concept' that goes beyond traditional state-to-state military concerns to include foreign policies that emphasize mutual stability founded on negotiations on a basis of mutual respect and economic development for all.[15] However, a hegemonic China may not have much patience for those states that fail to invest in human capital and institutions, or squander resources because of grand political corruption or ineptitude. In such cases, China might either simply walk away, if the risks to China were minimal, or seek to replace the existing regime, if the risks were greater.

Peaceful co-existence or coming conflict?

As for whether China will be aggressive toward the US and its neighbors, all one can say for sure is that only time will tell. The view that China has never or rarely engaged in aggression in its long history is surely a one-sided view of how China came to possess Tibet and Xinjiang, much less of the military conflicts with Korea in 1950, India in 1962, the Soviet Union in 1969, and Vietnam in 1979 and 1988. Although China has avoided military conflict since 1989, it has fired missiles and engaged in war games in the Taiwan straits in the mid-1990s and had a number of non-military skirmishes with its neighbors over various islands in the region.

By way of comparison, in the last twenty-five years, the US has been involved in some forty military actions, including wars in Iraq, Afghanistan, Yugoslavia, regime-changing invasions in Grenada, Panama, and Haiti, military assistance to rebel groups in Angola, El Salvador, and Nicaragua, and missile attacks on Lebanon, Libya, Yemen, and Sudan.[16]

During the war in Yugoslavia, NATO mistakenly bombed the Chinese embassy, although many Chinese to this day believe the bombing was intended to teach China a lesson for blocking US efforts to obtain UN approval for intervening. In 2001, a US spy plane and a Chinese fighter plane collided some 70 miles off China's coast, causing the Chinese plane to crash and the death of the pilot, while forcing the US plane to make an emergency landing in Chinese territory. Chinese authorities detained and questioned the crew, and searched the plane, notwithstanding protests from the US. After the US issued an apology, the Chinese government released the crew and the plane. In contrast, the US never formally apologized for the 1993 Yinhe incident, where the US navy stopped and boarded a Chinese freighter believed to be carrying illegal chemicals, although no chemicals were found on board. Such incidents have led to impassioned denunciations of the US in Internet chatrooms, and calls for Chinese leaders to stand up to what some Chinese see as US bullying and intimidation. It is possible that the rise of nationalism may cause Chinese leaders to be more aggressive in standing up to the US and other states should similar events occur in the future.

Supporters of the democratic peace theory would argue that a democratic China would not be a risk to geopolitical stability, or at least would be a lesser risk. Yet China becoming democratic is no guarantee of peace. The democratic theory may hold for wealthy, consolidated democracies, but it does not hold for poor and unconsolidated democracies, which are prone to internal and external conflicts.[17] Moreover, China would not just be any democracy, but a new upstart challenging US hegemony. Major powers go to war more often than minor powers, especially when dominance of the existing hegemon is being challenged.

One potential conflict is over increasingly scarce oil and natural resources. Some fear China's quest to secure oil and other resources will cause China to support dictators. According to US Congressman Christopher Smith: 'China is playing an increasingly influential role on the continent of Africa and there is concern that the Chinese intend to aid and abet African dictators, gain a stranglehold on precious African natural resources, and undo much of the progress that has been made on democracy and governance in the last 15 years in African nations.'[18] How or why China's policies would be any different than the policies to date of the US and other G8 countries is not made clear. Presumably the idea is that as an authoritarian socialist state China is less concerned about democracy and human rights than the US and European countries are. Yet Western countries' history of colonialism, support for dictators during the Cold War, and continued support for authoritarian regimes in oil-rich countries in the Mid East suggest caution in drawing any hard and fast distinctions based on regime type. Whether democratic or not, China may very well end up working more closely with some of the more authoritarian regimes in the world. However, if so, the main reason will be that the geopolitical and economic dominance of the US and Europe leaves few alternatives.

The most likely source of military conflict is the impasse over Taiwan. The best way to avoid a conflict is to maintain the status quo. Yet domestic political pressures are making that increasingly difficult. The 2004 election in Taiwan suggested that the demand for independence is growing, and that Taiwan's politicians may need to play the independence card to get elected. The perceived wisdom is that there would be a greater chance for reunification if China were democratic. However, reunification under even the most generous self-determination framework would require relinquishment of de facto sovereignty in many areas, and would not likely be supported by the majority in Taiwan unless the costs in decreased sovereignty were outweighed by significant benefits. Such benefits would presumably be economic in nature—though perhaps the threat of forced reunification also creates an unwelcome incentive. On the other hand, it is hard to imagine any administration, whether democratic or not, ceding independence to Taiwan in the face of massive popular opposition fanned by Chinese nationalists.

While China might go to war over Taiwan, China is not going to export revolution around the globe in the hopes of spreading communism. Within China, socialism as an ideology is increasingly incoherent and obsolete as a basis for policy-making, and no amount of money spent on reprinting or reinterpreting classical Marxist texts will be able to put Humpty Dumpty back together again. The Cold War is over. At least the first Cold War is over. If there is going to be a new Cold War with China, political ideology and cultural issues are not going to be the main sources of contention. The conflict will be due to realpolitik concerns over national security and economic interests.

There is no shortage of contentious issues—on both sides. China objects to US efforts to develop a missile defense system that would allow the US to fire nuclear missiles at China without fear of counterattack and mutual destruction. It also takes a dim view of US efforts to create offensive weapons in space and to deploy satellites that would disrupt other country's satellites, as well as arms sales to Taiwan. Nor does China appreciate the US led efforts to censure China for rights violations, or US pressure to let the RMB appreciate further, the limits on dual-use technologies, agricultural subsidies to US farmers, the invocation of surge mechanisms, or the reliance on anti-dumping cases to protect US industries.[19] The US for its part objects to nuclear testing by China, arms sales to countries that are not US allies, violations of agreements to prevent the spread of weapons of mass destruction, market access restrictions, intellectual property violations, and a host of other commercial issues.

Meanwhile, both sides are watching warily the other's efforts to form alliances and enter into bilateral and multilateral trade and security agreements in Asia.

For all of the possible sources of conflict, there are many areas where the interests of both parties are aligned. Both China and the US want to prevent North Korea from obtaining nuclear weapons and destabilizing the region, even if they don't always see eye to eye on how best to achieve that. Both sides joined arms, albeit for different reasons, in opposing efforts to expand the UN Security Council. They are allies in the war on terror. Neither supports the ICC. Their cooperation is essential for progress on global environmental issues and international money laundering. Their economies are mutually dependent: Chinese purchases of US Treasury securities are underwriting US trade and budget deficits; American purchases of Chinese products are fueling growth in China. Perhaps most importantly, both sides share a common interest in continued stability in China, and therefore in ensuring that economic, legal, and political reforms continue.

History shows that the rise of a new power usually leads to conflict. However, a knock-down, drag-out battle with China for world supremacy is not inevitable. This is a different era. There is less emphasis on territory as a source of power. Economic globalization has led to greater codependence. A more developed international trade regime has clarified many of the rules of the game, and the WTO is available to resolve disputes peacefully. The world is better informed about what is happening thanks to the global media.

Most importantly, there is a significant role for human agency in avoiding conflict. Although there will inevitably be conflicts from time to time, major conflict can be avoided if both sides are able to overcome their suspicions of each other and work through their differences in a frank but open-minded and constructive way. US policy will have to abandon neoconservative policies that seek to contain China, which is the surest way to bring about the kind of military conflict and economic trade war that all hope to avoid. Portraying China as a threat that must be contained fuels animosity and undermines those constituencies in China working to ensure that China's rise to power is peaceful. The US will also have to stop demonizing China on trade issues and applying double standards on human rights, which just inflames a vengeful nationalism. Chinese leaders for their part will have to resist the tendency to dismiss every criticism of human rights violations or expression of concern for Taiwan as an infringement on its sovereignty and an insult to the dignity of the Chinese people.

Both sides will have to make greater efforts to understand each other. Regular meetings of high level officials, cooperative efforts on economic and legal reform such as the United States Trade and Development Agency program to improve banking practices and the State Department's rule of law programs, and private sector programs to train government officials or explore ways to address the needs of the most vulnerable members in society—all are steps in the right direction.

In addition to trying harder to understand the other side, both sides will need to be more self-critical about their own shortcomings with respect to human rights, rule of law, trade, and external aggression. Neither side is beyond reproach. Both sides have legitimate complaints and concerns. Both sides face numerous obstacles in resolving their own problems and domestic pressures that politicize and complicate the situation. More humility is needed, especially but not only on the US side. US officials cannot just lecture Chinese officials, as if they were recalcitrant children who needed to be reprimanded by an older and wiser parent. There is a tendency to attribute differences with regard to democracy and human rights to cognitive dissonance—they just don't get it. But there are legitimate differences in values and interests at stake. Conversely, Chinese officials cannot rely on misty-eyed invocations of cultural practices to allay concerns that China's rising will be far from peaceful, especially while insisting that all US actions be viewed through a cold neo-realist prism of state interests.[20] Genuine dialogue is essential to work through these issues. Politicizing debates, reducing complex issues to sound bites, exaggerating problems, distorting facts, and demonizing the other side do not help.[21]

Genuine dialogue means being able to air differences. There will inevitably be hard negotiations as China continues its march to superpower status. Chinese leaders and negotiators have demonstrated that they are no pushovers. They have resisted foreign pressure to democratize, to mimic Western rule of law, to subject infant industries to global competition, and to prematurely engage in financial liberalization. The development process has been driven primarily by domestic concerns, and what the government has perceived to be in China's interest. That approach has been remarkably successful so far. But as China grows, it will have to assume the responsibilities that come with being a superpower, and forgo some of the self-interested policies (from greenhouse gas emissions to violations of international labor standards to intellectual property violations) that may be justified for developing states trying to catch up but are not acceptable for one of the world's great economic and political powers.

US–CHINA RELATIONS AS A JOINT VENTURE

In a recent speech that may represent a change in US–China relations, Deputy Secretary of State Robert Zoellick encouraged China to be a responsible stakeholder in the international order.[22] In so doing, Zoellick acknowledged that China is now a major power, drew a clear distinction between China and the Soviet Union, and rejected containment and balance-of-power strategies. He also allowed that China's economic policies, including a depressed currency rate, have been beneficial to China, although warning that China has now reached the point where it must compete on more equal terms. While noting that economic reforms must be matched with further political reforms, Zoellick did not call for democratization now, suggesting a more business-oriented approach.

Rhetorically, the tone of the speech was on the whole balanced and measured, although at times Zoellick's remarks appeared condescending, preachy, and hypocritical—such as when he cautioned that 'China needs to recognize how its actions are perceived by others. China's involvement with troublesome states indicates at best a blindness to consequences and at worst something more ominous.'

Substantively, China was offered a place at the table, but on terms that decidedly served US interests: lower currency rates, more protection of intellectual property, more transparency on military spending and future military plans, and financial support for the war in Iraq, including debt reduction, even though China opposed the war. Chinese concerns over US military and economic policies were not addressed, while the many challenges that China as a relatively poor developing country faces were briefly noted but quickly dismissed. The message appeared to be, now that China is a world power, it should join forces with the US and other world powers to maintain the international order that serves their interests, even if at the expense of other countries. China should help the US prevent other countries such as Iran and North Korea from obtaining nuclear capabilities; it should uphold intellectual property rights and support the international trade regime that has so richly benefited the rich; and it should cooperate rather than compete in securing oil and developing other energy sources to avoid strengthening the hand of the oil cartels and driving up oil prices. Zoellick also warned that until China toes the line, other countries will be forced to 'hedge relations with China.'

Zoellick's speech is praiseworthy, particularly given the domestic political context. After all, the Bush administration came into office with a policy of China as strategic competitor, and there are still significant voices advocating containment. Zoellick's proposals may provide the basis for a more coherent China policy. However, at this point, China is being offered a minority stake in a joint venture with little input on major policies and few veto rights over key decisions. As a nuclear power, a member of the Security Council, one of the US's leading trading partners, and the holder of an enormous amount of US Treasury bonds, China is already a stakeholder. The US may have to offer China more in the way of positive inducements before China will sign on. It may also have to give up some of the more coercive tools such as the annual censuring of China in Geneva for human rights problems. If so, China might be willing to go along even as a junior partner—for now. But at some point, China's leaders will want to increase their share in the joint venture, and have more say over major policies and future developments. Whether China's rising is peaceful will depend in large part on the willingness of the US and other world powers to recognize and accommodate China's legitimate interests and growing power, and to continually renegotiate the terms of the venture accordingly. While the relative shares of the existing powers may decrease, the hope is that they will still be better off with a smaller piece of a much bigger—or better—enterprise. But even should China's rise lead to relative net losses for existing powers, the alternative of superpower conflict is likely to leave all concerned less well off. For this venture to succeed, *all* the stakeholders will have to be responsible.

Conclusion

China's refusal to democratize has been a source of great contention. However, democratic elections will not solve most of the problems China is facing or causing other countries, and may exacerbate some of them. Given the rapid progress to date without democracy, the lack of most of the preconditions for a successful consolidation of democracy, and the success of other East Asian states that have followed the EAM and postponed democracy in contrast to the failure of those that democratized prematurely, the decision of Chinese leaders to put democracy on the back burner would appear to be correct. At minimum, it is entirely understandable why leaders of the largest country in the world would not want to risk chaos given the empirical record.

Democracy proponents claim that a democratic China would be able to implement similar policies—investing in human capital and institutions, attending to the inequalities that arise from economic globalization and the transition to markets, forcing through deeply contested economic and legal reforms—while maintaining political and social stability without repression. Unless China democratizes in the near future, we will never know if they are right. However, the empirical record of other countries that have democratized at lower levels of wealth, including in Asia, suggest that the more likely result would fall considerably short of the noble aspirations of democracy advocates. Democracy advocates might attribute the empirical shortcomings in other countries to a stunted form of electoral democracy:

what is needed is a more genuinely democratic system, a substantive or progressive democracy that gives voice to and addresses the concerns of the poor and marginalized. Unfortunately, substantive democracy exists as an ideal rather than a reality, especially in developing countries that lack the resources to provide robust welfare benefits and to ensure individuals have what is necessary to make the most of their capabilities. Chinese leaders would have to be considerably more risk preferring, and considerably less pragmatic, than they are now to take the chance on democracy of any kind at this stage.

Whether democratic or not, China's rise to power will present significant challenges to the current world order. Perhaps the best reason for hoping that major conflict can be avoided, despite the many risks, is that the costs to everyone of failing to overcome the obstacles in a peaceful way are just too high.

CHAPTER NINE

Conclusion: modernity with modesty. The strengths and limits of the EAM

China, the heart of the mysterious Orient, has fascinated Westerners for centuries. China has been much admired as a great civilization, the home of philosophers Confucius, Lao Zi, and Zhuang Zi, the source of delicate porcelain pottery and dancing calligraphy, the land of the Great Wall and imperial palaces with their majestic gardens.

Conversely, many Western commentators have portrayed China in harshly negative ways that often revealed more about their own normative biases and intellectual assumptions than about China. China was an unchanging, despotic regime where the lack of individualism reduced human beings to selfless servants of the greater authoritarian state. Chinese culture precluded the possibility of adopting manifestly superior Western institutions, including democracy, constitutionalism, and rule of law. Blinded by a misguided sense of cultural superiority, Chinese mistakenly believed they had no need for the material goods being flogged by the West, with the Emperor Qianlong dismissing the British ambassador with the comment: 'We have never valued ingenious articles, nor do we have the slightest need of your country's manufactures.' Adding insult to economic injury, Chinese rulers had the supreme arrogance to insist that foreign dignitaries actually follow Chinese practices by dropping to their knees to kowtow.

China's perceived shortcomings justified imperialistic attempts to impose Western ways. The failure of China's legal system to comply with Western conceptions of rule of law justified extraterritorial jurisdiction. The United States' Chinese exclusion laws were 'justified in part on the premise that the Chinese, as born slaves of Oriental despots, were incapable of understanding the notion of individual rights and could therefore never assimilate into America's Republican values.'[1] China's indifference to the offerings of the outside world and the haughty arrogance in requiring foreign dignitaries to pay tribute led to the gunboat diplomacy that forced China to open its markets to foreign companies. When the desire for Chinese products and the lack of desire for Western products led to a growing trade deficit, Western companies peddled massive quantities of opium, in violation of Chinese laws, thereby recapturing some of the precious silver—the foreign exchange medium of its day—piling up in the middle kingdom.

Today, the fascination with China continues, with China still perceived in two radically opposed ways, both slightly mysterious: it is, on the one hand, an enigmatic threat to the West, and on the other, a model for the much poorer Rest of the world seeking to modernize while maintaining indigenous lifeforms in this era of globalization. Just as the difficulties in coming to grips with China continue, so do the oftentimes heavy-handed attempts to remake China in the prevailing image of the West. Chinese are still taken to task for failing to properly appreciate the importance of human rights and democracy. Western governments are still trying to pry open Chinese markets, and to force China to play by the rules of the game—rules which they as the dominant world powers have largely designed to promote their own economic interests.

China's challenges

It is of course still too early to sit in final judgment of China's efforts to modernize. We do not know whether China will succeed in its efforts to achieve the same level of wealth as Japan, South Korea, Taiwan, Singapore, or Hong Kong. Nor do we know whether it will be as successful in implementing rule of law as they have been, or in achieving the same level of success on human rights measures and other indicators of human well-being. Nor do we know when it will democratize or when, if ever, it will become a 'liberal democracy.'

How middle income countries break through to the upper echelons remains mysterious, in part because so few countries have made it into the top ranks since the eighteenth and nineteenth centuries. The only viable model for most countries seems to be the EAM, although countries that now seek to follow the model face different challenges than the East Asian states that rose to power in the latter half of the twentieth century. China is certainly facing many challenges, some of them not encountered by its predecessors in Asia, including greater pressure to democratize, to protect an expanded range of human rights, and to comply with a more comprehensive and onerous international trade regime.

One of the biggest challenges will be to bring the political system more into line with the economic system. That will involve deeper institutional reforms in all sectors. The role of the CCP in daily governance needs to be clarified, with greater separation between the CCP and the state. That does not mean that the CCP will have no role to play. In some cases, the Party is the only entity with the ability to break deadlocks in the power struggle between central and local governments, different regions, or different state organs. Nevertheless, the proper role of the CCP needs to be reconsidered and formalized in a way consistent with the principle of legality and the requirements of rule of law. The legislative system would benefit from further professionalization, with full-time rather than part-time delegates in the NPC and local people's congresses. The experimentations with local elections should continue by allowing elections at increasingly higher levels of government. The administrative system needs to be improved to ensure government officials are more accountable to the public. All of the various mechanisms for limiting abuse of power need to be strengthened, including administrative reconsideration, administrative litigation, administrative supervision, the Party discipline system, and the letters and visits system. The role of civil society in decision-making and monitoring state actors should also be increased. One way would be to establish consultative committees that include citizens to review local policing policies, allegations of torture, and government land confiscation and relocation decisions. The media must become a better watchdog, with greater freedom to report on important issues, including corruption. The government must also find ways to reduce central–local tensions and regional protectionism.

The authority and competence of the courts must be further strengthened if the judiciary is to meet the new challenges and play the role expected of it by increasingly rights-conscious citizens. Deep institutional reforms of the judicial system are required, including changing the way judges are appointed and courts are funded. The excessive limitations on civil and political rights must also be addressed, especially in cases involving discussion of legitimate issues of public concern such as corruption, government takings, and abuse of power. The growing tendency of local government officials to use defamation laws or other laws to attack citizens who express critical views should be nipped in the bud. All parties should be given their day in court, and entitled to a fair trial. Procedural justice must be taken more seriously.

There are still doubts about whether Chinese bureaucrats raised in a planned economy are sufficiently market oriented and technically competent to oversee the transition. The fear is that they will hang on to power too long, and move too slowly in streamlining the approval process, dismantling monopolies, and separating government agencies from corporate activities. State-owned enterprise reform, including downsizing and liquidation of money-losing and insolvent enterprises, is an ongoing process, as is the accompanying development of a functional social security system. Much remains to be done to address the many problems of the banking system and securities markets, and to address shortcomings in corporate governance. The government must also decide how fast to liberalize trade, whether to allow the RMB to appreciate further, and a host of other issues that have led to economic crisis in other developing countries. While the government has been more open to foreign direct investment than other Asian states, it has emphasized openness as a means to catch up to the West. However, the emphasis on economic nationalism and a stronger China may be at odds with heavier reliance on foreign capital,[2] and may give rise to a protectionist backlash, particularly if other countries continue to impose quotas on Chinese traders or block acquisitions of companies by Chinese firms.

At the same time, the government must deal with a number of pressing social issues, including a breakdown of the moral order, which has resulted in a turn toward religion for some and a cut-throat acquisitive materialism for most. The growing disparities in wealth between the eastern region and the rest of China, between rural and urban residents, and even within cities are potentially destabilizing—and in any event dehumanizing. Perhaps even more destabilizing is the widespread view that many of the rich have become wealthy through government connections, corruption, and other illicit means. Then there are the problems of rapid industrialization and urbanization, including the large influx of migrant workers, rising crime, and more social order problems, as well as severe environmental degradation.

These are difficult issues. There will be reasonable disagreements about how best to address these problems, and about the pacing and sequencing of reforms.

Nevertheless, China's performance to date has exceeded expectations, and there are reasons to be optimistic about the future. It is a large country, with considerable room for further growth. As rule of law and good governance are highly correlated with wealth, there is reason to expect that the legal system and government institutions will continue to improve as China becomes richer. The leaders and the citizenry are pragmatic and committed to restoring China to its former glory. And the experiences of other Asian countries demonstrate that success is possible if China continues to follow the EAM, and resists the pull of inertia or the siren call of conservatives to cut back on or slow the pace of reforms. This is not a time for the weak-willed or faint of heart. Decisive, progressive leadership is essential to break through logjams and maintain the forward momentum built up over the last twenty-five years, and to address the needs of those who have been left behind by economic reforms.

Chinese citizens may be willing to accept shortcomings if they feel steady progress is being made. They may feel the government is doing its best, or at least reasonably well, given the circumstances.

But their patience has limits. The EAM social contract requires that the government show results in exchange for the broad powers granted it. Chinese leaders have no choice but to continue with economic, legal, and political reforms. The general direction of reforms is clear, even if the timing, sequencing, and details of specific reforms are not. China need only look at its more successful neighbors to get a general sense of the way forward.

What others can learn from China and successful Asian countries

The success of China and other Asian countries suggests several important lessons for developing countries. First, much of the Washington Consensus was right, especially the points that focused on sound macroeconomic principles for the domestic economy such as fiscal discipline, a broad tax base, and public expenditure on health care, education, and infrastructure. Other aspects, especially those that involved opening the domestic economy to foreign competition or reflected particular views about the role of the state in the economy popular at the time among neoliberals such as privatization or financial and trade liberalization, have proven to be incorrect or to require adaptation by developing states in light of their particular circumstances. China's restrictions on trade and foreign investment, its undervalued currency, and the prudent pace of financial liberalization, may upset politicians and their constituencies in rich countries, but they have served China's economic interests well—just as the restrictions and subsidies in rich countries have served their national economic interests well. China has enjoyed high growth rates without the shocks including a sharp drop in GDP levels experienced in Eastern Europe or the financial crisis that affected some of its Asian neighbors. While economists continue to debate the proper sequencing of reforms, China's experience supports a prudential approach that promotes competition within the domestic economy while gradually opening the domestic economy to international competition, and delays financial liberalization and in particular capital account convertibility until late in the game.[3]

Second, developing countries must continue to invest in human resources and institutional development. Contrary to some critical accounts, rule of law is essential for sustained economic growth. This does not mean that poor countries need to import wholesale the political-legal institutions found in rich states—they cannot and generally should not. Rather, they must take advantage of local resources to develop institutions that respond to local needs. Over time, there may be more convergence in institutions and practices as countries become wealthier and are able to afford the costly infrastructure of developed countries. But even then, there is ample room for institutional variation consistent with general rule of law principles.

Nor does the importance attached to rule of law assume that any legal system actually plays the role or lives up to the ideals sometimes suggested in civic textbooks. Legal systems are complex. There is always considerably more discretion, as well there should be, than some of the interpretations of rule of law as a formalistic rule of rules would suggest. But as anyone knows who attempts to establish a business, or who is arrested, or who wants to challenge the government's seizure of his property in Bangladesh, China, and the US, rule of law matters, and there is a big difference in how well legal systems meet the generally accepted principles of a thin rule of law. To be sure, differences in normative systems and social-political philosophies will lead to different thick conceptions of rule of law. China's socialist rule of law, Singapore's soft-authoritarian or communitarian rule of law, Islamic rule of law, and liberal democratic rule of law will produce different outcomes in particular cases because the laws and practices reflect different values.

Third, and related, laws must reflect social norms and conditions. Liberal laws are not always appropriate. When laws are radically at odds with the deeply held views of the dominant majority, they are rarely implemented. This creates a gap between law on the books and actual practice that undermines respect for the legal system and rule of law, and fuels a resentful nationalism in Asia and other developing countries over the neo-imperialistic imposition of contested values. The title of a recent book captures a more appropriate attitude: *Human Rights with Modesty*. In explaining the growing unease about universal claims, the book's editor Andras Sajo points out, 'the unity of humankind under the current terms, to the extent unity is at all on offer, is unconvincing to those who feel that this comes at their expense . . . [P]roblems that came up time and again include lack of validity, bias, or even complete irrelevance of universal legal solutions to fundamental human problems . . . Further, human rights thinking and action often suffer from the predominance of double standards, arrogance, and incompetent absolutism of bystanders.'[4] The crisis over universalism reflects concerns about the increasingly specific and comprehensive policy advice being given to developing countries, as well as the increasingly coercive means of enforcement, including the imposition of sanctions and in the extreme the use of military force to effect regime change in the name of humanitarian intervention and democracy.

There is undoubtedly much in the ever-expanding human rights corpus that people in developing states will find attractive. China has accepted much of the human rights agenda, and amended its laws to reflect basic human rights principles. However, it has been selective in its adaptation, rejecting some basic principles, and interpreting or implementing other principles in light of existing conditions. In that sense, it has adopted a pragmatic approach that seeks to particularize what are oftentimes exceedingly broad and abstract principles.

Fourth, developing countries should take seriously the rising inequality that often attends development. Higher inequality leads to resentment, even if the poor lack the political clout to do much about it. The government should adopt economic reforms that benefit the broad majority first, as China and other East Asian states have done.[5] Sacrificing economic efficiency in the name of equity and social justice is sometimes justified. As noted, China has limited bankruptcies of state-owned enterprises to minimize lay-offs and enhance social stability. This admittedly has created additional problems for the banking system, which is burdened with bad loans provided to insolvent SOEs to keep them afloat. Sooner or later, these issues will need to be addressed, and the cost may be higher if the problems are addressed later rather than sooner. But at that point, the country may be more stable, and at a higher level of development, and thus better able to afford the higher costs.

Fifth, political stability is essential. China has been able to maintain stability, though it has done so at considerable cost, including to the exercise of civil and political rights. This is a bitter pill to swallow. But sometimes it is necessary to take bitter medicine to ensure healthy development.

Sixth, and another bitter pill, democratization at lower levels of wealth is likely to be counterproductive, as it generally has been in other developing countries.

Seventh, and perhaps the most important lesson for other countries, is that a pragmatic approach to reforms is essential. One of the keys to success in China and East Asia more generally has been the willingness to experiment, to try different approaches to solving common problems, and then to evaluate the results free of economic, normative, or political dogma. Although China is often portrayed as a country dominated by the rigid ideology of Leninist socialism, in fact Chinese leaders have been resolutely pragmatic, as captured in Deng Xiaoping's homey advice that the color of the cat matters not as long as it captures mice. Ironically, nowadays, it is the Western liberal democracies, particular the US, that appear to be dogmatic and fundamentalist—at least when it comes to giving advice to others on how to run their country.

Limits of the EAM and China as paradigm for developing states

Can other countries follow in China's large footsteps? To what extent will the EAM work for them? Other countries that have managed to succeed in the last fifty years have arguably followed a roughly similar path, with rapid growth occurring under an authoritarian regime, democratization occurring at higher levels of development, and ongoing reforms aimed at strengthening institutions. Greece, Spain, and Portugal all democratized at relatively high levels of wealth. In Eastern Europe, the wealthier countries such as Poland,

Hungary, and the Czech Republic have been more successful in the transition from authoritarianism than the poorer countries such as Albania and Romania. In Latin America, Chile stands out as the closest example, although Mexico may also fit the model to some extent.[6]

There will be additional test cases in the future. Vietnam and Laos are now following the model, so far with impressive results. There are a number of Middle Eastern countries that also are beginning to show improvements in rule of law and achieving economic growth within a nondemocratic political structure.

There are obviously many differences within these countries that require attention and analysis—but that is another project for another time. Here I can only offer a few general observations about the applicability of the EAM to other countries. Although the success of countries following the EAM is impressive, there are ample reasons to be cautious about taking the EAM as the latest off-the-shelf blueprint for developing states.

First, there are significant variations among these Asian countries in economic policy, legal institutions, and political systems, and with respect to particular legal doctrines and practices. Singapore and Hong Kong are small city-states, with economies that rely heavily on trade through their ports, whereas the others are much bigger states whose economy depends more on domestic markets. Small family businesses have played a large role in Taiwan's economy, while large industrial conglomerates played a dominant role in Korea and Japan. Export policies and foreign investment regimes differed both among states and within states over time.[7] Most countries avoided fiscal deficits—some through balanced budget laws, others through reliance on technocratic policy-makers—but others had deficits as high as in other developing countries, although none so high as to destabilize the economy.[8] While East Asian states generally kept labor on a tight leash, labor–management relations were decidedly more harmonious in Japan than in Korea.

On the other hand, that countries with such wide diversity were able to succeed by following the general principles of the EAM suggests that there is something to them, and that the EAM may travel better than might be expected at first glance. However, the generality with which the EAM is stated will still force policy-makers to make tough decisions.

A second and related concern is that there are still doubts about the utility of some of the specific policies adopted by China and other Asian countries. Economists continue to debate the wisdom of supporting infant industries, whether exchange rates should be fixed, free-floating, or flexible, and when and how trade and financial liberalization should occur. Moreover, some of the policies and practices adopted by Asian countries have been problematic. Support for domestic industries has sometimes led to the bailout of inefficient companies, often for political reasons. Governments have sometimes moved too slowly to liberalize and open up key sectors to foreign competition. The close relationship between government and particular companies, including in some cases a direct economic stake in the company, has exacerbated problems of local protectionism in China. And the tight control on unions has resulted in inferior working conditions and safety problems. Other countries will want to experiment with ways to avoid some of these shortcomings.

Third, even assuming agreement on the superiority of some of the economic policies adopted by China and other Asian countries, many developing states may not be able to implement them. Some failed states are simply too weak to govern effectively. But even in relatively more stable developing countries, the government's ability to set economic policy is now more constrained by the international trade regime. States are less able to protect domestic industries and promote exports as a result of the WTO, the increasing reach of intellectual property regimes, and multilateral and bilateral trade agreements.[9] Rich states increasingly rely on anti-dumping actions, surge mechanisms, countervailing duties, and the imposition of quotas to limit imports from developing countries or to retaliate against perceived distortions in 'free trade' practices. Countries that want to become members of the EU must open their markets, adopt rule of law, and protect human rights as a condition for entry. Poor countries in other parts of the world are often forced to adopt economic policies and institutional reforms as a condition for aid, including allowing greater access for multinational corporations to natural resources and key market sectors. In response to such pressures, the Commission on Africa declared that there should be no other conditions on aid except that the funds are used for development and elimination of poverty, and that government spending is transparent and accountable.

Increased competition may also be undermining the ability of states to protect workers and support a generous social welfare system. The Wal-Mart phenomenon may be pushing down margins everywhere. If poorer countries must increasingly answer to the global agencies of capitalism—the IMF, World Bank, and WTO—richer countries must answer to avid consumers who want the highest quality product for the lowest possible price regardless of place of origin.

But a race to the bottom is not inevitable. The financial crisis in South Korea 'facilitated the transformation of a developmental state into a welfare state by not only bringing social inequality and welfare to the core of social and political discourses, but also paving the way for the new policy of productive welfare.'[10] The government can offset the impact of globalization to some extent by adopting policies that minimize unemployment and create jobs, by retraining workers, and by strengthening medical, work injury, unemployment, and pension insurance schemes. The effects of globalization in any country will be a function of state capacity, leadership commitment, technocratic competence, resource availability, domestic politics, and institutions.

China is relatively fortunate—it is a large, politically powerful developing country that has long had nuclear capabilities. Other developing countries will be much more vulnerable to external pressures. Not many developing countries dare to go toe to toe with the US, issuing their own reports criticizing the US for human rights violations or unfair trade practices. Even if they did, it would not matter. To be sure, China is not immune to foreign pressure, as evidenced by the revaluation of the currency, the compromise over textiles, and the attempts to address intellectual property violations.

Conversely, while other developing states may have less room for maneuver than China does, they are still not completely powerless. Some developing states clearly have chosen better policies than others. And the WTO and other international trade laws do provide some room for developing states to promote exports and assist domestic companies through improvements in the regulatory regime that make exporting easier; use of export credit agencies; encouragement of export-oriented foreign investors; support of research and development or improvements in infrastructure in areas where domestic companies are weak or are likely to be able to export; and entrance into regional or bilateral trade agreements that may provide access to domestic companies to other markets on preferable terms or offer other competitive advantages not generally available to all countries. Developing countries may also unite in calling for a reconsideration of WTO rules that prohibit them from adopting the same successful policies that East Asian states—and developed states—used in the past.

Fourth, many countries have already democratized, and those that have not are under tremendous pressure to do so. Once a country has democratized, government leaders may not be able to ignore the demands of powerful constituencies or favor one group at the expense of others. Consumers and laborers, for their part, may no longer be willing to sacrifice their own interests at the altar of the development state. The expansion of the human rights corpus to include social and economic rights has increased citizens' expectations of government. Yet many developing countries lack the resources to deliver. They are thus unable to delay political reforms by buying off the populace with higher material standards of living.

Countries that follow China in postponing democracy will be subject to widespread criticism. Despite China's impressive achievements, those who take civil and political rights and 'democracy now, not later,' as the metrics regularly judge China a failure. But then the other Asian countries would also have been deemed failures at similar points in their developmental arc. Indeed, these Asian states might still be judged a failure by those who insist on a liberal interpretation of rights, as these countries continue to score lower on civil and political rights measures than others in their income class, and to limit rights in ways consistent with a communitarian or collectivist interpretation. But then many in Asia judge Western countries a failure by their preferred normative standards.

While authoritarian regimes are likely to incur the wrath of Western critics, a modified EAM along the lines found in Singapore, Malaysia, and Thailand where a democratically elected leader runs the country in accordance with the basic principles of the EAM may be somewhat more palatable. To be sure, human rights activists, among others, would still denounce the government, as we have seen. However, the general public is generally more supportive—as long as the government delivers the goods.

The proliferation of nonliberal democracies and soft-authoritarian regimes has blurred the lines between democracy and authoritarianism. Rather than simply classifying regimes as democratic or authoritarian, and then turning a blind eye to what goes on in democracies while shining a floodlight on every shortcoming in authoritarian states, we need to examine how all states actually operate, to hold all states equally accountable, and to avoid painting all authoritarian regimes with the same broad brush. In defending his administration against liberal critics, Lee Kuan Yew observed: 'Our citizens live with freedom and dignity in an environment that is safe, healthy, clean and incorrupt. They have easy access to culture, recreational and social amenities, good standards of education for our children and prospect of a better life for future generations.'[11]

Fifth, just as Singapore's Lee Kuan Yew did not claim that what worked in Singapore would work in every country, neither do Chinese leaders claim that they have discovered the one true path to riches and the good life. The most basic premise of China's approach is that reforms must be pragmatic and build on local circumstances. Blindly copying all of the details of China's approach will almost inevitably lead to failure. Which aspects of the EAM will work for other countries is ultimately to be determined by the same pragmatic methods of experimentation.

Various factors may affect the outcome, and produce different results in Asia. Cultural differences may be one factor. The success of East Asian countries has been attributed in part to 'Asian values' and the impact of Confucianism, which led to an emphasis on education, hard work, high levels of personal savings, a nationalistic desire for a strong state, and a willingness to sacrifice personal interest in the name of the overall good.

Political economies differ. China and other East Asian countries have benefited from traditional beliefs that government officials are supposed to be *junzi*—morally exemplary persons who ensure the material and spiritual well-being of the citizens. Of course, the reality has often been considerably different. Nevertheless, despite grand political corruption, Chinese leaders have taken seriously their duty to improve the lives of the people, and to contribute to a stronger China. There have been limits to clientelism and corruption. As we have seen, the political economy of other countries has been less hospitable, with clientelism and abuse of power for personal or narrow ethnic ends often undermining efforts to improve government institutions and resulting in the diversion of resources from a broad-based investment in all members of the society.

The development path of countries may also diverge because of differences in colonial history. The impact of colonialism on future development depends on who the colonizers were, how deep the penetration was, how long it lasted, and the particular policies and institutional development of the colonial rulers.[12]

Many other factors will also come into play—as they have in Asia—including the strength and role of the military, the nature and extent of ethnic diversity, the prevalence of religious beliefs, the role of religion in social and political life, neighborhood effects from others in the region, and relations with the US and other global powers.

Pragmatism has always been about the application of creativity and intelligence to contemporary problems in order to devise novel and ameliorative solutions—which themselves will lead to further problems and the need to continue to experiment with an open mind. Reformers cannot afford to look only West or only East, only up to the state or only down to grass-roots movements, only to culture, politics, or economics. A more context-sensitive approach is needed. Fortunately, no one seriously engaged in reforms in China seems to think there is any other alternative. Other developing countries will also have to feel their own way across the stones—as they say in China—adopting, modifying, or rejecting aspects of the EAM, the Beijing Consensus, and the Washington Consensus as need be.

Finally, at the risk of restating the obvious, China is far from perfect; on the other hand, it is far from the worst. We must not lose sight of China's achievements, its relative success in attacking many problems, or the dismal failure of other states, including developing and developed democracies, to overcome many similar problems. Other countries may learn from China's experiences. Other countries may also be able to improve on China's performance—and then China may be able to learn from their experiences. Learning, whether among developing countries or between rich and poor countries, is a two-way street. China must do better in many ways if it is to meet the expectations of its citizens and the world community. But then so must other countries, both rich and poor.

Endnotes

CHAPTER 1

1. While it is unlikely China will become the largest economy by 2020, in a survey of a dozen Nobel Prize winners in economics, most predicted that China would have the largest economy in the world in 75 years. See Wessel and Walker (2004).
2. A Pew Research Center survey of attitudes in sixteen countries found that more than half of the respondents in eleven countries viewed China favorably. Similar majorities in thirteen countries had a favorable view of France, Germany, and Japan, whereas majorities in only six countries viewed the US favorably. Of seven European countries, only Poland viewed the US more favorably. Even in the UK, the strongest ally of the US in the war on terrorism and the war in Iraq, 65% viewed China favorably as compared to just 45% for the US (Dinmore 2005). On the 'Four No's,' see Ramo (2004).
3. See Gordon Chang (2001), predicting at the time the book was written that China would collapse around 2006.
4. See, generally, Murphy (2004); Deller et al. (2003); van der Vyver (1998); Gunn (2002); Malone and Yuen Foong Khong (2003); and Danchin (2002).
5. See e.g. Clarke (2003).
6. Upham (2002: 1). While much of his article focuses on Japan and the US, Upham explicitly appeals to China's economic success to buttress his arguments.
7. McCormick (2000: 5).
8. Bernstam and Rabushka (2002).
9. Kim (2000: 131, 143).
10. Huntington (1996).
11. Wang (2000) discusses, and dismisses as applicable to contemporary China, three reasons for this view. Authoritarian regimes often are based on radical ideologies such as fascism or communism that are

all-encompassing and take world domination as the ultimate foreign policy goal; political power is often highly concentrated in the hands of a paramount leader such as Mao or Stalin; regimes that rely on repression to maintain control domestically are more likely to rely on force to achieve their ends internationally.

12. Bernstein and Munro (1997); Mearsheimer (2005).
13. See e.g. Zakaria (2004); Ramo (2004); Chan (2002).
14. Stiglitz (2003); Rodrik (2003); Godoy and Stiglitz (2006).
15. Evans et al. (1985); Lowi (2002: 47); Rocamora (2002: 85); Stiglitz (2003).
16. See Ramo (2004); *The 'Washington Consensus' and the 'Beijing Consensus'* (2005).
17. Williamson (2004).
18. For a more comprehensive discussion of neoliberalism and its negative impact on equality both between and within countries, see Rapley (2004).
19. Most commentators, although not apparently Ramo, include economic reforms before political reforms, with democratization only at a high level of wealth, as part of the BC. See e.g. Bernstam and Rabushka (2002).
20. Ramo (2004: 3).
21. Ibid. 4.
22. Zhao (2000: 32–4); Pan Wei (2003).
23. See e.g. World Bank (2005); Commission for Africa (2005). The Commission for Africa goes to great lengths to emphasize the need to take into consideration and build on African cultural values and practices if reforms are to succeed. The Commission also insisted that Africans have a greater voice in the reform process, and called for greater African representation in the World Bank and IMF, as well as a seat on the UN Security Council.
24. 'China,' 'the state,' and the 'Chinese Communist Party' are all abstractions. These abstract entities consist of individuals and groups or factions, themselves consisting of individuals, who hold diverse views on many issues. The official position of the government will often differ from the views of particular government officials and Chinese citizens, who themselves often hold diverse views. Nevertheless, the strength of different views in society can be measured through polls. Some views are more dominant than others. And speaking of 'the state's view' or 'China's position' still makes sense when referring to official government positions. In any event, for stylistic reasons, the 'country (or state, or Party) as person' metaphor can hardly be avoided.

25. In addition to providing a succinct statement of the affirmative and admittedly optimistic view, Howard-Hassman (2005) sketches a more pessimistic scenario. Nevertheless, she remains optimistic. Claiming that opponents of globalization tend to exaggerate the detrimental consequences, she depicts globalization's woes as short-term obstacles that may be overcome, although doing so will require class action and social movements. As she acknowledges, the optimistic model is 'not so much a prediction as a rough description of what happened in Western Europe and in North America' in previous centuries. To her credit, she acknowledges that non-Western states can no longer follow the exact same path as Western powers because the contemporary concern for human rights would prevent them from engaging in colonialism, practicing slavery, and committing genocide. One might add that states today are also under pressure to democratize, to respect a much broader range of civil and political rights than in the past, and to treat social and economic rights as justiciable—as real rights—rather than aspirations honored mainly in the breach.
26. See Trakman (1997); Aziz (1999); Mutua (1996); Smolin (1995/1996). Bartholomew (2003) suggests the way to overcome the imperialism in the current human rights movement is to extend the principles of Habermasian deliberative democracy to the international arena to ensure the legitimacy of human rights.
27. Mutua (2001).
28. Przeworski et al. (2000: 270).
29. UNDP Human Development Report 2003, at 1.
30. Paul (2003: 310).
31. UNDP Human Development Report 2003, at 8, citing Gini coefficients of .66 globally compared to .61 for Brazil. In 2005, the global Gini was .67, exceeded only by Namibia. UNDP (2005: 38).
32. UNDP 2003: 2.
33. Ibid.
34. Commission for Africa (2005: 27, 280). The US provides almost $4 billion in subsidies each year to cotton growers alone. This is more than three times the amount of US aid to Africa. *Cutting Agricultural Subsidies* (n.d.).
35. Commission for Africa (2005: 280).
36. Ibid. 280.
37. UNDP (2005: 10)
38. United Nations Conference on Trade and Development (1999). Srinivasan (2002) concludes that on balance, the Uruguay Agreement

that established the WTO was tilted against poor countries. Developing countries undertook wide-ranging and costly institutional reforms, including the establishment of patent and copyright systems and technical, sanitary, and phytosanitary standards. They agreed under TRIPs to 20-year patents and 50-year copyrights, even though the empirical evidence on whether patents are even needed to stimulate innovation is weak and the evidence that 50 years is too long for copyrights is convincing. In exchange, they received limited tariff reduction in the manufacturing sector and even more limited relief in the agricultural sector. The UNDP (2005: 135) reports that 96% of patent royalties go to companies in developed countries. Athukorala (2002) observes that the setting of 'dirty tariffs' (setting bound rates well above applied rates) by developed countries (and some developing countries) further limited the benefits for poor countries of the Uruguay Round. In addition, developed countries have also imposed various technical barriers to importation of processed food from developing countries. As a result, developing countries are only able to export the raw product, to be processed in the developed countries. Developing countries have complained that the Sanitary and Phytosanitary Agreement allows developed countries too much discretion in setting standards and denying access to imported products no matter how minimal the risk. Standards also vary considerably by country, making compliance difficult and costly for exporters.

39. Boughton and Quereshi (2004: 44). The impact on particular developing countries will vary depending on whether they are net importers or exporters of agricultural products, and whether they would be able to shift production toward agricultural and industrial products for export.
40. UNDP Human Development Report 2003, at 8.
41. Ibid. 5. Overall the absolute number of people living on less than $1 per day dropped by at least 200 million to 1.2 billion by 1998. Much of the decrease is due to the success of India and China, neither of which followed the full range of Washington Consensus policies. China was successful at lifting 150 million people out of poverty between 1990 and 1999. Other studies put the total number of people lifted above the $1/day line in China at between 250 and 400 million. Ramo (2004: 11).
42. Boughton and Quereshi (2004: 44).
43. Commission for Africa (2005: 64).
44. UNDP (2005: 85, 94). In 2003, the US spent twenty-five times as much on the military as it did on development assistance. Although the US gives just 0.18% of GNI in aid, the Senate and House cut nearly half of

the $2.3 billion increase proposed by President Bush for 2005. *Where's That Veto Threat* (2005).

45. World Bank (2000: 120). Dittmer (2002: 23) notes that the wave of financial liberalization that occurred after the collapse of the Bretton Woods agreement in 1972 was followed by financial crises in Finland, Norway, and Sweden between 1990 and 1993, in Europe between 1992 and 1993, in Mexico between 1994 and 1995, and in Russia in 1998.
46. UN (1999: 24).
47. Commission for Africa (2005: 122).
48. Rocamora (2002: 84).
49. While most people's intentions may be honorable, many may still be faulted for failing to attend to the actual consequences of democratization in developing countries, and for their complicity in the structural causes of global inequality that benefit richer countries at the expense of poorer countries. Pogge (2005) argues that citizens of affluent countries are harming the global poor by defending the present radically unequal distribution and the international order that produces it.
50. For an assessment of the variety of capitalism literature, see Hall (1999). Redding (1990) argues for a distinct type of 'Chinese capitalism.'
51. See e.g. Hollingsworth and Boyer (1999), noting that the authors contributing to the volume differ as to whether social systems of production will continue to have a strong national flavor or tend toward convergence.
52. Boyer (1999).
53. UNDP (2005: 116–17). Rich countries still account for two-thirds of world exports. Moreover, most of the increase in developing countries' market share of manufacturing goods is from East Asia and a handful of other countries. Seven countries, including China, account for 70% of low technology exports and 80% of high technology exports from developing countries.
54. Kaufmann et al. (2005: 14). The World Bank's country policy and institutional assessment (CPIA) ratings measure economic management, structural policies, public sector management and institutions, and policies for social inclusion/equity. The overall CPIA ratings of developing countries improved slightly from 1999 to 2004. However, progress on governance and institutional reforms, as measured by public sector management and institutions, while still marginally positive overall, was the weakest of all indicators. Moreover, there are significant regional differences and differences among countries within regions. Sub-Saharan Africa in particular lags behind in simplifying

procedures to start a business, securing property rights, strengthening contract enforcement, establishing rule of law and controlling corruption. World Bank Global Monitoring Report 2005.

55. Bhagwati (2004).
56. Wolf (2004).
57. Cited in Chomsky (2003: 209).
58. It is helpful to distinguish between *majoritarian democracy*, as a form of government in which the people exercise their right of self-determination and decide political issues through the majoritarian decision-making process and elections; *constitutional democracy* as a particular form of democracy that emphasizes individual rights as a check on the majoritarian decision-making process; and *liberal democracy*, which is a particular type of constitutional democracy that emphasizes individual rights and autonomy to a greater extent than communitarianism, for example. Constitutional democracy proponents worry that the majoritarian decision-making process may subject individuals and minorities to the tyranny of the majority. To protect the rights and interests of individuals and minorities, constitutional democracy places limits on the majoritarian voting process by removing certain issues from the legislative arena. My use of 'liberal democracy' may be narrower than for some who use the term to refer to what I have called 'constitutional democracy.' In general however, when commentators call for 'liberal democracy,' they mean a particular form of constitutional democracy where rights are interpreted in a liberal way. In any event, the notion that there must be limits of the majoritarian process is widely accepted: democracy today is constitutional democracy rather than majoritarian democracy. The controversy is over what the limits should be, who gets to decide, and on what basis the decision should be made. *Liberal democracy* is also often contrasted with *illiberal democracy*. I shall refer to communitarian, collectivist, Islamic, or other versions of constitutional democracy that may be normatively attractive to nonliberals as *nonliberal democracy*. I shall use the more pejorative 'illiberal democracy' to refer to repressive regimes that are formally democratic but fail to protect human rights.
59. The scare quotes reflect reservations about whether there is a single model. The main reservations are that the common features are stated at a high level of abstraction; there is considerable diversity with respect to specific issues and policies; and the essence of the East Asian approach has been pragmatism—which emphasizes flexibility and adaptation rather than dogmatic adherence to specific guidelines. That

said, there are significant 'family resemblances' (to borrow Wittengstein's phrase) or patterns among East Asian states. Thus, the World Bank (1993: 367), while denying that there is a single model or recipe for success, then turns around and summarizes a number of principles and lessons for other developing countries. In the end, not much hinges on whether these principles, lessons, and patterns are referred to as a 'model' or 'suggestive guidelines that must be interpreted and adapted to fit local circumstances.' Given the absence of any methodological or substantive standards for distinguishing between a 'model' and 'suggestive guidelines,' I will continue to refer to the East Asian Model (EAM) or the model—without scare quotes.

60. I have discussed this role of the legal system in China's growth at length elsewhere, and thus will not focus on that aspect of the problem. See Peerenboom (2002: 450–512) and (2003*a*), and the cites therein to the general literature and to the China-specific literature.
61. For a more detailed discussion, see Peerenboom (2002); Lubman (1999); Chen Jianfu (2002); and Chen (2004).
62. See Figure 5 below. The index is part of the World Bank's Good Governance Indicators. See Kaufmann et al. (2003) and (2005). Data for 2004 came out after the tables and charts for this manuscript were initially prepared. The World Bank's good governance numbers cited herein will be to the data as reported in 2003 rather than in 2005 unless otherwise noted.
63. The empirical studies, tables, and figures provide a snapshot summary of performance on a variety of rights and other indicators of well-being for the Asian region, China, several Asian countries, and other selected countries from around the world as comparison points. The studies define variables in different ways, use different data sets, rely on data from different years, are subject to wide margins of error, and so on. Thus, the tables are no substitute for more in-depth studies. Nevertheless, they are useful in providing a general sense of the range of difference within Asia on rights issues, and also in showing how Asian states compare to other states in other parts of the world at similar stages of economic, political, and legal development. On the advantages and disadvantages of empirical studies, the problems measuring human rights, and the pros and cons of different data sets and approaches, see generally Landman (2002); Barsh (1993); Bollen (1986); Haas (1996). Official government statistics on unemployment, the rate of growth, and so on have also been questioned. Accordingly, I also cite non-government sources for key figures where possible.

64. See e.g. *FM Spokesman on China's Efforts to Promote Human Rights* (2000).
65. I have argued (2002: 513–46) that China is likely to democratize in the long run for at least three reasons: to overcome what is likely to become a growing legitimacy deficit, to address accountability problems, and to ameliorate intensifying social cleavages.

CHAPTER 2

1. World Bank (1993).
2. Quoted in Sanger (1998).
3. Stiglitz (2003); Williamson (2004); Yao (2005). Ariff and Khalid (2005) attribute the crisis to financial fragility from financial liberalization together with the lack of institutional capacity to manage prudentially the risks, leading to over-reliance on foreign capital, along with overvalued currencies relative to China that decreased export competitiveness.
4. Fukuyama (2001). See also Chan (2002); Jomo (2001).
5. Haggard (2001: 133–6).
6. Chang (2000).
7. Yoshimatsu (2003).
8. Bell (2006).
9. Tat Yan Kong (2004) describes the continued viability of the Korean corporatist model, which is socially inclusive but politically exclusive. See also Moon and Yang (2002); Jeong and Lee (2001).
10. See Wang Jiangyu (2006), discussing analyses by Kaplan and Rodrik, and Stiglitz.
11. Bell (2006). See also Jomo (2001).
12. Krugman (1994).
13. Lardy (1998: 10).
14. Ibid.
15. Wade (1990); Amsden (1989).
16. Callon (1995).
17. More specifically, the World Bank (1993: 24–5) claimed that promotion of specific industries did not work; mild financial repression of interest rates on deposits and loans combined with direct credit to specific companies worked in some cases but was a risky approach; and export strategies were effective, but that changes in the international economic order including GATT rules reduced the ability of developing

states to rely on such strategies. The Bank also explained some of the interventions as justified even on neoclassical terms as they addressed coordination problems, information asymmetries, externalities, and other market failures.

18. The following is based on Williamson (2000) and (2004).
19. Williamson preferred at the time and continues to prefer an intermediate regime of limited flexibility to the more popular choice of either a firmly fixed or freely floating exchange rate. He now concedes that the preference for either a firmly fixed or freely floating exchange rate was a more accurate reflection of Washington opinion. In any event, he suggests successful East Asian states 'by and large' have had competitive exchange rates. The World Bank (1993: 114–15, 125–6) holds a similar view, noting that the general pattern was to move from fixed-rate regimes, to fixed-but-adjustable regimes with occasional steep devaluations, to a managed-float regime. However, the Bank acknowledges that some countries maintained a 'slightly undervalued' exchange rate versus the US dollar to boost exports.
20. China has learned this lesson the hard way. As we shall see, while China has done reasonably well in addressing poverty, the focus on aggregate economic growth has led to rising inequality. In addition, the relatively low amount of public spending on education and health, combined with a turn toward market forces in the health sector, have increased social tensions. In recent years, the government has begun to increase public spending on education, health, and welfare services.
21. Fuller (1976). On the differences between thin (procedural) and thick (substantive) theories of rule of law, see Peerenboom (2002: 65–71), and the cites therein. Briefly put, a thin theory stresses the formal or instrumental aspects of rule of law—those features that any legal system allegedly must possess to function effectively as a system of laws, regardless of whether the legal system is part of a democratic or non-democratic society, capitalist or socialist, liberal or theocratic. Although proponents of thin interpretations of rule of law define it in slightly different ways, there is considerable common ground, with many building on or modifying Lon Fuller's influential account that laws be general, public, prospective, clear, consistent, capable of being followed, stable, and enforced. In contrast to thin versions, thick or substantive conceptions begin with the basic elements of a thin conception, but then incorporate elements of political morality such as particular economic arrangements (free-market capitalism, central planning, etc.), forms of government (democratic, single party socialism, etc.), or conceptions

of human rights (liberal, communitarian, collectivist, 'Asian values,' etc.). There is relatively little controversy over the merits or elements of a thin rule of law in China, or for that matter anywhere these days. However, there are competing thick conceptions of rule of law, and considerable disagreement over particular aspects of particular thick conceptions in China, Asia, and elsewhere. See Peerenboom (2004*a*).

22. See generally Peerenboom (2004*a* and 2004*b*); Gillespie and Nicholson (2005). Although Hong Kong is now part of China and Taiwan's status remains contested, I will follow standard practice and refer to Hong Kong and Taiwan as states or countries for stylistic reasons.
23. Thaksin at one point rejected the EAM because of the low rates of growth in the more mature economies and the overdependence on cheap labor to fuel growth. However, he later recanted, claiming that his government was not abandoning the EAM but trying to build on and improve it. Thaksinomics involves running the country like a company, emphasizing equitable growth, promoting competition through marketization while protecting and directing credit to certain domestic industries, depressing the exchange rate to promote exports, promoting regional trade and bringing the informal economy into the formal sector. See Pasuk and Baker (2004: 99–133).
24. Laos and Myanmar have average growth rates over 6% between 1991 and 2001, suggesting that government officials may be beginning to realize the virtues of the EAM. Even North Korea shows signs of change.
25. See e.g. Carothers (2003). Brooks (2003: 280) concludes that '[d]espite billions of aid dollars, programs to promote the rule of law have been disappointing.' Lindsey (2006*b*) declares a consensus that many if not most legal reform projects in developing countries have failed. Dezalay and Garth (2002: 246) claim that most legal transplants either fail or are largely unsuccessful, although allowing that optimists might view the reforms as half-successful.
26. These include Antigua and Barbuda, Barbados, the Bahamas, Bermuda, the Cayman Islands, Malta, Martinique, Mauritius, Puerto Rico, and Samoa, in addition to Oman, Qatar, Bahrain, Kuwait, and the United Arab Emirates. Several of the island states rely heavily on tourism and the provision of financial services to companies looking for tax havens for economic development. Most have populations between 50,000 and 500,000.
27. Using time series data, Chang and Calderon (2000) find that the causal relationship between institutions and economic growth runs in both

directions, although the impact of growth on institutional development is stronger than the impact of institutions on growth. See also Rigobon and Rodrik (2005). Kaufmann et al. (2005: 38) agree that wealth matters to some extent but claim that the causal impact of income on governance is small and that 'most of the correlation between governance and per capita incomes reflects causation from the former to the latter.'

28. I summarize the main theoretical arguments for the relationship between rule of law and economic development as well as the critiques elsewhere. See Peerenboom (2002: 451–8) and the cites therein. See also Godoy and Stiglitz (2006).
29. See Upham (2002); Ohnesorge (2003); Clarke (2003). Even assuming these Asian countries were exceptions, individual country studies (much less reliance on individual cases or even studies of a particular industry or sector) cannot disprove the general correlations found in larger empirical studies. China, for instance, clearly has advantages that other countries may not have, including potentially large markets and a wealthy and entrepreneurial force of overseas Chinese to draw on.
30. For the argument that law played a greater role than normally suggested, see Pistor and Wellons (1999); Ramseyer and Nakazato (1999); Peerenboom (2002).
31. Rowen (1998). Other studies have found similar results. Chan (2002: 203) cites two surveys in which Hong Kong and Singapore receive the highest ranking, with Japan, Taiwan, and South Korea just slightly behind the US.
32. Rowen (1998). Thailand, Malaysia, and Indonesia grew more slowly, at around 3.5% per year. Seven countries, including North Korea, Mongolia, Vietnam, Cambodia, Laos, Philippines, and Myanmar, averaged less than 2% growth.
33. See Kaufmann et al. (2003).
34. For a variety of criticisms of current measures of rule of law, see Davis (2004).
35. Barro (1997).
36. Peerenboom (2003*a*).
37. See e.g. Ohnesorge (2003); Upham (2002); Clarke (2003).
38. Chan (2002: 192–9); World Bank (1993: 181–8).
39. A number of articles from a conference in Hong Kong on Social Networks and Civil Society: A Comparative Approach, which examined the role of social networks in the economy, were published in *Global Economic Review*, vol. 31 (2002). Articles from the same

conference examining the role of social networks in politics were published in Hahm and Bell (2004).

40. See Peerenboom (2002), ch. 3, discussing thin and thick conceptions of rule of law, and ch. 9, discussing administrative law. See also the country chapters in Peerenboom (2004*a*).
41. On the old and new law and development movements, see Trubek (1972, 1974, 1996); Faundez (1997); Peerenboom (2002: 148–53). Jensen (2003) distinguishes between five waves of reforms.
42. The World Bank's (1999) Comprehensive Development Framework, for example, includes a broad conception of development that encompasses recognition of the human dignity of individuals, access to justice, poverty reduction, women's rights and concerns about environmental degradation, and sustainable growth. This broader conception of development builds on the work of Sen (1999, 1993) and the capabilities approach.
43. Meyer (1996) found that GNP is the biggest contributor to civil, political, social, and economic rights. Hofstede (2001: 251) found wealth was the main factor affecting rights compliance, although individualism mattered in rich countries. Mitchell and McCormick (1988) found that higher levels of economic well-being were associated with better physical integrity rights records. Apodaca (1998) found that higher GDP was associated with better performance on women's rights.
44. The table is based on UNDP rankings for social and economic rights in 2002 as measured by the Human Development Index. Some scholars have complained about the quality of the UN data. However, other studies using an alternative measure of physical quality of life have also found a very strong correlation between wealth and indicators of well-being, including subsistence rights, life expectancy, infant mortality, and literacy. Using the Physical Quality of Life Index developed by Morris, Milner et al. (2004) observed that the strong relationship between wealth and better physical quality of life found in their study is consistent with earlier results of other scholars.
45. The UNDP's Gender Development Index (GDI) index is also highly correlated with the HDI index ($r = .99$), suggesting that they capture largely the same phenomena. Accordingly, I have not produced a separate scatterplot for GDI as the graph is virtually identical to the HDI graph.
46. The World Bank's voice and accountability index is a measure of civil and political rights.
47. See Kaufmann et al. (2003).

48. A chart comparing a country's performance to the average performance in its income class can be readily generated using the World Bank interactive data set by simply selecting the country and the good governance indicators, or selecting several countries for a particular indicator, and then selecting 'income category average.' See Kaufmann et al. (2003 and 2005).
49. Other Asian countries that underperform relative to income are Myanmar, Laos, and North Korea.
50. Other Asian countries that outperform the average are Mongolia, Cambodia, and East Timor.
51. See UNDP (2003: 41), Table 2.3.
52. Yao (2005) provides a detailed analysis of, and an explanation of the reasons for, the rise in inequality and enduring poverty.
53. See Khan (2006).
54. UNDP (2000) also notes that more than one in five adults in the US is functionally illiterate.
55. Gledhill (1997: 72–3). The UNDP (2005: 69) notes that the US and Mexico are the only two OECD members with child poverty rates over 20%
56. UNDP (2005: 58).
57. World Bank (1993: 44–6).
58. UNDP (2003).
59. The Gini index measures inequality over the entire distribution of income or consumption. A value of 0 represents perfect equality (every person earns the same), and a value of 1.00 perfect inequality (all earnings accrue to one person).
60. According to the World Bank (1993: 72–4), Malaysia's average Gini coefficient was approximately .50 for 1965–70, .48 for 1971–80, .43 for 1980–90. It then rose again to .49 in 2002. Malaysia has developed along lines consistent with the EAM to a considerable extent, including moderate state-led development, political stability, a readiness to invoke internal security regulations to limit the exercise of civil and political rights, labor discipline, and a pragmatic approach to reforms. Two notable differences are the concessions to Malays to offset the economic dominance of the Chinese minority and the early turn toward financial liberalization. See Nathan (2005); World Bank (1993).
61. Like other socialist countries, China was relatively successful in alleviating poverty and improving human development even before implementing economic reforms. However, like other socialist countries, China was not able to sustain the growth that is necessary if not sufficient to maintain improvement in human development.

62. World Bank (1993: 72–4). While the World Bank estimates the Gini coefficient in 2002 to be 40.3, the official PRC press has reported higher numbers of 42.4 in 1996 to 45.8 from 1998 to 2000. Li (2001).
63. Przeworski et al. (2000: 120).
64. World Bank (1993: 198).
65. Comments by the Chinese Government (2003: 3). China Economic Quarterly (2005: 20), citing the Ministry of Education. In 2006, the Minister of Education more cautiously promised to increase spending to 4.0%.
66. Information Office of the State Council of China (2004).
67. World Bank (1993: 199).
68. UNESCO/OECD (2005) found that spending on tertiary education increased by 77% in 19 middle income countries between 1995 and 2003, compared to a 43% increase in rich countries. Private spending on tertiary education increased on average from 13% in 1995 to 37% in 2003. In China, there has been a boom in tertiary education, with enrollments more than doubling. In 2003, private spending in the form of tuitions accounted for 29% of tertiary education, donations, and other fees accounted for 23% and government spending for 48%. Government spending also accounted for 47% of high school expenditures, in contrast to 74% for middle school and 81% for primary school. *China Economic Quarterly* (2005: 25–6).
69. Yao (2005: 210–11). Another study reporting aggregate data found a similar pattern of rising returns as one went up the educational scale, although with lower amounts at each step. *China Economic Quarterly* (2005: 26).
70. Bell (2006) notes that in the early 1990s, 40% of public expenditure in Sweden and the United States was for social welfare, whereas public spending on social welfare in Japan, South Korea, Taiwan, Singapore, and Hong Kong ranged from 14 to 31%. Underlying philosophies vary considerably from country to country. China and Vietnam have little problem reconciling broad welfare policies with state socialism. In contrast, Singapore emphasizes the need to avoid welfare dependency while providing individuals the opportunities and resources to become self-sustaining, as captured in the slogan: give me a fish, and I eat for a day; teach me to fish and I eat for a lifetime. Nevertheless, the government provides subsidized housing, schooling, and medical care. Hong Kong, despite its commitment to laissez-faire economic principles, also provides subsidized housing, schooling, and medical care. Holliday (2000); Petersen (2006: 244–50).

71. See Table 5 and Chapter 5.
72. China Europe International Business School (2005) citing data from the WHO.
73. See *Rumsfeld warns China on Military* (2005); *Pentagon's 'China Threat' Paranoia* (2005).
74. The UNDP (2005: 22, 29) claims that economic growth has outstripped social progress, noting that China advanced 32 places on global wealth rankings but just 20 places on the HDI. While the rate of child mortality continued to decline, the rate of progress slowed in the 1990s, although much depends on what reference years are used. India has experienced a similar pattern. One explanation is that once broad-based reforms have been carried out, the marginal costs of further improvements increase.
75. Liu Jian (2004), head of the State Council Leading Group Office of Poverty Alleviation and Development, attributes China's success to the leading role of the government, social participation by civil society, the self-initiative of the poor, economic growth, and comprehensive and coordinated poverty reduction and development planning.
76. Liu Jian (2004) claims that 'poverty reduction work in the new era emphasizes the poor villages as the basic poverty reduction unit, applying lump sum planning methods, distributing funds by year, implementing poverty reduction projects by phase, and solving the poverty problems village by village.'
77. UNDP (2005: 63).
78. Malaysia has a consociational system that provides political and economic guarantees to ethnic Malays. Under the quota system in place until 2002, 55% of university enrollment was reserved for Malays and 10% for Indians. The steady improvement in the fortunes of Malays over the years led to calls by non-Malays for more even-handed treatment. Nathan (2005).
79. Yao (2005) found that 24% of laid-off workers thought the reforms were right while another 53% thought the reforms were right for the state but not for the workers.
80. See the chart at **http://info.worldbank.-org/governance/kkz2002/sc_chart.asp**.
81. The patterns continue in the new data for 2004, albeit with China receiving somewhat lower scores in all areas except political stability. See Kaufmann et al. (2005).
82. On the disappointing results in Latin America, see generally the Proceedings of the Fourth Annual Legal and Policy Issues in the

Americas Conference (2004); Daniels & Trebilcock (2004). Of course Latin American countries differ in significant ways that affect the paths of legal reforms. Space limitations permit me to paint with only the broadest of brushes. For a more detailed discussion, see Dezalay & Garth (2002).

83. Rigobon and Rodrik (2005) found that greater rule of law produces more democracy and vice versa but the effects are not strong. Barro (1997) notes that there is little empirical evidence that rule of law promotes political freedom.
84. Zakaria (2004).
85. Tan (2002).
86. Thio (2004); Peerenboom (2004*b*).
87. Thio (2004).
88. Singapore's rating for 2002 on the Polity IV scale was 2.
89. Chen (2002); Report of the Joseph R. Crowley Program (1999); US Department of State (2001).
90. Rigobon and Rodrik (2005) found that while democracy and rule of law are both related to higher GDP levels, the impact of rule of law is much stronger. For a discussion of other studies, see Peerenboom (2005) and the cites therein.
91. Pinkney (2003: 65).
92. Przeworski et al. (2000); Barro (1996).
93. Przeworski et al. (2000: 78–127).
94. Ibid. 111.
95. Ibid. 78–127. See also Boix and Stokes (2003).
96. While emphasizing the importance of income inequality, Boix and Stokes (2003) argue that higher wealth does lead to democracy. However, while countries tended to democratize at lower levels of wealth prior to 1949, wealth has had less of an impact on democratization in authoritarian regimes since 1950. Przeworski et al. (2000) also find a small but significant effect of wealth on democratization at higher levels of wealth. However, the number of cases is small, thus reducing the reliability of statistical studies of the impact of wealth on democratization in reasonably rich countries.
97. Przeworski et al. (2000: 78–127) note that countries with income over $4,000 per capita (PPP) that democratize are not likely to revert to authoritarianism, and no country with an income over $6,055 has ever reverted.
98. Przeworski et al. (2000: 158) note that 96% of countries under $1,000 are dictatorships.

99. See e.g. Przeworski et al. (2000: 178), who also claim that not one study published after 1987 concluded in favor of dictatorships. However, one study employing sophisticated statistical techniques did conclude that economic development causes democracy but democracy does not cause economic development. Burkhart and Lewis-Beck (1994). Further, Barro (1997) found that at the extremely low levels of development, introducing greater political freedoms contributes to growth. That is, in the worst dictatorships, the lack of limitations on government power deters investment and growth. However, once a moderate amount of political freedom has been attained, democracy inhibits growth. At higher levels of development, the demand for democracy rises.
100. Przeworksi et al. (2000: 176–7).
101. Dowdle (2002) describes the processes of constitutional development in authoritarian and transitional states, with references to East Asian countries, and a detailed analysis of constitutional development in China. As he shows, emphasizing elections before the strengthening of governing institutions and the development of a constitutional order is to put the cart before the horse: 'effective electoral institutions are more the product of effective constitutional development than the motor for effective constitutional development' (p. 21). Similarly, he cautions against focusing too narrowly on the courts and judicial review, noting that constitutional review is usually the product of constitutional development rather than the source of constitutional development, and that courts and judicial review played little catalyzing role in the third wave of democratization. Even in Euro-America, the powers of judicial review were generally developed long after states became democratic and known for rule of law. Aggressive attempts by the judiciary to assert authority over other branches have resulted in political crisis in many countries, including South Africa in 1950, India and Korea in the 1970s, Malaysia in 1988, and Russia and Peru in the 1990s.
102. Zakaria (2004); Chan (2002).
103. Wang (2002); Hahm (2004); Ginsburg (2003).
104. Dick (2006).
105. Pangalangan (2004).
106. Muntarbhorn (2004: 362).
107. Baxi (2004: 339) notes that Indian activists 'remain familiar with the meandering nature of judicial activism.' Cassels (1989: 515) warns that India's activist judges have been criticized for violating rule of law, and that not all judicial decisions have favored the oppressed and less fortunate.

108. See Peerenboom (2004*b*); Pangalangan (2004); Hahm (2004).
109. For a discussion of physical integrity rights and derogation of rights in times of emergency, national security laws, and the effects of the war on terrorism in Asia, see generally Peerenboom et al. (2006).
110. See Peerenboom (2004*c*); Peerenboom et al. (2006).
111. Hahm (2006).
112. Juwana (2006).
113. Pasuk and Baker (2004: 149–55); see also Muntarbhorn (2006).
114. *Asia's Media Have Few Reasons to Celebrate World Press Freedom Day* (2004).
115. Baxi (2006).
116. Matsui (2006).
117. For empirical studies showing different value orientations in Asia, see Peerenboom (2002 and 2004*c*); Albritton and Bureekul (2003). Gillespie (2006) points out that current restrictions in Vietnam also reflect the appreciation on the part of the ruling regime that free speech and media destabilized the former colonial regime.
118. Levitsky and Way (2002).
119. Mosley and Uno (2002) found that the Asian and Pacific regions were not as protective of labor rights as Western, Central, and Eastern Europe, although they were more protective than the Middle East, North Africa, and Latin America, and on par with Sub-Saharan Africa.
120. Apodaca (1998) found that strong regional coefficients play a larger role than GNP in the achievement of women's economic and social rights, although the regional identification of Asian and African explains less variation than the Middle East regional designation. She observes that various literatures suggest that the explanation lies in 'culturally specific attitudes towards women's status, developed under differing historical and economic conditions.'
121. Reilly (2003).
122. Licht et al. (2002).
123. Smith et al. (2002) summarize various multiple country studies that find similarities on various dimensions of values within the Asian region, particularly along the dimensions of individualism versus collectivism, autonomy versus social embeddedness, and hierarchy versus egalitarianism.
124. Cross (1997) finds that cultural values are an important determinant of rights and that Western nations have a higher level of freedom from government intrusion even after controlling for GDP and other factors.
125. See generally Peerenboom et al. (2006).
126. Peerenboom (2004*b*: 29–31).

127. Sunstein (1996) argues against making social and economic rights justiciable. In contrast, Scheppele (2004) argues that courts need to support social rights, if more in a directive fashion that provides the legislature flexibility in implementation rather than by specifying an immediate particular minimum level of entitlement for individuals, because such decisions may provide governments the political leverage to resist the harmful prescriptions of international financial organizations regarding democratization and marketization.
128. Hahm (2006).
129. 1945 Constitution of the Republic of Indonesia, art. 28H (amended 2002). See also Sen (1993); Nussbaum (1997).
130. Banpasirichote (2004).
131. Pasuk and Baker (2004).
132. Muntarbhorn (2006).
133. Human Rights Watch (2005).
134. Albritton and Thawilwadee (2003).
135. Banpasirichote (2004: 222).
136. Branstetter and Lardy (2005: 12).
137. See the Catalogue for the Guidance of Foreign Investment Industries, Dec. 7, 2004.
138. Gallagher (2005) argues that early FDI liberalization strengthened the authoritarian regime and helped delay political liberalization because it made possible a more gradual and less painful reform process for the urban workforce. In addition, the expansion of the foreign-investment sector has led to the fragmentation and diversification of the industrial working class, and allowed the state to renegotiate the social contract with workers. The superior performance of foreign-invested enterprises legitimates the downsizing of SOEs even among laid-off SOE employees who recognize the need for SOEs to become more efficient in the face of increased competition and who support the nationalistic goal of an economically, and hence politically, more powerful China. In short, the logic of a market economy has displaced to a considerable extent the logic of a social welfare state.
139. Wolf (2005).
140. Rawski (2005).
141. See Peerenboom (2002).
142. Wang (2006) notes approvingly that Asian countries have moved slowly to open the banking sector to foreign competition.
143. US–China Business Council (2005).

144. Bush shared his visions in his second inaugural address: 'America's vital interests and our deepest beliefs are now one. From the day of our founding, we have proclaimed that every man and woman on this Earth has rights, and dignity and matchless value because they bear the image of the maker of heaven and Earth. Across the generations, we have proclaimed the imperative of self-government, because no one is fit to be a master, and no one deserves to be a slave. Advancing these ideals is the mission that created our nation. It is the honorable achievement of our fathers. Now it is the urgent requirement of our nation's security and the calling of our time. So it is the policy of the United States to seek and support the growth of democratic movements and institutions in every nation and culture, with the ultimate goal of ending tyranny in our world.'
145. Brooks (2005).
146. The World Bank (1993: 86–8, 106–20) also emphasizes the pragmatic approach of the successful East Asia countries, and provides numerous examples to illustrate how governments abandoned failed experiments.
147. Williamson (2000).

CHAPTER 3

1. Information Office of the State Council of China (2004).
2. Kent's (1999) impressively detailed study of China's interactions with UN human rights organs shows how, over time, China learned the rules and how to manipulate them to achieve its ends, and how it used its political and economic power to defeat attempts at censure. Kent argues that China improved with respect to procedural compliance but showed less progress with respect to substantive compliance. She suggests this may be a problem of cognitive learning or lack of internalization of norms. However, in many cases there may be a legitimate difference of opinion over the substantive norms and how they are to be interpreted and implemented. In other cases, it may not be cognitive deficiencies as much as a hard-headed calculation of what is in China's interests. Overall, the picture that emerges is of China complying when it can and it is in its interest to do so, but resisting otherwise. When not in its interest, China uses a range of techniques to resist, including procedural ploys, political pressure, economic pressure, and

normative arguments. Whether China is significantly different in that regard from other countries is doubtful. See also Foot (2000) for a discussion of the relationship between China's perceived national interests and its response to international human rights pressure.

3. Kim (2000: 147–9). For empirical evidence to support Beijing's view, see Wheeler (1999) and Chapter 6.
4. Shen (2003).
5. Information Office of the State Council of China (2004).
6. Information Office of the State Council of China (1991).
7. Peerenboom (2003*b*: 16, 56–63).
8. Ramo (2004) notes that when asked in a recent survey where stability ranked as a social value, Chinese ranked it number two. In contrast, stability ranked on average 23rd for citizens from other nations. Chen (2004) reports that one poll of Beijing residents in the late 1990s found that over 90% preferred a stable and orderly society to a freer society that could be prone to disruption. For many other studies that show the high value assigned to order and economic growth in China and Asia more broadly, and the limited demand for democracy in China, see Peerenboom (2002).
9. See for example China's reservations to art. 22 of the ICERD, and to art. 29(1) of the CEDAW.
10. Although China allowed Manfred Nowak, the Special Rapporteur on Torture, to visit, the trip ended badly. Nowak described torture as 'widespread,' and claimed that the government obstructed his investigations. China's foreign ministry spokesperson demanded that Nowak retract his statement, which he said lacked an empirical basis, noting that Nowak was only in China for two weeks and only visited three cities. He also denied that Nowak was closely monitored and that police prevented family members from meeting with him. *China denies torture widespread, slams UN envoy* (2006).
11. Pisik (1998) reports that in response to a report by UN Special Rapporteur describing capital punishment in the US as arbitrary and racially discriminatory, US legislators huffily declared such monitoring constituted UN harassment. In the past, powerful Western countries raised little objection to the human rights movement as long as rights organizations concentrated on exporting liberal values to developing countries. Today, however, the growing power of the international human rights movement has led to a backlash in both developing and developed countries as they have begun to feel the movement's bite. Citizens everywhere are increasingly worried about

the lack of democratic accountability of human rights organizations including UN bodies, regional rights organizations, the ICC, and NGOs. See Goldsmith (2000). As Helfer (2002) points out, some states have taken the dramatic and unprecedented step of withdrawing from rights treaties rather than conform their policies to what they consider to be the unreasonable demands of international rights bodies out to impose one-size-fits-all solutions on countries whose contingent national circumstances render compliance impossible. I have noticed in teaching human rights law over the years that students react very differently to ICCPR Committee reports criticizing certain US practices and recommending changes than they do to criticism of other countries. When it comes to the US, they are much quicker to raise concerns about distant, unelected rights organs telling the US what to do. The different reaction cannot be attributed completely to the sense that other countries have more serious rights problems and thus the ICCPR's criticisms are more legitimate as they do not react as strongly to ICCPR criticisms of similar practices in European countries. Why should unelected administrators in international bodies set policies for Americans?

12. Information Office of the State Council of China (2004).
13. Ibid.
14. The United States was also upset over the failure of China to make good on certain commitments negotiated the year before, and thus wanted to send the signal that such 'backsliding' would not be tolerated.
15. The US could not sponsor a motion in 2002 when it lost its seat on the Human Rights Commission, although it could and did cosponsor a number of other resolutions with its allies. While the government expressed disappointment that it was unable to persuade its allies to put forth a motion, it is hard to believe that the United States could not have managed to persuade a single friendly state to take the lead had it really wanted to spend the political resources to do so. This is especially true given the close cooperation between the US, the EU, and other Western countries in the past, even allowing that European states have been less keen on such high profile motions since 1995. In any event, that no country was willing to sponsor a motion, even though many regularly vote in favor of US-sponsored motions, suggests some degree of political expediency rather than pure principled commitment on the part of Western allies.
16. In 2000, then-Secretary of State Madeleine Albright (2000) preached perseverance in the face of terrorism, rising crime and a breakdown in

social order in Uzbekistan: '[T]he United States will not support any and all measures taken in the name of fighting drugs and terrorism or restoring stability. One of the most dangerous temptations for a government facing violent threats is to respond in heavy-handed ways that violate the rights of innocent citizens. Terrorism is a criminal act and should be treated accordingly—and that means applying the rule of law fairly and consistently. We have found, through experience around the world, that the best way to defeat terrorist threats is to increase law enforcement capabilities while at the same time promoting democracy and human rights.' These sagacious words of moral exhortation were delivered just one year before the US declared its own war on terrorism, arrested up to 5,000 suspected terrorists many of whom have ended up being detained incommunicado for years without access to a lawyer or even the chance to notify their families, and authorized the use of military tribunals where defendants without the right to a lawyer of their choice or even to know the charges against them would be tried in closed proceedings before military personnel with the normal rules of evidence suspended and no right of appeal whatsoever of a guilty verdict, which could be based on a lower standard of proof than the usual 'beyond a reasonable doubt.' Dickinson (2002: 1414–18) points out that Secretary of Defense Rumsfeld has stated that prisoners may continue to be detained even if the military tribunals acquitted them. Cole (2003: 26) notes that of the estimated 5,000 people arrested by May 2003, not one had been charged with involvement in the attacks on Sept. 11 and only a handful have been charged with terrorist-related crimes.

17. *Patterns of Abuse* (2005).
18. Amnesty International (1998: 17, 19, 26, 43): 'There is a widespread and persistent police brutality across the USA. Thousands of individual complaints about police abuse are reported each year . . . Police officers have beaten and shot unresisting suspects; they have misused batons, chemical sprays and electro-shock weapons; they have injured or killed people by placing them in dangerous restraint holds . . . Common forms of ill-treatment are repeated kicks, punches or blows with batons or other weapons, sometimes after a suspect has already been restrained or rendered helpless. There are also complaints involving various types of restraint hold, pepper (OC) spray, electro-shock weapons and firearms . . . [V]ictims include not only criminal suspects but also bystanders and people who questioned police actions or were involved in minor disputes or confrontations.'
19. Blanton (2003); Cole (2003).

20. Paust (2001 and 2002).
21. Gibney (2004*a*).
22. Keith and Poe (2002) note that civil war and then violent rebellion lead to more violations of personal integrity rights.
23. Juwana (2006).
24. Hahm (2006).
25. Muntarbhorn (2006).
26. Gibney (2004*b*).
27. US Department of State (2004*a*).
28. Amnesty International (2004*a*) refers to an estimate based on unspecified internal Chinese Communist Party documents that on average 15,000 people per year were killed in the four years from 1997–2001, although this figure includes people killed during police operations including pursuit and apprehension. The accuracy of the estimate is hard to evaluate without knowing more about the inputs and assumptions that were relied on in coming up with the final tally, or the source of the numbers.
29. Saiget (2004).
30. US Department of State (2004*a*).
31. For instance, China's Supreme Court has revoked its delegation over final review to lower level courts and required that appeals be heard in open court.
32. Report of the Special Rapporteur on Extrajudicial, Summary or Arbitrary Executions (1998), citing US Supreme Court opinions.
33. Peerenboom (2004*d*) and cites therein.
34. See e.g. Amnesty International (2001*a*).
35. Ibid. 2.
36. Amnesty International (1998: 1, 17, 26, 43).
37. Rahn (2000: 170).
38. Information Office of the State Council of China (2004). See also Chan (2004).
39. For recommendations, see Human Rights in China (2000).
40. Amnesty International (2001*a*: 42).
41. ICCPR, art. 9(4). The ICCPR Human Rights Committee has declared that authorities should not delay for more than a few days before bringing detainees before a judge. UN Office of the High Commissioner for Human Rights, Right to Liberty and Security of Persons (Art. 9) CCPR General Comment 8, 16th Sess., ¶ 2 (1982). The general comments and case holdings of the ICCPR Committee are nonbinding.

42. The Working Group suggested that the Administrative Committee's review would suffice if the Committee provides 'safeguards equivalent to those of a court.' UN Working Group on Arbitrary Detention (1998). However, the Group noted that the Committee did not currently provide such safeguards, and recommended review by a judge, perhaps according to the simplified procedures set out in the CPL.
43. Huber *v*. Switzerland, 188 Eur. Ct. H.R. (ser. A) at 18 (1990). The Court however has taken a dimmer view of relying on prosecutors in new entrants to the E.U. such as Hungary with less trustworthy legal systems. Kulomin *v*. Hungary, Communication 521/1992.
44. See Ministry of Public Security Regulations for the Procedures for Administrative Reconsideration Cases Handled by the Public Security (effective Jan. 1, 2004).
45. Empirical studies show that, in England, detention is almost always authorized, and the idea of a custody officer as an independent check has proven chimerical. Reiner (2000: 181) notes one study found that detention was refused in only one case out of 4,246. According to Hodgson (2002: 796–7), authorization for detention is granted routinely in France unless there is clearly no legal basis. Furthermore, the transmission by police to procureur is given by phone or fax and is characterized as communication of information that does not require a response. Johnson (2002: 62) notes that Japanese judges refused a prosecutor's request for detention only 110 times out of 77,545. They also denied the prosecutor's request for an arrest warrant on average only once every 1,233 times. In the US, the Foreign Intelligence Surveillance Court that grants warrants for wiretaps, telephone record traces, and physical searches in investigations of persons thought to be terrorists or spies approved 18,748 warrants while rejecting just five requests between 1979 and 2004 (Leonning 2006). Nevertheless, the low percentage of refusals does not mean that the process is entirely useless or ineffective. The procedure's existence itself may send a signal to prosecutors that arbitrary arrests are unacceptable and thus may cause prosecutors to exercise more self-restraint.

    On the other hand, Chinese prosecutors already exercise some check on the police. In 2004, prosecutors rejected 7.7% of police requests for an arrest in criminal cases (not administrative detention cases). Prosecutors then released 2.2% of those arrested prior to trial. Less than 1% of criminal defendants were acquitted, although an additional 1.6% avoided criminal punishments (CECC 2005: 134). Conviction rates are generally higher in civil law countries than in common law countries, in large part because of the extended period of pre-trial detention and investigation. By the time the investigation is over, the innocence or guilt of the suspect will be for the most part already determined. Thus, conviction rates are 99.8% in Japan (described by some as an adversarial system, but one that still functions like an inquisitorial one), 99.6% in Korea, and 97% in Germany. In contrast, the conviction rate in US district courts is 88.2% and 90.3% in Britain. However, in Japan and civil law countries, a higher percentage of suspects are released after investigation, and thus the prosecution rate is much lower—68.1% in Japan compared to 90.6% in the United States (Chu 2001).

46. See Fairchild (2000: 125–7).
47. Information Office of the State Council of China (2004).
48. Ibid.
49. See generally Peerenboom (2004*d*) and cites therein.
50. Chen Ruihua (2002: 9, 13).
51. Peerenboom (2004*d*).
52. US Department of State (2004).
53. LaFave (2003: 121) points out that the United States' common law rule states that someone whose conviction is final is not released if the criminal statute on which the person is convicted is subsequently repealed.
54. Munro (2000: 67).
55. Amnesty International (2004*b*).
56. See Hom (2004).
57. US Department of State (2004). Several pages later, the report states that Amnesty International has identified 211 persons still in prison or on medical parole, and rather unhelpfully 'identifies' the credible source for the higher 2000 numbers as 'other NGOs.'
58. Some protesters burned vehicles and destroyed property, and some assaulted and killed soldiers and police. Therefore it is possible that some could still be in prison for such offenses, although most would have been released by now except for those held for the most serious offenses, for which some would have been sentenced to life in prison. Amnesty International is careful not to label all of those in detention for Tiananmen-related offenses as prisoners of conscience.
59. Of course, the authorities and others who feel the restrictions are justified would see the fact that many others are deterred from such behavior as desirable—one of the main purposes for the punishments is to deter what they see as unacceptable behavior.

60. This figure includes prisoners of conscience of all stripes in all forms of detention.
61. ICCPR, art. 4.
62. The Siracusa Principles on the Limitation and Derogation Provisions in the International Covenant on Civil and Political Rights.
63. ICCPR, art. 4(2).
64. Wood (2003: 460).
65. American Communications Ass'n *v.* Douds, 339 US 382, 415 (1950).
66. See generally Yourow (1996).
67. Ireland *v.* United Kingdom, 25 Eur. Ct. HR (ser. A) at 78–9, 82 (1978).
68. Nathan et al. (2001: 318–64).
69. Spencer (2004).
70. Amnesty International (2001*b*).
71. Amnesty International (2004*a*).
72. Information Office of the State Council of China (2002*a*).
73. Mackerras (2004).
74. US State Department Counterterrorism Office (2002: 17) describes ETLO as a cause for concern, along with the East Turkestan Islamic Party, which was founded in the early 1980s with the goal of establishing an independent state of Eastern Turkestan and advocates armed struggle. Cloud and Johnson (2004) also note that an ETIM member acknowledged the group's ties to Osama bin Laden and the group's use of violent means to overthrow the PRC government.
75. See e.g. *Ethnic Tension Rising in Southern Xinjiang, Says Official* (2004), reporting an increase in ethnic and religious tensions in southern Xinjiang and the arrests of seventy-five people, including eight for endangering the state, and others for various offenses including 'illegal religious activities.'
76. Amnesty International (2003*a*). See also *Executed Uyghur Refugee Left Behind Tapes Detailing Chinese Torture* (2004).
77. Amnesty International (2003*b*), citing unconfirmed reports that police fired into the crowd, and tortured and killed some of those citizens detained in relation to the incident.
78. *Wang Bingzhang Convicted of Terrorist Activities and Espionage* (2003).
79. The court's judgment is available at **www.cdjp.org/wbz/panjueshu.htm** (last visited Dec. 20, 2004). See also *Hunger Strike Helps Improve Conditions for Jailed Chinese Dissident—Report.*
80. Pan (2004*a*).
81. *US Resident Jailed in China Threatens Hunger Strike* (2003).
82. Hom (2004); Congressional-Executive Commission on China (2003).
83. Ibid. 2.

84. Weaver (2003), quoting Chinese Foreign Ministry spokeswoman Zhang Qiyue.
85. See the preamble of the PRC Constitution (1982, as amended).
86. Comments by the Chinese Government (2003: 11).
87. See Chang (2004); Cheung (2004); Evans (2002).
88. US Department of State (2004*a*).
89. Information Office of the State Council of China (2004).
90. Ibid.
91. For example, religious organizations below the central level require government approval to publish religious materials. Individuals and groups other than those recognized by the government are not allowed to publish religious materials. In July and August 2005, 200 Muslims were arrested for possessing illegal religious texts (CECC 2005: 52).
92. Information Office of the State Council of China (2004).
93. Rahn (2000: 170).
94. Peerenboom (2002: 91–102); Chang (2004).
95. Kahn (2004), describing violence between religious sects and abusive behavior on part of sect leaders.
96. Peerenboom (2002: 95–6); Evans (2002: 763–5).
97. US Department of Statc (2004*a*).
98. Ibid.
99. Ibid.
100. Sautman (2003: 208–14).
101. US Department of State (2004*a*). China forbids hate speech. Articles 149 and 250 of the Criminal Law prohibit 'incitement of national enmity or discrimination' by any organization or individual.
102. US Department of State (2004*a*).
103. Ibid. at 22.
104. *Japan Ignores Tokyo University Student Jailed in China* (2002).
105. Ibid.
106. Information Office of the State Council of China (1991).
107. Luo Yongzhong Inciting Subversion Case (Changchun Intermediate Ct., Oct. 14, 2003), at **http://171.64.233.179/articles/luo/luo001.htm**.
108. Wang Zechen Subversion Case (Anshan Intermediate Ct., Sept. 4, 2002), at **www.bignews.org/200202904.txt**.
109. See Reporters without Borders (2004).
110. Ibid.
111. Judgment of the Yang Zili, Xu Wei, Jin Haike, Zhang Honghai case (Beijing First Intermediate Ct., May 28, 2003), at **www.peacehall.com/news/gb/china/2004/01/200401311031.shtml**.

112. Xu Wei's statement is available at **www.peacehall.com/news/gb/china/2003/11/200311120832.shtml** (last visited Dec. 22, 2004).
113. Pan (2004*b*). According to the news report, the four defendants claimed that they were physically and psychologically abused while in detention. Other due process concerns involved the lengthy detention before trial. The defendants were detained on March 13, 2001, and formally arrested on April 20, 2001. The intermediate court met three times to decide the case on September 28, 2001, April 4, 2003, and May 28, 2003. The defendants were in custody therefore from March 2001 until May 2003.
114. *China Releases Three Arrested Members of 'Tiananmen Mothers'* (2004).
115. Hu is known for his work on AIDS issues and the environment, as well as his support for the release of the 'Stainless Steel Mouse' for Internet violations. *Aids Activist Released After Hunger Strike* (2004).
116. US Department of State (2004*a*).
117. The Judgment of Huang Qi Case (Chengdu Intermediate Ct., Feb. 23, 2003), at **www.peacehall.com/news/gb/china/2003/05/200305171038.shtml**. Huang's appeal apparently was also rejected. Amnesty International (2003*b*: 8).
118. *Yang Ming, Sichuan Government Official Li Zhen Sentenced to Eight Years for Exposing Corruption on Internet* (2003); *Sichuan Interneter Li Zhi Arrested* (2003).
119. *Well-Known Anti-Corruption Activist An Jun Sentenced to Four Years This Morning for Subversion* (2000).
120. Amnesty International (2003*b*).
121. Dickie (2003: 5).
122. Information Office of the State Council of China (2004).
123. See the Judgment of Song Yue case, Wuhu Intermediate Ct., at **www.yecao.net/Html/20044324116-1.Html**. While the plaintiff won the suit in that the court quashed the act to deny him employment, the court could not order the defendant to provide a job as the post had already been filled.
124. US Department of State (2004*a*: 15–16). China Information Center (2004), listing the ten topics that the Chinese government warned the media not to discuss. See also CECC (2005: 12).
125. The case report can be found at **www.szonline.net/Channel/2003/200306/20030603/Preview_20030603_1.html**.
126. Human Rights Watch (2004: 218).
127. Kurtenbach (2004).
128. Zittrain and Edelman (2003). Ironically, this site was not accessible when I tried from Beijing on April 19, 2004.
129. Morris (2004).

130. Pan (2003).
131. *Security Official Confirms Chinese Man Arrested for Internet 'Subversion'* (2004).
132. *Chinese Internet Dissident Found Guilty of Subversion, but Given Probation* (2004).
133. For the text of the petition, see Petition for Judicial Interpretation of Anti-Subversion Law, Laogai Research Foundation, **www.laogai.org/news/newsdetail.php?id=2044** (June 6, 2004).
134. Ibid.
135. Liebman (2005).
136. Horsley (2004).
137. See generally Minzner (2006).
138. Zittrain and Edelman (2003: 71), concluding that the Chinese government has not relied on commercial filtering programs to block access to pornographic websites.
139. *Couple Watching Porno DVD Case Continues* (2002).
140. US Department of State (2004*a*: 19).
141. Ibid.
142. Ibid.
143. Ibid.
144. Amnesty International (2002) discusses the growing number of work-related protests and demonstrations in China.
145. McGregor (2006), citing figures from the Public Security Ministry. The number of demonstrations has increased rapidly, from 8,700 in 1993 to 32,000 in 1999, to 74,000 in 2004. Tanner (2004) describes changing tactics on the part of protesters and the authorities.
146. McGregor (2006); *Attacks on Chinese police rising* (2005).
147. Pan (2005); CECC (2005: 11).
148. Cody (2005).
149. *China sacks officials after pollution riots* (2005).
150. Sautman (2003: 177–96) discusses the lack of a foundation in international law for the concepts of 'cultural genocide' and 'ethnocide' on which the Tibetan émigré ideology is based and argues that claims of cultural genocide and ethnocide are inapposite legally and empirically.
151. Brandenburg *v.* Ohio, 395 US 444 (1969).
152. Question of the Human Rights of All Persons Subjected to Any Form of Detention or Imprisonment: Promotion and Protection of the Right to Freedom of Opinion and Expression—Report of the Special Rapporteur, Mr. Abid Hussain, Pursuant to Commission on Human Rights Resolution 1993/45, U.N. ESCOR, 52nd Sess., U.N. Doc. E/CN.4/1996/39 (1996).

153. In Dennis *v.* US, 341 US 494, 501 (1951), the US Supreme Court rejected 'any principle of government helplessness in the face of preparation for revolution, which principle, carried to its logical conclusion, must lead to anarchy.'
154. See United Nations High Commissioner (1993), § 6, art. 19.
155. Blanton (2003). See also Lawyers Committee for Human Rights (2003).
156. See Yourow (1996).
157. Przeworski and Limongi (1997: 161).
158. Ibid. Authoritarian regimes become more stable at levels above $6,000.
159. UNDP HDI (2003).
160. Blanton (2003).
161. The lawyer for Du Daobin apparently had his license to practice cancelled as a result of his efforts, although the details of the case are unclear. The sentencing of well-known Beijing defense lawyer Zhang Jianzhong to two years for fabricating evidence in a corruption case led to a protest petition signed by 600 lawyers. Shanghai housing advocate Zheng Enchong was also sentenced to three years for revealing state secrets. Zheng faxed an article from an internal publication for government officials to an overseas human rights organization, noting the source on the fax. The court's judgment states that Zheng confessed, and that he knowingly sent the internal document to foreign organizations in part to enlist support in his struggle to get the local justice bureau to renew his license to practice. The court does not discuss why Zheng would have encountered problems renewing his license. See also Cohen (2002). According to the *Legal Daily*, lawyers were acquitted in 11 of 18 completed cases in which they were charged with falsifying evidence. Another study found that 80% of lawyers charged with various types of wrongdoing were eventually found innocent (CECC 2005: 31–2, 133–4). Recent regulations and reforms have attempted to strengthen the position of criminal defense lawyers, though they do not seem to have had much impact in practice. See e.g. Regulations to Guarantee the Lawful Practice of Lawyers in Criminal Cases, Supreme People's Procuracy, Feb. 10, 2004. On the problems of environmental groups, see CECC (2005: 12).
162. Color revolutions were made possible in part by multi-party elections. Nevertheless, the government in China fears mass demonstrations calling for political change.
163. Huang (2006) reports that Party leaders recently decided to invite 3,000 Marxist theorists and Beijing to compile 100 to 150 volumes on

Marxism, at a cost of up to RMB 200 million. Funds have also been earmarked for international conferences on Marxism.

164. See, generally, CECC (2005: 11–12).
165. State Council (2005).
166. Bueno de Mesquita and Downs (2005). The study found that restricting coordination goods does not prevent economic growth, except at the highest levels of per capita income. The authors recommend attaching conditions to international aid to force authoritarian regimes to allow greater civil liberties and press freedom. Aid conditionalities have generally not been very successful, with economic sanctions often harming citizens in the targeted country. It is unlikely that authoritarian regimes will be willing to hasten the end of their own regime by agreeing to such conditions. China in particular is unlikely to accept any such conditions. China usually has been able to avoid most of the conditions imposed by the Asian Development Bank or IMF on smaller developing countries that need financial assistance.

CHAPTER 4

1. Yao (2005).
2. UNDP HDI (2003).
3. See generally Yao (2005).
4. UNDP HDI (2003), citing survey data from 1998. Unfortunately, data reported varies by year depending on availability, with the year not clearly indicated in some cases.
5. *China's Reforms Cause Dramatic Widening Gap between Rich and Poor* (2003).
6. UNDP HDI (2003). Yao (2005: 212) estimates there are 103 to 187 million rural poor, which is four to six times the official number. In addition, he estimates that there are 5 to 15 million urban poor.
7. UNDP HDI (2003: 223).
8. State Council of China (2004).
9. Ibid.
10. Information Office of the State Council of China (2004).
11. Khan and Riskin (2005) cite Gini coefficients around .45 during this period.
12. Khan and Riskin (2005) found the decrease in *urban* inequality was due mainly to a reduction in interprovincial inequality, even though urban

inequality within the majority of provinces surveyed increased. In contrast, inequality in *rural* income decreased both among and within most provinces. Khan and Riskin (2005) found that urban to rural inequality increased from 2.47 in 1995 to 2.89 in 2002, while Sicular et al. (2006) calculate an increase from 2.7 to 3.3 during the same period, excluding income from housing.

13. Sicular et al. (2006) found that the relative gap rose in the western and central regions but declined in the east. They suggest that the gap will stabilize and narrow as China becomes more developed and prosperity spreads to the inner regions.
14. See Several Opinions on Promoting New Rural Socialist Construction, issued Feb. 22, 2006, available in Chinese at **http://club.china.alibaba.com/club/post/view/129_9567394.html**.
15. Khan (2006). In contrast, the UNDP (2005: 34) claims that most of the decline in extreme poverty occurred between 1990 and 1996. Much depends on how poverty is defined. In Khan's study, the urban thresholds are twice the rural thresholds in income values, although the rural thresholds are lower as a percentage of per capita income. The lower rural threshold is similar to the official PRC poverty line while the higher threshold is closer to the World Bank's standard of PPP$1/day. The higher urban threshold is twice the level of the World Bank's standard, while the lower threshold is approximately 40% higher than the World Bank standard.
16. UNDP (2005: 34).
17. WHO (2005).
18. UNDP HDI (2003: 247).
19. See Implementation of the International Covenant on Economic, Social and Cultural Rights: Initial Reports Submitted by States Parties Under Articles 16 and 17 to the Covenant—Addendum People's Republic of China, UN Economic and Social Council, UN Doc. E/1990/5/add.59, at 11 (2004) [hereinafter Implementation of the ICESCR].
20. Ibid.
21. The government claims that the number of people covered by medical insurance increased by 14.95 million between 2002 and 2003. According to the report, 108.95 million people now have medical insurance coverage. Information Office of the State Council of China (2004). However, Blumenthal and Hsiao (2005) point out that almost half of urban residents still have no insurance. They note that the government has begun to address the problems 'with remarkable pragmatism, uninhibited by ideology and often importing (after careful examination) solutions pioneered in other countries.'

22. Comments by the Chinese Government (2003: 3). In its report to the ICESCR Committee, China cited 2000 census data that showed adult literacy at 91.3% and literacy for those under forty at 95.2%. Implementation of the ICESCR, ¶ 220.
23. Yao (2005: 72), citing the World Bank.
24. Information Office of the State Council of China (2004).
25. Report of Committee on the Elimination of Discrimination Against Women, UN General Assembly, 45th Sess., ¶ 257, UN Doc. A/54/38 (1999), citing statement from China's representative [hereinafter, CEDAW Report].
26. Information Office of the State Council of China (2004).
27. Comments by the Chinese Government (2003: 5).
28. The Right to Education, Report Submitted by the Special Rapporteur, Katarina Tomaševski, UN ESCOR Human Rights Comm., 60th Sess., Agenda Item 10, ∂ 9, UN Doc. E/CN.4/2004/45/Add.1 (2003) [hereinafter The Right to Education Report].
29. Ibid. at ¶ 16; see also Peerenboom (2004c), noting that of the countries in the study, only Malaysia met the 6% level.
30. Comments by the Chinese Government (2003: 2–3).
31. The Right to Education Report: ¶¶ 9 & 11.
32. Comments by the Chinese Government (2003: 3–4).
33. See China Economic Quarterly (2005).
34. Human Rights in China (1999: 13).
35. State Council Administrative Measures for Assistance to Indigent Vagrants and Beggars in Urban Areas (2003); Ministry of Civil Affairs Detailed Implementing Rules for the Administrative Measures for Assistance to Indigent Vagrants and Beggars in Urban Areas (2003).
36. See Reply of the Supreme People's Court on Whether Persons Who Infringe upon the Basic Right of Citizens to Receive Education Protected by the Constitution of the People's Republic of China by Means of Infringing upon the Right of Personal Name Shall Bear Civil Liabilities (Supreme People's Court, July 24, 2001).
37. Wang Lei (2003).
38. For details, see Yu (2004), who also reports another case where a student who did not meet the requirements to take the graduate student exam, but was nevertheless permitted to do so, was rejected by the Chinese Academy of Social Sciences even though others who did not meet the minimal score were admitted. After losing in administrative reconsideration and in both the Beijing Intermediate and High Courts, the student took his case to the Supreme Court, where it is pending.
39. *Highlights of Major Beijing-Based Newspapers* (2002).

40. Law Publishing House (2002: 144). In the past, the percentage of punishments over five years was even higher. Tanner (1999: 98–9) notes that during the first strike-hard campaign from 1983 until 1987, 38% of those convicted received a punishment of five years or more.
41. Amnesty International (2001*b*).
42. US Department of State (2004*a*).
43. About 500 Chinese women commit suicide a day, a rate that the World Bank estimates to be five times the global average. Report of the Special Rapporteur on Violence against Women, Its Causes and Consequences, Ms. Radhika Coomaraswamy, 59th Sess., Agenda Item 12(a), ¶ 963, UN Doc. E/CN.4/2003/75/Add.1 (2003) [hereinafter Violence against Women Report].
44. See State Statistics Bureau, National Population and Family Planning Commission of China, **www.npfpc.gov.cn/data/sfpcdatamar3.htm**.
45. Zhang Hong (2001).
46. The GDI is a composite indicator that measures the average achievement of a population in the same dimensions as the HDI. However the GDI adjusts to take into account gender inequalities in the level of achievement in the three basic aspects of human development. The GDI uses the same variables as the HDI, disaggregated by gender.
47. Violence against Women Report, ¶ 959.
48. CEDAW Report, ¶ 299–301.
49. CEDAW Report, ¶ 257.
50. As of 2001, women constituted 39% of the non-agricultural workforce. UNDP HDI (2003: 203). Zhu Ling (2002) notes that studies in 1988 and 1995 show that differences in male and female poverty are not substantial, and that relative female poverty has not increased significantly in the 1990s.
51. CEDAW Reports, ¶ 277.
52. Ibid. ¶ 281.
53. Concluding Observations Adopted by the Committee on the Rights of the Child: China, UN Convention on the Rights of Child, 12th Sess., ¶ 34, UN Doc. CRC/C/15/Add.56 (1996).
54. CEDAW Report,¶ 293. The Committee recommended using the talent bank of the All China Women's Federation to increase the percentage of women in all public bodies.
55. Ibid. ¶ 298, at 33.
56. Ibid. ¶ 303, at 34.
57. Keith et al. (2003).
58. CEDAW Report, ¶¶ 285–6.

59. See ibid. ¶ 289.
60. Peerenboom (2004*d*: 992).
61. Biddulph (2003: 234).
62. Tanner (1999: 149). In part, this may reflect the broad definition of prostitution, which includes sex-related occupations such as hostessing, nude dancing, and those who work in massage parlors or saunas where the range of service goes beyond certain ill-defined limits. But it may also simply reflect the view among those with limited economic prospects that prostitution is a lucrative profession.
63. CEDAW Report, ¶ 299.
64. Ibid. ¶ 299(*a*).
65. As of 1998, there were five autonomous regions, thirty autonomous prefectures, 120 autonomous counties, and 1,256 ethnic townships. Among the fifty-five ethnic minorities, forty-four have their own autonomous areas, with a population of 75% of the total of the ethnic minorities and an area of 64% of the area of the whole country. Information Office of the State Council of China (2000).
66. One reason the legal system has not played a major role in struggles over cultural rights is that individuals in special autonomous regions presumably realize that to challenge local regulations at odds with generally applicable laws would be pointless because judges assume that the NPC has already reviewed any such deviations and given its approval. Judges therefore simply follow the local regulations. Critics also argue that the 388 separate regulations and 68 alterations to national laws are vaguely worded and address a limited set of relatively insignificant topics (CECC 2005: 16). A more common scenario is where generally applicable laws and regulations conflict with noncodified local customs. For example, some acts considered to be serious crimes under PRC law may not be considered serious crimes or crimes at all in some localities. Areas of conflict include property rights and disputes over access to land, grazing rights, and inheritance rights; marriage laws and disputes over dowries, arranged marriages, and bigamy; and criminal law, including what constitutes rape and what count as mitigating circumstances in homicides. Outcomes in such cases differ widely, from strict application of the law to wide deference to local customs. See generally Liang Zhiping (2001). In some cases, parties prefer to settle the disputes in accordance with local norms rather than going to the courts.
67. See Racism, Racial Discrimination, Xenophobia and All Forms of Discrimination, Report by Mr. Maurice Glèlè Ahanhanzo, Special

Rapporteur on Contemporary Forms of Racism, Racial Discrimination, Xenophobia and Related Intolerance, UN ESC Human Rights Commission, 58th Sess., Prov. Agenda Item 6, UN Doc. E/CN.4/2002/24 (2002).

68. CECC (2005: 13).
69. Information Office of the State Council of China (2004).
70. Ibid.
71. US Department of State (2004*a*: 45), citing complaints that of 38,000 people hired to work on the Qinghai-Tibet railroad, only 6,000 were Tibetans.
72. Mackerras (2004). CECC (2005: 17) reports that minorities constitute only 6.3% of Party membership and that all of the 125 regional, prefectural, municipal, and county first secretaries in Xinjiang were Han.
73. Sautman (2003: 177).
74. Mackerras (2004). Fischer (2004) claims that concerns about social exclusion and Tibetans being overrun by Hans reflects an urban-centric viewpoint as Hans concentrate in cities, and that within cities 'the critical factors generating exclusion and fuelling conflict are the differentials between groups, such as urbanisation rates and education levels, rather than base line characteristics, such as population shares or poverty levels.'
75. CECC (2005: 20), noting that in April 2005 the government reserved 500 out of 700 new civil servant positions for Hans in southern Xinjiang.
76. Information Office of the State Council of China (2001).
77. Comments by the Chinese Government (2003: 6).
78. Information Office of the State Council of China (2004).
79. Report of the Committee on the Elimination of Racial Discrimination: China, 56th Sess., Supp. No. 18 ¶ 245 UN Doc. A/56/18 (2001).
80. US Department of State (2004*a*). In 1996, Tibetan was the main language in 98% of TAR primary schools. Virtually all Tibetans in the TAR speak Tibetan and over 90% of Tibetans outside of the TAR speak Tibetan, while only about 5% of Tibetans in the TAR speak Mandarin. Sautman (2003: 221, 225).
81. US Department of State (2004*a*).
82. See CECC (2005: 51).
83. Cultural factors are evident in women's issues, including domestic violence, the rights of the child, female infanticide and the preference for male children, the reliance on the family to pick up the slack left by a poor state welfare system, and in preferences for group over individual interests across a range of issues.

84. Peerenboom (1995).
85. Peerenboom (1998).
86. See US Embassy Beijing (2000).
87. See *PRC Survey: Most Guangzhou Residents Satisfied with Public Order* (2001).
88. *Beijing Succeeds in Crackdown on Crimes* (2001).
89. Hu (2002).
90. Ibid.
91. Bakken (2000: 395), also noting that a survey of 15,000 people showed that almost 60% thought the state was too lenient in handling criminals, while only 2% thought it was too strict.
92. *Residents Eager for Drug Fight* (1997).
93. See Peerenboom (2002: 302–9).
94. CEDAW Report, ¶ 257.
95. Van Boven (1991).
96. Pangalangan (2006).
97. Matsui (2006).
98. Muntarbhorn (2006) points out that while Buddhism is not mentioned expressly as the state religion in the Thai constitution, it is implied.
99. As Wheeler (1999: 81, 88) points out only twenty-two states were the subject of UN resolutions for systematic violations of rights between 1982 and 1997. China is part of a small group that includes Iraq, Myanmar, Iran, Equatorial Guinea, and Haiti, all of which were the subject of proposed motions to censure in Geneva in at least ten years between 1990 and 2004. As Wheeler's study ended in 1997, I have updated the results through 2004.

CHAPTER 5

1. See e.g. Human Rights Defenders in China (2005): 'The human rights situation in China continues to be grave. China has secured a prominent position in the international arena . . . However, this has not been accompanied by a parallel improvement in human rights.' See also Amnesty International (2004*a*).
2. See e.g. *China Evades Human Rights Censure* (2004), quoting China's Assistant Foreign Minister Shen Guofang, who accused the United States of practicing 'double standards.'
3. *Students' Attitudes Toward Human Rights Surveyed* (1999).
4. Gedda (2003).

5. See e.g. Information Office of the State Council of China (2002*b*).
6. See Zhao Xi (2003). Pew Global Attitudes Project (2005: 4) found that only 42% of Chinese had a favorable view of the US, in comparison to 71% of Indians.
7. See generally Gries (2004), discussing the role that Chinese resentment of Western criticism has played in the resurgence of Chinese nationalism.
8. For other evidence of a growing nationalism that has led to conflicts between Asian governments and international rights NGOs as well as between domestic and international rights groups, see generally Peerenboom et al. (2006).
9. I do not discuss the possibility of racism as an explanatory factor for the double standards, because racism would not explain why China is subject to such intense criticism and not other Asian or predominantly non-white states. Nevertheless, I do not mean to exclude racism as a possible contributing factor. For earlier accounts of racism in US foreign policy toward China, see Ruskola (2005).
10. Table 3; Figure 4; Table 8. Whereas China scores poorly on civil and political rights (voice and accountability), India scores highly. However, China does much better in terms of political stability. Like China, India actually does better relative to the average country in its income class on most good governance indicators. As Ray (2002) notes, from the 1950s to the 1990s, India relied primarily on an indigenous development model that produced low but relatively equal growth, with intermittent periods where a more neoliberal program was adopted. During the last decade and half, India has pursued greater economic liberalization. The result has been much higher growth rates, albeit with increased inequality, more people living in poverty, and growing regional differences. India is a low income country, while China is a lower-middle income country. Hence, China would be expected to outperform India on these indicators.
11. The following discussion of the rights situation in India is drawn from the US Department of State Report India (2004*b*). I cite this report extensively to demonstrate that the US government is well aware of the many human rights violations in India, and yet it has failed to sponsor a motion against it. Whatever the reason for the government's differing treatment of China and India, it is not because the government is unaware that human rights violations in India are as serious, if not more serious, than the violations in China.
12. The State Department report claims that there were no political detainees. However, the report also notes that several people were

arrested for expressing support for the banned LTTE terrorist group, even though the Supreme Court has held that mere moral support for a terrorist organization does not constitute an offense under the Prevention on Terrorism Act.

13. An empirical study by Ovsiovitch (1996: 91, 93) found bias against communist regimes and that the presence of a news bureau in the country leads to more reports of human rights violations.
14. Wheeler (1999: 75).
15. Ibid. at 86.
16. Donnelly (1988: 288).
17. Wheeler (1999).
18. Grunfeld (2001) argues that media reporting on China generally, and human rights in particular, is so negative and unrealistic that many Americans hold highly distorted views on modern China. Granted, the media's negative reporting on China resembles media coverage elsewhere. Reporters in the US tend to emphasize murders by strangers and violent crime, even though most murder victims know their killers and most crimes are property crimes. As a result, the public often exaggerates the seriousness of crimes and the likelihood of being a victim of violent crime. Politicians then respond to the public's misinformed demands to crack down on crime with harsher punishments and other confrontational measures. Beale (2003); Pettit (2002).

    Nevertheless, the public has a better sense of the situation in its own country than in other distant countries. Thus, 'normal' negative reporting on events in China will create a more negative impression in the minds of American citizens or others not familiar with China because they lack the counterbalancing positive, less-newsworthy experiences from everyday life. The negative impact is likely to be even greater when the reports tap into long-held stereotypes often favored by editors eager to peddle papers. Moghalu (2002: 34–5) points out that the Western media paid more attention to the International Criminal Tribunal for the Former Yugoslavia than the International Criminal Tribunal for Rwanda and that coverage of the ICTR was more critical. The author explained that 'the most important reason why the ICTR receives a steady stream of criticism and critical reporting is the stereotypical, biased, and long standing negative image and neglect of the African continent in the global media,' complemented by 'a mixture of ignorance, misunderstanding, and calculated editorial decision making by the editors of various global media.'

19. Amnesty International and other NGOs have traditionally excluded economic rights from their mandate, although they have recently begun to focus more on poverty and economic development issues.
20. To give credit where credit is due, the general media does often cover such stories of economic hardship.
21. US Department of State (2004*a*).
22. In her testimony before the US Congress, Executive Director of Human Rights Watch in China Sharon Hom (2004), stated:

    Although there have been areas of improvement—increased average living standards, access to information, greater government participation in the international human rights regime—the human rights situation is generally worsening in other respects for the vast majority of China's people . . . .[T]he human rights situation has overall deteriorated seriously and is marked by growing social inequalities and poverty; massive unemployment; and environmental degradation reaching crisis dimensions; severe restrictions on freedom of expression, including crack-downs on ethnic minorities, religious groups (Falun Gong, underground churches), independent political parties or unions, independent media; use of torture and mistreatment of prisoners, arbitrary detentions and arrests. Lawyers taking on cases that are politically sensitive may find themselves intimidated or themselves the target of prosecution.

    Whereas claims of steady deterioration in 'human rights' are usually based on increased violations only in some areas of civil and political rights, Hom suggests a broader deterioration. There may be ups and downs with respect to some issues and new problems may arise from time to time, as is true everywhere. Nevertheless, claims of deterioration across the board for the vast majority of Chinese citizens are not consistent with the empirical evidence showing generally steady improvement in the last twenty-five years in all main categories, albeit with more limited and less consistent progress on civil and political rights. Despite problems with unemployment, growing income differentials and even environmental degradation, the vast majority of Chinese citizens are far better off as a result of economic reforms during the last two decades. As demonstrated, infant mortality rates are down, education enrollments are up, people are living longer, and poverty has been reduced. Moreover, the international human rights regime has not yet recognized a right to a particular distribution of wealth. Nor have the rights to employment or to particular environmental standards become justiciable in most countries. Perhaps more importantly, the proposed solution is unclear. No doubt Chinese leaders would prefer full employment, a clean environment, and zero poverty. However, the transition from a poor, underdeveloped country with an economy dominated by rural agriculture and state-owned enterprises to a modern, affluent, industrialized society with a large urban population and a market-based economy is always accompanied by growing unemployment, widening income differentials and environmental degradation. See also Christie and Roy (2001: 219, 232), noting that while serious problems remain, 'the CCP can truthfully claim that the average Chinese is better off than before the establishment of the CCP regime, and indeed the total human rights situation (that is, including socioeconomic as well as civil/political rights) today is the best in China's history.'

23. US Department of State (1998).
24. US Department of State (1994).
25. For a discussion, see Peerenboom (2002: 142–5, 559–68).
26. Russia's software piracy rate (93%) was actually slightly higher than China's in 2003 (92%). See USTR (2004).
27. Russia was put on the Priority Watch List. But only a Priority Foreign Country designation allows for the imposition of sanctions after an investigation. Dimitrov (2004: 87–90).
28. Ibid. Less noble concerns over economic self-interest may also have played a role: intellectual property violations in China cost US companies more than similar violations in Russia, and American businesses stand to gain more from access to Chinese markets than to Russian markets. The USTR estimates copyright violations in China result in losses of US$2.5 billion per year, as compared to $1.1 billion in Russia. These numbers rely on the absurd assumption that people in a low income country such as China would actually pay full price for products they now purchase at a tenth or twentieth of the full price. See USTR 2004.
29. Bush (2002).
30. The White House (2002: 3).
31. Persaud (2004).
32. Jochnick and Normand (1994).
33. Albright (2000).
34. Holsti (2000: 131–55) cites polling data showing a decline in the public's interest in the state of human rights abroad since the end of the Cold War.

CHAPTER 6

1. Gilley (2004) is a particularly egregious example, blaming everything from higher crime rates to environmental degradation to rising inequality to the tourist boats eating away at the Buddhist carvings on the riverside in Guilin on the lack of democracy. When confronted with areas where the government has been successful, he claims that China would have enjoyed even greater success under a democratic regime; conversely, when confronted with the empirical reality of dramatically inferior performance in India or other developing democracies, he claims that the situation there would have been even worse under an authoritarian regime. But clearly democracy is no guarantee of good governance, as the low World Bank scores of many democracies show.
2. Watson (1993). The Chinese Academy of Social Sciences (2004) recently devoted a special issue to yet another round on legal transplants.
3. Teubner (1998).
4. Langer (2004).
5. Xu Zhangrun (2004).
6. Orücü (2002).
7. Pistor and Wellons (1999).
8. Potter (2004).
9. Evans (2003) describing institutional monocropping as the imposition on developing countries of idealized versions of Anglo-American institutions, which are presumed to transcend national circumstances, level of development, position in the global economy and culture, and claiming that the processes has produced 'profoundly disappointing results.'
10. Su Li (1995).
11. 'Harmony but not identity' is typically associated with cultural assimilation and the relationship between Chinese and non-Chinese. However, it is equally applicable to legal reforms that involve some element of assimilation of foreign models.
12. The metaphor of legal translations leads into the murky waters of postmodernism on the one hand, and analytic philosophy of language, including discussions of incommensurability and holistic systems of meaning, on the other.
13. Turn of the century legal and political reforms were often described in terms of an impact-response model, which is similar to legal transplants in emphasizing the Western origins of legal reforms and in being unidirectional. Just as the notion that contemporary legal reforms are

simply imported from abroad fails to capture the complexity of the dynamics of reform today, so too the notion that China's turn of the century reforms were driven by the sudden realization that China lagged behind Western countries in technical, military, and legal-political matters was too simple. For a critique of the impact-response model, see Cohen (1970).

14. These shortcomings do not mean that the metaphors are not useful for the intended purpose of shedding light on legal development or a particular aspect of legal development. Nor is it surprising that descriptive metaphors are not that useful in prediction as these are different tasks. A hammer may be useful for pounding but not cutting. It also bears noting that the metaphors have then been interpreted and applied to the legal reform process in various ways, including at times in ways at odds with the original views of the authors. For example, different commentators may disagree over whether, or the extent to which, legal transplant implies a teleological convergence in legal systems.
15. See generally Dowdle (2002); Cai (2005/2006).
16. This same criticism applies generally to the notion of mixed legal systems. On the growing use of 'mixed systems' as a descriptive category in comparative law, scc Rcid (2003).
17. See generally, Peerenboom (2002: 153–6) and the cites and examples therein.
18. Developing their regulatory theory in the context of a liberal democracy, Dorf and Sabel (1998) refer to their approach as a directly deliberative polyarchy based on democratic experimentalism. For a discussion of the applicability and limits of this approach for China, see Peerenboom (2002: 424–31).
19. For an early attempt to predict success or failure of transplants, see Kahn-Freund (1974), emphasizing political factors including interest group politics over social, economic, and cultural factors. Daniels and Trebilcock (2004) group obstacles to rule of law into three general categories—resource and institutional capacity shortcomings; social-cultural-historical problems; and political-economy barriers. They argue that political-economy obstacles, including opposition by key interest groups, have been the biggest barriers in Latin America and Central and Eastern Europe. Brooks (2003), Kahn (1999), Licht et al. (2002), Friedman and Perez-Perdomo (2003) all emphasize cultural factors. Cooter (1996) highlights the importance of law complying with efficient social norms. Friedman (1960) calls for more attention to *legal* culture.

20. There are vast literatures containing numerous empirical studies on the transition to and consolidation of democracy, the relationship between law and development, and factors affecting the implementation of human rights. See e.g. Carey and Poe (2004) for empirical studies of human rights. There is also a growing empirical literature on the establishment and implementation of rule of law, with 'rule of law' taken as the dependent variable. In addition, several systematic empirical studies look at particular features of the legal system in relation to economic development and the protection of rights. See generally, Peerenboom (2005) and the cites therein.
21. See Peerenboom (2004*e*); Linnan (2006).
22. Ravich (2000) argues that marketization leads to development of civil society and a process of democratic learning on the part of citizens that is crucial for legal and political reforms. Zakaria (2004) attributes problems in development of rule of law and establishment of democracy in the Mid East in part to a business class and citizenry dependent on easy money from oil. Easy money tends to produce a corporatist or clientelist relationship between the elite and the government, and allows the government to buy off the populace and delay political reforms.
23. See Raustiala (2000).
24. A change that can make at least one individual better off, without making any other individual worse off is a Pareto improvement: an allocation of resources is Pareto efficient when no further Pareto improvements can be made. An outcome is Kaldor–Hicks efficient if those that are made better off could in theory compensate those that are made worse off and produce a Pareto optimal outcome. However, Kaldor–Hicks does not require that those made worse off are in fact compensated, and thus may lead to negative distributional consequences.
25. Clarke (1998–9) cautions against the teleological assumption that the end state of legal reform is meant to be, or likely to be, the 'Western rule of law ideal.'
26. Peerenboom (2002 and 2004*a*).
27. Clarke (1998–9) questions whether China has a *legal* system; Lubman (1999) questions whether China has a legal *system*. For a response to Clarke and Lubman's claims that China lacks a legal system and an attempt to sort out different approaches to defining the minimal requirements of rule of law and answer the question whether we will know rule of law when we see it, see Peerenboom (2002: 130–41, 565–8). Briefly stated, I argue that there is considerable agreement about the elements of a thin (or procedural) rule of law. However, there

is considerable disagreement about thick (or substantive) conceptions of rule of law in China and elsewhere.

28. One type of Orientalism denies China could ever establish rule of law given its cultural traditions. Another attempts to impose on China a particularly thick conception of liberal democratic rule of law as the only appropriate model worth pursuing. See also Ruskola (2002).
29. Licht et al. (2002) found that countries that emphasized autonomy and egalitarianism had higher levels of rule of law and accountability and less corruption, whereas countries that emphasized embeddedness and hierarchy had a lower level of rule of law and accountability and worse corruption. In short, Euro-America scored significantly higher than other regions. The authors suggest that cultural orientation in East Asia may make it more difficult to implement rule of law, restrict corruption, and increase accountability, and that 'good governance' in Asia may differ in some respects from 'good governance' in Western liberal democracies.

    Good governance in Asian countries no doubt differs in significant respects from good governance in rich, liberal democratic Western countries once one examines in more detail the broad variables of rule of law, accountability, and corruption. Kasian Thechapira for instance describes three different versions of good governance—autocratic, liberal, and communitarian—each of which has different positions on civil society, the state, markets, and democracy. The autocrat emphasizes the need for a strong state to ensure economic development, root out corruption, and maintain social order. The liberal favors broader participation by civil society in fair competition both in the market and political arena. The communitarian sees civil society as promoting social justice through pressure on the state to overcome the growing inequality associated with globalization and neoliberal markets (Banpasirichote 2004: 224). Nevertheless, Asian states have outperformed other regions in terms of rule of law on the same World Bank good governance scales used by Licht et al., suggesting that culture may not be as important at least in Asia as the authors suggest.
30. Of course, judicial corruption is not only a matter of low salaries.
31. For a more extensive discussion of adversarial and inquisitorial systems, see Langer (2004).
32. For a discussion and critique of the amendments, see Hecht (1996); Clarke (1998).
33. Wiegand (1996). Langer (2004) argues that while the US's influence may be producing deep changes in other legal systems, these systems may

still diverge in important ways. Amann (2000) discusses the reservations regarding the adoption of common law norms and practices with respect to the International Criminal Tribunal for Rwanda.

34. Cohen (2002); Yu Ping (2002).
35. Kurczewski and Sullivan (2002: 281–2). Hammergren (1998: 10) points out that Latin Americans have also reacted to increased crime by curtailing liberal reforms.
36. Although Japan has adopted a more adversarial system since the Second World War, the system retains many of the features of an inquisitorial system, including the emphasis on the search for truth carried out by impartial and professional prosecutors, the distrust of defense counsel and the limits on counsel's ability to meet with the accused and conduct discovery, the long periods of detention during investigation, the limited access to bail for those who have not confessed, and the relaxed rules of evidence that allow for consideration of hearsay evidence and the introduction of illegally obtained evidence. While such features seem alien to an American lawyer steeped in the adversarial tradition (with trial by a lay jury), and, while such features may in certain cases lead to abuse or miscarriages of justice, they must be viewed in terms of a highly professional procuracy that goes to great lengths to ensure that the facts of the case are clear, the punishment both fits the defendant and the crime, and that the punishment is consistent with other similarly situated defendants whose circumstances are explored in great detail. Furthermore, the Japanese system seeks not only or even primarily punishment in most cases. Rather, the emphasis is on rehabilitation and reintegration of the accused into society. Johnson (2002: 74, 84) notes that in Japan, '[l]awyers are not permitted to be present during interrogation;' suspects have the right to remain silent, but may be and often are interrogated for hours at a time for up to twenty-three days; fewer than 10% of suspects secure the services of a lawyer during the investigative phase; prosecutors typically limit contact between the lawyer and the accused to three short visits of fifteen minutes each if the accused has not yet confessed; and '[p]rosecutors, police and prison guards may censor written communications between the accused and defense counsel.' Despite some areas of concern, Johnson concludes the 'normative bottom line' is that 'the Japanese way of justice is uncommonly just,' especially in comparison to the punitive and highly dysfunctional criminal justice system in the United States.
37. In recent years, the Constitutional Court in Taiwan has exercised its newfound authority by greatly expanding the rights of criminal suspects,

notwithstanding similar views among the Taiwanese public, as in China, regarding the need to wage war on crime. In 1991, 58% of Taiwanese approved of executing criminals in public, 68% endorsed passing special laws to attack crime, and 59% believed that punishment was more important than compensation for the injured. In 1999, over two-thirds thought punishments were too lenient, while only 1% thought punishments were too harsh. Furthermore, over 42% believed that suspects could be detained even if there was not sufficient evidence to prove them guilty of serious crime, as long as there was reasonable suspicion. See Chen (2003), arguing that without broader public support for the protection of human rights, it is doubtful that rule of law can be realized in Taiwan—or at least the liberal democratic version of rule of law entailed by such rights.

38. There is little if any chance that China will revert back to an inquisitorial system: the global trend is toward an adversarial (if not American) model; human rights organizations would have a fit; domestic reformers and legal academics, many of them trained in the US, would oppose the changes; and central authorities are unlikely to reverse themselves so soon after the decision in the mid-1990s to move toward an adversarial model.
39. Supreme People's Court's Several Opinions on Applying Summary Procedures to Try Cases of Public Prosecution (2003).
40. Several Opinions on Applying Ordinary Procedure to Try 'Cases in Which the Defendant Pleaded Guilty' (Trial Implementation) (2003).
41. See Langer (2004).
42. For critical accounts, see Alschuler (1983); Langbein (1978); Schulhofer (1992). For positive accounts, see Scott and Stuntz (1992). For a thought-provoking description by a former public defender and prosecutor, see Lynch (1994). He points out that in seven state counties in the US, 100% of convictions were obtained by guilty pleas without jury trials; some judges threatened—and imposed—draconian punishments for defendants who refused to plea bargain; judges, prosecutors, and defense counsel favored plea bargains because jury trials were much more work and fraught with professional risk for the judge if the case was overturned on appeal, for the prosecutor if the defendant was acquitted, and for defense counsel if the defendant was found guilty and subject to a much heavier punishment; meanwhile, prosecutors, far from agonizing over appropriate sentences, made snap decisions usually within three minutes for misdemeanors and ten minutes for serious felonies based on only a cursory knowledge of the facts of the case.

43. Scott and Stuntz (1992: 1911–12).
44. See Peerenboom (2004*d*).
45. Ministry of Public Security, Doc. No. 52. The Notice also calls on public security officers to punish activities of hooliganism that disrupt public order despite exhortations to halt such activities, such as panhandling; camping in the open; provoking disturbances; and inciting crowds to fight in or around such public places as offices, schools, hospitals, public squares, movie theaters, and famous scenic spots.
46. For instance, Inner Mongolian regulations emphasized that the problems of migrancy and vagrancy could only be addressed through the combined efforts of government, society, and families. The regulations require local governments to pick up the tab for return transportation and to help solve the economic difficulties of migrants so that they do not head back to the cities. In addition, the regulations call for the education of families regarding their responsibility to look after vagrants. They also ominously, if vaguely, warn that those who fail to provide support will be 'strictly dealt with according to law.' The Mongolian government also emphasized that the relief centers were only for the temporary assistance of those in dire circumstances, who lacked the ability to meet basic living needs. The vast majority of those who come to centers will still be sent back to their homes. In addition to reiterating that the maximum stay is ten days unless the next higher level government department approves an extension, the regulations limit vagrants to two stays within a six-month period. If vagrants refuse to leave after their time is up, relief services will be terminated. If the relief centers cannot track down the families of minors, seniors, handicapped people, and the mentally impaired, after fifteen days the center staff is to contact the same level government to arrange for their relocation. The regulation is silent as to where they will be relocated. The centers may also deny services to anyone who refuses to provide accurate information about their identity, residence, and financial resources. See Inner Mongolian Autonomous Region Government, Notice To Carry Out Well the Relief Management Work for Urban Indigent Vagrants and Beggars (Aug. 15, 2003).
47. The procedure is referred to as *kangsu* or protest when the challenge is brought by the procuracy.
48. The legislature in most legal systems may be able to pass new laws that would result in a different income on similar facts in future cases, but they generally do not have the power to alter the results for the parties in cases already decided by the court. Some legal systems also have

three tiers of review as part of their normal appeal process, in comparison to the trial plus one-appeal system in China.

49. Each year, the courts handle approximately 6 million cases, of which less than 2% end up being retried. Only a minuscule fraction—between 0.3% and 0.4% of all cases handled by the courts—result in a changed verdict (Peerenboom 2006).
50. The ratio of cases reversed to those supervised is in the aggregate rather high, although it varies by type of supervision, type of case, and from place to place (Peerenboom 2006).
51. This is not surprising at least for reforms introduced via laws as the NPC lawmaking process typically involves both domestic and foreign input. Drafters will usually collect relevant laws from many different countries for reference. A drafting committee will then tour China to get a sense of the problems people working in the system are facing and their proposed solutions. A drafting group, often headed by a legal scholar or at least involving academics, will then prepare a draft for discussion. The draft will then be circulated to relevant departments and interested parties, including in some cases foreign businesses or their representatives such as the American Chamber of Commerce. Drafts of important laws such as the Marriage Law and Property Law are also made available for public comment.
52. Biebesheimer and Payne (2001) discuss various problems with the available quantitative data including that measuring instruments are too general to be of much use. Taylor (2006) discusses and evaluates four popular measures for evaluating legal systems and legal reforms. Carothers (2003) claims that the lack of systematic empirical studies has hindered development of our knowledge base.
53. Daniels and Trebilcock (2004).
54. Ignatieff (2003) questions whether states that have failed because of ethnic conflict should be maintained intact, and whether the international community should intervene at all in places like Somalia or just walk away given that periodic aid may exacerbate conflicts as factions fight over the bounty, while the international community often lacks the political will and resources for the kind of sustained occupation that ultimately is required to turn the state around.
55. Several of the essays in the Holzgrefe and Keohane (2003) volume contemplate a more expanded scope of humanitarian intervention that includes nation building, in some cases in contexts where sovereignty is compromised under forms of protectorate or trusteeship. Keohane (2003), for example, argues that effective post-intervention measures requires

limitations on sovereignty, and that states in 'bad neighborhoods' might have to go through a process of nominal sovereignty where authority over domestic affairs rests with the UN or some outside authority, limited sovereignty where the UN or outside authority has veto power over key decisions by local actors, and then integrated sovereignty where nationals make their own decisions subject to a supranational court. Williams and Pecci (2004) discuss the earned sovereignty approach, which may involve phased, conditional, or constrained sovereignty as a possible approach to conflicts over self-determination.

56. See e.g. Carothers (2003).
57. Neilson (2006) reminds us that bankruptcy laws pushed by the international community in Indonesia have not been implemented due to limited state and public sector capacity, opposition by local stakeholders and ideological concerns about the negative consequences of neoliberal economic policies, many of which were forced upon Indonesia as conditions for economic aid during the Asian financial crisis. Stewart (2005) points out that the remarkable consensus of the international community on tax reforms ignores local politics, emphasizes efficiency over equity and the distributional effects of tax rules, and has failed to produce the expected results in many countries.
58. An experimental approach is consistent with a deep streak of pragmatism running through Chinese political philosophy and culture (Hall and Ames 1999).
59. Kaufmann et al. (2005) concede the difficulties of assessing trends in a particular country indicator given the large margins of error. The decreases may be attributable to the addition of new data sets and more importantly large margins of error (standard deviation of .12 for rule of law). After new data sets were added, China's scores from earlier years were lower than reported previously. For example, China's 2002 rule of law ranking is now listed as the 48.5 percentile rather than the 51.5 percentile previously given when the data came out in 2003. Other indicators for 2002 are also anywhere from 2 to 4.5 percentage points lower now than when reported in 2003. The World Bank index aggregates results from several other data sets that rely on subjective judgments by business people and others familiar to one degree or another with China. Thus, there is also the possibility that subjective impressions are out of line with objective circumstances, particularly when it comes to a technical area such as legal reforms. Nonspecialists in particular might have been disappointed that China's accession to the WTO did not miraculously lead to a rule of law compliant legal system overnight.

60. Funneling compensation claims for the taking of land, farms, and houses in the countryside and cities into the courts forces courts to decide the controversial issuse of who is entitled to the windfall from rising real estate prices. Urban residents, especially those that worked for the government or state-owned enterprises, are often living in housing originally allocated to them by the state for free, and then sold to them at heavily subsidized rates. When the land is requisitioned, the court must decide how much the homeowners should be compensated. Should the current residents be entitled to fair market value for their housing *and* the land use rights, even though the land use rights may be unclear and they obtained the housing at subsidized prices? Those affected may argue that they worked hard for the state for years for low wages, and deserve the windfall. But they have already benefited relative to others who did not have the opportunity to purchase their housing at below-the-market prices. Similar issues arise in the countryside, although farmers may have a greater normative claim to the sales from land use rights given the discriminatory policies that transferred wealth from rural to urban areas through artificially low prices for agricultural products and the large wealth differential between rural and urban areas today.
61. Very roughly, a *xiaokang* refers to a society in which the differences between the rich and poor are not so great as to undermine social stability. A harmonious society is a much higher standard, which entails much more than the minimal compromises and accommodations required to achieve a *xiaokang* society. A harmonious society would require in addition that individuals are given the opportunity to achieve a certain degree of self-fulfillment—a notion vaguely akin to the capabilities approach adopted by Sen (1993) and Nussbaum (1997). An even loftier idea would be *datong*—literally 'great unity.' This state is a utopian ideal, capable of various interpretations ranging from the Marxist ideal of 'to each according to their needs' or a Millian state in which all obtain self-realization and fulfillment to a state in which procedural and substantive notions of equality would merge.
62. Bugaric (2001) argues that in Eastern Europe, courts decided cases based on neoliberal economic dogma that did not always fit the times and conditions. Similarly, in the Philippines, a recurring complaint is that the courts interfere too much in 'economic decision-making' by second-guessing government policy-makers. Pangalangan (2004) describes how the desire of the Filipino courts to please the public has led to an outcome-oriented jurisprudence, 'as if the courts were in

a perpetual popularity contest refereed by polling groups and single-interest lobbies, all of them oblivious to the professional demands of the legal craftsman.' On the other hand, Halmai and Scheppele (1997) point out that Hungarian constitutional court enjoyed strong public support even though it adopted a strict legalistic or 'rule of law approach' to transitional justice issues, striking several of the more punitive laws passed by the democratically enacted legislature for being retroactive.

More generally, the expanding role of the courts in transitional states raises questions about the preferred form of constitutional review and whether relying too heavily on the judiciary may hinder the development of political processes needed to consolidate and sustain democracy. Courts are increasingly being plunged into the middle of political disputes. In Russia, the judiciary faced the issue of Chechnya's claim to independence; in Egypt, courts have decided cases involving Sharia principles that determine the nature of public life; in South Africa, courts have decided on the legality of amnesty provisions and even the constitutionality of the constitution (Hirschi 2002). Whatever the long-term impact on the development of other political institutions, these decisions by the court are driven more by policy considerations than law. They highlight the differences in social, economic, political, and normative beliefs that support competing thick conceptions of rule of law in a society. As a result, parties on all sides of the issue will invoke 'rule of law' to support their preferred outcome and to criticize the courts if the court's decision does not comport with their preferences, leading to doubts about the meaning and value of rule of law.

63. Pluralism as used here refers to the view that there are multiple, irreducible fundamental values that may conflict in particular circumstances. This is both a factual and normative claim.
64. Tyler (1990).
65. Pei (2006).

CHAPTER 7

1. Lawrance (2004).
2. Vitug (2004).
3. *Amateurism Impairs Roh Regime* (2004).
4. *Asia: The Greatest Show on Earth* (2004).
5. CIA (2005).

6. See e.g. Lawrance (2004). See also Gilley (2004).
7. *Asia: The Greatest Show on Earth* (2004).
8. Lele and Quadir (2004*b*: 3).
9. Rocamora (2004).
10. Angeles (2004: 196).
11. David (1994: 24–5).
12. Rocamora (2004: 204–5).
13. Co (2004).
14. Lindsey (2004: 312).
15. Linnan (2006).
16. See generally Lindsey (2006*a*).
17. Robinson (2002: 103).
18. Linnan (2006).
19. CIA (2005).
20. Ibid.
21. On the positive side, the UNDP (2005: 46) points out that Bangladesh was able to make notable improvements in human development, admittedly from a very low base, despite low growth.
22. CIA (2005).
23. McCann and Gibney (1996: 23–5). Reilly (2003) notes that over the period 1976–96, the number of countries with the best score actually decreased, countries with the worst score increased, while the mean remained about the same.
24. Fein (1995).
25. Davenport and Armstrong (2002) found that 'authorities do not perceive any change in the costs and benefits of repression until the highest levels of democracy have been achieved.' Keith and Poe (2002) found that democracy has only a minor impact on personal integrity rights, although the transition from the lowest level to the highest level produces a more substantial impact. Zanger (2000) found that democracy leads to improvement in human rights performance within the first year of holding elections, but then leads to increased repression in following years. In contrast, while a regime change from democracy to authoritarianism brings repression in its first year, it results in a decrease in repression in subsequent years. Moreover, the study distinguished between democracies, authoritarian regimes, and mixed regimes—i.e. those regimes that score in the middle of the Polity III index, as most new democracies are likely to do. Transitions from an authoritarian regime to a mixed regime lead to more repression in the year of change, a decrease in the first year, and then an increase in

the second year. In sum, the results support the argument that human rights improvements are consistently obtained only in full democracies.

26. Bueno de Mesquita et al. (2005: 439).
27. Ibid. at 440.
28. Lak (2002).
29. Przeworski et al. (2000: 270).
30. Gu (1997).
31. Chan (1993).
32. Hagopian (1998) points out that Latin America elections are also often more about choosing persons than policies, and that the presidential system encourages presidents who treat parties, congress, and courts as a nuisance. Examples include Collar in Brazil, Fujimori in Peru, Serrano in Guatemala.
33. Helgesen (2002: 82).
34. See Bell (2000: 153).
35. Hahm (2004).
36. Ling and Shih (1998).
37. Albritton and Thawilwadee (2003).
38. Pasuk and Baker (2004: 5).
39. Cited in Pasuk and Baker (2004: 171).
40. Peng (1998).
41. Kim (2004: 201) considers two common explanations. The first emphasizes cultural factors. Korean civil society is still rooted in traditional patters of associational life, and remains particularistic and closed. The second suggests that the state has co-opted political associations and thus undermined the necessary tension between state and civil society. He argues both fail to appreciate that civil society was originally intended and has historically served to complement the state, rather than simply oppose the state, by ameliorating some of the negative effects of capitalism, including poverty, inequality, moral decay, and the social stability that then follows. Han (2005: 106) points out that Korean NGOs are hampered by 'poor financial conditions due to the lack of a membership fee payers, an overly professionalized support base, and project-oriented activities with little participation of citizens.'
42. Helgesen (2002: 82).
43. Park and Shin (2004).
44. Albritton and Thawilwadee (2003). However, only 25% agree that free speech is not worth it if that means having to put up with a threat of

social disorder, while over 90% believe that the political leaders should tolerate views of challengers, suggesting that Thais are aware of the misuse of restrictions on free speech in the name of public order and the use of defamation laws to curtail political opposition.

45. Pinkney (2003: 232). In addition to a handful of countries that have enjoyed continuous democracy since becoming independent, Pinkney counts Uruguay as the only clear-cut case of consolidation among those making a transition from authoritarianism, with some support for Argentina, Chile, and perhaps South Africa and Ghana. McFaul (2002) notes that twenty-two of the twenty-eight former soviet republics are 'various shades of dictatorships or unconsolidated transitional regimes.'
46. O'Donnel and Schmitter (1986: 69).
47. Bell and Keenan (2004: 346–7) point out that once in power even the rights-friendly Nelson Mandela criticized NGOs, claiming that 'many of our nongovernmental organizations are not in fact NGOs, both because they have no popular base and the actuality that they rely on the domestic and foreign governments, rather than the people, for their material sustenance.'
48. As Rapley (2004) and Dezalay and Garth (2002) note, many elite in developing countries—often trained in prestigious American universities—supported neoliberal policies.
49. Chua (2003) shows that the combination of globalization, economic liberalization, and democratization may be particularly problematic in countries where there is an economically dominant minority. Ethnic minorities with market skills are better able to take advantage of economic liberalization. As the gap in inequality grows, ethnic tensions rise. The poorer ethnic majority takes advantage of the increased political space provided by democracy to vent their anger, often spurred on by demagogues who rise to power by stirring up ethnic hatred. This scenario frequently leads to three types of backlash. The first is against economic liberalization, as the dominant majority elects populists who reject both the positive and negative elements of the Washington Consensus in favor of limits on imports and foreign direct investment, nationalization of companies, confiscation of land owned by members of the minority and foreigners, and redistribution of income, as in Mugabe's Zimbabwe and Chavez's Venezuela. The second is against democracy, as the economically dominant minority joins forces with authoritarian leaders, as in Suharto's Indonesia. The third reaction is ethnic violence, even genocide, as in Rwanda and the former

Yugoslavia. Given that democratization and economic liberalization may lead to conflict in heterogeneous societies, one possible implication is that economic reforms (albeit with more sensitivity to distributional effects and greater investment in human capital and institutions) should precede political reforms, and that democratization should be postponed until a higher level of wealth is obtained. This is consistent with the general empirical literature that shows democratization at lower levels of wealth is likely to fail and that the better protection of human rights generally occurs only once democratization is consolidated. Chua herself resists this conclusion, suggesting instead various ways members of the dominant ethnic minority, leaders of developing countries, and the international community might be able to mitigate the problems. To be sure, democratization and market reforms have not led to problems in all countries with a dominant economic minority. Yet even assuming all of her recommendations were taken together, it is doubtful that they would be sufficient in many cases to prevent the backlashes.

50. Quadir (2004: 91).
51. Angeles (2004: 189).
52. Latinobarometer (2002).
53. Carothers (2002); Diamond (1999).
54. Diamond (1999).
55. Carothers (2002). See also McFaul (2002).
56. I have discussed these and other factors elsewhere, concluding that China is not likely to become democratic in the near future, although democratization in the long run is likely (Peerenboom 2002: 513–46).
57. Eurobarometer 62 (2005).
58. Pew Global Attitudes Project (2002). Interestingly, Asian citizens are generally satisfied with their own lives and optimistic about the future, with between half and three-quarters of respondents in India, China, the Philippines, South Korea, Vietnam, Indonesia, and Bangladesh believing their lives would improve in the next five years and less than 10% worried that their lives would not improve during the same period. Japan, where 39% of people felt they lost ground in recent years, was the exception. Only 34% of Japanese are optimistic about the chances of improvement in the next few years, with 27% anticipating being worse off. However, beliefs about future growth and improvement in personal circumstances do not necessarily translate into satisfaction with the current government in democratic states. One can only speculate about what the implications for democracy would be if

people came to believe they would be worse off in the future under a democratic regime. Thailand is a notable exception to the general discontent with democracy in Asia. Albritton and Thawilwadee (2003) report that an astounding 90% of Thais are satisfied with the way democracy works, with 85% maintaining that democracy is always preferable to authoritarianism. The strong support reflects the long history of military coups that have undermined efforts to democratize for much of the twentieth century.

59. Freedom House (2004).
60. Chu et al. (2001: 124).
61. Helgesen (2002: 84).
62. Elections without meaning (2004).
63. Dezalay and Garth (2002).
64. Herman and Chomsky (1988). There are similar complaints about the media in Asia: 'In much of Asia today, major political parties, institutions of formal education and the internationalized "media of communication" are playing the role of citizen pacification, of manufacturing consent and legitimization of actually undemocratic regimes (whether formally democratic or not), as has already happened in other older capitalist democracies' (Lele and Quadir 2004*b*: 11). Han (2005) attributes the widespread perception that the Korean mass media represents a superpower out of control to the dominance of the press by entrenched conservative interests.
65. De Luca and Buell (2005).
66. Latinobarometer (2002). Forero (2004) points out that massive discontent in Latin America has led to the downfall of six elected leaders after violent unrest, growing support for neo-authoritarian leaders, and the granting of extrajudicial powers to effective leaders. There have even been calls in Peru for the return of the authoritarian leader Alberto Fujimori, who was run out of office on corruption charges.
67. E-mail from Tianjin Shi (Aug. 13, 2004), citing data from a nationwide survey conducted in 2002.
68. Pew Global Attitudes Project (2002).
69. Chu et al. (2001: 127).
70. Pew Global Attitudes Project (2002); Pew Global Attitudes Project (2005). The sample in these studies was disproportionately urban. Chen Jie (2004) reports that public opinion surveys in Beijing from 1995 to 1999 found that contrary to the widespread assumption outside of China that the CCP lacks support, the CCP still enjoys legitimacy, at least among urban residents in Beijing, although citizens were

concerned about rising inequality, diminishing job security and corruption. Dowdle (2002: 32–5) cites a number of other polls showing support for government policies and general satisfaction with life in China. The UNDP (2005: 121) notes that Vietnam has achieved impressive growth rates of 5% a year since the 1980s, while managing to maintain equality, with only a slight rise in the Gini coefficient from .35 to .37 during the 1990s. Vietnam's HDI ranking is 16 places higher than its wealth ranking, demonstrating that it has used available resources effectively to promote human well-being.

CHAPTER 8

1. For a more comprehensive discussion of the various paths to democracy and the likely impact of democratizing or not democratizing on a range of issues, see Bachman (2000), who believes gradual democratization more likely, and Gilley (2004), who believes that CCP rule will end with a bang rather than a whimper. While agreeing with most of Bachman's assumptions and conclusions, I think there is a greater chance for the CCP to evolve into some sort of social democratic party and then maintain power for years. Although I also agree that rule of law will require significant changes in social values, I see the main obstacles at present as institutional rather than cultural. Gilley (2004: 191) provides a much more optimistic picture regarding the benefits of democratization, while acknowledging the possibility of chaos and the probability of 'much violence and many deaths.' He suggests (p. 153) that democracy will not fail in China, as it has in so many other developing countries, although the transition to democracy 'will likely be ugly, very ugly at first.' Gilley asserts that limited violence may be necessary and morally acceptable for a greater justice, and that the world should be willing to pay the cost of 'some degree' of chaos in China. He also suggests Chinese citizens would find the 'great deal of bloodshed' and the political, social, and economic disruption worth it, just as people in other countries allegedly have. However, the many polls showing widespread disenchantment of citizens in developing countries with democracy and the willingness to sacrifice elections and civil liberties for economic growth suggest that many people will *not* find the bloodshed and social disorder worth it. This is all the more likely to be the case for Chinese citizens given the higher value placed on social order,

the memory of violent chaos and political instability for much of the last 200 years, and the dire consequences for social, economic, and political disruption on the hundreds of millions living below or near the poverty line.

2. Han (2005: 82).
3. Ethnic conflicts in Bosnia, the rise of Islamic fundamentalism, the struggle for power between Kurds, Sunnis, and Shiites in Iraq, the popularity of extreme right-wing parties in Europe, the rioting by Muslims in France, and the Québécois quest to secede from the rest of Canada all reflect a global trend toward greater awareness of ascriptive and affiliative identities, growing recognition of the need for policies that give due consideration to multiculturalism, and a more worrisome rise in identity politics. Asia is no exception to the general trend, as evidenced by the emergence of conservative Hindu nationalism in India, the rising Islamic fundamentalism in Indonesia and Malaysia, the New Confucian attempts to articulate a normatively attractive conception of modernity consistent with Confucian principles in China, Singapore, and South Korea, and the heated debates over Asian values. In Thailand, anger at the IMF and its role in the Asian financial crisis has fanned a general distrust of international institutions, as reflected in Thaksin's dismissive retort to UN criticism that 'the UN is not my father' (Pasuk and Baker 2004: 164, 17). In South Korea, rising nationalism is manifest in a tendency to emphasize the 'uniqueness' of Korea and Korean people; in the growing assertion of sovereignty and independence in foreign relations, particularly with the US; and in opposition to the economic offshoots of globalization, such as free-trade agreements, the opening of the service sector in education and law, and policies to foster increased labor market flexibility. International NGOs, which are highly critical of North Korea, have also clashed with domestic rights groups that favor reconciliation with North Korea (Hahm 2006).
4. World Bank Chief Economist Nicholas Stern claims that protectionism on the part of developed countries in just the textile sector results in a loss of 27 million jobs in developing countries. *Cutting Agricultural Subsidies* (n.d.).
5. *Greenspan, Snow warn against China sanctions* (2005).
6. See e.g. Johnston (2001).
7. Ironically, many Asian critics of liberal democracy were trained in elite Western universities, where they were exposed to the arguments and

discourses of orientalism, postmodernism, and post-colonialism, and to Western critics of democracy and liberalism.

8. For New Confucianism, see Hall and Ames (1999); Makeham (2003); Tan (2003); Bell and Hahm (2003). For the Asian values debates, see Peerenboom (2003*b*) and the cites therein. See also Discussion: Asian Values (2001).
9. The various pieces of the puzzle are now beginning to fall into place. To cite just a small portion of the literature available in English, Hall and Ames (1999) provide the philosophical foundation for a Deweyean–Confucian alternative to liberalism; de Bary (1998) argues for a more liberal form of Confucian communitarianism; and Tan (2003) splits the difference by attempting a Confucian synthesis of communitarianism and liberalism. Bell (2000) contains both a theoretical discussion of nonliberal democracy and consideration of institutions and specific issues. The Bell and Hahm edited volume (2003) *Confucianism for the Modern World* focuses on institutions. Peerenboom (2002, 2004*a*) discusses nonliberal conceptions of rule of law and accompanying institutions and outcomes on specific issues in China and Asia more broadly. Peerenboom et al. (2006) surveys outcomes in Asia on a range of rights issues. Bell (2006) contrasts Asian and liberal perspectives on a number of specific policy issues.
10. State Council (2005).
11. This is a theme of several best-selling books such as Song et al. (1996) *A Powerful China Can Say No* [*Da Zhongguo keyi shuo bu*].
12. Supporters of the universality of human rights have sought to discredit the notion of Asian values or Chinese values by pointing to the tremendous diversity within the region and China. However, if such diversity precludes the possibility of common values within China and the Asian region, then it also precludes *a fortiori* the possibility of universal values. Alternatively, one could claim that there are common values within China and the Asian region but they are not distinctive. However, what common values do exist are so abstract and so 'thin' that they lead to widely divergent outcomes on specific issues, many of which are not consistent with current human rights standards as interpreted by the ICCPR Human Rights Committee and liberal rights activists. Moreover, as we have seen, large multiple country empirical studies have consistently identified statistically significant regional differences in values, in rights performance, and in the impact of differences in values on rights performance. Both the regional studies and

more specific studies suggest that the liberalism that provides the thicker ideological basis for the human rights movement today is not widely accepted within China and other Asian countries.

13. Wang (2004).
14. Chivers (2005) notes China offered support for President Islam A. Karimov of Uzbekistan, who was facing criticism for the crackdown against an antigovernment rally.
15. Wang Yizhou (2003*b*: 41).
16. Grossman (2004).
17. Mansfield and Snyder (2005) show that democratizing states—especially those that democratize before establishing rule of law and other government institutions for checking executive power—are significantly more likely to start wars than either democracies or authoritarian regimes.
18. Fisher-Thompson (2005).
19. Ministry of Commerce (2005) sets out a long list of what China considers to be discriminatory or unfair practices by the US. Noting the parallel to the demonization of Japan in the 1980s, Bown and McCulloch (2005) describe 'unprecedented' discriminatory policies against China by the US that protect domestic industries and favor China's competitors. For example, Chinese companies face the most anti-dumping actions, are the most likely to have duties imposed, and suffer the highest duties—a 'China premium' of an additional 80%—making China 'public enemy number one.' They argue that such policies are likely to have unintended consequences for the global economy and US interests.
20. Li Shaojun (2003: 69–70) provides a fairly typical account of what many Chinese perceive to be their more ethical approach toward foreign relations:

    Strategic culture can explain many things that cannot be explained by realpolitik or realism. In fact, realpolitik and realism in international relations do influence China's choices of nuclear arms control and disarmaments, but the development model of Chinese civilization and the traditional political culture influence Chinese behavior as well. A contrast of the two reveals that the latter influence is at a much deeper and substantive level.

    . . . During the historical process of thousands of years of Chinese civilization, invasions by peripheral tribes and punitive expeditions by central dynasties were common occurrences . . . According to historical records, Chinese dynasties sometimes engaged in war, but most times implemented policies of peace with peripheral tribes, such as establishing friendly relations, trading, intermarrying, enfeoffing, and moving them to the hinterland. The trade-off between war-like policies and peaceful policies consisted of the following: (1) China engaged in wars generally under conditions beyond its endurance. The basic purpose was to remove external threats, not to expand territory. Therefore, the Chinese military would always return after a victory. (2) For the Chinese dynasties, war was a means and peace was [the] object. The ancient politicians knew that invaders would return if peace were not established. After winning a battle China would seek a friendly relationship and indicate its power and kindness. (3) During conflicts with peripheral tribes, China emphasized its civilizing role. Ancient Chinese politicians thought that China could realize unification 'under Heaven' through the spread of its culture, which was characterized by benevolence.

21. The Schumer report (2005) on the 'one-way street' for foreign investment is an example of a political hack job that hinders rather than facilitates resolution of tough trade issues. The report contains serious misstatements of PRC foreign investment laws that anyone with even the least familiarity with China business would know are clearly false, such as PRC law forces foreign companies to enter into a joint venture with a Chinese partner rather than allowing them to set up wholly foreign owned companies. The whole notion of foreign investment being a one-way street because China does not allow or excessively restricts foreign investment is absurd. According to the Ministry of Commerce (2005), over 45,000 US companies have set up companies in China, almost 4,000 in 2004 alone. In contrast, 883 Chinese companies have set up shop in the US, 87 in 2004. The total amount of contracted FDI from US companies is almost $100 billion, in comparison to $1 billion for Chinese investors in the US. As noted, China stands out among developing states, including East Asian states during their economic rise, for its openness to foreign investment and import trade.

On the other hand, amidst all the distortion and hyperbole, the report does raise the legitimate concern that China limits or prohibits foreign investment in certain sectors to the detriment of US companies, and has sought to encourage foreign parties to bring high technology, although that is generally not a requirement for investment as the report states. Clearly some of the restrictions are meant to protect infant industries. The report does not consider the substantive merits of such policies. Needless to say, the report does not consider China's complaints about US unfair trade practices.

22. Zoellick (2005).

CHAPTER 9

1. Ruskola (2005). The US is generally not perceived in the US or even in China as having been a colonial power in China. Ruskola however recounts the forgotten story of US imperialism where the US forced a weakened China to sign treaties and agreements opening the country to foreign trade while granting extraterritorial jurisdiction whereby US citizens were largely immune from Chinese laws. At the same time, despite the so-called Open Door policy to ensure free trade, the US adopted blatantly racist and discriminatory policies against Chinese immigrants. The excluded Chinese, for all of their alleged lack of understanding of individual rights, immediately challenged the discriminatory laws for being unconstitutional. However, the Supreme Court held against them, on the ground that the United States had an absolute right to exclude aliens from its territory.
2. Gallagher (2005).
3. For a recent summary of the literature on the proper sequencing of reform, see Ariff and Khalid (2005: 346–51). While warning that there is much disagreement about the proper sequence and that local differences may preclude a single optimal model, they recommend generally that market reforms and competition in the domestic real sector be introduced first, with import tariffs, barriers for foreign investment, and protections for infant industries reduced gradually. Budget deficits should be dealt with before reform of the labor markets. Capital account convertibility should be postponed, with financial liberalization occurring when a regulatory framework has been created to manage and supervise the sector.
4. Sajo (2004: 1, 5).
5. The World Bank (1993: 157–89) describes the various ways in which Asian states have sought to share growth, including land reforms, affirmative action policies that favor particular minorities or disadvantaged groups, investments in education, financial support for small and medium-sized business, government subsidized housing and health services, and an emphasis on redistribution of wealth in some countries.

6. Zakaria (2004) provides a general overview of countries that have followed to one degree or another a path similar to the EAM.
7. See generally Chan (2002: 199); World Bank (1993).
8. World Bank (1993: 106–8).
9. UNDP (2005: 134).
10. Moon and Yang (2002: 135).
11. Thio (2004).
12. Pinkney (2003).

References

Abou el Fadl, Khaled. 2003. Islam and the Challenge of Democratic Commitment. *Fordham International Law Journal* 27:4.

Adhikari, Ramesh, and Prema-chandra Athukorala. 2002. *Developing Countries in the World Trading System: The Uruguay Round and Beyond*. Cheltenham, UK, and Northampton, MA, USA: Edward Elgar.

Aids Activist Released After Hunger Strike. 2004. *South China Morning Post*. Apr. 6.

Albright, Madeleine. 2000. Speech at University of World Economy and Diplomacy, Tashkent, Uzbekistan. Apr. 17. **htttp://secretary.state.gov/www/statements/2000/000417.html**.

Albritton, Robert B. and Bureekul Thawilwadee. 2003. The Meaning of Democracy in a Developing Nation. **http://www.kpi.ac.th/en/meaning_of_democracy1.htm**.

Alschuler, Albert W. 1983. Implementing the Criminal Defendant's Right to Trial: alternatives to the plea bargaining system. *University of Chicago Law Review* 50:931.

Amann, Diane Marie. 2000. Harmonic Convergence? Constitutional criminal procedure in an international context. *Indiana Law Journal* 75:809.

Amateurism Impairs Roh Regime. 2004. *Korean Times*. May 27.

Amnesty International. 2004*a*. Amnesty International Report 2004: China. **http://web.amnesty.org/report2004/chn-summary-eng**.

—— 2004*b*. The Shadow of Tiananmen. **http://web.amnesty.org/web/wire.nsf/June2004/China**.

—— 2003*a*. China: Further Information on Fear of Forcible Return. **http://web.amnesty.org/library/Index/ENGASA170372003?open&of=ENG-393**.

—— 2003*b*. Continuing Abuses Under a New Leadership—A Summary of Human Rights Concerns, ASA 17/035/2003. Oct. 1.

—— 2003*c*. No Justice for the Victims of the 1997 Crackdown in Gulja. ASA 17/011/2003. Feb. 4.

—— 2002. People's Republic of China: Labour Unrest and the Suppression of the Rights to Freedom of Association and Expression.

Amnesty International. 2001*a*. People's Republic of China: Torture—A Growing Scourge in China—Time for Action. **http://web.amnesty.org/library/pdf/ASA17004200 1english/$File/ASA1700401.pdf**.

—— 2001*b*. China: 'Striking Harder' Than Ever Before. **http://web.amnesty.org/library/Index/engASA170222001**.

—— 1998. *United States of America: Rights for All.* **http://web.amnesty.org/library/Index/ENGAMR510351998?open&of=ENG-USA**.

—— 1993. Amnesty International Report 1993. **http://www.amnesty.org/ailib/aireport/ar93/index.html**.

Amsden, Alice. 1989. *Asia's Next Giant: South Korea and Late Industrialization*. New York: Oxford University Press.

Angeles, Leonara C. 2004. Grassroots Democracy and Community Empowerment: The Quest for Sustainable Poverty Reduction in Asia. In Lele and Quadir 2004*a*.

Antons, Christoph, ed. 2003. *Law and Development in East and Southeast Asia*. New York: RoutledgeCurzon.

Apodaca, Clair. 1998. Measuring Women's Economic and Social Rights Achievement. *Human Rights Quarterly* 20:139.

Ariff, Mohamed and Ahmed Khalid 2005. *Liberalization and Growth in Asia: 21st Century Challenges*. Cheltenham, UK, and Northampton, MA, USA: Edward Elgar Publishing, Inc.

Asia: The Greatest Show on Earth; India's Election. 2004. *The Economist*. April 17.

Asia's Media Have Few Reasons to Celebrate World Press Freedom Day. 2004. *Agence France Press*. May 2.

Athukorala, Prema-chandra. 2002. Asian developing countries and the global trading system for agriculture, textiles and clothing. In Adhikari and Athukorala 2002.

Attacks on Chinese police rising. 2005. *BBC News*. Sept. 28.

Aziz, Nikhil. 1999. The Human Rights Debate in an Era of Globalization: Hegemony of Discourse. In Van Ness 1999.

Bachman, David. 2000. China's Democratization: What Difference Would It Make for U.S.–China Relations. In Friedman and McCormick 2000.

Bakken, Borge. 2000. *The Exemplary Society: Human Improvement, Social Control, and the Dangers of Modernity in China*. Oxford: Oxford University Press.

Banpasirichote, Chantana. 2004. Civil Society and Good Governance: A New Chapter in Thailand's Political Reform? In Lele and Quadir 2004*a*.

Barro, Robert. 1997. *Determinants of Economic Growth*. Cambridge: MIT Press.

—— 1996. Democracy: A Recipe for Growth? In *Current Issues in Economic Development: An Asian Perspective*. Edited by M. G. Quibria and J. Malcolm Dowling. New York: Published for the Asian Development Bank by Oxford University Press.

Barsh, Russel Lawrence. 1993. Measuring Human Rights: Problems of Methodology and Purpose. *Human Rights Quarterly* 15:87.

Bartholomew, Amy. 2003. The Ideology of Human Rights. *Virginia Journal of International Law* 36:589

Bauer, Joanne R. and Daniel A. Bell, eds. 1999. *The East Asian Challenge for Human Rights*. Cambridge: Cambridge University Press.

Baxi, Upendra. 2006. Protection of Human Rights and Production of Human Rightlessness in India. In Peerenboom et al. 2006.

—— 2004. Rule of Law in India: Theory and Practice. In Peerenboom 2004*a*.

Beale, Sara Sun. 2003. Still Tough on Crime? Prospects for Restorative Justice in the United States. *Utah Law Review* 2003:413.

Beijing Succeeds in Crackdown on Crimes. 2001. *People's Daily Online*. Dec. 1.

Bell, Christine, and Johanna Keenan. 2004. Human Rights Nongovernmental Organizations and the Problems of Transition. *Human Rights Quarterly* 26.

Bell, Daniel A. 2006. *Beyond Liberal Democracy: Political Thinking for an Asian Context*. Princeton: Princeton University Press.

—— 2000. *East Meets West: Human Rights and Democracy in East Asia*. Princeton: Princeton University Press.

—— and Hahm Chaibong, eds. 2003. *Confucianism for the Modern World*. Cambridge: Cambridge University Press.

—— et al. 1995. *Towards Illiberal Democracy in Pacific Asia*. London and New York: MacMillan/St Anthony's College and St Martin's Press.

Berger, Suzanne. 1999. Introduction. In Berger and Dore 1999.

Berger, Suzanne and Ronald Dore. 1999. *National Diversity and Global Capitalism*. Ithaca, NY: Cornell University Press.

Bernstam, Michael and Alvin Rabushka. 2002. Beijing Consensus for Russia? *Hoover Institution Public Policy Inquiry, The Russian Economy*.

Bernstein, Richard, and Ross Munro. 1997. *The Coming Conflict with China*. New York: Knopf.

Bhagwati, Jagdish. 2004. *In Defense of Globalization*. Oxford: Oxford University Press.

Biddulph, Sarah. 2003. The Production of Legal Norms: A Case Study of Administrative Detention in China. *UCLA Pacific Basin Law Journal* 20:217.

Biebesheimer, Christina and J. Mark Payne. 2001. IDB Experience in Justice Reform: Lessons Learned and Elements of Policy Formulation. Inter-Am. Dev. Bank, No. SGC-101, 2001. **http://www.iadb.org/sds/doc/sgc-IDBExperiences-E.pdf**.

Bishop, Bernard. 2003. APEC, industry policy, and the role of law. In Antons 2003.

Blanton, Thomas. 2003. National Security and Open Government in the United States: Beyond the Balancing Test. In *National Security and Open Government: Striking the Right Balance*. Campbell Public Affairs Institute. **http://www.maxwell.syr.edu/campbell/opengov/Chapter%202.pdf**.

Blumenthal, David, and William Hsiao. 2005. Privatization and Its Discontents: The Evolving Chinese Health Care System. *New England Journal of Medicine* 353: 1165.

Bollen, Kenneth. 1986. 'Political Rights and Political Liberties in Nations: An Evaluation of Human Rights Measures, 1950–1984.' *Human Rights Quarterly* 8(4).

Boix, Carlos, and Susan Stokes. 2003. Endogenous Democratization. *World Politics* 55.

Boughton, James M. and Zia Quereshi. 2004. From Vision to Action. *Finance and Development*.

Bown, Chad P. and Rachel McCulloch. 2005. U.S. Trade Policy Toward China: Discrimination and its Implications. **http://ssrn.com/abstract=757124**.

Boyer, Robert. 1999. The Convergence Hypothesis Revisited: Globalization but Still the Century of Nations. In Berger and Dore 1999.

Branstetter, Lee and Nicholas Lardy. 2005. China's Embrace of Globalization. *Asia Program Special Report*. Woodrow Wilson International Center for Scholars.

Brooks, David. 2005. Liberals, Conservatives and Aid. *New York Times*. June 26.

Brooks, Rosa Ehrenreich. 2003. The New Imperialism: Violence, Norms and the 'Rule of Law.' *Michigan Law Review* 101:2275.

Bueno de Mesquita, Bruce et al. 2005. Thinking Inside the Box: A Closer Look at Democracy and Human Rights. *International Studies Quarterly* 49(3):439.

—— and George Downs. 2005. Development and Democracy. *Foreign Affairs*. Sept./Oct.

Bugaric, Bojan. 2001. Courts as Policy-Makers: Lessons from Transition. *Harvard International Law Journal* 42.

Burkhart, Ross E., and Michael S. Lewis-Beck. 1994. Comparative Democracy: The Economic Development Thesis.' *American Political Science Review* 88.

Bush, George W. 2002. Remarks at the Graduating Class of 2002 at the United States Military Academy, May 23.
Cai, Dingjian. 2005/2006. The Social Transformation and the Development of Constitutionalism in Contemporary China. *Columbia Journal of Asian Law*.
Callon, Scott. 1995. *Divided Sun: MITI and the Breakdown of Japanese High-Tech Industrial Policy, 1975–1993*. Stanford, CA: Stanford University Press.
Carey, Sabine C. and Steven C. Poe, eds. 2004. *Understanding Human Rights Violations*. Aldershot, United Kingdom: Ashgate.
Carothers, Thomas. 2003. *Promoting the Rule of Law Abroad—The Problem of Knowledge*. Washington: Carnegie Endowment for International Peace.
—— 2002. The End of the Transition Paradigm. *Journal of Democracy* 13.
—— 1999. *Aiding Democracy Abroad: the learning curve*. Washington: Carnegie Endowment for International Peace.
Cassels, Jamie. 1989. Judicial Activism and Public Interest Litigation in India: Attempting the Impossible? *American Journal of Comparative Law* 37:495.
Chan, Heng Chee. 1993. *Democracy and Capitalism: Asian and American Perspectives*. Singapore: Institute of Southeast Asian Studies.
Chan, Sylvia. 2002. *Liberalism, Democracy and Development*. Cambridge: Cambridge University Press.
Chan Siu-sin. 2004. Officers To Be Held To Account Over Deaths of Detainees. *South China Morning Post*. Aug. 4.
Chang, Alberto and Cesar Calderon. 2000. Causality and Feedback between Institutional Measures and Economic Growth. *Economics and Politics* 12:69.
Chang, Gordon. 2001. *The Coming Collapse of China*. New York: Random House.
Chang, Maria Hsia. 2004. *Falun Gong, The End of Days*. New Haven: Yale University Press.
Chang Seung Wha. 2000. The Role of Law in Economic Development and Adjustment Process: The Case of Korea. *International Lawyer* 34:267.
Chen, Albert. 2004. An Introduction to the Legal System of the People's Republic of China. 3rd edn. Hong Kong: LexisNexis/Butterworths.
—— 2002. Hong Kong's Legal System in the New Constitutional Order. In Chen Jianfu et al. 2002.
Chen Jianfu et al., eds. 2002. *Implementation of Law in the People's Republic of China*. The Hague/Boston/London: Kluwer Law International.
Chen Jie. 2004. *Popular Political Support in Urban China*. Stanford, CA: Stanford University Press.

Chen Ruihua. 2002. Laodong Jiaoyang De Lishi Kaocha Yu Fansi [Survey of and Reflections on the History of ETL]. In *Lixing Yu Zhixu: Zhongguo Laodong Jiaoyang Zhidu Yanjiu* [*Rationality and Order: Research on China's Education Through Labor System*]. Edited by Chu Huaizhi et al. Beijing: Falu Chubanshe.

Chen Tsung-fu. 2003. The Rule of Law in Taiwan: culture, ideology, and social change. In *Understanding China's Legal System*. Edited by Stephen Hsu. New York: New York University.

Cheng, Allen T. 2004. Rich–Poor Gap Among the Worst, Study Finds. *South China Morning Post*. Feb. 26.

Cheung, Anne S. Y. 2004. In Search of a Theory of Cult and Freedom of Religion in China: The Case of Falun Gong. *Pacific Rim Law and Policy Journal* 13:1.

China denies torture widespread, slams UN envoy. 2006. *Reuters*. Dec. 6.

China Economic Quarterly. 2005. Building human capital: education in China. Vol. 9, issue 4.

China Europe International Business School. 2005. Health Care Issues in China. July 8. **http://www.ceibs.edu/today/news/archive/6062.shtml**.

China Evades Human Rights Censure. 2004. *BBC News*. Apr. 15.

China Information Center. 2004. The Chinese Authorities Issue 'Ten Forbiddens' for the Media. **http://www.cicus.org/news/newsdetail.php?id=2159**.

China Releases Three Arrested Members of 'Tiananmen Mothers.' 2004. *Agence France-Presse*. Apr. 2.

China sacks officials after pollution riots. 2005. *Reuters*. Dec. 30.

China's Reforms Cause Dramatic Widening Gap Between Rich and Poor, 2003. *Agence France-Presse*. Mar. 9.

Chinese Academy of Social Sciences. 2004. Legal Transplants in Contemporary China. *Social Sciences in China* 25.

Chinese Internet Dissident Found Guilty of Subversion, but Given Probation. 2004. *Agence France-Presse*. June 11.

Chivers, C. J. 2005. China Backs Uzbek, Splitting With US on Crackdown. *New York Times*. May 25.

Christie, Kenneth and Denny Roy. 2001. *The Politics of Human Rights in East Asia*. London: Pluto Press.

Chomsky, Noam. 2003. *Hegemony or Survival: America's Quest for Global Dominance*. New York: Henry Holt and Company.

Chu, Mike. 2001. Criminal Procedure Reform in the People's Republic of China: The Dilemma of Crime Control and Regime Legitimacy. *UCLA Pacific Basin Law Journal* 18.

Chu Yun-han et al. 2001. Halting Progress in Korea and Taiwan. *Journal of Democracy* 12:122.

Chua, Amy. 2003. *World on Fire: How Exporting Free Market Democracy Breeds Ethnic Hatred and Global Instability*. New York: Anchor Books.

CIA. 2005. The World Factbook. **http://www.cia.gov/cia/publications/factbook/docs/faqs.html**.

Cingranelli, David Louis, ed. 1996. *Policy Studies and Developing Countries*. Greenwich, CT: Jai Press.

Clarke, Donald. 2003. Economic Development and the Rights Hypothesis: The China Problem. *American Journal of Comparative Law* 51:89.

—— 1998–9. Alternative Approaches to Chinese Law: beyond the 'Rule of Law' paradigm. *Waseda Proceedings of Competition Law* 2:49.

—— 1998. *Wrongs and Rights: a human rights analysis of China's revised Criminal Code*. New York: Lawyers Committee for Human Rights.

Cloud, David S. and Ian Johnson. 2004. Friend or Foe, in Post-9/11 World, Chinese Dissidents Pose U.S. Dilemma—Uighur Nationalists Have Peaceful, Violent Wings. *Wall Street Journal*. Aug. 3.

Co, Edna A. 2004. Education as an Instrument of Democratization. In Lele and Quadir 2004*a*.

Cody, Edward. 2005. Chinese Police Bring Villagers To Heel After Latest Uprising. *Washington Post*. Dec. 1.

Cohen, Jerome. 2002. The Plight of Criminal Defense Lawyers, Statement at the Congressional-Executive Commission on China Roundtable Discussion on Challenges for Criminal Justice in China. **www.cecc.gov/pages/roundtables/072602/cohen.php**, accessed 3 June 2005.

Cohen, Paul. 1970. Ch'ing China: confrontation with the West, 1850–1900. In *Modern East Asia: essays in interpretation*. Edited by James B. Crowley. New York: Harcourt, Brace & World.

Cole, David. 2003. *Enemy Aliens: Double Standards and Constitutional Freedoms in the War on Terrorism*. New York: The New Press.

Comments by the Chinese Government on the Report on the Mission of the Special Rapporteur on the Right to Education to the People's Republic of China, U.N. ESCOR Human Rights Comm., 60th Sess., Agenda Item 10, at 11, U.N. Doc. E/CN.4/2004/G/16 (2003).

Commission for Africa. 2005. Our Common Interest. **http://www.commissionforafrica.org/english/report/introduction.html#report**.

Congressional-Executive Commission on China (CECC). 2005. Annual Report. Washington: U.S. Government Printing Office.

Congressional-Executive Commission on China (CECC). 2003. The Execution of Dobsang Dondrub and the Case Against Tenzin Deleg: The Law, the Courts and the Debate on Legality. **http://www.cecc.gov/pages/news/lobsang.php**.

Cooter, Robert. 1996. The Rule of State Law and the Rule-of-Law State: Economic Analysis of the Legal Foundations of Development. *Annual World Bank Conference on Development Economics* 1996:196.

Couple Watching Porno DVD Case Continues. 2002. *Xinhua News Agency*. Dec. 22. **http://news.xinhuanet.com/newscenter/2002-12/22/content_666765.htm**.

Cross, Frank B. 1997. International Determinants of Human Rights and Welfare: Law, Wealth or Culture. *Indiana International and Comparative Law Review* 7:265.

Cutting Agricultural Subsidies. n.d. **http://globalenvision.org/library/6/309**.

Danchin, Peter G. 2002. U.S. Unilateralism and the International Protection of Religious Freedom: The Multilateral Alternative. *Columbia Transnational Law* 41:33.

Daniels, Ronald J. and Michael J. Trebilcock. 2004. The Political Economy of Rule of Law Reform in Developing Countries. **http://www.wdi.bus.umich.edu/global_conf/papers/revised/Trebilcock_Michael.pdf**.

Davenport, Christian and David Armstrong. 2002. Democracy and the Violation of Human Rights: A Statistical Analysis of the Third Wave. **http://apsaproceedings.cup.org/Site/abstracts/011/011002ArmstrongD.htms**.

David, Randolph. 1994. Redemocratisation in the Wake of the 1986 People Power Revolution: Errors and Dilemmas. *Karasnlan* 11:20.

Davis, Kevin. 2004. What Can the Rule of Law Variable Tell Us About Rule of Law Reforms? *NYU Law and Economics Research Paper*. No. 04-026.

De Bary, Wm. Theodore. 1998. *Asian Values and Human Rights: A Confucian Communitarian Perspective*. Cambridge: Harvard University Press.

Deller, Nicole et al. eds. 2003. *Rule of Power or Rule of Law? An Assessment of U.S. Policies and Actions Regarding Security-Related Treaties*. Washington: Institute for Energy and Environmental Research.

De Luca, Tom and John Buell. 2005. *Liars, Cheaters, Evildoers: Democratization and the End of Civil Debate in American Politics*. New York. NYU Press.

Dezalay, Yves and Bryant G. Garth. 2002. *The internationalization of palace wars: lawyers, economists, and the contest to transform Latin American states*. Chicago: University of Chicago.

Diamond, Larry. 1999. *Developing Democracy: Toward Consolidation.* Baltimore: Johns Hopkins University Press.
—— 1996. Is the Third Wave Over? *Journal of Democracy* 7:20.
—— 1994*a*. Introduction: Political Culture and Democracy. In *Political Culture and Democracy*. Edited by Larry Diamond. Boulder, CO: Lynne Rienner.
—— 1994*b*. Toward Democratic Consolidation. *Journal of Democracy* 5:4.
Dick, Howard. 2006. Why Law Reforms Fail: Indonesia's Anti-corruption Reforms. In Lindsey 2006*a*.
Dickie, Murie. 2003. China Frees Aids Official. *Financial Times*. Oct. 20.
Dickinson, Laura. 2002. Using Legal Process to Fight Terrorism: Detentions, Military Commissions, International Tribunals, and the Rule of Law. *Southern California Law Review* 75:1407.
Dimitrov, Martin Kostadinov. 2004. Administrative Decentralization, Legal Fragmentation, and the Rule of Law in Transitional Economies: The Enforcement of Intellectual Property Rights (IPR) Laws in China, Russia, Taiwan, and the Czech Republic. Ph.D. dissertation, Department of Political Science, Stanford University.
Dinmore, Guy. 2005. Anti-Americanism gives China the edge in poll. *Financial Times*. June 24.
Discussion: Asian Values. 2001. *The Korea Journal* 41.
Dittmer, Lowell. 2002. Globalization and the twilight of Asian exceptionalism. In Kinnvall and Jonsson 2002.
Donnelly, Jack. 1988. Human Rights at the United Nations, 1955–1985: The Question of Bias. *International Studies Quarterly* 32:275.
Dorf, Michael and Charles Sabel. 1998. A Constitution of Democratic Experimentalism. *Columbia Law Review* 98:267.
Dowdle, Michael. 2002. Of Parliaments, Pragmatism, and the Dynamics of Constitutional Development: The Curious Case of China. *New York University Journal of International Law and Politics* 35:1.
Elections without meaning. 2004. *New York Times*. Feb. 21.
Englehart Neil A. State Capacity and Democracy: A Theoretical Argument with a Burmese Case Study and a Time-Series Cross-Section Analysis. **http://www.apsanet.org/mtgs**.
Ethnic Tension Rising in Southern Xinjiang, Says Official. 2004. *Agence France-Presse*. Aug. 2.

Eurobarometer 62. 2005. **http://europa.eu.int/comm/public_opinion/archives/eb/eb62/eb_62_en.pdf**.

Evans, Carolyn. 2002. Chinese Law and the International Protection of Religious Freedom. *Journal of Church and State* 44:749.

Evans, Peter. 2003. Development as Institutional Change: The Pitfalls of Monocropping and the Potentials of Deliberation. *Studies in Comparative International Development* 38:30.

—— et al. eds. 1985. *Bringing the State Back In*. Cambridge: Cambridge University Press.

Executed Uyghur Refugee Left Behind Tapes Detailing Chinese Torture. 2003. *Radio Free Asia*. Oct. 23.

Fairchild, Erika. 2000. *Comparative Criminal Justice Systems*. 1st edn. Belmont, CA: Wadsworth Publishing.

Faundez, Julio. 1997. Introduction: Legal Technical Assistance. In *Good Government and Law*. Edited by Julio Faundez. New York: St. Martin's Press.

Fein, Helen. 1995. More Murder in the Middle: Life-Integrity Violations and Democracy in the World, 1987. *Human Rights Quarterly* 17:170.

Filkins, Derek. 2004. Guard's Abuse Trial to Be Public in Iraq. *International Herald Tribune*. May 11.

Fischer, Andrew Martin. 2004. Urban Fault Lines in Shangri-La: Population and Economic Foundations of Inter-Ethnic Conflict in the Tibetan Areas of Western China. **http://www.crisisstates.com/Publications/wp/wp42.htm**.

Fisher-Thompson, Jim. 2005. China No Threat to United States in Africa, US Official Says. *USINFO East Asia*. July 29.

FM Spokesman on China's Efforts To Promote Human Rights. 2000. *People's Daily*. Nov. 21.

Forero, Juan. 2004. Latin America is Growing Impatient with Democracy. *New York Times*. June 24.

Foot, Rosemary. 2000. *Rights Beyond Borders: The Global Community and the Struggle over Human Rights in China*. Oxford: Oxford University Press.

Freedom House. 2004. Freedom in the World 2003: Survey Methodology. **http://www.freedomhouse.org/research/freeworld/2003/methodology.htm**.

Friedman, Edward and Barret McCormick, eds. 2000. *What If China Doesn't Democratize? Implications for War and Peace*. New York: M.E. Sharpe.

Friedman, Lawrence M. 1969. On Legal Development. *Rutgers Law Review* 24:11.

—— and Rogelio Perez-Perdomo, eds. 2003. *Legal Culture in the Age of Globalization—Latin America and Latin Europe*. Stanford, CA: Stanford University Press.

Fukuyama, Francis. 2001. Asian Values in the Wake of the Asian Crisis. In Iqbal and You 2001.

Fuller, Lon. 1976. *The Morality of Law*. New Haven: Yale University Press.

Gallagher, Mary. 2005. *Contagious Capitalism: Globalization and the Politics of Labor in China*. Princeton: Princeton University Press.

Gedda, George. 2003. U.S. Won't Reproach China on Human Rights. *Associated Press*. Apr. 11.

Gibney, Mark. 2004*a*. Notes on Levels of Political Terror Scale. **http://www.unca.edu/politicalscience/faculty-staff/gibney_docs/Notes%20on%20Levels%20of%20Political%20Terror%20Scale.doc**.

—— 2004*b*. Terror Scale Scores 1980–2003. **http://www.unca.edu/politicalscience/faculty-staff/gibney_docs/pts.xls**.

Gill, Bates et al. eds. 2004. Defusing China's Time Bomb: Sustaining the Momentum of China's HIV/AIDS Response. Center for Strategic & International Studies. **http://csis.org/china/040617_China_AIDS_Timebomb.pdf.**

Gillespie, John. 2006. Evolving Concepts of Human Benefits and Rights in Vietnam. In Peerenboom et al. 2006.

—— and Pip Nicholson, eds. 2005. *Asian Socialism & Legal Change: The Dynamics of Vietnamese and Chinese Reform*. Canberra: Asia Pacific Press and Australia National University E Press.

Gilley, Bruce. 2004. *China's Democratic Future*. New York: Columbia University Press.

Ginsburg, Thomas. 2003. *Judicial Review in New Democracies: Constitutional Courts in Asian Cases*. New York, Cambridge University Press.

Gledhill, John. 1997. Liberalism, Socio-Economic Rights and the Politics of Identity: From Moral Economy to Indigenous Rights. In *Human Rights, Culture and Context*. Edited by Richard Wilson. London: Pluto Press.

Godoy, Sergio and Joseph Stiglitz. 2006. Growth, Initial Conditions, Law and Speed of Privatization in Transition Countries: 11 Years Later. NBER Working Paper No. W11992.

Goldsmith, Jack. 2000. Should International Human Rights Law Trump US Domestic Law? *Chicago Journal of International Law* 1:327.

Greenspan, Snow warn against China sanctions. 2005. *Reuters*. June 23.

Gries, Peter Hays. 2004. *China's New Nationalism: Pride, Politics, and Diplomacy*. Berkeley: University of California Press.

Grossman, Zoltan. 2004. A Partial List of U.S. Military Interventions from 1890 to 2004. **http://www.uwec.edu/grossmzc/interventions.html**.

Grunfeld, A. Tom. 2001. Human Rights and the People's Republic of China. *Touro International Law Review* 9:71.

Gu, Edward X. 1997. Elitist Democracy and China's Democratization. *Democratization* 4:84.

Gunn, T. Jeremy. 2002. American Exceptionalism and Globalist Double Standards: A More Balanced Alternative. *Columbia Journal of Transnational Law* 41:137.

Gustafsson, Björn, Li Shi, and Terry Sicular, eds. *Inequality and Public Policy in China*. Cambridge: Cambridge University Press, forthcoming.

Haas, Michael. 1996. Empirical Dimensions of Human Rights. In Cingranelli 1996.

Haggard, Stephan. 2001. The Politics of Governance: Lessons from the East Asian Crisis. In Iqbal and You 2001.

Hagopian, Frances. 1998. Democracy and Political Representation in Latin America in the 1990s: Pause, Reorganization, or Decline? In *Fault Lines of Democratization in Post-Transition Latin America*. Edited by F. Aguero and J. Stark. Miami: North–South Center.

Hahm, Chaihark. 2006. Human Rights in Korea. In Peerenboom et al. 2006.

—— 2004. Rule of law in South Korea: Rhetoric and Implementation. In Peerenboom 2004*a*.

—— and David Bell, eds. 2004. *The Politics of Affective Relations: East Asia and Beyond*. Lanham, MD: Lexington Books.

Hall, David, and Roger Ames. 1999. *Democracy of the Dead: Dewey, Confucius and the Hope for Democracy in China*. Chicago: Open Court.

Hall, Peter. 1999. The Political Economy of Europe in an Era of Independence. In *Continuity and Change in Contemporary Capitalism*. Edited by Herbert Kitschelt et al. Cambridge: Cambridge University Press.

Halmai, Gabor and Kim Lane Scheppele. 1997. Living Well is the Best Revenge: The Hungarian Approach to Judging the Past. In *Transitional Justice and Rule of Law in New Democracies*. Edited by A. James McAdams. Notre Dame, IN: University of Notre Dame Press.

Hammergren, Linn. 1998. Institutional Strengthening and Justice Reform. U.S. Agency for Int'l Dev., PC-ACD-020. **http://www1.worldbank.org/publicsector/legal/Institutional%20Strengthening.pdf**.

Han, Sang-jin. 2005. Democratic Transformation and Non-Traditional Security Challenges of Republic of Korea. In Zhang Yunling 2005.

Hathaway, Oona. 2002. Do Human Rights Treaties Make a Difference? *Yale Law Journal* 111:1935.

Hecht, Jonathan. 1996. *Opening to Reform: An Analysis of China's Revised Criminal Procedure Law*. New York: Lawyer's Committee for Human Rights.

Helfer, Laurence. 2002. Overlegalizing Human Rights: International Relations Theory and the Commonwealth Caribbean Backlash Against Human Rights. *Columbia Law Review* 102:1832.

Helgesen, Geir. 2002. Imported Democracy: The South Korean Experience. In Kinnvall and Jonsson 2002.

Herman, Edward S., and Noam Chomsky. 1988. *Manufacturing Consent*. London: Pantheon Books.

Highlights of Major Beijing-Based Newspapers. 2002. *Xinhua News Agency*. Oct. 30.

Hirschi, Ran. 2002. Restituating the Judicialization of Politics: Bush v. Gore as a Global Trend. *Canadian Journal of Law and Jurisprudence* 15.

Hodgson, Jacqueline. 2002. Suspects, Defendants and Victims in the French Criminal Process: The Context of Recent Reform. *International and Comparative Law Quarterly* 51:781.

Holliday, Ian. 2000. Productivist Welfare Capitalism: Social Policy in East Asia. *Political Studies* 48:706.

Hollingsworth, J. Rogers, and Robert Boyer. 1999. Coordination of Economic Actors and Social Systems of Production. In *Contemporary Capitalism: The Embeddedness of Institutions*. Edited by J. Rogers Hollingsworth and Robert Boyer. New York: Cambridge University Press.

Hofstede, Geert. 2001. Culture's Consequences: Comparing Values, Behaviors, Institutions and Organizations Across Nations. 2nd edn. Newbury Park, CA: Sage.

Holsti, Ole. 2000. Public Opinion on Human Rights in American Foreign Policy. In *The United States and Human Rights: Looking Inward and Outward*. Edited by David Forsythe. Lincoln: University of Nebraska.

Holzgrefe, J. L. and Robert Keohane, eds. 2003. *Humanitarian Intervention: Ethical, Legal and Political Dilemmas*. New York: Cambridge University Press.

Hom, Sharon. 2004. Testimony Before the United States Congressional-Executive Commission on China. **//www.cecc.gov/pages/hearings/060304/hom.php**.

Horsley, Jamie. 2004. Shanghai Advances the Cause of Open Government Information in China, *Freedominfo.org*. Apr. 20. **http://chinalaw.law.yale.edu/shanghai_article.pdf**.

Howard-Hassmann, Rhoda E. 2005. The Second Great Transformation: Human Rights Leapfrogging in the Era of Globalization. *Human Rights Quarterly* 27:1.

Hu Yunteng. 2002. Application of the Death Penalty in Chinese Judicial Practice. In Chen Jianfu et al. 2002.

Huang, Cary. 2006. Millions pledged to revive Marxism. *South China Morning Post*. Jan. 20.

Human Rights Defenders. 2005. Human Rights Defenders in China. **www.humanrightsfirst.org/defenders/hrd_China/hrd_China.htm**.

Human Rights in China. 2000. Impunity for Torturers Continues Despite Changes in the Law.

—— 1999. Not Welcome at the Party: Behind the 'Clean-up' of China's Cities—A Report on Administrative Detention Under 'Custody and Repatriation.'

Human Rights Watch. 2005. Thailand: Elections Amid an Assault on Rights. **http://hrw.org/english/docs/2005/02/03/thaila10120.htm**.

—— 2004. Human Rights Watch World Report 2003: China and Tibet.

Hunger Strike Helps Improve Conditions for Jailed Chinese Dissident—Report. 2004. *Agence France-Presse*. Jan. 27.

Huntington, Samuel P. 1996. *The Clash of Civilizations: The Remaking of World Order*. New York: Simon and Simon.

Ignatieff, Michael. 2003. State failure and nation-building. In Holzgrefe and Keohane 2003.

Information Office of the State Council of China. 2004. Progress in China's Human Rights Cause in 2003. **http://www.china.org.cn/e-white/20040330/index.htm**.

—— 2002*a*. 'East Turkistan' Terrorist Forces Cannot Get Away with Impunity. *Beijing Review* 45:15.

—— 2002*b*. Human Rights Record of the United States in 2001. **http://www.china.org.cn/e-white/20020313/index.htm**, Mar. 11.

—— 2001. Tibet's Modernization Achievements. **http://www.china.org.cn/e-white/20011108/3.htm**.

—— 2000. Regional Autonomy for Ethnic Minority, in National Minorities Policy and Its Practice. **http://www.china.org.cn/e-white/4/4.3.htm**.

—— 1991. Human Rights in China: Active Participation in International Human Rights Activities. **http://www.china.org.cn/e-white/7/7-L.htm**.

Inglehart, Ronald. 1997. *Modernization and Postmodernization: Cultural, Economic and Political Change in 43 Societies*. Princeton, NJ: Princeton University Press.

Iqbal, Farrukh and Jong-Il You, eds. 2001. *Democracy, Market Economics and Development: An Asian Perspective*. Washington, DC: The International Bank for Reconstruction and Development/The World Bank.

Japan Ignores Tokyo University Student Jailed in China. 2002. *Asian Political News*. Sept. 23.

Jensen, Erik G. 2003. The Rule of Law and Judicial Reform: The Political Economy of Diverse Institutional Patterns and Reformers' Response. In *Beyond Common Knowledge: Empirical Approaches to the Rule of Law*. Edited by Eric G. Jensen and Thomas C. Heller. Stanford, CA: Stanford University Press.

Jeong, Kap-Young and Yeon-ho Lee. 2001. Convergence or Divergence? The South Korean State After the Asian Financial Crisis. *Global Economic Review* 30:66.

Jochnick, Chris af and Roger Normand. 1994. The Legitimation of Violence: A Critical History of the Laws of War. *Harvard International Law Journal* 35:49.

Johnson, Chalmers. 1987. Political Institutions and Economic Performance: The Government–Business Relationship in Japan, South Korea and Taiwan. In *The Political Economy of New Asian Industrialism*. Edited by Frederick C. Deyo. Ithaca, NY: Cornell University Press.

Johnson, David T. 2002 *The Japanese Way of Justice*. New York: Oxford University Press.

Johnston, Alastair Iain. 2001. US Scholars on Relations between China and International Organizations. *World Economy and Politics* 8:48.

Jomo, K. S. 2001. Rethinking the Role of Government Policy in Southeast Asia. In *Rethinking the East Asian Miracle*. Edited by Shahid Yusuf and Joseph Stiglitz. New York: Oxford University Press.

Juwana, Hikmahanto. 2006. Human Rights in Indonesia. In Peerenboom et al. 2006.

Kahn, Joseph. 2004. Violence Taints Religion's Solace for China's Poor. *New York Times*. Nov. 25.

Kahn, Paul W. 1999. *The Cultural Study of Law: reconstructing legal scholarship*. Chicago: The University of Chicago Press.

Kahn-Freund, Otto. 1974. On Uses and Misuses of Comparative Law. *Modern Law Review* 37:1.

Kaufmann, Daniel et al. 2005. Governance Matters III: Governance Indicators for 1996–2004. **http://www.worldbank.org/wbi/governance/pdf/govmatters3.pdf**.

—— et al. 2003. Governance Matters III: Governance Indicators for 1996–2002. **http://ideas.repec.org/p/wpa/wuwpdc/0308001.html**.

Keith, Linda Camp. 1999. The United Nations International Covenant on Civil and Political Rights: Does It Make a Difference in Human Rights Behavior? *Journal of Peace Research* 36:95.

—— and Steven C. Poe. 2002. Personal Integrity Abuse during Domestic Crises. **http://apsaproceedings.cup.org/Site/papers/046/046004PoeSteveno.pdf**.

Keith, Ronald et al. 2003. The Making of a Chinese NGO: The Research and Intervention Project on Domestic Violence. *Problems of Post-Communism* 56:38.

Kent, Ann. 1999. *China, the United Nations and Human Rights: the Limits of Compliance*. Philadelphia: University of Pennsylvania Press.

Keohane, Robert. 2003. Political authority after intervention: gradations in sovereignty. In Holzgrefe and Keohane 2003.

Khan, Azizur Rahman. 2006. Growth, Inequality and Poverty: A Comparative Study of China's Experience in the Periods Before and After the Asian Crisis. In Gustafsson et al. 2006.

—— and Carl, Riskin. 2005. China's Household Income and its Distribution, 1995 and 2002. *China Quarterly* 182 (June).

Kim, Samuel. 2000. Human Rights in China's International Relations. In Friedman and McCormick 2000.

Kim Sung Ho. 2004. Democracy in Korea and the Myth of Civil Society. In Hahm and Bell 2004.

Kinnvall, Catarina and Kristina Jonsson eds. 2002. *Globalization and Democratization in Asia: The construction of identity*. London and New York: Routledge.

Krugman, Paul. 1994. The Myth of Asia's Miracle: A Cautionary Fable. *Foreign Affairs*.

Kurczewski, Jacek and Barry Sullivan. 2002. The Bill of Rights and the Emerging Democracies. *Law & Contemporary Problems* 65:251.

Kurtenbach, Elaine. 2004. Chinese Experts Urge Retrial of Editors. *Associated Press*. Apr. 9.

LaFave, Wayne R. 2003. *Criminal Law*. 4th edn. St. Paul, MN: Thomson West.

Lak, Daniel. 2002. Kingdom on the Brink of Catastrophe. *South China Morning Post*. May 12.

Landman, Todd. 2002. Comparative Politics and Human Rights. *Human Rights Quarterly* 24:890.

Langbein, John H. 1978. Torture and Plea Bargaining. *University of Chicago Law Review* 46:3.

Langer, Maximo. 2004. From Legal Transplants to Legal Translations: the globalization of plea bargaining and the Americanization thesis in criminal procedure. *Harvard International Law Journal* 45:1.

Lardy, Nicholos R. 1998. *China's Unfinished Economic Revolution*. Washington, DC: Brookings Institution.

Latinobarometer: Public Opinion in Latin America. (2002). **http://www.latinobarometro.org/index.php?id=147**.

Law Publishing House. 2002. *Zhongguo Falü Nian Jian [China Law Yearbook]*. Beijing.

Lawrance, Anthony. 2004. Nobody Said Democracy Is a Tea Party. *South China Morning Post*. March 27.

Lawyers Committee for Human Rights. 2003. *Imbalance of Powers: How Changes to U.S. Law and Security Since 9/11 Erode Human Rights and Civil Liberties*. **http://www.humanrightsfirst.org/us_law/loss/imbalance/powers.pdf**.

Lele, Jayant and Fahimjul Quadir, eds. 2004*a*. *Democracy and Civil Society in Asia*. Vols. i & ii. 2004*a*. New York: Palsgrave Macmillan.

—— 2004*b*. Introduction: Democracy and Development in Asia in the 21st Century: In Search of Popular Democratic Alternatives. In Lele and Quadir 2004*a*.

Leonning, Carole D. 2006. Secret Court Judges Were Warned About NSA Spy Data. *Washington Post*. Feb. 9.

Levitsky, Steven and Lucan Way. 2002. Autocracy by Democratic Rules: The Dynamics of Competitive Authoritarianism in the Post-Cold War Era. *Journal of Democracy* 13.

Li Heng. 2001. How Wide Is the Gap of China's Individual Income? *People's Daily Online*. Aug. 31.

Li Shaojun. 2003. International Regimes of Nuclear Nonproliferation and China. In Wang Yizhou 2003*a*.

Liang Zhiping. 2001. Xiangtu Shehui Zhong de Falu yu Zhixu [On Law and Order in Rural Societies], pts. I & II. **http://www.usc.cuhk.edu.hk/wk_wzdetails.asp?id=1351**.

Licht, Amir et al. 2002. *Culture Rules: the foundations of Rule of Law and other norms of governance*. **http://www.faculty.idc.ac.il/licht/CR11.pdf**.

Liebman, Benjamin. 2005. Watchdog or Demagogue? The Media in the Chinese Legal System. *Columbia Law Review* 105:1.

Lindsey, Tim, ed. 2006*a*. *Law Reforms in Developing and Transitional States*.
—— 2006*b*. Preface. In Lindsey 2006*a*.
—— 2004. Indonesia: Devaluing Asian values, rewriting rule of law. In Peerenboom 2004*a*.
Ling, L. H. M. and Chih-yu Shih. 1998. Confucianism with a Liberal Face: The Meaning of Democratic Policies in Postcolonial Taiwan. *Review of Politics* 60:1.
Linnan, David K. 2006. Like a Fish Needs a Bicycle: Public Law Theory, Civil Society and Governance Reform in Indonesia. In Lindsey 2006*a*.
Lipset, Seymour Martin. 1959. Social Requisites of Democracy: Economic Development and Political Legitimacy. *American Political Science Review* 53:69.
Liu Jian. 2004. China's Comprehensive Approach to Poverty Reduction. **http://www1.worldbank.org/devoutreach/oct04/textonly.asp?id=267**.
Lubman, Stanley B. 1999. *Bird in a Cage: legal reforms in China after Mao*. Stanford, CA: Stanford University Press.
Lynch, David. 1994. The Impropriety of Plea Agreements: a tale of two counties. *Law and Social Inquiry* 19:115.
Lowi, Theodore. 2002. Progress and Poverty Revisited: Toward Construction of a Statist Third Way. In Tulchin and Brown 2002.
McCann, James. A. and Mark Gibney. 1996. An Overview of Political Terror in the Developing World, 1980–1991. In Cingranelli 1996.
McCormick, Barret. 2000. Introduction. In Friedman and McCormick 2000.
McFaul, Michael. 2002. The Fourth Wave of Democracy *and* Dictatorship: Noncooperative Transitions in the Postcommunist World. *World Politics* 54.
McGregor, Richard. 2006. Data show social unrest on the rise in China. *Financial Times*. Jan. 19.
Mackerras, Colin. 2004. Why Terrorism Bypasses China's Far West. *Asia Times*. Apr. 23.
Mansfield, Edward, and Jack Synder. 2005. *Electing to Fight: Why Emerging Democracies Go to War*. MIT Press.
Makeham, John, ed. 2003. *New Confucianism: A Critical Examination*. New York: Palgrave MacMillan.
Malone, David M. and Yuen Foong Khong, eds. 2003. *Unilateralism and US Foreign Policy: International Perspectives*. Washington: Center on International Cooperation Studies in Multilateralism.
Matsui, Shigenori. 2006. The Protection of Fundamental Rights in Japan. In Peerenboom et al. 2006.

Mearsheimer, John. 2005. The rise of China will not be peaceful at all. *The Australian*. Nov. 18, 2005.

Meyer, William H. 1996. Human Rights and MNCs: Theory Versus Quantitative Analysis. *Human Rights Quarterly* 18:368.

Milner, Welsey et al. 2004. Providing Subsistence Rights: Do States Make a Difference? In *Understanding Human Rights Violations*. Edited by Sabine Carey and Steven Poe. Aldershot: Ashgate.

Minzner, Carl. 2006. Xinfang: An Alternative to the Formal Legal System. *Stanford Journal of International Law* 42.

Ministry of Commerce. 2005. Foreign Market Access Report 2005. **http://gpj.mofcom.gov.cn/table/2005en.pdf**.

Moghalu, Kingsley Chiedu. 2002. Image and Reality of War Crimes Justice: External Perceptions of the International Criminal Tribunal for Rwanda. *Fletcher Forum of World Affairs* 26:21

Moon Chung-in and Yang Jae-jin. 2002. Globalization, Social Inequality and Democratic Governance in South Korea. In Tulchin and Brown 2002.

Morris, Peter. 2004. China Cracks Down on Chat Rooms on Eve of NPC. *Asia Times*. Mar. 4.

Mosley, Layna and Saika Uno. 2002. Racing to the Bottom or Climbing to the Top? Foreign Direct Investment and Human Rights. **http://www.nd.edu/~mmosley/mosleyunomay2004.pdf**.

Mitchell, Neil J. and James M. McCormick. 1988. Economic and Political Explanations of Human Rights Violations. *World Politics* 40:476.

Munro, Robin. 2000. Judicial Psychiatry in China and Its Political Abuses. *Columbia Journal of Asian Law* 14:1.

Muntarbhorn, Vitit. 2006. Human Rights in the Era of 'Thailand Incorporated (Inc.).' In Peerenboom et al. 2006.

—— 2004. Rule of Law and Aspects of Human Rights in Thailand: From Conceptualization to Implementation. In Peerenboom 2004*a*.

Murphy, John. 2004. *The United States and the Rule of Law in International Affairs*. Cambridge: Cambridge University Press.

Mutua, Makau wa. 2001. Savages, Victims and Saviors: The Metaphor of Human Rights. *Harvard International Law Journal* 42:201.

—— 1996. The Ideology of Human Rights. *Virginia Journal of International Law* 36:589.

Nathan, Andy et al., eds. 2001. *The Tiananmen Papers*. New York: Public Affairs.

Nathan, K. S. 2005. The Role of the State in Managing Social Transition: The Malaysian Experience. In Lele and Quadir 2004*a*.

Neilson, William A. W. 2006. Competition Laws for Asian Transitional Economies: Adaptation to Local Legal Cultures in Vietnam and Indonesia. In Lindsey 2006*a*.

Nussbaum, Martha C. 1997. Capabilities and Human Rights. *Fordham Law Review* 66:273.

O'Donnell, Guillermo A., and Philippe Schmitter. 1986. Tentative Conclusions. In Guillermo A. O'Donnell, Philippe Schmitter, and Laurence Whitehead, eds. *Transitions from Authoritarian Rule*, 4 vols. Baltimore: John Hopkins University Press.

Ohnesorge, John K. M. 2003. The Rule of Law, Economic Development and the Developmental States of Northeast Asia. In Antons 2003.

Orücü, Esin. 2002. Law as Transposition. *International & Comparative Law Quarterly* 51: 205.

Ovsiovitch, Jay. 1996. A Distorted Image? Factors Influencing the U.S. Media's Coverage of Human Rights. *Policy Studies and Developing Nations* 4:85.

Pan, Phillip P. 2005. Five Chinese Nuns Hospitalized After Land Dispute. *Wash. Post*. Dec. 1.

—— 2004*a*. China Tries Dissident out of View; Permanent Resident of U.S. Held as Spy. *Wash. Post*. Aug. 5.

—— 2004*b*. A Study Group Is Crushed in China's Grip. *Wash. Post*. Apr. 23.

—— 2003. China Releases 3 Internet Writers, but Convicts 1 Other. *Wash. Post*. Dec. 1.

Pan, Wei. 2003. Toward a Consultative Rule of Law Regime in China. *Journal of Contemporary China* 12:3.

Pangalangan, Raul. 2006. Human Rights in the Philippines. In Peerenboom et al. 2006.

—— 2004. The Philippine 'People Power' Constitution, Rule of Law, and the Limits of Liberal Constitutionalism. In Peerenboom 2004*a*.

Park Chong-min and Shin Doh Chull. 2004. Do Asian Values Deter Popular Support for Democracy? The Case of South Korea. **http://www.aasianst.org/absts/2004abst/Interarea/intertoc.htm**.

Pasuk Phongpaichit and Chris Baker. 2004. *Thaksin: The Business of Politics in Thailand*. Chiang Mai: Silkwork Books.

Patterns of Abuse. 2005. *New York Times*. May 23.

Paul, Joel R. 2003. Do International Trade Institutions Contribute to Economic Growth and Development? *Virginia Journal of International Law* 44:285.

Paust, Jordan J. 2002. Antiterrorism Military Commissions: The Ad Hoc DOD Rules of rocedure. *Michigan Journal of International Law* 23:677.

—— 2001. Antiterrorism Military Commissions: Courting Illegality. *Michigan Journal of International Law* 23:1.

Peerenboom, Randall. 2006. Judicial Accountability and Judicial Independence: An Empirical Study of Individual Case Supervision in the People's Republic of China. *The China Journal*.

—— 2005. Human Rights and Rule of Law: What's the Relationship? *Georgetown International Law Review* 36.

—— 2004*a*. (editor). *Asian Discourses of Rule of Law: Theories and Implementation of Rule of Law in Twelve Asian Countries, France and the U.S.* London, New York: RoutledgeCurzon.

—— 2004*b*. Varieties of Rule of Law. In Peerenboom 2004*a*.

—— 2004*c*. Show Me the Money: The Dominance of Wealth in Determining Rights Performance in Asia. *Duke International Law Journal* 15:75.

—— 2004*d*. Out of the Pan and into the Fire: Well-intentioned but Misguided Recommendations to Eliminate Administrative Detention in China. *Northwestern Law Review* 98:991.

—— 2004*e*. Social Networks, Civil Society, Democracy and Rule of Law: A New Conceptual Framework. In Hahm and Bell 2004.

—— 2003*a*. Networks, Rule of Law and Economic Growth in China: The Elusive Pursuit of the Right Combination of Public and Private Ordering. *Global Economic Review* 31:2.

—— 2003*b*. Beyond Universalism and Relativism: The Evolving Debates about 'Values in Asia.' *Indiana International and Comparative Law Review* 14:1.

—— 2002. *China's Long March Toward Rule of Law*. Cambridge: Cambridge University Press.

—— 1998. Confucian Harmony and Freedom of Thought: The Right to Think Versus Right Thinking. In *Confucianism and Human Rights*. Edited by Wm. Theodore de Bary and Tu Weiming. New York: Columbia University Press.

—— 1995. Rights, Interests, and the Interest in Rights in China. *Stanford Journal of International Law* 31:359.

—— et al., eds. 2006. *Human Rights in Asia: A Comparative Legal Study of Twelve Asian Jurisdictions, France and the U.S.* London: RoutledgeCurzon.

Pei Minxin. 2006. *China's Trapped Transition: the Limits of Developmental Autocracy*. Cambridge: Harvard University Press.

—— 2001. Political Institutions, Democracy and Development. In Iqbal and You 2001.

Peng Yali. 1998. Democracy and Chinese Political Discourses. *Modern China* 24:4.

Pentagon's 'China Threat' Paranoia. 2005. *People's Daily Online*. July 22.

Persaud, Randolph B. 2004. Shades of American Hegemony: The Primitive, the Enlightened, and the Benevolent. *Connecticut Journal of International Law* 19:263.

Personn, Torsten. 2006. Democracy and Development: The Devil is in the Details. NBER Working Paper No. 11993.

Petersen, Carole. 2006. From British colony to special administrative region of China: Embracing human rights in Hong Kong. In Peerenboom et al. 2006.

Pettit, Philip. 2002. Is Criminal Justice Politically Feasible? *Buffalo Criminal Law Review* 5:427.

Pew Global Attitudes Project. 2005. Prosperity Brings Satisfaction—and Hope. China's Optimism. **www.pew.global.org**.

—— 2002. What Do Asians Think About Their Own Lives? In *What the World Thinks in 2002*. **http://international.ucla.edu/asia/news/02pewpolla.asp**.

Pinkney, Robert. 2003. *Democracy in the Third World*. 2nd edn. Boulder, CO: Lynne Rienner.

Pisik, Betsy. 1998. Human Rights Probes Irk U.S. *Wash. Times*. June 29.

Pistor, Katharina and Phillip Wellons. 1999. *The Role of Law and Legal Institutions in Asian Economic Development 1960–1995*. New York: Oxford University Press.

Pogge, Thomas. 2005. World Poverty and Human Rights. *Ethics and International Affairs* 19:1.

Potter, Pitman B. 2004. Legal Reform in China: Institutions, Culture, and Selective Adaptation. *Law & Social Inquiry* 29:465.

PRC Survey: Most Guangzhou Residents Satisfied with Public Order. 2001. *Xinhua*. Dec. 14.

Proceedings of the Fourth Annual Legal and Policy Issues in the Americas Conference. 2004. *Florida Journal of International Law* 55.

Przeworski, Adam et al. 2000. *Democracy and Development: Political Institutions and Well-being in the World, 1950–1990*. Cambridge: Cambridge University Press.

—— and Fernando Limongi. 1997. Modernization: Theories and Facts. *World Politics* 49:155.

Pye, Lucian W. 1985. *Asian Power and Politics*. Cambridge, MA: Belknap Press.

Quadir, Fahimul. 2004. Going Beyond the Mainstream Discourse: Democratic Consolidation and Market Reforms in Bangladesh. In Lele and Quadir 2004.

Rahn, Patsy. 2000. The Falun Gong: Beyond the Headlines. *Cultic Studies Journal* 17:168.

Ramo, Joshua Cooper. 2004. *The Beijing Consensus*. London: Foreign Policy Centre.

Ramseyer, Mark, and Minoro Nakazato. 1999. *Japanese Law: An Economic Approach*. Chicago: University of Chicago Press.

Rapley, John. 2004. *Globalization and Inequality: Neoliberalism's Downward Spiral*. Boulder, CO: Lynne Rienner Publishers, Inc.

Raustiala, Kal. 2000. Compliance and Effectiveness in International Regulatory Cooperation. *Case Western Reserve Journal International* Law 32:387.

Ravich, Samantha. 2000. *Marketization and Democracy: East Asian Experiences*. Cambridge: Cambridge University Press.

Rawski, Thomas. 2005. China's Economy: Retrospect and Prospect. *Asia Program Special Report*. Woodrow Wilson International Center for Scholars.

Ray, Aswini K. 2002. Globalization and democratic governance: the Indian experience. In Kinnvall and Jonsson 2002.

Redding, Gordon. 1990. *The Spirit of Chinese Capitalism*. New York: De Gruyter.

Reid, Kenneth G. C. 2003. The Idea of Mixed Legal Systems. *Tulane Law Review* 78:5.

Reilly, David. 2003. Diffusing Human Rights. **proceedings@apsanet.org**.

Reiner, Robert. 2000. *The Politics of the Police*. 3rd edn. Aldershot, UK: Dartmouth Publishing.

Report of the Joseph R. Crowley Program. 1999. One Country, Two Legal Systems: The Rule of Law; Democracy, and Rights in Post-Handover Hong Kong. *Fordham International Law Journal* 23:1.

Reporters Without Borders. 2004. Reporters without Borders Concerned About Health of Cyberdissident He Depu. Mar. 2. **http://www.rsf.fr/print.php3?id_article=8475**.

Report of the Special Rapporteur on Extrajudicial, Summary or Arbitrary Executions, U.N. ESCOR Human Rights Comm., 54th Sess., Agenda Item 10, at 34, U.N. Doc. E/CN.4/1998/68/Add.3 (1998).

Residents Eager for Drug Fight. 1997. *Xinhua News Agency*. Aug. 18.

Rigobon, Roberto and Dani Rodrik. 2005. Rule of Law, Democracy, Openness, and Income: Estimating the Interrelationships. *Economics of Transition* 13:533.

Robinson, Richard. 2002. Which sort of democracy? Predatory and neo-liberal agendas in Indonesia. In Kinnvall and Jonsson 2002.

Rocamora, Joel. 2004. Formal Democracy and Its Alternatives in the Philippines: Parties, Elections and Social Movements. In Lele and Quadir 2004*a*.

—— 2002. A Clash of Ideologies: International Capitalism and the State in the Wake of the Asian Crisis. In Tulchin and Brown 2002.

Rodrik, Dani. 2003. Economic Reforms without Rules of Thumb. **http://www2.gsb.columbia.edu/faculty/jstiglitz/festschrift/Papers/Stig-Rodrik.pdf**.

Rowen, Henry S. 1998. The Political and Social Foundations of the Rise of East Asia. In *Behind East Asian Growth*. Edited by Henry S. Rowen. New York: Routledge.

Rumsfeld warns China on Military. 2005. *CNN.com*. June 4.

Ruskola, Teemu. 2005. Canton is not Boston: The Invention of American Imperial Sovereignty. *American Quarterly*.

—— 2002. Legal Orientalism. *Michigan Law Review* 101:179.

Saiget, Robert. 2004. China Executes 10,000 People a Year: NPC Delegate. *Agence France-Presse*. Mar. 15.

Sajo, Adras, 2004. Introduction: Universalism with Humility. In *Human Rights with Modesty: The Problem of Universalism*. Leiden/Boston: Martinus Nijhoff.

Sanger, D. 1998. Greenspan sees Asian crisis moving world to Western capitalism. *New York Times*. Feb. 13.

Sarat, Austin and Thomas R. Kearns, eds. 1996. *Historical and Philosophical Perspectives*. Ann Arbor: The University of Michigan Press.

Sautman, Barry. 2003. 'Cultural Genocide' and Tibet. *Texas International Law Journal* 38:173.

Scheppele, Kim Lane. 2004. A Realpolitik Defense of Social Rights. *Texas Law Review* 82:1921.

Schulhofer, Stephen J. 1992. Plea Bargaining as Disaster. *Yale Law Journal* 101: 1979.

Schumer, Charles. 2005. China's One-Way Street on Foreign Direct Investment and Market Access. **http://schumer.senate.gov/SchumerWebsite/pressroom/special_reports/2005/08.18.05%20China%20Report.pdf**.

Scott, Robert and William Stuntz. 1992. Plea Bargaining as Contract. *Yale Law Journal* 101:1909.

Security Official Confirms Chinese Man Arrested for Internet 'Subversion.' 2004. *BBC Monitoring Asia Pacific*. Feb. 17.

Sen, Amartya. 1999. *Development as Freedom*. Oxford: Oxford University Press.

—— 1993. Capability and Well-being. In *The Quality of Life*. Edited by Martha Nussbaum and Amartya Sen. Oxford: Oxford University Press.

Shen, Kui. 2003. Is it the Beginning of the Era of the Rule of the Constitution? Reinterpreting China's First Constitutional Case. *Pacific Rim Law and Policy Journal* 12:199.

Sichuan Interneter Li Zhi Arrested. 2003. *BBC*. Sept. 24. **http://www.peacehall.com/news/gb/china/2003/09/200309242141.shtml**.

Sicular, Terry et al. 2006. The Urban–Rural Gap and Income Inequality in China. Manuscript on file with author.

Smith, Peter B. et al. 2002. Cultural Values, Sources of Guidance, and their Relevance to Managerial Behavior—A 47-Nation Study. *Journal of Cross-Cultural Psychology* 33:188.

Smolin, David. 1995/1996. Will International Human Rights Be Used as a Tool of Cultural Genocide? The Interaction of Human Rights Norms, Religion, Culture and Gender. *Journal of Law and Religion* 12:143.

Song Qiang et al. 1996. *Da Zhongguo keiyi shuo bu* [A Powerful China Can Say No]. Beijing. Zhonghua gongshang lianhe chubanshe.

Spencer, Richard. 2004. Tiananmen: Victory for Capitalism. *Spectator (London)*. June 12.

Srinivasan, T. N. 2002. Emerging issues in the world trading system. In Adhikari and Athukorala 2002.

State Council of China. 2005. White Paper: Building of Political Democracy in China.

—— 2004. Government Work Report 2004.

Stewart, Miranda. 2005. Global Trajectories of Tax Reform: The Discourse of Tax Reform in Developing and Transition Countries. In Lindsey 2006*a*.

Stiglitz, Joseph E. 2003. *Globalization and Its Discontents*. New York: Norton.

Students' Attitudes Toward Human Rights Surveyed. 1999. *BBC Summary of World Broadcasts*. May 4.

Su Li. 1995. Bianfa, Fazhi Jianshe ji qi Bentu Ziyuan [Change of Law, Establishment of the Rule of Law and its Native Resources]. *Zhongwai Faxue* 5:1.

Sunstein, Cass R. 1996. Against Positive Rights. In *Western Rights? Post Communist Application*. Edited by Andras Sajo. The Hague: Kluwer Law International.

Tan, Eugene K. B. 2002. 'WE' v 'I': Communitarian Legalism in Singapore. *Australian Journal of Asian Law* 4:1.

Tan Sor-Hoon. 2003. *Confucian Democracy: A Deweyan Reconstruction*. Albany: SUNY Press.

Tanner, Harold. 1999. *Strike Hard: Anti-Crime Campaigns and Chinese Criminal Justice, 1979–1985*. Ithaca, NY: Cornell University Press.

Tanner, Murray Scot. 2004. Shades of Tiananmen: Protests Now Flourish in China. *Int'l Herald Tribune*. June 3.

Tat Yan Kong. 2004. Neo-liberalization and Incorporation in Advanced Newly Industrialized Countries: A View from South Korea. *Political Studies* 52:1.

Taylor, Veronica. 2006. The Law Reform Olympics: Measuring the Effects of Law Reform in Transition Economies. In Lindsey 2006*a*.

Teubner, Gunter. 1998. Legal Irritants: good faith in British Law or how unifying law ends up in new divergences. *Modern Law Review* 61:11.

The Politics of Affective Relations: East Asia and Beyond. 2004. Edited by Hahm Chaihark and Daniel Bell. Lanham, MD: Lexington Books.

The 'Washington Consensus' and the 'Beijing Consensus.' 2005. *People's Daily Online*. June 18. **http://english.people.com.cn/200506/18/eng20050618_190947.html**.

Thio, Li-Ann. 2004. Rule of law within a non-liberal 'communitarian' democracy: the Singapore experience. In Peerenboom 2004*a*.

—— 1997. An i for an I: Singapore's Communitarian Model of Constitutional Adjudication. *Hong Kong Law Journal* 27:152.

Trakman, Leon. 1997. Native Cultures in a Rights Empire: Ending the Dominion. *Buffalo Law Review* 45:189.

Trotz, Alissa. 2004. Engendering Globalization: Perspectives on Challenges and Responses. In Lele and Quadir 2004*a*.

Trubek, David. 1996. Law and Development: Then and Now. *American Society of International Law Proceedings*.

—— 1974. Scholars in Self-Estrangement: Some Reflections on the Crisis in Law and Development Studies in the United States. *Wisconsin Law Review* 1974:1062.

—— 1972. Toward a Social Theory of Law: An Essay on the Study of Law and Development. *Yale Law Journal* 82:1.

Tulchin, Joseph and Amelia Brown, eds. 2002. *Democratic Governance & Social Inequality*. Boulder, CO: Lynne Rienner.

Tyler, Tom. 1990. *Why People Obey the Law*. New Haven: Yale University Press.

UN 1999. *The World Economy in 1999*. New York: UN Department of Economic & Social Affairs.

UN Working Group on Arbitrary Detention, Report on the Visit to the People's Republic of China, 54th Sess., Agenda Item 8, ¶ 96(a), U.N. Doc. E/CN.4/1998/44/Add.2 (1998).

UNESCO/OECD. 2005. Education Trends in Perspective: Analysis of the World Education Indicators 2005 Edition. Montreal.

United Nations Conference on Trade and Development (UNCTAD). 1999. *Trade and Development Report, 1999*. Geneva: United Nations.

United Nations Development Programme (UNDP). 2005. Human Development Report 20. 05; **http://hdr.undp.org/reports/global/2005/pdf/HDR05_complete.pdf**.

—— 2003. *Human Development Report 2003, Millennium Goals: A Compact Among Nations to End Human Poverty*. **http://www.undp.org/hdr2003/pdf/hdr03_overview.pdf**.

—— Human Development Index (2003). **http://www.undp.org/hdr2003/indicator/indic_4_1_1.html**.

—— *Human Development Report 2000: human rights and human development*. **http://hdr.undp.org/reports/global/2000/en/pdf/hdr_2000_back1.pdf**.

United Nations High Commissioner (1993). Freedom of Expression Manual. **http://www.article19.org/docimages/811.htm**.

Upham, Frank. 2002. Mythmaking in the Rule of Law Orthodoxy. *Carnegie Endowment for International Peace Working Papers, No. 30*.

US–China Business Council. 2005. China's WTO Scorecard: Selected Three-year Commitments. **http://www.uschina.org/public/documents/2005/05/wto_scorecard.pdf**.

US Department of State. 2004*a*. Country Reports on Human Rights Practices 2003: China (2004). **http://www.state.gov/g/drl/rls/hrrpt/2003/27768.htm**.

—— 2004*b*. U.S. State Department Country Reports on Human Rights Practices, India—2003. **http://www.state.gov/g/drl/rls/hrrpt/2003/27947.htm**.

—— 2001. United States Report on Hong Kong. **http://www.usconsulate.org.hk/ushk/pi/20010731.htm**.

—— 1998. U.S. State Department's Country Reports on Human Rights Practices for 1997.

—— 1994. Oversight of the State Department's Country Reports on Human Rights Practices for 1993 and U.S. Human Rights Policy.

U.S. Embassy Beijing. 2000. Beijing Environment, Science and Technology Update, Nov. 3. **http://www.usembassy-china.org.cn/sandt/estnews1103.htm**.

US Resident Jailed in China Threatens Hunger Strike. 2003. *BBC Monitoring International Reports*. Dec. 11.

U.S. State Department Counterterrorism Office. 2002. Patterns of Global Terrorism 2001.

USTR 2004. 'Special 301' Decisions on Intellectual Property: IIPA's 2003 Estimated Trade Losses Due to Copyright Piracy and Piracy Levels In-Country. **http://www.iipa.com/pdf/IIPA_USTR_2004_Special_301_DECISIONS_FINAL_050304.pdf.**

van Boven, Theo. 1991. Advances and Obstacles in Building Understanding and Respect Between People of Diverse Religions and Beliefs. *Human Rights Quarterly* 13:437.

van der Vyver, Johan D. 1998. Universality and Relativity of Human Rights: American Relativism. *Buffalo Human Rights Law Review* 4:43.

Van Ness, Peter, ed. 1999. *Debating Human Rights: Critical Essays From the United States and Asia*. London: Routledge.

Verma, Vidhu. 2002. *Malaysia: State and Civil Society in Transition*. Boulder: Lynne Reinner.

Vitug, Marites Danguilan. 2004. Star Power Holds Perils for the Philippines; Celebrity Politics. *Int'l Herald Tribune*. Feb. 20.

Wade, Robert. 1990. *Governing the Market: Economic Theory and the Role of Government in East Asian Industrialisation*. Princeton: Princeton University Press.

Wang Bingzhang Convicted of Terrorist Activities and Espionage. 2003. *Xinhuanet*. Feb. 10. **http://news.xinhuanet.com/english/2003-02/10/content_722148.htm/**.

Wang Jiangyu. 2006. Financial Liberalization in East Asia: Lessons from Financial Crises and the Chinese Experience of Controlled Liberalization. *European Business Law Review*.

—— 2004. China's Regional Trade Agreements: The Law, Geopolitics, and Impact on the Multilateral Trading System. *Singapore Yearbook of International Law* 8:119.

Wang Jianwei. 2000. Democratization and China's Nation Building. In Friedman and McCormick 2000.

Wang Lei. 2003. *Xuanzi Xianfa [To Choose Constitutional Law]*. Beijing: Law Press.

Wang Tay-sheng. 2002. The Legal Development of Taiwan in the 20th Century: Toward a Liberal and Democratic Country. *Pacific Rim Law and Policy Journal* 11:531.

Wang Yizhou, ed. 2003*a*. *Construction within Contradiction: Multiple Perspectives on the Relationship Between China and International Organizations*. China Development Publishing House.

—— 2003*b*. Briefing Multiple Perspectives on Relations between China and International Organizations. In Wang Yizhou 2003*a*.

Watson, Alan. 1993. *Legal Transplants*. Athens: University of Georgia Press.

Well-Known Anti-Corruption Activist An Jun Sentenced to Four Years This Morning for Subversion. 2000. *Xiaocankao Daily News*. Apr. 19. **http://www.bignews.org/20000419.txt**.

Weaver, Lisa Rose. 2003. China Defends Tibetan Execution. Jan. 8. **http://www.cnn.com/2003/WORLD/asiapcf/east/01/28/china.execution/index.html**.

Wessel, David, and Marcus Walker. 2004. Good News for the Globe; Nobel Winners in Economics Are Upbeat About the Future As China and India Surge. *Wall Street Journal (Eastern Edition)*. Sept. 3.

Wheeler, Ron. 1999. The United Nations Commission on Human Rights, 1982–1997: A Study of 'Targeted' Resolutions. *Canadian Journal of Political Science* 32:75.

Where's That Veto Threat? 2005. *New York Times*. Nov. 4.

White House. 2002. The National Security Strategy of the United States of America. **http://www.whitehouse.gov/nsc/nss.pdf**.

Wiegand, Wolfang. 1996. Americanization of Law: Reception or Convergence. In *Legal Culture and Legal Profession*. Edited by Lawrence Friedman and Harry Schreiber. Boulder, CO: Westview Press.

Williams, Paul R. and Francesca Jannotti Pecci. 2004. Earned Sovereignty: Bridging the Gap between Sovereignty and Self-Determination. *Stanford Journal of International Law* 40:347.

Williamson, John. 2004. The Washington Consensus as Policy Prescription for Development. Institute for International Economics. **http://www.iie.com/publications/papers/williamson0204.pdf**.

—— 2000. What Should the World Bank Think about the Washington Consensus? *The World Bank Research Observer* 15:151.

Wolf, Martin. 2005. China's rise need not bring conflict. *Financial Times. FT.com*. Sept. 14.

—— 2004. *Why Globalization Works*. New Haven: Yale University Press.

Wood, Diane P. 2003. The Rule of Law in Times of Stress. *University of Chicago Law Review* 70:455.

World Bank. 2005. *Global Monitoring Report*. Washington, DC: World Bank.

—— 2000. *Global Development Finance 2000*. Washington, DC: World Bank.

—— 1999. *Entering the 21st Century: World Development Report 1999/2000*. New York: Oxford University Press.

World Bank. 1998. *World Development Report: From Plan to Market.* Washington, DC: World Bank.

—— 1993. *The East Asian Miracle: Economic Growth and Public Policy.* New York: Oxford University Press.

World Health Organization. 2005. China: Health Situation. **www.wpro.int/countries/chn/health_situation.htm**.

Xu Zhangrun. 2004. Western Law in China: transplantation or transformation—four cases and Liang Shuming's responses. *Social Sciences in China* 25: 3.

Yang Ming. 2003. Sichuan Government Official Li Zhen Sentenced to Eight Years for Exposing Corruption on Internet. *Epoch Times*. Dec. 11.

Yao Shujie. 2005. *Economic Growth, Income Distribution and Poverty Reduction in Contemporary China.* London and New York: RoutledgeCurzon.

Yoshimatsu, Hidetaka. 2003. *Japan and East Asia in Transition: Trade Policy, Crisis and Evolution, and Regionalism.* Houndmills: Palgrave Macmillan.

Yourow, Howard Charles. 1996. *The Margin of Appreciation Doctrine in the Dynamics of European Human Rights Jurisprudence*. London, New York, The Hague: Martinus Nijhoff Publishers, Kluwer Press.

Yu Meisun. 2004. Cong Jiaoyubu Dang Beigao de Liangan, Kan Zhaosheng Zhidu Chuangxin de Poqiexing [On the Exigency of Renovating the College Recruiting System, Judging From the Two Cases Where the Ministry of Education is the Defendant]. *Epochtimes.com*. Apr. 23.

Yu Ping. 2002. Glittery Promise vs. Dismal Reality: the role of the criminal lawyer in the People's Republic of China After the 1996 Revision of the Criminal Procedure Law. *Vanderbilt Journal of Transnational Law* 35: 827.

Zakaria, Fareed. 2004 *The Future of Freedom: Illiberal Democracy at Home and Abroad*. New York : W.W. Norton.

Zanger, S.C. 2000. A Global Analysis of the Effect of Regime Changes on Life Integrity Violations, 1977–93. *Journal of Peace Research* 37:213.

Zhang Hong. 2001. It Is Difficult Not To Be Confused About Extramarital Affairs. *Renmin Fayuan Bao* (Internet edition). Mar. 29.

Zhang Yunling, ed. 2005 *State and Civil Society in the Context of Transition: Understanding Non-Traditional Security in East Asia.* Beijing: World Affairs Press.

Zhao Suisheng. 2000. We are Patriots First and Democrats Second: The Rise of Chinese Nationalism in the 1990s. In Friedman and McCormick 2000.

Zhao Xi. 2003. Jin Shinian Lai Zhongmei Guanxi Diaocha Zhong de Minjian Renzhi [Public Opinion in Surveys of China–US Relations in the Last 10

Years]. *New Weekly Magazine*. May 22. **http://cul.sina.com.cn/s/2003-05-22/34512/html**.

Zhu Ling. 2002. Poverty Alleviation During the Transition in China. In *Poverty, Income Distribution and Well-Being in Asia During the Transition*. Edited by Aiguo Lu and Manuel F. Montes. New York: Palgrave MacMillan.

Zittrain, Jonathan and Benjamin Edelman. 2003. Internet Filtering in China, IEEE Internet Computing. **http://ssrn.com/abstract_id=399920**.

Zoellick, Robert B. 2005. Wither China: From Membership to Responsibility? **http://www.state.gov/s/d/rem/53682.htm**.

Index